AL
DU
PRE

PL
RUG
ANNUAL 1999-2000

4th edition

Edited by Stuart Farmer and Brendan Gallagher

HEADLINE

First published in 1999
by HEADLINE BOOK PUBLISHING

Cover photographs Front, left to right: Richard Cockerill (Leicester Tigers and England), Joost van der Westhuizen (Northern Transvaal and South Africa) and Mike Catt (Bath and England); back: Neil Back (Leicester Tigers) – *Colorsport*

10 9 8 7 6 5 4 3 2 1

ISBN 0 7472 6133 4

Typeset by
Letterpart Limited, Reigate, Surrey

Printed in England by
Clays Ltd, St Ives plc

HEADLINE BOOK PUBLISHING
A division of the Hodder Headline Group
338 Euston Road
London NW1 3BH

www.headline.co.uk
www.hodderheadline.com

Contents

Editorial Preface

Is rugby in a state of terminal anarchy and self-destruction or has it reached new levels of excellence and excitement? Remarkably it was possible to draw both conclusions at the end of the 1998-99 season, such was the roller-coaster ride that professional rugby endured. Of course it should have settled down by now, but alas not. It's nearly four years since the IRB made the fateful decision to declare the game open yet still we are making massive and costly mistakes. Many individuals and clubs have been hurt, friendships have been lost, confidences broken. The general public despairs of trying to understand what is going on, potential sponsors have turned lukewarm, old supporters of the game have had their patience tested like never before. And yet . . . when you recall some of the astonishing action that unfolded last season and gasp at the sheer spectacle of top-class international rugby it's tempting to ignore the prophets of doom. That would be foolish – there are huge and genuine problems facing our game – but let's try, firstly, to accentuate the positive. There remains plenty to enthuse over.

Who will ever forget Scotland's triumph in the final Five Nations tournament, the most unexpected but deserving of championship titles? Coach Jim Telfer, in his final Five Nations season, fashioned an exciting young side determined to play fluid, free-running rugby. Their motives were not just altruistic, though Gregor Townsend on more than one occasion commented on the sheer fun and enjoyment of playing and watching such rugby. Rather, Scotland shrewdly assessed that their best chance of winning lay with such an approach, that it best suited the players they had available. New stars were born – the Leslie brothers, Scott Murray, Glen Metcalfe and Stuart Grimes – while more experienced individuals such as Gary Armstrong, Eric Peters, Alan Tait and Gregor Townsend were rejuvenated figures. Scotland's five-try burst in 20 minutes against France in Paris will go down in history – nor should one underestimate the quality of their performances against Ireland and England, even though they narrowly lost to the latter at Twickenham.

Wales' heartening revival under Graham Henry, which started with encouraging pre-Christmas performances against South Africa and Argentina, looked to be another false dawn after disappointing defeats against Scotland and Ireland early in the Championship. The Welsh, however, recovered in truly astonishing style to record an amazing 34-33 win over France at the Stade de France in one of the all-time classic Five Nations encounters. Not content with that, Wales then broke English hearts at Wembley when Scott Gibbs powered over in the third minute of injury time to secure a famous 32-31 victory. In one fell swoop Gibbs sent the Welsh supporters home delirious with joy, denied England the Grand Slam and handed the Championship to the deserving Scots. Rarely, if ever, has a try resulted in such emotional turmoil. The Welsh success story, happy to relate, continued in Argentina during their summer tour, a prelude to their historic 29-19 win over South Africa at the Millennium Stadium in June. The host nation can approach the World Cup in good heart and with everything to gain.

Elsewhere, too, there was much to celebrate. Ulster's march to victory in the European Cup was the stuff of fairytales, the unfancied Irish province taking the competition by storm and defeating three top French sides – Toulouse, Stade Francais and Colomiers – en route to the final. Ulster's day out at Lansdowne Road against Colomiers was one of the great rugby stories of recent times, a wonderful boost to the rugby community in Northern Ireland who have suffered, along with everybody else, during that province's political problems. Leicester's flinty, durable and utterly professional squad were impressive winners of the Allied Dunbar Premiership, though Northampton ensured the final months were not a complete stroll in the park. Captain Martin Johnson was simply immense, the undisputed Premiership player of the season, though he was pipped by Scott Murray for the international awards.

Further afield rugby took the Commonwealth Games in Malaysia by storm, proving arguably the most popular event in the multi-sport Games. Given the Commonwealth's sporting preferences the competition was virtually a rerun of the 1997 World Championships though Scotland, shamefully, did not send a side and England were considerably under-strength due to a full league programme back home. The tournament would have profited from being two rather than three days in duration but the action on the final afternoon was simply breathtaking, New Zealand finishing strongly to take the title from old rivals Fiji. David Campese, playing representative rugby for Australia for positively the final time, led his young squad to the bronze medal. The IRB are locked into serious negotiations with the IOC about rugby's reappearance at the Olympic Games and it is now a matter of when, not if. Though the IRB originally suggested sevens it is understood that the Olympic movement is strongly in favour of a 15-a-side competition.

And the negative? Where do you begin? Is it really possible that we started the Allied Dunbar Premiership last season without a fixture list? Even a year later it seems staggering that the sport could treat its club supporters in such a cavalier fashion. Then there was Sir John Hall's strategic withdrawal at Newcastle, the calamitous state of affairs at Bedford where nobody knew where the next pay cheque was coming from and the sad demise of Richmond, who, along with London Scottish, were taken over by London Irish. Clubs across the board at least agreed to a salary cap for the coming season but the desperate struggle for survival continues. In Wales the season was scarred by a seemingly needless dispute between the WRU and Swansea and Cardiff. The two clubs were reduced to playing a series of friendlies against Premiership teams which, despite the brave words of both parties, proved virtually meaningless. As a consequence the Welsh domestic season was stillborn, Llanelli's Premiership title being seriously devalued. At least the season finished on an upbeat note, Cardiff and Swansea finally signing an eight-year loyalty agreement with the WRU and being included in this season's European Cup competition. And then there was the damage caused to the sport by the appearance of Will Carling and Lawrence Dallaglio on the front page of every newspaper in the land. The merits of either case are not strictly relevant here but the consequence of yet more negative publicity for the game must be considered.

So what's going on? Nothing unusual really. Rugby must come to terms with the fact that the flipside of professionalism is accountability. Players and administrators must be prepared to justify and defend their every action and decision – in which case everything should be thought through just that little bit more carefully. The biggest disappointment of all is that rugby, still awash with highly intelligent, educated individuals, has unfailingly taken one bad decision after another. Successful businessmen who are major success stories in their specialist fields appear complete novices in the fledgling world of professional rugby. Very few lessons have been learnt.

And so to the World Cup – the perfect antidote to all that is wrong with the game. Fantastic stadia, huge crowds, great rugby. For a month at least the world will see rugby at its intoxicating best. It will be a timely renewal of faith, because it's been four bitterly hard and long years since the glories of South Africa in 1995.

Acknowledgements

We are particularly indebted this year to David Llewellyn of the *Independent* who stepped in at short notice to render invaluable assistance. As ever officials from the RFU, SRU, IRU and WRU readily provided information as did Peter McMullen and Michelle Tracey at the International Rugby Board. Others to provide much needed help were Andrew Harley, Bill McMurtrie, John Harding, Westgate Sports Agency, James Clarke at the RFU, Mary Gallagher and Janet Berry. We are also hugely indebted to typesetter Chris Leggett at Letterpart and our editor Lorraine Jerram.

Brendan Gallagher
Stuart Farmer
August 1999

Guide to Allied Dunbar Premiership Club Section

The following is a guide to the clubs and players in the two divisions of the Allied Dunbar Premiership. The information concerning individual players is set out as follows:

DAWSON, Matthew James Sutherland (Scrum-half)
Born Birkenhead, 31.10.72. 5′11″, 12st 10lb. **Rep hons**: England (22, WS95, 5t, 2c, 3pg-38pts), A (11, Fr93, 7t-35pts), Barbarians (94). **ADPR**: Northampton (1991-99, 112, 29t, 23c, 24pg, 1dg-265pts).

After listing place of birth, date of birth, height and weight, details of Matt Dawson's international career are set out. To date he has played 22 England internationals, making his debut against Western Samoa in 1995. During that time he has scored five tries, kicked two conversions and three penalty goals to total 38 points. At A level he represented England on 11 occasions, making his debut against France in 1993, scoring seven tries to total 35 points.

Records of A/B appearances also include tour games against such opposition as B Col (British Columbia), S Aus (South Australia), Vic (Victoria), Nat (Natal). International records for this year's book end on 30 June. Barbarians (94) indicates that Dawson made his Barbarians debut in 1994.

For Northampton he has made 112 League appearances, scoring 29 tries, kicking 23 conversions, 24 penalties and one dropped goal to total 265 points. Where a player has scored points for more than one League club, his points total is given by club. After a player's ADPR there follow details about him, his playing career, interests etc. Where details of birth, height, weight are not given it is because we have been unable to track down such information.

Abbreviations for various countries are standard:

ARG	(Argentina)	NZ	(New Zealand)
AUS	(Australia)	ROM	(Romania)
CAN	(Canada)	SA	(South Africa)
ENG	(England)	SC	(Scotland)
FIJ	(Fiji)	SP	(Spain)
FR	(France)	TON	(Tonga)
IRE	(Ireland)	USA	(USA)
IT	(Italy)	WAL	(Wales)
JAP	(Japan)	WS	(Western Samoa)
NAM	(Namibia)	ZIM	(Zimbabwe)

RUGBY WORLD CUP 1999

Just 12 years ago the major rugby-playing nations of the world, and a few emerging hopefuls, gathered in New Zealand and Australia for a bit of a jolly. A handful of visionaries, led by John Kendall-Carpenter, had come up with the idea of a World Cup. Nobody knew whether it would be a one-off but it would be a chance for rugby folk to meet and share a few beers. Now, as we approach the millennium, it is already established as the third biggest sporting event on this planet behind soccer's World Cup and the Olympics. Rugby, at least on the international stage, continues to grow, as RWC99 will demonstrate throughout October and November. There have been teething problems on the way – the Welsh Rugby Union left the completion of their magnificent Millennium Stadium perilously late and there is still a feeling of vague disquiet that, as in 1991, the tournament is to be spread among Europe's Five Nations countries. Yet again those sides competing in France run the risk of feeling isolated and barely involved in the tournament proper. But that apart, we should be in for a treat. What other sporting event in the world can boast arenas of the calibre of the Millennium Stadium, Stade de France, Twickenham, Murrayfield, Hampden Park and Lansdowne Road?

The sense of expectation has been building almost since that wonderful moment in 1995 when Francois Pienaar was presented with the Webb Ellis Trophy by President Nelson Mandela, resplendent in his Springbok shirt. The action was so good four years ago that you never wanted it to stop. Will the tournament spawn another superstar like Jonah Lomu? Almost certainly – when the world's best gather only the truly special emerge from the pack. Can anybody match South Africa, New Zealand and Australia – the southern hemisphere giants who walked off with the first three trophies? Can Western Samoa continue their remarkable rise up the world rankings and can Pacific neighbours Fiji and Tonga begin to perform to their full potential? Can the minnows, such as Uruguay and Spain, avoid crushing embarrassment and can the home countries and France cash in on home advantage? We'll all know soon enough.

Over 80 nations are now registered with the International Rugby Board. Rugby's popularity, on a global scale, grows by the day and the World Cup is the game's major showpiece occasion. The scene is set; the fans and players alike can't wait. RWC99 promises to see the millennium out in style.

1999 World Cup Schedule

Fri 1 Oct:	Pool D:	Wales v Argentina (Cardiff, 1400)
Fri 1 Oct:	Pool C:	Fiji v Namibia (Beziers, 1900)
Sat 1 Oct:	Pool C:	France v Canada (Beziers, 1200)
Sat 2 Oct:	Pool A:	Spain v Uruguay (Galashiels, 1400)
Sat 2 Oct:	Pool B:	England v Italy (Twickenham, 1600)
Sat 2 Oct:	Pool E:	Ireland v USA (Lansdowne Road, 1800)
Sun 3 Oct:	Pool D:	Western Samoa v Japan (Wrexham, 1200)
Sun 3 Oct:	Pool B:	New Zealand v Tonga (Bristol, 1400)
Sun 3 Oct:	Pool A:	Scotland v South Africa (Murrayfield, 1600)
Sun 3 Oct:	Pool E:	Australia v Romania (Belfast, 1800)
Fri 8 Oct:	Pool A:	Scotland v Uruguay (Murrayfield, 1500)
Fri 8 Oct:	Pool C:	France v Namibia (Bordeaux, 1900)
Sat 9 Oct:	Pool C:	Fiji v Canada (Bordeaux, 1130)
Sat 9 Oct:	Pool D:	Wales v Japan (Cardiff, 1330)
Sat 9 Oct:	Pool B:	England v New Zealand (Twickenham, 1530)

Sat 9 Oct:	Pool E:	USA v Romania (Lansdowne Road, 1800)
Sun 10 Oct:	Pool D:	Argentina v Western Samoa (Llanelli, 1200)
Sun 10 Oct:	Pool E:	Ireland v Australia (Lansdowne Road, 1400)
Sun 10 Oct:	Pool A:	South Africa v Spain (Murrayfield, 1600)
Sun 10 Oct:	Pool B:	Italy v Tonga (Leicester, 1800)
Thu 14 Oct:	Pool B:	New Zealand v Italy (Huddersfield, 1200)
Thu 14 Oct:	Pool D:	Wales v Western Samoa (Cardiff, 1400)
Thu 14 Oct:	Pool E:	Australia v USA (Limerick, 1600)
Thu 14 Oct:	Pool C:	Canada v Namibia (Toulouse, 1830)
Fri 15 Oct:	Pool B:	England v Tonga (Twickenham, 1200)
Fri 15 Oct:	Pool A:	South Africa v Uruguay (Glasgow, 1600)
Fri 15 Oct:	Pool E:	Ireland v Romania (Lansdowne Road, 1800)
Sat 16 Oct:	Pool C:	France v Fiji (Toulouse, 1200)
Sat 16 Oct:	Pool A:	Scotland v Spain (Murrayfield, 1400)
Sat 16 Oct:	Pool D:	Argentina v Japan (Cardiff, 1900)

Quarter-final play-offs:

Wed 20 Oct:	Runner-up B v Runner-up C (H) (Twickenham, 1200)
Wed 20 Oct:	Runner-up A v Runner-up D (G) (Murrayfield, 1430)
Wed 20 Oct:	Runner-up E v Best 3rd place (F) (Lens, 1700)

Quarter-finals:

Sat 23 Oct:	Winner D v Winner E (M): (Cardiff, 1400)
Sun 24 Oct:	Winner A v Winner H (J): (Stade de France, 1200)
Sun 24 Oct:	Winner B v Winner G (K): (Murrayfield, 1430)
Sun 24 Oct:	Winner C v Winner F (L): (Lansdowne Road, 1700)

Semi-finals:

Sat 30 Oct:	Winner J v Winner M (Twickenham, 1400)
Sun 31 Oct:	Winner K v Winner L (Twickenham, 1400)

Play-off:

Thu 4 Nov: Third place play-off (Cardiff, 2000)

Final:

Sat 6 Nov: (Cardiff, 1500)

THE POOLS AND TEAMS

Pool A

SCOTLAND

What a difference a year makes. Just 12 months ago Scotland were still fearful of the future after the crushing disappointments of the 1997-98 season, but after their 1999 Five Nations triumph they can approach the tournament with real confidence. Nobody will relish meeting them, especially at Murrayfield. Coach Jim Telfer – who has always insisted he will sign off after the World Cup – has got the entire squad playing a loose, exciting, native style of rugby that is wonderful to watch and invigorating to play. The addition to the squad last year of New Zealand-reared brothers John and Martin Leslie has proved the catalyst but individuals have raised their game throughout the team. Alan Tait and Gary Armstrong will be anxious to impress in their final World Cups, Gregor Townsend is at the height of his powers, Gordon Bulloch, Scott Murray and Stuart Grimes could take the tournament by storm and Eric Peters will be anxious to repeat the conspicuous success of his '95 campaign. A developmental tour of South Africa in the summer provided a low profile preparation for the World Cup but with nearly half his first choice team deciding to rest injuries, or simply rest, Telfer took the opportunity to evaluate squad players who could yet be required on the big occasion. A record of two wins and two losses was about what Scotland's coach expected. Scotland have proved rugged World Cup competitors, losing with some honour to eventual winners New Zealand in the 1987 quarter-finals, going down by just three points to England in the semi-finals four years later and again giving a good account of themselves in South Africa when they lost a high-scoring quarter-final to New Zealand. With all due respect to Uruguay and Spain, the key to Scotland's group will be their opening game against South Africa at a packed Murrayfield on Sunday 3 October – already the sense of anticipation is building. The winner of that game is virtually guaranteed a quarter-final in Paris against the runner-up either of England's or France's group. Even if Scotland lose to South Africa there will still be much to play for – a home quarter-final play-off against the runners-up of the Welsh group and then a home quarter-final against the winners of England's group.

Key players: John Leslie, Scott Murray, Gregor Townsend.

1987: *Pool*: Scotland 20 France 20; Scotland 60 Zimbabwe 12; Scotland 55 Romania 28. *Quarter-final*: Scotland 3 New Zealand 30.

1991: *Pool*: Scotland 47 Japan 9; Scotland 51 Zimbabwe 12; Scotland 24 Ireland 15. *Quarter-final*: Scotland 28 Western Samoa 6. *Semi-final*: Scotland 6 England 9. *3rd/4th play-off*: Scotland 6 New Zealand 13.

1995: *Pool*: Scotland 89 Ivory Coast 0; Scotland 41 Tonga 5; Scotland 19 France 22. *Quarter-final*: Scotland 30 New Zealand 48.

1999: Qualification: *European qualifying tournament*: Scotland 85 Portugal 11; Scotland 85 Spain 3.

SOUTH AFRICA

South Africa have experienced an enormous number of highs and lows since their triumph in 1995 but, despite everything, Nick Mallett's squad are likely to start favourites to lift the trophy again. Only Joost van der Westhuizen, Japie Mulder and Mark Andrews are likely to reappear from that 1995 side, which underlines the constant state of flux within the South African game. Coaches have come and gone – notably Andre Markgraaf and Carel du Plessis – older players have been discarded, possibly prematurely, and exciting new talent has immediately been thrown in at the deep end. South African rugby is all about proving yourself, time and time again. With a back division boasting the likes of Percy Montgomery, Peter Rossouw, Andre Snyman and Stefan Terblanche as well as van der Westhuizen, hopefully restored to full health after a serious knee injury, South Africa offer a potent threat out wide but a successful defence of their world crown will ultimately depend on whether their occasionally vulnerable pack can lift their game. With the marvellously gifted Bobby Skinstad and the ultra-competitive Johan Erasmus there will be no lack of quality in the backrow, though they could yet regret discarding Gary Teichmann as captain whose workmanlike qualities were vastly underrated. Additionally can Andrews' creaking joints get him through another tournament and can their front row rediscover their once fearsome scrummaging skills? South Africa identified their forwards as a possible area of weakness after their pre-Christmas tour of Britain in 1998 and have been working hard to rectify the faults ever since. On the evidence of their disappointing 29-19 defeat against Wales at the Millennium Stadium in June their pack can still appear vulnerable and the return to fitness and form of mighty prop Os du Randt would be a huge bonus. Generally, however, they have every reason to be optimistic, especially with Nick Mallett directing operations as coach. Shrewd and innovative, he is also a master of public relations and South Africa are certain to be popular as well as formidable. His biggest task could again be to defuse the race issue which flared once more in the summer with SARFU again unhappy at the representation of black and coloured players in the Springboks team. The Springboks will barely raise a sweat in defeating Spain and Uruguay but their clash against Scotland will a be a full-on, winner-take-all Test with the victors certain to win Pool A. After that nobody will fancy tackling South Africa, who showed yet again four years ago that the higher the stakes, the tougher they get.

Key players: Bobby Skinstad, Os du Randt, Joost van der Westhuizen.

1987: Did not compete

1991: Did not compete

1995: *Pool*: South Africa 27 Australia 18; South Africa 21 Romania 8; South Africa 20 Canada 0. *Quarter-final*: South Africa 42 Western Samoa 14. *Semi-final*: South Africa 19 France 15. *Final*: South Africa 15 New Zealand 12.

1999: Qualification: As 1995 champions.

SPAIN

Spain, who will be making their debut at the World Cup finals, may face an awesome task to avoid humiliation against South Africa and Scotland, but no team can have worked harder in preparation for the tournament. Despite limited facilities and the fact that their team are amateurs, the Spaniards organised short tours to France and Romania in the summer and then contested internationals against Japan, Fiji and Italy prior to the start of the competition. A flying visit to South America in July did little to help morale with Spain losing a friendly against Chile 21-18. Outclassed against Scotland in the European qualifying tournament, when they were humiliated 85-3 by the home side, Spain's only realistic aim is to adopt damage-limitation tactics against the Springboks and the Scots and make a dash for glory against Uruguay at Galashiels. Spain should be captained by durable flanker Alberto Malo, who has represented the French Barbarians on a number of occasions and also played for a World XV against Argentina in April 1999. Much depends on their more experienced French-based players such as Dax prop Asier Altuna, Lourdes prop Jonadeb Diez, Castres flanker Jose Diaz and Colomiers wing Rafael Bastide. Another important player could be fly-half Andrei Kovalenko, their Ukrainian-born goal-kicker who landed six penalties in their vital 21-17 win over Portugal in the European zone qualifying game at Murrayfield last December. Coach Alfonso Feijoo, Spain's best ever centre who once represented a World XV, and assistant Tomas Pardo face a huge task. Spain's road to the finals was an unsatisfactory combination of matches they either couldn't lose or couldn't win. Andorra, the Czech Republic and Germany provided little threat and their only pool game of any consequence was their 33-22 win over Iberian neighbours Portugal. Then came their disaster against Scotland, followed by another narrow but crucial win over Portugal. Rugby in Spain is based in Madrid and Barcelona and the Spanish Federation has been a member of FIRA since 1934, with the national side competing regularly in Division One. There are, however, just 62 clubs throughout the country and the sport in Spain remains strictly amateur. Without doubt Spain's finest moment came in 1986 at the New South Wales Centenary Sevens when Spain, whose players had to sit down and watch videos before the game in an attempt to understand what sevens was all about, picked the game up so quickly that they beat not-so-mighty England 24-6. They also defeated the Netherlands before losing 12-6 to Argentina in the quarter-finals. No such upsets are likely in the sterner atmosphere of 15-a-side rugby, but Spain intend to enjoy themselves.

Key players: Andrei Kovalenko, Jose Diaz, Alberto Malo.

1987: Did not compete

1991: Did not qualify for finals

1995: Did not qualify for finals

1999: Qualification: *Europe Round B*: Spain 62 Andorra 3; Spain 39 Czech Republic 8; Spain 24 Germany 9; Spain 33 Portugal 22. *European qualifying tournament*: Spain 3 Scotland 85; Spain 21 Portugal 17.

URUGUAY

Uruguay's steady improvement is reflected by their first-ever appearance at the World Cup finals after a long and arduous qualification process. After beating Chile, another rapidly improving nation, 20-14 and outclassing Paraguay they narrowly failed to secure an automatic place by going down 21-16 to the USA in the Americas qualifying tournament in Buenos Aires. Reverting to the repechage system, they took full advantage of the home and away games against Portugal and Morocco to train and play together on an almost daily basis, something they had never experienced before as amateurs. Uruguay, known as the Teros, only has 12 senior clubs, with less than 1,000 players in all. Most of their top players are with the Carrasco Polo Club which competes regularly against top sides in neighbouring Argentina. Like their South American cousins, the Uruguayans have a reputation for being formidable scrummagers and already one of their props, Pablo Lemoine, has made his mark with Bristol, helping them to win promotion to Premiership One last season. Lemoine, who tips the scales at over 20 stone, is Uruguay's only professional rugby player who is tipped to become a real power in the game by Bristol coach Bob Dwyer. His influence is such that Uruguayan Rugby Union President Andres Sangninetti made a flying visit to England in March to ensure Lemoine would be released for their vital repechage games against Morocco. The Teros are likely to be captained by veteran No 8 Diego Ormachea, who has won over 100 caps since first being capped in 1979! Ormachea, who will be 40 when the competition begins and probably the oldest player ever to appear in the World Cup finals, is a prolific try-scorer, having grabbed two against Portugal in their first repechage game and another against Morocco. The Teros' other main source of points has often been goal-kicking scrum-half Federico Sciarra, who landed six penalties in the second-leg game against Morocco to book their place in RWC99. The Uruguayan Union was founded in 1951, though rugby had been played, largely by expats, before and during World War Two. For many years it was firmly based on the Montevideo Club, though gradually other sides were formed. Before the recent emergence of the national side, Uruguay's best-known player was probably wing Roberto Canessa, who toured South Africa with the 1980 Pumas.

Key players: Pablo Lemoine, Diego Ormachea, Federico Sciarra.

1987: Did not compete

1991: Did not compete

1995: Did not qualify for finals

1999: Qualification: *Americas Round C*: Uruguay 20 Chile 14; Uruguay 43 Paraguay 3. *Americas qualifying tournament*: Uruguay 15 Canada 38; Uruguay 0 Argentina 55; Uruguay 16 USA 21. *Repechage*: Uruguay 46 Portugal 9; Uruguay 33 Portugal 24 (Uruguay win 79-33 on aggregate). Uruguay 18 Morocco 3; Uruguay 18 Morocco 21 (Uruguay win 36-24 on aggregate).

Pool B

ENGLAND

If any side is to challenge the southern hemisphere's domination of the World Cup it could be England, but despite all the brave words – and home advantage – Clive Woodward's team, at best, are only fourth or fifth favourites, just about on a par with Scotland, France, Wales and Western Samoa. Absolutely everything will have to go right if England are to emerge victorious at the Millennium Stadium on 6 November. The Lawrence Dallaglio affair was a distraction they could have done without, but a month in Australia proved useful as Woodward built on a solid if unspectacular Five Nations campaign. But for Scott Gibbs' late try at Wembley England would have claimed a Grand Slam, but they were far from the finished article. A huge question mark hung over Mike Catt at fly-half – hence Jonny Wilkinson's move to No 10 on tour in Australia – and Dan Luger apart, the back three has yet to show genuine international class. In the pack the back five are among the best in world rugby but the front row occasionally creaked. Wilkinson's emergence as an international-class goal-kicker was encouraging and the return of Will Greenwood and young prop Phil Vickery could also bolster the squad. England's 22-15 defeat against Australia at the Olympic Stadium in Sydney again showed that they have a pack to compete with the best but lack a real cutting edge behind the scrum, although Matt Perry is beginning to look like the finished article at full-back. Final warm-up games against USA and Canada and EFDR XVs in September will provide Clive Woodward with a final opportunity to fine tune. England have enjoyed mixed fortunes in the tournament to date. In 1987 it was treated very much as a jolly and ended with one of their poorest performances in recent history, when they lost 16-3 to Wales in the quarter-finals. Four years later, under the Geoff Cooke/Will Carling axis, they were much more focused and competitive and, on the back of their formidable pack, beat a way through to the final before Australia triumphed 12-6 in an uninspiring game. In South Africa in 1995 they failed to impress in pool games against Argentina, Italy and Western Samoa but hinted at better things when Rob Andrew's drop goal secured a famous quarter-final win over Australia at Newlands. Alas, the joy was short-lived as England were dismantled 45-29 a week later by New Zealand and then lost disappointingly in the 3rd/4th place play-off.

Key players: Neil Back, Martin Johnson, Jonny Wilkinson.

1987: *Pool*: England 6 Australia 19; England 60 Japan 7; England 34 USA 12. *Quarter-final*: England 3 Wales 16.

1991: *Pool*: England 12 New Zealand 18; England 36 Italy 6; England 37 USA 9. *Quarter-final*: England 19 France 10. *Semi-final*: England 9 Scotland 6. *Final*: England 6 Australia 12.

1995: *Pool*: England 24 Argentina 18; England 27 Italy 20; England 44 Western Samoa 22. *Quarter-final*: England 25 Australia 22. *Semi-final*: England 29 New Zealand 45. *3rd/4th play-off*: England 9 France 19.

1999: Qualification: *European qualifying tournament*: England 110 Netherlands 0; England 23 Italy 15.

ITALY

Italy enter the most challenging season in their history – after the World Cup they can look forward to making their Six Nations debut – in a state of disarray after humiliating defeats against South Africa: 74-3 at Port Elizabeth and 101-0 at King's Park Durban. Denied key players through injury and tired from their domestic season, the results were a huge setback. Shortly after their return coach Georges Coste resigned, to be replaced by former national captain Massimo Mascioletti who played as a centre in the 1987 World Cup. All of this came on top of a tough international season in Europe. Their 23-15 reverse against England in their World Cup qualifier at the McAlpine Stadium, Huddersfield, probably represented their best performance – indeed, but for a crass decision by the referee when scrum-half Alessandro Troncon was denied a clear-cut try, the Italians might have claimed the most famous win in their history. In the other matches, however, their strength in depth was badly exposed when key players were absent and they are still struggling to find second-rows of genuine international class. Despite the best efforts of French coach Georges Coste they also showed worrying signs of reverting to their old ill-disciplined ways, giving away far too many penalties. On the positive side, they possess one of the world's best place-kickers in Argentinian-born Diego Dominguez, a centre of enviable talent in Christian Stoica and a brilliant wing in Paulo Vaccari, who was badly missed while recovering from a complicated broken hand. Captain Massimo Giovanelli is a tower of strength at blindside flanker and Italy unearthed a real star of the future against England when young Padova openside Mauro Bergamasco made a big impression. In past World Cups Italy have always been hampered by being drawn in the same pool as either England or New Zealand – indeed in 1991, and again this year, the Azzurri have been pitted against both superpowers at the pool stage. Their best World Cup moments have been victory over Fiji in 1987, the late and much-missed Ivan Francescato's brilliant individual try against USA at Otley four years later and a thoroughly competent 31-25 win over Latin cousins Argentina in South Africa in 1995.

Key players: Diego Dominguez, Massimo Giovanelli, Christian Stoica.

1987: *Pool*: Italy 6 New Zealand 70; Italy 16 Argentina 25; Italy 18 Fiji 15.

1991: *Pool*: Italy 30 USA 9; Italy 6 England 36; Italy 21 New Zealand 31.

1995: *Pool*: Italy 18 Western Samoa 42; Italy 20 England 27; Italy 31 Argentina 25.

1999: Qualification: *Europe Round B*: Italy 102 Denmark 3; Italy 31 Georgia 14; Italy 48 Russia 18; Italy 39 Croatia 27. *European qualifying tournament*: Italy 67 Netherlands 7; Italy 15 England 23.

NEW ZEALAND

Forget, for a moment, their disappointing results in 1998 when they lost five consecutive internationals against South Africa and Australia, and indeed any vagaries of form over the summer. New Zealand have lost just two games in the history of the World Cup and will be nothing less than formidable again this time around. Their reservoir of talented players is bigger than any other country – and their recent blip was largely the result of a freak mass retirement of key players such as Sean Fitzpatrick, Zinzan Brooke, Frank Bunce, Walter Little and Olo Brown. Fitzpatrick's departure through injury was the biggest setback. The teak-tough Auckland hooker has played in every New Zealand World Cup game bar one – he was rested against Japan four years ago. Replacing such a leader has proved a major headache, though at least his experience will be harnessed this autumn with Fitzpatrick due to accompany the team as an advisor. Certainly their early performances this summer suggested a return to their very best form with crushing wins over Western Samoa and France. Christian Cullen has switched to the wing with Jeff Wilson, the team's best all-round footballer, reverting to full-back. Elsewhere the emergence of Tana Umaga at centre has been a major plus as their World Cup line-up begins to take shape. New Zealand romped to victory on home soil in the inaugural competition in 1987 but were far less impressive four years later in England when, again, an experienced and hitherto successful side were beginning to break up. These things are all relative of course – the All Blacks were undefeated in a pool containing England – but they looked unusually vulnerable in their quarter-final against Canada in the rain at Lille and were comprehensively outplayed by Australia when they lost the semi-final 16-6 at Lansdowne Road. By 1995 Laurie Mains had revolutionised New Zealand's approach and the All Blacks, with Jonah Lomu proving a sensation in the backs, provided marvellous entertainment as they powered through their pool and then dismissed Scotland and England in the quarter-final and semi-final respectively. The final against a Nelson Mandela-inspired South Africa proved another story, though, as the Springboks stopped New Zealand at source with almost suicidal tackling and then fed off the adrenaline of the home crowd.

Key players: Josh Kronfeld, Andrew Mehrtens, Jeff Wilson.

1987: *Pool*: New Zealand 70 Italy 6; New Zealand 74 Fiji 13; New Zealand 46 Argentina 15. *Quarter-final*: New Zealand 30 Scotland 3. *Semi-final*: New Zealand 49 Wales 6. *Final*: New Zealand 29 France 9.

1991: *Pool*: New Zealand 18 England 12; New Zealand 46 USA 6; New Zealand 31 Italy 21. *Quarter-final*: New Zealand 29 Canada 13. *Semi-final*: New Zealand 6 Australia 16. *3rd/4th play-off*: New Zealand 13 Scotland 6.

1995: *Pool*: New Zealand 43 Ireland 19; New Zealand 34 Wales 9; New Zealand 145 Japan 17. *Quarter-final*: New Zealand 48 Scotland 30. *Semi-final*: New Zealand 45 England 29. *Final*: New Zealand 12 South Africa 15.

1999: Qualification: As 1995 runners-up.

TONGA

Which Tonga will appear at the World Cup? The disorganised, underfunded, understrength, underperforming squad that has roamed ineffectively around the international circuit for the past decade or a full-strength, professional and highly motivated team that could cause the world's best a problem? Tongans have talent in abundance – unfortunately their best players have been ruthlessly poached by Australia and New Zealand over the years. In the past two years alone Australia have fielded four Tongan backrow forwards at Test level – Willie Ofahengaue, Toutai Kefu, Fili Finau and Daniel Manu. The All Blacks, meanwhile, have capped mighty No 8 Isitolo Maka, rugged utility forward Charles Reichelmann and prop Carl Hoeft. Throw in Australian rugby league's hitman Solomon Haumono or maybe move Jonah Lomu, the world's most famous Tongan, to his schoolboy position of lock and you would have the makings of a truly terrifying, hard-running, big-hitting pack. But Tonga's South African coaches, Phil Pretorious and Dave Waterston, are beginning to lure a few back, like former Australia Sevens stars Semi Taupeaafe and Ipolito Fenukitau. In addition, New South Wales hooker Timote Tavalea, ex-Leeds full-back Sateki Tu'ipulotu, Pontypridd prop Ngalu Ta'u, Ebbw Vale utility back Siua Taumalolo (man of the match in the 1998 SWALEC Cup final), club colleague and lock Kuli Faletau and Llanelli's cultured centre Selisi Finau should all be available in October. And in New Zealand, Otago Highlanders' electric centre Pita Alatini and Wellington Hurricanes' openside flanker Kupu Vanisi might yet opt for the land of their fathers, though both have been included in the All Blacks' preliminary squad. If these can be combined with the exciting home-grown talents of players like flanker Jonny Koloi, Tonga have the potential to trouble the best. Koloi was outstanding during their repechage games and after playing for Gauteng Lions in the Currie Cup will be moving to Llanelli after the World Cup. After making a slow start in this summer's Epson Cup, Tonga finished strongly with a win over Canada, a draw against Western Samoa and a narrow defeat against Fiji. They also recorded a memorable win over France. Certainly Tonga won't be physically intimidated. To date their only win in the World Cup finals was against Ivory Coast four years ago, but already the Tongans are targeting their game against Italy at Welford Road on 10 October.

Key players: Selisi Finau, Jonny Koloi, Sateki Tu'ipulotu.

1987: *Pool*: Tonga 4 Canada 37; Tonga 16 Wales 29; Tonga 9 Ireland 32.

1991: Did not compete

1995: *Pool*: Tonga 10 France 38; Tonga 5 Scotland 41; Tonga 29 Ivory Coast 11.

1999: Qualification: *Pacific Round B*: Tonga 10 Fiji 20; Tonga 68 Cook Islands 12. *Australasia qualifying tournament*: Tonga 20 Western Samoa 28; Tonga 0 Australia 74. *Repechage*: Tonga 37 Georgia 6; Georgia 28 Tonga 27 (Tonga win 64-34 on aggregate). Tonga 58 South Korea 26; South Korea 15 Tonga 82 (Tonga win 140-41 on aggregate).

Pool C

CANADA

Always tough and competitive, Canada will be looking to repeat their achievement of 1991 by qualifying for the quarter-final play-offs and then the quarter-finals from the French group. On this occasion, as then, they will be opposed by France and Fiji, the only difference being Namibia's presence instead of Romania. With Gareth Rees directing operations in his fourth tournament Canada have every chance of troubling the best. With world-class forwards such as Al Charron and Mike James and formidable grafters like Mike Schmid and John Tait they can live with the best up front, while in the backs Dave Lougheed made an excellent impression with championship-winning Leicester last season, John Graf has a wealth of experience at scrum-half and young Fred Asselin is developing rapidly. A full summer in the competitive Pacific Rim tournament, albeit occasionally with a less than full-strength squad, ultimately proved disappointing though the Canadians as a squad tend to use these experiences. Canada finished bottom of the table without a win in five games. Particularly galling, and worrying, was a rare 18-17 defeat against North American rivals USA. The Canadians will complete their preparations with testing games in August against Wales, at the Millennium Stadium, and England at Twickenham. Canada have appeared in all three World Cup finals with some distinction. In 1987 they were impressive 37-4 winners over Tonga before losing to both Ireland and Wales, and in 1991 they defeated Fiji and Romania en route to a quarter-final against New Zealand, where they covered themselves in glory against the All Blacks. In South Africa, after again disposing of Romania, they made the Springboks and Australia work extraordinarily hard for victory. Often forgotten amidst the controversy of having two players sent off against South Africa was a superbly brave and committed performance that was scarcely reflected in the score. Qualification for this year's tournament, after comparatively routine wins over the USA and Uruguay, ended with a disappointing 54-28 defeat by Argentina which served as a timely warning that Canada need to tighten their scrummaging technique. Having absorbed the lessons, they will be disappointed with anything less than a place in the quarter-final play-offs.

Key players: Al Charron, John Graf, Gareth Rees.

1987: *Pool*: Canada 37 Tonga 4; Canada 19 Ireland 46; Canada 9 Wales 40.

1991: *Pool*: Canada 13 Fiji 3; Canada 19 Romania 11; Canada 13 France 19. *Quarter-final*: Canada 13 New Zealand 29.

1995: *Pool*: Canada 34 Romania 3; Canada 11 Australia 25; Canada 0 South Africa 20.

1999: Qualification: *Americas qualifying tournament*: Canada 38 Uruguay 15; Canada 31 USA 14; Canada 28 Argentina 54.

FIJI

One of the great enigmas of world rugby, Fiji have rarely done themselves justice on the international stage though there were signs in the recently completed Pan-Pacific tournament that the Pacific islanders, under their New Zealand coach Brad Johnstone, are just beginning to fulfil their potential. Certainly a 40-29 win over Canada suggested that their forwards are beginning to tighten up, something which must happen if their exciting backs are ever to be unleashed. Waisale Serevi may or may not appear, depending on how the politics of Fijian rugby unravel, and Marika Vunibaka, star of the 1997 World Sevens Cup, may also be absent after falling into dispute with the Union midway through their Epson Cup campaign this summer. We should, however, be able to enjoy the running talents of Fero Lasagavibau and the Little brothers, Nicky and Lawrence. Up front, former Waikato and New Zealand U21 hooker Greg Smith has added steel to the front row and often captains the side while Sale lock Simon Raiwalui is a fine line-out operator and extremely mobile. The side began to show a little more like their known form in this summer's Epson Cup, being responsible for Japan's solitary defeat. Fiji's best performance came in the 1987 World Cup, when they managed to defeat Argentina 28-9 and ran eventual finalists France close in the quarter-finals before losing 31-16. A breakthrough really did seem imminent. Yet four years later, possibly distracted by a full-scale revolution back home, it was a sorry tale as they failed totally to adapt to French conditions and a foreign culture and were whitewashed in a pool containing Romania, Canada and France. Even worse was to follow, as the nation's preoccupation with sevens took a grip to such an extent that they failed even to qualify for the 1995 tournament. That situation has, to a certain extent, been turned around and Fiji demonstrated some real determination in clinching second place in the Australasia qualifying tournament last August, defeating Western Samoa and Tonga after a heavy reverse against Australia. The Fijians have never travelled well when leaving the southern hemisphere, but if they can learn to relax in the warm autumn sunshine and get the French crowd on their side against Canada and Namibia they can pose a real threat. One day, somewhere in the world, somebody is going to be on the wrong end of a superlative Fijian performance.

Key players: Fero Lasagavibau, Greg Smith, Waisale Serevi.

1987: *Pool*: Fiji 28 Argentina 9; Fiji 13 New Zealand 74; Fiji 15 Italy 18. *Quarter-finals*. Fiji 16 France 31.

1991: *Pool*: Fiji 3 Canada 13; Fiji 9 France 33; Fiji 15 Romania 17.

1995: Did not qualify for finals

1999: Qualification: *Pacific Round B*: Fiji 20 Tonga 10; Fiji 53 Cook Islands 7. *Australasia qualifying tournament*: Fiji 20 Australia 66; Fiji 26 Western Samoa 18; Fiji 32 Tonga 15.

FRANCE

After their disastrous 1999 Five Nations tournament, when they started as favourites to complete a third consecutive Grand Slam and finished as wooden-spoon winners, it's impossible to predict exactly how France will fare in the World Cup. But on the assumption that they cannot play with such a lack of focus and passion two years in succession, it's probably safest to assume that they will return to something like their known form – in which case they will be a considerable threat, especially on home soil. In partial mitigation, last season injury did deprive them of key players such as Jean-Luc Sadourny, Stephane Glas, Christophe Lamaison and Olivier Magne, but French rugby has made light of such absences in the past. Their biggest failing was up front, where their pack lacked the strength and intimidating qualities of yesteryear – they badly need a front five forward of the stature of Abdelatif Benazzi to come through before the World Cup. Indeed it was no surprise when coach Jean-Claude Skrela recalled the man himself for their first international of the summer, when they thrashed Romania 62-8 at Castres. That win, however, was not built upon. With Benazzi injured and forced to return home, France slumped to defeat against Tonga and then suffered a record 54-7 reverse against New Zealand. The situation could not get much worse. The French had become arrogant and complacent after two years of success, believing they could play what assistant coach Pierre Villepreux calls the 'beautiful game' without completing the hard graft up front first. All that has got to change if they are to stand any chance. Statistically France have a good record in the World Cup, their 75 per cent win ratio placing them equal third behind South Africa and New Zealand. Their campaign in 1987 will be remembered for their miraculous 30-24 semi-final win over Australia rather than their disappointing 29-9 defeat against New Zealand in the final, when they were tired and produced an unusually flat performance. In 1991, after an unimpressive series of pool victories, they were outpsyched and outplayed by England at the Parc des Princes, but four years ago in South Africa they improved steadily as the tournament progressed – so much so that they were distinctly unlucky to lose in the pouring rain against South Africa in the Durban semi-final. All that seems a long time ago as they prepare for the 1999 tournament without confidence and without the swagger normally associated with French rugby.

Key players: Christian Califano, Thomas Castaignede, Olivier Magne.

1987: *Pool*: France 20 Scotland 20; France 55 Romania 12; France 70 Zimbabwe 12. *Quarter-final*: France 31 Fiji 16. *Semi-final*: France 30 Australia 24. *Final*: France 9 New Zealand 29.

1991: *Pool*: France 30 Romania 3; France 33 Fiji 9; France 19 Canada 13. *Quarter-final*: France 10 England 19.

1995: *Pool*: France 38 Tonga 10; France 54 Ivory Coast 18; France 22 Scotland 9. *Quarter-final*: France 36 Ireland 12. *Semi-final*: France 15 South Africa 19. *3rd/4th play-off*: France 19 England 9.

1999: Qualification: As 1995 play-off winners.

NAMIBIA

Namibia, formerly South West Africa, break new ground by competing in the World Cup finals for the first time. Their preparation has been far from ideal, starting back in April when a row broke out regarding the alleged failure of the Namibian Federation to instigate previously agreed measures to stamp out racial inequality within the Namibian game, both in the national side and at domestic club level. At one stage the argument became so protracted that the Namibian Sports Council was threatening to withdraw the national side from the World Cup, but eventually a compromise settlement was found. Then in June came the sacking of national coach Johan Venter after his side won just one of their 14 Vodacom Cup games. In an emergency measure he was replaced by Rudy Joubert, the manager of coaching in South Africa, who has been seconded to the Namibians until the end of their World Cup campaign, having already helped out with their development programme. Joubert immediately arranged a warm-up game against a Springbok Development XV in June, while Namibia were due to continue with a two-match series against old rivals Zimbabwe and a training camp in Italy where they were scheduled to play the hosts, Spain and Fiji, before completing their preparations at home. 'Our pool gives us an enormous challenge but I'm really keen to give our players the best possible chance to be competitive,' declares Joubert. 'Our players are amateurs but I still believe we can have professional attitudes and if the right structures are in place the players will achieve their potential.' With barely 1,000 individuals to choose from it's difficult to envisage anything but heavy defeats for Namibia, but at least their extensive Vodacom Cup campaign enabled them to train and play together like a club side and the heat in south-west France should also be much to their liking. They have players who could catch the eye – Attie Samuelson is a clever runner if he can be put into space and full-back Leane van Dyk is another talented all-round footballer. The trouble, as with all the smaller nations, will be trying to secure enough possession to become competitive. Namibia are used to being underdogs – after their disappointing showing in their pool games they approached the African qualifying tournament in Casablanca with some trepidation – but they emerged as impressive winners, improving as the week progressed until they signed off with a thumping 39-14 win over Zimbabwe.

Key players: Quinn Hough, Attie Samuelson, Rudi van Vuuren.

1987: Did not compete

1991: Did not compete

1995: Did not qualify for finals

1999: Qualification: *Africa Round C*: Namibia 17 Tunisia 20; Namibia 32 Zimbabwe 26. *African qualifying tournament*: Namibia 22 Cote D'Ivoire 10; Namibia 17 Morocco 8; Namibia 39 Zimbabwe 14.

Pool D

ARGENTINA

Argentina won't win the World Cup, they probably won't even win their pool, but with their forward power and competitive instincts they are a team that nobody will relish playing. Always awesome in the front row – rest assured a world-class prop to accompany the rejuvenated Federico Mendez and Roberto Grau will be found – they also possess a world-class line-out operator in captain Pedro Sporleder and a tough-tackling backrow. Half-backs Agustin Pichot and Lisandro Arbizu are as busy and inventive as anybody around but it is out wide that Argentina are invariably found out. They were bitterly disappointed with their 2-0 series defeat against Wales in June, the first time they have ever lost a home series to a British or Irish side. Without a potent attacking runner of their own, they also lack the pace to live with attack-minded countries. Nonetheless, boosted by their professional Europe-based players, they will be a tough side to defeat and in the evenly matched and unpredictable Group D could yet clinch a place in the quarter-final play-offs. For all their qualities, Argentina have yet to do themselves full justice in the World Cup finals. They managed just a 25-16 win over Italy in 1987, when a calamitous 28-9 defeat against Fiji deprived them of an expected quarter-final place. Four years later, based in Wales, they badly misfired, losing all three games, and four years after that in South Africa they again departed without a win. This time, however, there was honour in defeat, outscoring England 2-0 in tries, running Western Samoa close in a minor classic and going down narrowly to Italy. The entire front row of Patricio Noriega, who has since emigrated to Australia where he now plays his international rugby, Mendez and Matias Corral, who has moved to New York and given the game up, would probably have been voted en bloc into the team of the tournament. The Americas qualification tournament boded well this time around with comprehensive wins over USA and Uruguay and an impressive 54-28 victory over Canada – though the margin possibly flattered Argentina. It's about time that Argentina fired on the big occasion. So tight is their group that it is possible to envisage them winning all three games, or losing all three. If nothing else it will make for exciting viewing.

Key players: Lisandro Arbizu, Federico Mendez, Agustin Pichot.

1987: *Pool*: Argentina 9 Fiji 28; Argentina 25 Italy 16; Argentina 15 New Zealand 46.

1991: *Pool*: Argentina 19 Australia 32; Argentina 7 Wales 16; Argentina 12 Western Samoa 35.

1995: *Pool*: Argentina 18 England 24; Argentina 26 Western Samoa 32; Argentina 25 Italy 31.

1999: Qualification: *Americas qualifying tournament*: Argentina 52 USA 24; Argentina 55 Uruguay 0; Argentina 54 Canada 28.

JAPAN

Japan may have found themselves in one of the toughest groups – along with hosts Wales, Western Samoa and Argentina – but the 1999 World Cup represents their best-ever chance of making an impact on the world scene. After settling in Japan following the 1995 World Cup, when they represented New Zealand in the final, Jamie Joseph and Graeme Bachop qualified to play for Japan in May 1999 and made an immediate impact as their new side raced to three home victories in the Epson Cup, defeating Canada 23-21, Tonga 44-17 and Western Samoa 37-34 when Joseph scored the winning try on the final whistle. They also defeated USA and suffered just one defeat, away to Fiji, en route to the title. An important corner has been turned and Japan can no longer be treated lightly. Two further talented Kiwis – lock Robert Gordon and flanker Greg Smith – are important members of the squad, having also served the necessary three-year qualification period, while centre Andrew McCormick is a naturalised Japanese citizen and frequently captains the national side. Add in some exciting home-grown talent and Japan have the makings of their best-ever side. Wing Daisuke Ohata showed with his wonder try against Scotland in the 1999 Hong Kong Sevens that he is one of the game's best broken-field runners, and subsequently scored four tries in the Epson Cup during the summer, while fly-half Keiji Hirose scored 34 points in that win over Tonga, including a world record nine penalties. Japan's only victory in the World Cup finals to date came at Ravenhill in 1991 when they recorded an exhilarating 52-8 triumph over Zimbabwe. They had come close against USA four years earlier, when they went down 21-18, but elsewhere it has been a case of facing up to heavy defeats. In 1987 they were trounced 60-7 by England, but much worse was to follow eight years later in Bloemfontein when they were ruthlessly crushed 145-17 by New Zealand, who scored 21 tries en route to their record-breaking win – Marc Ellis alone scored six tries and Simon Culhane kicked 20 conversions, as well as scoring a try himself. Although they handled themselves with dignity, Japan found it a deeply humiliating experience and thereafter there was never any doubt that they would turn to their 'Kiwis' as soon as they became eligible. Coached by Seiji Hirao, they feel their time is coming.

Key players: Graeme Bachop, Jamie Joseph, Keiji Hirose.

1987: *Pool*: Japan 18 USA 21; Japan 7 England 60; Japan 23 Australia 42.

1991: *Pool*: Japan 9 Scotland 47; Japan 16 Ireland 32; Japan 52 Zimbabwe 8.

1995: *Pool*: Japan 10 Wales 57; Japan 28 Ireland 50; Japan 17 New Zealand 145.

1999: Qualification: *Asian qualifying tournament*: Japan 40 South Korea 12; Japan 134 Taiwan 6; Japan 47 Hong Kong 7.

WALES

Not so long ago it seemed as if the honour of hosting the 1999 World Cup was going to prove an acute embarrassment for Wales as their national side struggled from disaster to disaster, culminating in two horrendous defeats against England and France – 60-26 and 51-0 respectively – in the 1998 Five Nations. Director of rugby Terry Cobner then travelled to New Zealand to persuade Graham Henry to accept the toughest job in rugby as Wales coach and since that time there has been a steady improvement. Wales still have much to do – they slipped to sloppy defeats against Scotland and Ireland – but nothing can take away from the quality and courage of the attacking play they produced in that sensational 34-33 win over France in Paris in the 1999 Five Nations and they demonstrated great patience at Wembley three weeks later to deprive England of the title. Henry will have hoped to build on that during their summer tour of Argentina, while a one-off international against South Africa in June to celebrate the opening of the Millennium Stadium was also a big test. They passed with flying colours, overcoming fatigue and staleness after a ten-month season to record an historic 29-19 win over South Africa, their first ever win over the Springboks. That victory above all others convinced the sceptics that they could yet prosper at RWC 99. Objectively Wales' major weaknesses are that they concede too many tries – they must introduce more organisation into their defence – and they badly need a second international-class line-out jumper to back up the splendid Chris Wyatt, who waged a solitary battle in the 1999 Five Nations. Top sides will recognise that by 'dealing' with Wyatt they can reduce Wales' line-out possession to almost nothing. To date Wales' only notable World Cup campaign came in 1987 when they recovered superbly from a 49-6 mauling against New Zealand in the semi-final to defeat Australia in the 3rd place play-off, Paul Thorburn landing a magnificent touchline conversion. Four years later it was a sorry tale, although in retrospect their infamous 16-13 defeat against Western Samoa doesn't look so bad – the Samoans were a class act and only lost by six points to eventual champions Australia later in the tournament. Wales' 1995 campaign was ill-starred from the start, Alan Davies being dumped as coach just before the tournament. A plucky display against New Zealand was probably the highlight, an abysmal first-half showing against Ireland the nadir.

Key players: Colin Charvis, Shane Howarth, Neil Jenkins.

1987: *Pool*: Wales 13 Ireland 6; Wales 29 Tonga 16; Wales 40 Canada 9. *Quarter-final*: Wales 16 England 3. *Semi-final*: Wales 6 New Zealand 49. *3rd/4th play-off*: Wales 22 Australia 21.

1991: *Pool*: Wales 13 Western Samoa 16; Wales 16 Argentina 7; Wales 3 Australia 38.

1995: *Pool*: Wales 57 Japan 10; Wales 9 New Zealand 34; Wales 23 Ireland 24.

1999: Qualification: As host country.

WESTERN SAMOA

Two World Cup finals and two quarter-final places. The remarkable Western Samoans – small in numbers but a proud and highly physical island race – were star turns in 1991 and again four years later, and although finding themselves in a highly competitive group are again favoured to do well. That natural talent has always been there but under former All Black wing Bryan Williams' shrewd management and Pat Lam's astute captaincy, they are now paying more attention to detail and are as well prepared as any side. Williams has managed to negotiate a significant sponsorship deal with Adidas to ease their financial burdens and many of Samoa's top players have been playing professionally abroad in New Zealand and in Britain, gaining valuable experience of varying weather conditions. Former All Blacks Va'aiga Tuigamala and Stephen Bachop have returned to the land of their fathers, Lam is playing better than ever, Trevor Leota has emerged as one of the game's 'big-hitters', Terry Fanolua, veteran centre To'o Vaega, George Leaupepe and Earl Va'a have been lapping up the experience of Premiership rugby, while Brian Lima has continued to look one of the best wings in the Super 12. The only major disappointment to date is that a serious neck injury seems certain to prevent powerhouse flanker Junior Paramore from playing. Western Samoa know that they must continue to work hard on their front five, who remain comparatively lightweight by international standards. They must also keep the lid on their explosive temperaments – the dismissals of Leota and Leaupepe in quick succession cost them a famous victory against France in Apia in June. Such is Western Samoa's standing within the game that it seems unbelievable they did not qualify for the initial World Cup twelve years ago. Stunned by the disgrace, they concentrated on blooding exciting new talent at the Hong Kong Sevens and contacting expatriates in New Zealand – such as Lam and Frank Bunce – who formed the hard core of the 1991 squad. Their 16-13 win over Wales is now the stuff of legends but even more impressive were their 35-12 win over Argentina and a brave 9-3 defeat to eventual champions Australia in alien, muddy conditions at Pontypool Park. Although suffering a pool defeat against England in South Africa, they claimed victories over Argentina and Italy before losing to the eventual winners in a rugged quarter-final at Ellis Park.

Key players: Pat Lam, Trevor Leota, Va'aiga Tuigamala.

1987: Did not compete

1991: *Pool*: Western Samoa 16 Wales 13; Western Samoa 3 Australia 9; Western Samoa 35 Argentina 12. *Quarter-final*: Western Samoa 6 Scotland 28.

1995: *Pool*: Western Samoa 42 Italy 18; Western Samoa 32 Argentina 26; Western Samoa 22 England 44. *Quarter-final*: Western Samoa 14 South Africa 42.

1999: Qualification: *Australasian qualifying tournament*: Western Samoa 28 Tonga 20; Western Samoa 18 Fiji 26; Western Samoa 13 Australia 25.

Pool E

AUSTRALIA

Definitely one of the teams to beat, Australia seem to have done nothing but play against South Africa and New Zealand in recent seasons and their success against both demonstrates their World Cup-winning potential. They do need a little break – if that's the right word – from injuries, however. Key players such as John Eales, Matt Burke, Jason Little, Ben Tune and Steve Larkham have all suffered serious injuries over the summer and although they will have benefited from a prolonged rest, there is no substitute for regular games as the biggest competition of all looms. At least coach Rod MacQueen has been able to examine all his options as Australia's squad strength has been fully tested. He will have been moderately satisfied with two wins over Ireland – the Aussies struggled a little in the second Test at Perth – and very pleased with a thoroughly competent win over England at the Olympic Stadium, Sydney. Australia in full flight should be an exciting side to watch – their backrow three of Burke, Tune and Joe Roff bears comparison with any in the world, half-backs Larkham and George Gregan have pace and wit and the strapping James Holbeck has been a major discovery at centre. The naturalisation of former Argentinian World Cup prop Patricio Noriega has added steel to the front row, 1991 veteran Phil Kearns has been back to his best and Eales, when fully fit, is simply the world's best all-round forward. Apart from injuries the only possible weakness would seem to be the backrow, where despite an array of available talent, the correct balance has sometimes proved elusive. Australia were unhappy with their showing in South Africa four years ago and not just with that agonising quarter-final defeat against the old enemy, England. They failed to fire in the pool, but in a relatively straightforward group – surely only Ireland will seriously test them – they should have ample opportunity to build a head of steam this time around. In 1987 they were also slightly disappointed to finish only fourth but in 1991 they were, of course, deserving all-purpose champions, able to outpass and outrun New Zealand in the semi-finals and then out-think and out-defend England in the Twickenham final. Strongly fancied to do well this time around and emulate their cricketing brothers by claiming another world title for Australia.

Key players: Matt Burke, John Eales, Steve Larkham.

1987: *Pool*: Australia 19 England 6; Australia 47 USA 12; Australia 42 Japan 23. *Quarter-final*: Australia 33 Ireland 15. *Semi-final*: Australia 24 France 30. *3rd/4th play-off*: Australia 21 Wales 22.

1991: *Pool*: Australia 32 Argentina 19; Australia 9 Western Samoa 3; Australia 38 Wales 3. *Quarter-final*: Australia 19 Ireland 18. *Semi-final*: Australia 16 New Zealand 6. *Final*: Australia 12 England 6.

1995: *Pool*: Australia 18 South Africa 27; Australia 25 Canada 11; Australia 42 Romania 3. *Quarter-final*: Australia 22 England 25.

1999: Qualification: *Australasian qualifying tournament*: Australia 66 Fiji 20; Australia 74 Tonga 0; Australia 25 Western Samoa 13.

IRELAND

Given home advantage and a group in which there will be no excuses if they do not qualify for the quarter-final play-offs, Ireland would seem to have the springboard for a useful World Cup – but the men in green have flattered to deceive too often in the past for supporters to hold out many genuine hopes of success. In last season's Five Nations they went into the tournament on the back of a promising performance against South Africa and Ulster's morale-lifting win in the European Cup, yet still disappointed bitterly. All the old problems remained – the inability to score tries clinically when the opportunity presents itself, the lack of class in midfield and the absence of an obvious scrum-half to partner David Humphreys. Hopefully a four-week summer tour to Australia, with the emphasis on squad training as well as two Test matches, will have gone some way to resolving the problems, along with a testing warm-up game against Argentina. Their performance in the second Test at Perth, when they scored three tries and narrowly lost 32-26, offered much-needed cheer after a disappointing 46-10 defeat at Ballymore the previous week. There were some pluses last season. The scrum remains solid, Jeremy Davidson is beginning to recapture his Lions form after a career-threatening knee injury and South African-reared Dion O'Cuinneagain was an outstanding newcomer in the backrow. Now Ireland need to get world-class lock Malcolm O'Kelly fully fit after his shoulder injury, discover the best way of employing Eric Miller's talents in the backrow, use Keith Wood more sparingly on the charge and somehow incorporate the powerful Rob Henderson in the backs. Get it right and they can challenge anybody on their day. In the past three World Cups Ireland have never failed to reach the quarter-finals, indicating that at least they play up to their known ability and occasionally beyond. In 1987 they gave a good account of themselves before losing 33-15 to Australia and four years later they enjoyed their finest moment, taking the lead three minutes from time against the same opponents before Michael Lynagh's dramatic late try saved the eventual winners. In 1995 they never got to grips with France in the hot sun of Durban but performed better than most against New Zealand in the pool when they scored three good tries and their opponents were flattered by the 43-19 scoreline. With home advantage the stage is set; Ireland have the capability of producing one big shock in the tournament. Where and when is the question.

Key players: David Humphreys, Malcolm O'Kelly, Keith Wood.

1987: *Pool*: Ireland 6 Wales 13; Ireland 46 Canada 19; Ireland 32 Tonga 9.
Quarter-final: Ireland 15 Australia 33.

1991: *Pool*: Ireland 55 Zimbabwe 11; Ireland 32 Japan 16; Ireland 15 Scotland 24.
Quarter-final: Ireland 18 Australia 19.

1995: *Pool*: Ireland 19 New Zealand 43; Ireland 50 Japan 28; Ireland 24 Wales 23.
Quarter-final: Ireland 12 France 36.

1999: Qualification: *European qualifying tournament*: Ireland 70 Georgia 0; Ireland 53 Romania 35.

ROMANIA

Romania's glory years may have gone but they will certainly not be overawed by USA and Ireland, although they hold out little hope of success against Australia. The World Cup came along four years too late for the Romanians. Had it been staged in 1983 they were possible semi-final material but by 1987 they were enduring a frustrating dip in form. They started with a 21-20 win over Zimbabwe in Auckland and then rested a number of key players against France, with the predictable result that they were thrashed 55-12 in Wellington. The key match was against Scotland but too much momentum had been lost in that heavy defeat against France and Romania went down 55-28. Murariu scored two tries but, tragically, was gunned down at a checkpoint two years later in the revolution. Former Romania captain Raducu Durbac also perished in the hostilities, as did many grassroots players, supporters and coaches. Romanian rugby suffered grievously but they are a resistant bunch and were determined to take their appointed place in the 1991 finals. Although again finding themselves against the French, Romania would have ordinarily fancied their chances against Canada and Fiji. Despite heroic resistance in the opening 60 minutes, a 30-3 defeat against France in Beziers was no surprise but Canada also proved too hot to handle in Toulouse, Romania going down 19-11. Romania did well to recover against Fiji at Brive, scoring three tries in an unusually fluid performance. Four years ago Romania were outclassed 34-3 against the Canadians in Port Elizabeth but rallied to perform with superb courage against South Africa, the eventual champions, at Newlands. South Africa could only manage a 21-8 win and Romania scored the try of the game through flanker Andrei Guranescu. They ran out of steam a little in the final game, losing 42-3 to Australia, but at least served notice that Romanian rugby was not entirely without hope. And so to the 1999 World Cup. In their qualifying group there was little opportunity to extend themselves against Belgium, the Netherlands and Ukraine while in the European pool, when denied four of their first-choice front five players by club demands in France, they lost 53-35 to Ireland and scraped through their 'must win' contest against Georgia 27-23. The omens do not look good. A 62-8 drubbing against France in May only underlined their difficulties but Romania have struggled before and bounced back. A quarter-final place looks beyond them but they fully intend to record only their third victory at the World Cup finals when they play USA on 9 October at Lansdowne Road.

Key players: Tiberiu Brinza, Catalin Draguceanu, Gheorghe Solomie.

1987: *Pool*: Romania 21 Zimbabwe 20; Romania 12 France 55; Romania 28 Scotland 55.

1991: *Pool*: Romania 3 France 30; Romania 11 Canada 19; Romania 17 Fiji 15.

1995: *Pool*: Romania 3 Canada 34; Romania 8 South Africa 21; Romania 3 Australia 42.

1999: Qualification: *Europe Round B*: Romania 83 Belgium 13; Romania 42 Netherlands 3; Romania 74 Poland 13; Romania 39 Ukraine 17. *European qualifying tournament*: Romania 27 Georgia 23; Romania 35 Ireland 53.

USA

One day the USA is going to get its act together on the rugby pitch and the rest of the world will suffer – but in the meantime we have to make do with tantalising glimpses of their potential. They performed well in this summer's Pacific Rim contest – early home victories over Tonga and Fiji were particularly encouraging – and the promise of a professional national league could strengthen the game further, but they have yet to show any degree of consistency against the more established international sides. After failing to impress during qualification – they came perilously close to losing to Uruguay in Buenos Aires and being condemned to the repechage process – they have no reason to fear Ireland and Romania, though Australia could be another matter. The strength of the team undoubtedly lies in the forwards, led by Bath's talented No 8 Dan Lyle who has now made a full recovery from a career-threatening anterior cruciate knee ligament injury. He will be joined by experienced troopers such as towering locks David Hodges and Luke Gross, flanker Rob Lumkong, hooker Tom Billups, former American footballer Richard Tardits in the backrow and West Hartlepool lock Philippe Farner, who is French-born but has an American mother. They have unearthed a competitive goal-kicking scrum-half in the pugnacious Kevin Dalzell who is also a fine broken-field runner. Dalzell scored three tries in the Epson Cup and finished up as the tournament's second highest points-scorer with 50. A major discovery. A final warm-up game against England in August, under the floodlights at Twickenham, should give us an accurate indicator as to exactly how far this side has progressed. The USA missed out on qualification last time around but appeared in the first two World Cups. They won their first ever game, 21-18 against Japan, but have not tasted victory since. That initial success was followed by a 34-12 defeat against England and a 47-12 reverse against Australia. They also found the going tough four years later in England when they were outgunned 30-9 by Italy – a game they had expected to win – and were then defeated 46-6 by New Zealand at Gloucester and 37-9 by England at Twickenham when they provided stern resistance for much of the game. Coach Jack Clarke, aided by welcome sponsorship by Rupert Murdoch's Fox TV, has begun the process of making the national squad professional in approach and deed. Vast improvements have been made, but as yet we still await take-off.

Key players: Kevin Dalzell, Rob Lumkong, Dan Lyle.

1987: *Pool*: USA 21 Japan 18; USA 12 Australia 47; USA 12 England 34.

1991: *Pool*: USA 9 Italy 30; USA 6 New Zealand 46; USA 9 England 37.

1995: *Pool*: Did not qualify for finals

1999: Qualification: *Americas qualifying tournament*: USA 24 Argentina 52; USA 14 Canada 31; USA 21 Uruguay 16.

THE QUALIFYING PROCESS

By the time Wales run out against Argentina at the Millennium Stadium on Friday 1 October, the 1999 World Cup will actually be over three years old. The action from the qualifying tournament started in Riga in September 1996 when the home side, Latvia, made short work of Norway, and ended in May 1999 when Tonga crushed South Korea 82-15 in the final repechage game. In between, a host of rugby nations played their 'World Cup', relishing the competitive experience and enjoying the increased exposure the tournament gave them. There were many success stories. In South America Chile mounted a genuine challenge to Uruguay in an attempt to claim the fourth spot at the qualifying tournament in Buenos Aires. With their U19 sides performing well at their own World Cup, Chile are a side to watch carefully in the future. Uruguay themselves are also improving steadily, adding to the strength in depth on the South American continent, an area where perhaps the International Board should allocate more resources. In the Caribbean, Trinidad and Tobago showed signs of progress and there is every chance that in the qualifying process for 2003 the West Indies will field a joint side for the first time, incorporating players from Bahamas, Barbados, Trinidad and Tobago, Bermuda and a number of French-speaking islands. In Europe Croatia, bolstered by a number of expatriate New Zealanders such as Frano Botica and Pau flanker Scott Keith – there is a large contingent of Croatian fishermen in Auckland – made great strides and offered serious opposition to Italy in their half of the draw. There was also a welcome resurgence by the former Soviet states, notably the Ukraine and Georgia. The latter, who can boast one of the biggest packs in international rugby, learned a host of useful lessons against Romania and Ireland during the qualifying tournament in Dublin and acquitted themselves well in their repechage games against Tonga, winning their home tie in Tbilisi. In Africa the disappointment was the failure of the Ivory Coast to develop from 1995. Nobody in Asia is yet able to match Japan and South Korea, especially as the latter are now able to call on their New Zealand contingent – but look out for the appearance of China next time around. The Pacific was predictably dominated by Australia and the big Pacific islands – Fiji, Tonga and Western Samoa – but the Cook Islands made a useful debut and could capitalise on their many New Zealand-based players next time. Tahiti also made their tournament debut while Papua New Guinea continue to produce a number of outstanding individual players.

EUROPE

Round A, Pool 1

Ukraine 60 Yugoslavia 0 (Kiev); Austria 3 Yugoslavia 0 (w/o); Switzerland 0 Ukraine 30 (Nyon); Israel 15 Austria 3 (Tel Aviv); Israel 9 Switzerland 9 (Tel Aviv); Yugoslavia 8 Israel 0 (Belgrade); Austria 6 Ukraine 36 (Vienna); Yugoslavia 10 Israel 7 (Belgrade); Ukraine 51 Israel 15 (Odessa); Switzerland 31 Austria 3 (Basle). Pool winners: Ukraine.

Round A, Pool 2

Latvia 44 Norway 6 (Riga); Bulgaria 6 Moldova 14 (Sofia); Norway 7 Croatia 43 (Oslo); Moldova 3 Latvia 8 (Chisinau); Bulgaria 31 Croatia 46 (Sofia); Moldova 31 Norway 7 (Chisinau); Latvia 89 Bulgaria 0 (Riga); Croatia 60 Moldova 5 (Split); Croatia 43 Latvia 24 (Makarska); Norway 22 Bulgaria 7 (Oslo). Pool winners: Croatia.

Round A, Pool 3

Lithuania 26 Luxembourg 3 (Vilnius); Andorra 54 Lithuania 24 (Andorra La Vella); Sweden 39 Hungary 17 (Vanersborg); Luxembourg 3 Hungary 12 (Cessange); Andorra 21 Sweden 20 (Andorra La Vella); Luxembourg 16 Andorra 30 (Luxembourg); Sweden 48 Luxembourg 5 (Karlskrona); Lithuania 17 Sweden 84 (Plunge); Hungary 16 Lithuania 3 (Budapest); Hungary 5 Andorra 34 (Budapest). Pool winners: Andorra.

Round B, Pool 1
Georgia 29 Croatia 15 (Tbilisi); Denmark 8 Georgia 19 (Copenhagen); Croatia 23 Russia 16 (Makarska); Italy 102 Denmark 3 (Brescia); Italy 31 Georgia 14 (L'Aquila); Russia 18 Italy 48 (Krasnoiarsk); Russia 45 Denmark 9 (Penza); Denmark 6 Croatia 40 (Aalborg); Georgia 12 Russia 6 (Tbilisi); Croatia 27 Italy 39 (Makarska). Pool winners: Italy.

Round B, Pool 2
Belgium 13 Romania 83 (Brussels); Ukraine 45 Belgium 5 (Kiev); Netherlands 49 Poland 7 (Amsterdam); Netherlands 35 Ukraine 13 (Amsterdam); Poland 30 Belgium 10 (Gdynia); Belgium 16 Netherlands 9 (Brussels); Romania 42 Netherlands 3 (Bucharest); Romania 74 Poland 13 (Bucharest); Poland 8 Ukraine 19 (Gdansk); Ukraine 17 Romania 39 (Kharkov). Pool winners: Romania.

Round B, Pool 3
Czech Republic 45 Andorra 20 (Prague); Andorra 11 Germany 56 (Andorra La Vella); Germany 31 Czech Republic 17 (Hanover); Andorra 3 Spain 62 (Andorra La Vella); Spain 39 Czech Republic 8 (Santander); Portugal 30 Germany 6 (Lisbon); Czech Republic 10 Portugal 15 (Prague); Germany 9 Spain 24 (Heidelberg); Spain 33 Portugal 22 (Madrid); Portugal 53 Andorra 11 (Lisbon). Pool winners: Spain.

European Qualifying Tournaments

Europe 1 (Dublin)
Ireland 70 Georgia 0; Georgia 23 Romania 27; Ireland 53 Romania 35. Ireland and Romania qualify.

Europe 2 (Huddersfield)
England 110 Netherlands 0; Netherlands 7 Italy 67, England 23 Italy 15. England and Italy qualify.

Europe 3 (Murrayfield)
Scotland 85 Portugal 11; Spain 21 Portugal 17; Scotland 85 Spain 3. Scotland and Spain qualify.

ASIA

Round A
Singapore 11 Thailand 16 (Singapore); Thailand 15 Sri Lanka 30 (Bangkok); Sri Lanka 18 Singapore 15 (Kuala Lumpur). Pool winners: Sri Lanka.

Round B
Malaysia 15 Sri Lanka 37 (Kuala Lumpur); Chinese Taipei 51 Malaysia 13 (Taiwan); Sri Lanka 29 Chinese Taipei 34 (Bangkok). Pool winners: Chinese Taipei.

Asian Qualifying Tournament (Singapore)
Japan 40 South Korea 12; Hong Kong 12 Taiwan 30; Japan 134 Taiwan 6; Hong Kong 20 South Korea 11; South Korea 81 Taiwan 21; Japan 47 Hong Kong 7. Japan qualify.

AFRICA

Round A
Arabian Gulf 53 Botswana 13 (Bahrain); Zambia 30 Arabian Gulf 44 (Ndola); Botswana 13 Zambia 20 (Jwaneng). Pool winners: Arabian Gulf.

Round B
Kenya 37 Arabian Gulf 18 (Nairobi); Arabian Gulf 12 Tunisia 11 (Bahrain); Tunisia 52 Kenya 5 (Tunis). Pool winners: Tunisia.

Round C
Zimbabwe 43 Tunisia 9; Tunisia 20 Namibia 17; Namibia 32 Zimbabwe 26. Namibia and Zimbabwe progress to Africa qualifying tournament.

African Qualifying Tournament (Casablanca)
Morocco 15 Zimbabwe 9; Cote d'Ivoire 10 Namibia 22; Cote d'Ivoire 0 Zimbabwe 32; Morocco 8 Namibia 17; Zimbabwe 19 Namibia 39; Cote d'Ivoire 3 Morocco 6. Namibia qualify.

AMERICAS

Round A, Pool 1
Trinidad & Tobago 41 Brazil 0 (Port of Spain); Brazil bt Guyana (w/o); Trinidad & Tobago bt Guyana (w/o). Pool winners: Trinidad & Tobago.

Round A, Pool 2
Bahamas 3 Bermuda 24 (Nassau); Barbados 23 Bahamas 37 (Bridgetown); Bermuda 52 Barbados 3 (Hamilton). Pool winners: Bermuda.

Round B
Trinidad & Tobago 6 Chile 35 (Port of Spain); Bermuda 52 Trinidad & Tobago 6 (Hamilton); Chile 65 Bermuda 8 (Santiago). Pool winners: Chile.

Round C
Chile 54 Paraguay 6 (Santiago); Uruguay 20 Chile 14 (Punta del Este); Paraguay 3 Uruguay 43 (Asuncion). Pool winners: Uruguay.

Americas Qualifying Tournament (Buenos Aires)
Argentina 52 USA 24; Canada 38 Uruguay 15; Canada 31 USA 14; Argentina 55 Uruguay 0; USA 21 Uruguay 16; Argentina 54 Canada 28. Argentina, Canada and USA qualify.

PACIFIC

Round A
Cook Islands 22 Papua New Guinea 19 (Rarotonga); Papua New Guinea 92 Tahiti 6 (Port Moresby); Tahiti 0 Cook Islands 40 (Papeete). Pool winners: Cook Islands.

Round B
Fiji 20 Tonga 10 (Suva); Cook Islands 7 Fiji 53 (Raratonga); Tonga 68 Cook Islands 12 (Nuku'alofa). Pool winners: Fiji. Tonga also progress to Australasia qualifying tournament.

Australasia Qualifying Tournament (Sydney and Canberra)
Australia 66 Fiji 20; Western Samoa 28 Tonga 20; Australia 74 Tonga 0; Fiji 26 Western Samoa 18; Australia 25 Western Samoa 13; Tonga 15 Fiji 32. Australia, Fiji and Western Samoa qualify.

REPECHAGE

Round 1
Uruguay 46 Portugal 9 (Montevideo); Portugal 24 Uruguay 33 (Lisbon). Uruguay win 79-33 on aggregate. Netherlands 31 Korea 30 (Amsterdam); Korea 78 Netherlands 14 (Seoul). Korea win 108-45 on aggregate. Tonga 37 Georgia 6 (Nuku'alofa), Georgia 28 Tonga 27 (Tbilisi). Tonga win 64-34 on aggregate. Morocco bye.

Round 2
Uruguay 18 Morocco 3 (Montevideo); Morocco 21 Uruguay 18 (Casablanca). Uruguay win 36-24 on aggregate and qualify for Pool A. Tonga 58 South Korea 26 (Nuku'alofa); South Korea 15 Tonga 82 (Seoul). Tonga win 140-41 on aggregate and qualify for Pool B.

1999 Tournament Referees: Derek Bevan (Wales), Brian Campsall (England), Andrew Cole (Australia), Stuart Dickinson (Australia), Joel Dume (France), Wayne Erickson (Australia), Jim Fleming (Scotland), Colin Hawke (New Zealand), Paul Honnis (New Zealand), David McHugh (Ireland), Peter Marshall (Australia), Ed Morrison (England), Paddy O'Brien (New Zealand), Clayton Thomas (Wales), Andre Watson (South Africa), Chris White (England).

WORLD CUP RECORDS

Most points at World Cup finals:

	1987	*1991*	*1995*	*Total*
Gavin Hastings (Scotland)	62	61	104	227
Michael Lynagh (Australia)	82	66	47	195
Grant Fox (New Zealand)	126	44		170
Thierry Lacroix (France)		12	112	124
Jonathan Webb (England)	43	56		99
Didier Camberabero (France)	53	32		85
Rob Andrew (England)	6	79		85
Andrew Mehrtens (New Zealand)		84		84
Gareth Rees (Canada)	26	20	25	71
Ralph Keyes (Ireland)		68		68
Diego Dominguez (Italy)		29	39	68

Most tries at World Cup finals:

	1987	*1991*	*1995*	*Total*
Rory Underwood (England)	2	4	5	11
David Campese (Australia)	4	6		10
Gavin Hastings (Scotland)	3	1	5	9
Ivan Tukalo (Scotland)	3	4		7
John Kirwan (New Zealand)	6	1		7
Jonah Lomu (New Zealand)			7	7
Marc Ellis (New Zealand)			7	7
Ieuan Evans (Wales)	4	1	2	7
Jean-Baptiste Lafond (France)		6		6
Craig Green (New Zealand)	6			6
John Jeffrey (Scotland)	4	2		6

Most points by a team in a single game (includes qualifying):

164	Hong Kong 164 Singapore 13	1995
145	New Zealand 145 Japan 17	1995
104	Italy 104 Czech Republic 8	1995
102	Wales 102 Portugal 11	1995
102	Italy 102 Denmark 3	1999
97	Japan 97 Malaysia 9	1995
93	Hong Kong 93 Thailand 0	1995
92	Papua New Guinea 92 Tahiti 6	1999
90	South Korea 90 Singapore 3	1995
89	Scotland 89 Ivory Coast 0	1995
89	Latvia 89 Bulgaria 0	1999
84	Sweden 84 Latvia 15	1999
80	Hong Kong 80 Taipei 26	1995
74	Western Samoa 74 South Korea 7	1991
74	New Zealand 74 Fiji 13	1987
74	Australia 74 Tonga 0	1999
70	New Zealand 70 Italy 6	1987
70	France 70 Zimbabwe 12	1987
70	Argentina 70 Chile 7	1995

Most points by a player in a single game (includes qualifying):

50	Ashley Billington (Hong Kong) v Singapore (10T)	1995
45	Simon Culhane (New Zealand) v Japan (1T, 20C)	1995
44	Gavin Hastings (Scotland) v Ivory Coast (4T, 9C, 2P)	1995
34	Jamie McKee (Hong Kong) v Singapore (17C)	1995
31	Gavin Hastings (Scotland) v Tonga (1T, 1C, 8P)	1995
30	Didier Camberabero (France) v Zimbabwe (3T, 9C)	1987
30	Marc Ellis (New Zealand) v Japan (6T)	1995
30	Jaco Coetzee (Namibia) v Kenya (3T, 6C, 1P)	1995
30	Pierpaolo Rotilio (Italy) v Denmark (6T)	1999

Most points by a player in a single game (finals):

45	Simon Culhane (New Zealand) v Japan	1995
44	Gavin Hastings (Scotland) v Ivory Coast	1995
31	Gavin Hastings (Scotland) v Tonga	1995
30	Didier Camberabero (France) v Zimbabwe	1987

Most tries by a player in a single game (finals):

6	Marc Ellis (New Zealand) v Japan	1995
4	Ieuan Evans (Wales) v Canada	1987
4	John Gallagher (New Zealand) v Fiji	1987
4	Craig Green (New Zealand) v Fiji	1987
4	Gavin Hastings (Scotland) v Ivory Coast	1995
4	Chester Williams (South Africa) v Western Samoa	1995
4	Jonah Lomu (New Zealand) v England	1995

Most tries by a team in a single game (finals):

21	New Zealand v Japan	1995

Most penalties in World Cup finals:

31	Michael Lynagh (Australia)	1987, 91, 95
29	Thierry Lacroix (France)	1991, 95
27	Grant Fox (New Zealand)	1987, 91

Most penalties in a single game (finals):

8	Thierry Lacroix (France) v Ireland	1995

Most conversions in a single game (finals):

20	Simon Culhane (New Zealand) v Japan	1995

Most drop goals in World Cup finals:

5	Rob Andrew (England)	1987, 91, 95
3	Jonathan Davies (Wales)	1987
3	Andrew Mehrtens (New Zealand)	1995
3	Joel Stransky (South Africa)	1995

Most appearances in World Cup finals:

17	Sean Fitzpatrick (New Zealand)	1987, 91, 95

Playing records of all teams (finals):

	Tournaments	*P*	*W*	*%*
South Africa	1	6	6	100
New Zealand	3	18	16	88
Australia	3	16	12	75
France	3	16	12	75
England	3	16	10	62
Wales	3	12	7	58
Scotland	3	14	8	57
Ireland	3	12	6	50
Western Samoa	2	8	4	50
Canada	3	10	4	40
Italy	3	9	3	33
Argentina	3	9	2	22
Romania	3	9	2	22
Tonga	2	6	1	16
United States	2	6	1	16
Fiji	2	7	1	14
Japan	3	9	1	11
Ivory Coast	1	3	0	0
Zimbabwe	2	6	0	0

PAST WORLD CUPS

1987 World Cup

Final

NEW ZEALAND 29 FRANCE 9 (Auckland, 20 June 1987)

Favourites New Zealand took the inaugural World Cup final with an impressive no-nonsense performance in front of their own fans. The New Zealand authorities had worked so hard to get the tournament up and running that it seemed appropriate that David Kirk should be the first captain to lift the Webb Ellis trophy. Kirk himself had only been deputising throughout the tournament for Andy Dalton, who unfortunately sustained an injury and was unable to take any part in the competition. Before the final the game itself was being billed as a classic northern/southern hemisphere clash but in truth there was little clash in styles. Throughout the competition the All Blacks showed as much if not more flair behind the scrum as the French, while Jacques Foroux's France sides were always founded on forward power. The biggest difference on the day was that France looked a little tired and jaded – not surprising given their epic semi-final against Australia the previous week when Serge Blanco's try clinched their victory in injury time. The physical toll was high and France spent much of the subsequent week resting while, in comparison, New Zealand had cruised through their semi-final with a thumping 49-6 win over Wales. New Zealand's tries in the final fittingly came from three of their star players throughout the campaign – Kirk, powerful-striding wing John Kirwain and the amazing former Western Samoan flanker Michael Jones, who was just starting a long and illustrious career. The ever-reliable Grant Fox did the rest with a 17-point haul while France could only manage a try by Pierre Berbizier, converted by Didier Camberabero, who also added a penalty. The World Cup was up and running. The organisation wasn't perfect but for a first attempt it was to be commended. The competition was in place, huge public interest had been generated and everybody knew that henceforth, rugby union had a global showpiece of which to be proud.

New Zealand: J.Gallagher; J.Kirwan, J.Stanley, W.Taylor, C.Green; G. Fox, D.Kirk (capt); J.Drake, S.Fitzpatrick, S.McDowell, M.Pierce, G. Whetton, A.Whetton, M.Jones, W.Shelford.

Scorers: T: Jones, Kirk, Kirwan. C: Fox. P: Fox (4). DG: Fox.

France: S.Blanco; D.Camberabero, P.Sella, D.Charvet, P.Lagisquet; F. Mesnel, P.Berbizier; P.Ondarts, D.Dubroca (capt), J-P.Garuet, A.Lorieux, J.Condom, E.Champ, L.Rodriguez, D.Erbani.

Scorers: T: Berbizier. C: Camberabero. P: Camberabero.

Referee: K. Fitzgerald (Australia).

Third place play-off

AUSTRALIA 21 WALES 22 (Rotorua, 18 June 1987)

Australia: A.Leeds; P.Grigg, M.Burke, A.Slack (capt), D.Campese; M.Lynagh, B.Smith; C.Lillicrap, T.Lawton, A.McIntyre, S.Cutler, T.Coker, D.Codey, S.Poidevin, S.Tuynman.

Replacements: N.Farr-Jones for Grigg (40), E.Rodriguez for Lillicrap (40).

Sent off: Codey (7).

Scorers: T: Burke, Grigg. C: Lynagh (2). P: Lynagh (2). DG: Lynagh.

Wales: P.Thorburn; I.Evans, J.Devereux, M.Ring, A.Hadley; J.Davies, R.Jones; A.Buchanan, A.Phillips, S.Blackmore, R.Moriarty (capt), S.Sutton, R.Webster, G.Roberts, P.Moriarty.

Scorers: T: Roberts, P.Moriarty, Hadley. C: Thorburn (2). P: Thorburn (2).

Referee: F.Howard (England).

Semi-finals: France 30 Australia 24 (Sydney); New Zealand 49 Wales 6 (Brisbane).
Quarter-finals: New Zealand 30 Scotland 3 (Christchurch); Australia 33 Ireland 15 (Sydney); France 31 Fiji 16 (Auckland); Wales 16 England 3 (Brisbane).

Pool 1: Australia 19 England 6 (Sydney); USA 21 Japan 18 (Brisbane); England 60 Japan 7 (Sydney); Australia 47 USA 12 (Brisbane); England 34 USA 12 (Sydney); Australia 42 Japan 23 (Sydney).

Pool 2: Canada 37 Tonga 4 (Napier); Wales 13 Ireland 6 (Wellington); Wales 29 Tonga 16 (Palmerston North); Ireland 46 Canada 19 (Dunedin); Wales 40 Canada 9 (Invercargill); Ireland 32 Tonga 9 (Brisbane).

Pool 3: New Zealand 70 Italy 6 (Auckland); Fiji 28 Argentina 9 (Hamilton); New Zealand 74 Fiji 13 (Christchurch); Argentina 25 Italy 16 (Christchurch); Italy 18 Fiji 15 (Dunedin); New Zealand 46 Argentina 15 (Wellington).

Pool 4: Romania 21 Zimbabwe 20 (Auckland); France 20 Scotland 20 (Christchurch); France 55 Romania 12 (Wellington); Scotland 60 Zimbabwe 12 (Wellington); France 70 Zimbabwe 12 (Auckland); Scotland 55 Romania 28 (Dunedin).

1991 World Cup

Final

ENGLAND 6 AUSTRALIA 12 (Twickenham, 2 November 1991)

Australia, who showed themselves in their semi-final against New Zealand to be the class act of the 1991 tournament, duly beat England in the final in a game that confused, frustrated and excited in equal measure. England – with their massive predatory pack that had squeezed the life out of every previous opponent – suddenly started playing out of character by running the ball at every opportunity. The crowd roared, but in truth England rarely looked dangerous – a try never came – and you were left wondering if their usual, more pragmatic, approach may not have proved more effective. In contrast Australia, having entertained all-comers with the trickery of David Campese and others against New Zealand a week previously, battened down the hatches and played a shrewd percentage game, backing their underrated pack to win sufficient possession for captain Nick Farr-Jones and fly-half Michael Lynagh to run the game. This they achieved without alarm. Indeed the entire victory was achieved without alarm. Australia scored the game's only try in the first half when prop Tony Daly burrowed over from short range and had built a 9-0 lead through Lynagh's conversion and penalty before England got on the scoreboard with a penalty from Jonathan Webb. Lynagh and Webb exchanged two further penalties before the end, Webb's providing the game's only hint of controversy with many feeling that Campese's deliberate knock-on could have been penalised with a penalty try. A sharp break by Rob Andrew in the closing minutes offered England late hope but that marvellous athlete John Eales chased across like a wing three-quarter to drag the England fly-half down with an all-embracing tackle. Australia were worthy and popular winners, modest and magnanimous in victory at all times. They suffered a close call against Ireland in the quarter-finals in Dublin but, that apart, their triumph was almost routine and predictable, the hallmark of a truly exceptional side.

England: J.Webb; S.Halliday, J.Guscott, W.Carling (capt), R.Underwood; R.Andrew, R.Hill; J.Leonard, B.Moore, J.Probyn, P.Ackford, W.Dooley, M.Skinner, P.Winterbottom, M.Teague.

Scorers: P: Webb (2).

Australia: M.Roebuck; D.Campese, J.Little, T.Horan, R.Egerton; M.Lynagh, N.Farr-Jones (capt); T.Daly, P.Kearns, E.McKenzie, R.McCall, J.Eales, S.Poidevin, W.Ofahengaue, T.Coker.

Scorers: T: Daly. C: Lynagh. P: Lynagh (2).

Referee: D.Bevan (Wales).

Third place play-off

NEW ZEALAND 13 SCOTLAND 6 (Cardiff Arms Park, 30 October 1991)

New Zealand: T.Wright; J.Kirwan, C.Innes, W.Little, V.Tuigamala; J.Preston, G.Bachop; S.McDowell, S.Fitzpatrick, R.Loe, I.Jones, G.Whetton (capt), A.Earl, M.Jones, Z.Brooke.

Replacement: S.Philpott for Tuigamala (40).

Scorers: T: Little. P: Preston (3).

Scotland: G.Hastings; T.Stanger, S.Hastings, S.Lineen, I.Tukalo; C.Chalmers, G.Armstrong; D.Sole (capt), J.Allan, P.Burnell, C.Gray, D.Weir, F.Calder, J.Jeffrey, D.White.

Replacement: P.Dods for Stanger (47).

Scorer: P: G.Hastings (2).

Referee: S.Hilditch (Ireland).

Semi-finals: England 9 Scotland 6 (Murrayfield); Australia 16 New Zealand 6 (Lansdowne Road). *Quarter-finals*: Australia 19 Ireland 18 (Lansdowne Road); New Zealand 29 Canada 13 (Lille); England 19 France 10 (Paris); Scotland 28 Western Samoa 6 (Murrayfield).
Pool 1: New Zealand 18 England 12 (Twickenham); Italy 30 USA 9 (Otley); New Zealand 46 USA 6 (Kingsholm); England 36 Italy 6 (Twickenham); England 37 USA 9 (Twickenham); New Zealand 31 Italy 21 (Leicester).
Pool 2: Scotland 47 Japan 9 (Murrayfield); Ireland 55 Zimbabwe 11 (Lansdowne Road); Ireland 32 Japan 16 (Lansdowne Road); Scotland 51 Zimbabwe 12 (Murrayfield); Scotland 24 Ireland 15 (Murrayfield); Japan 52 Zimbabwe 8 (Belfast).
Pool 3: Australia 32 Argentina 19 (Llanelli); Western Samoa 16 Wales 13 (Cardiff); Australia 9 Western Samoa 3 (Pontypool); Wales 16 Argentina 7 (Cardiff); Australia 38 Wales 3 (Cardiff); Western Samoa 35 Argentina 12 (Pontypridd).
Pool 4: France 30 Romania 3 (Beziers); Canada 13 Fiji 3 (Bayonne); France 33 Fiji 9 (Grenoble); Canada 19 Romania 11 (Toulouse); Romania 17 Fiji 15 (Brive); France 19 Canada 13 (Agen).

1995 World Cup

Final

SOUTH AFRICA 15 NEW ZEALAND 12 (Ellis Park, Johannesburg, 24 June 1995)

An incredible occasion from start to finish and a nail-biting match that ended deep in extra time when Joel Stransky landed the drop goal to deliver the World Cup trophy to hosts South Africa. Over 68,000 spectators witnessed the miracle at Ellis Park, a win that made a significant contribution to bringing Nelson Mandela's South Africa – black and white – together. A perfect high veldt afternoon set the scene for an astonishing opening when a South African Airways Jumbo jet completed an impressive pre-match display by buzzing the stadium not once but twice. Then came the appearance of Mandela, showing solidarity with his team by wearing a Springbok No 6 shirt. And then came the match. It wasn't a classic, as the fear of failure often held sway, but the tension and excitement were unbearable. South Africa successfully contained the threat of Jonah Lomu by not allowing him to gather any momentum – Japie Mulder and Joost van der Westhuizen both covered themselves in glory with tackles on the big man and James Small also did an effective policing job all afternoon. At full time both sides were level on nine points apiece – neither side had scored a try and at no time did either have more than a three-point lead. Joel Stransky had landed two penalties and a drop goal to give South Africa a 9-6 lead, Andrew Mehrtens added a second-half drop goal to his two first-half penalties to draw the scores level. Mehrtens peppered the Springbok posts with drop-goal attempts as regular time drew to a close, narrowly missing on three occasions. In the first 15-minute period of extra time Stransky and Mehrtens added another penalty apiece before, deep in the second half, a scrum wheeled around on the New Zealand

22 and Stransky struck. There was still work to be done as New Zealand staged a late rally but the trophy was South Africa's. The Rainbow Nation could start celebrating.

South Africa: A.Joubert; J.Small, J.Mulder, H.Le Roux, C.Williams; J.Stransky, J.van der Westhuizen; O.du Randt, C.Rossouw, B.Swart, K.Wiese, J.Strydom, F.Pienaar (capt), R.Kruger, M.Andrews.

Replacements: G.Pagel for Swart (68), R.Straeuli for Andrews (90), B.Venter for Small (97).

Scorers: P: Stransky (3). DG: Stransky (2).

New Zealand: G.Osborne; J.Wilson, F.Bunce, W.Little, J.Lomu; A.Mehrtens, G.Bachop; C.Dowd, S.Fitzpatrick (capt), O.Brown, R.Brooke, I.Jones, M.Brewer, J.Kronfeld, Z.Brooke.

Replacements: J.Joseph for Brewer (40), M.Ellis for Wilson (55), R.Loe for Dowd (83), A.Strachan for Bachop (67-73).

Scorers: P: Mehrtens (3). DG: Mehrtens.

Referee: E.Morrison (England).

Third place play-off

FRANCE 19 ENGLAND 9 (Loftus Versveld, Pretoria, 22 June 1995)

France: J-L Sadourny; E.Ntamack, P.Sella, T.Lacroix, P.Saint-Andre (capt); F.Mesnel, F.Galthie; L.Benezech, J-M.Gonzalez, C.Califano, O.Merle, O.Roumat, A.Benazzi, A.Cigagna, L.Cabannes.

Replacement: O.Brouzet for Merle (34-39).

Scorers: T: Roumat, Ntamack. P: Lacroix (3).

England: M.Catt; I.Hunter, W.Carling (capt), J.Guscott, R.Underwood; R.Andrew, D.Morris; J.Leonard, B.Moore, V.Ubogu, M.Johnson, M.Bayfield, T.Rodber, S.Ojomoh, B.Clarke.

Scorer: P: Andrew (3).

Referee: D.Bishop (New Zealand).

Semi-finals: South Africa 19 France 15 (Durban); New Zealand 45 England 29 (Cape Town). *Quarter-finals*: France 36 Ireland 12 (Durban); South Africa 42 Western Samoa 14 (Ellis Park); England 25 Australia 22 (Cape Town); New Zealand 48 Scotland 30 (Pretoria).

Pool A: South Africa 27 Australia 18 (Cape Town); Canada 34 Romania 3 (Port Elizabeth); South Africa 21 Romania 8 (Cape Town); Australia 25 Canada 11 (Port Elizabeth); Australia 42 Romania 3 (Stellenbosch); South Africa 20 Canada 0 (Port Elizabeth).

Pool B: Western Samoa 42 Italy 18 (East London); England 24 Argentina 18 (Durban); Western Samoa 32 Argentina 26 (East London); England 27 Italy 20 (Durban); Italy 31 Argentina 25 (East London); England 44 Western Samoa 22 (Durban).

Pool C: Wales 57 Japan 10 (Bloemfontein); New Zealand 43 Ireland 19 (Ellis Park); Ireland 50 Japan 28 (Bloemfontein); New Zealand 34 Wales 9 (Ellis Park); New Zealand 145 Japan 17 (Bloemfontein); Ireland 24 Wales 23 (Ellis Park).

Pool D: Scotland 89 Ivory Coast 0 (Rustenburg); France 38 Tonga 10 (Loftus Versveld); France 54 Ivory Coast 18 (Rustenburg); Scotland 41 Tonga 5 (Pretoria); Tonga 29 Ivory Coast 11 (Rustenburg); France 22 Scotland 19 (Pretoria).

ALLIED DUNBAR PREMIERSHIP

Premiership One

BATH

Formation of club: 1865
Ground: The Recreation Ground, Bath BA2 6PW
Ticket office: 01225 460588
Capacity: 8,317 (Seated 4,027)
Colours: Blue, white and black
Honours: Cup Winners (10) – 1984, 1985, 1986, 1987, 1989, 1990, 1992, 1994, 1995, 1996. League Champions (6) – 1988-89, 1990-91, 1991-92, 1992-93, 1993-94, 1995-96.
Last season: Premiership One – 6th. Tetley's Bitter Cup – 4th round (lost 22-25 to Newcastle Falcons)
Owner: Andrew Brownsword (Greetings card magnate)
Head coach: Andy Robinson
Assistant: Jon Callard
Captain: TBC

ADEBAYO, Adedayo Adeyemi (Wing)
Born Ibadan, Nigeria, 30.11.70. 5′9″, 14st 7lb. **Rep hons:** England (6, It96, 2t-10pts), A (17, Sp91, 8t-38pts), Barbarians (96). **ADPR:** Bath (1989-99, 111, 50t-244pts). A regular in the Bath side who proved he has lost nothing of his potency as a finisher by scoring half a dozen Premiership tries, but the Kelly College and Swansea University-educated player is facing increasing competition for his place from the thrusting youngsters in the squad. Overcame a serious knee injury in 1991, toured Canada with an England XV in 1993 and South Africa with England in 1994.

ADEBAYO, Adetokunbo **'Tokunbo'** (Centre)
Born Hammersmith, 24.01.80. 6′2″, 13st 4lb. **ADPR:** Bath (1998-99, 4). Brother of Adedayo, the youngest of 17 sons of Nigerian Army major. Made his Allied Dunbar Premiership debut against West Hartlepool. Part of England Under 19 development squad and played for an England Under 21 A side which was beaten by South Africa Under 21 A.

BALSHAW, Iain Robert (Wing)
Born Lancashire, 14.04.79. 6′1″, 13st 2lb. **ADPR:** Bath (1997-99, 33, 14t, 1c-72pts). The searing pace of this former Stonyhurst schoolboy saw him score 13 Premiership tries, just one behind top try-scorer Jeremy Guscott. Although he can play at full-back he has settled well on the Bath right wing. Made a big impression on the England Schools tour to Australia in 1997. Made a further England U21 appearance against Wales.

BORTHWICK, Stephen William (Lock)
Born Carlisle, 12.10.79. 6′6″, 15st 12lb. **ADPR:** Bath (1998-99, 14). **Other clubs:** Preston Grasshoppers. Established himself as a regular for the latter half of Bath's Premiership campaign. Competitive, not to say abrasive line-out exponent and good scrummager.

BOYD, Clement Thomas (Prop)
Born Belfast, 08.11.73. 6′1″, 18st. **ADPR:** Bedford (1996-99, 51, 2t-10pts). **Other clubs:** Instonians, Edinburgh Univ, Currie. Ireland A prop who played for Instonians

and the Currie club in Scotland while a student at Edinburgh University. Noted for his fine singing voice, his rendition of 'Danny Boy' is credited with inspiring Bedford's victory over Harlequins last season.

BRYAN, Richard Michael (Flanker)
Born Bristol, 21.01.77. 6′3″, 16st. **ADPR:** Bath (1997-99, 17). Member of the Bath Academy whose appearances were restricted to a handful last season.

CALLARD, Jonathan Edward Brookes (Full-back)
Born Leicester, 01.01.66. 5′11″, 12st 10lb. **Rep hons:** England (5, NZ93, 3c, 21pg-69pts), A (3, Sp89, 1t, 2c, 5pg-23pts), Barbarians (94-95). **ADPR:** Bath (1989-99, 105, 24t, 170c, 196pg-1042pts). Settled more comfortably into the role of assistant coach but still called upon twice during the season, first to replace Jon Preston against Harlequins when he scored 13 points with the boot and again at Gloucester at full-back, converting Bath's solitary try in the defeat. The former Bassaleg Comprehensive and St Paul's College, Cheltenham, student made his senior debut for Newport against Bath before moving to the Rec and opting for England. Scored a try in Bath's 1990 Pilkington Cup triumph over Gloucester but then struggled to secure a First XV place as Jon Webb rediscovered his best form. Returned in style in 1993-94 season, making a victorious England debut against New Zealand and securing a dramatic victory over Scotland.

CATT, Michael John (Utility back)
Born Port Elizabeth, South Africa, 17.09.71. 5′10″, 13st 8lb. **Rep hons:** England (35, Wal94, 4t, 14c, 22pg, 2dg-120pts), A (1, NZ93). **ADPR:** Bath (1992-99, 100, 27t, 81c, 68pg, 5dg-516pts). **Other clubs:** Eastern Province (SA). Remained his club's first-choice outside half, but not his country's. He tussled with Paul Grayson for the No 10 shirt throughout the season until injury ruled out the Northampton man. Kicking duties for England were limited to one match. On the summer tour to Australia found himself in the centre for the one-off Test in Sydney. Scored more than 300 points in total in Premiership, Tetley's Bitter Cup and for England including eight tries (seven in the Premiership). It still needs to be decided which position he should aim for in England's World Cup squad. Mike was educated at Grey School, Port Elizabeth and played for Eastern Province U21 before moving to England, almost immediately winning selection for the England U21 squad to Australia (1993). Made his full England debut against Wales as a replacement in 1994.

CLARKE, Benjamin Bevan (Backrow)
Born Bishop's Stortford, 15.04.68. 6′5″, 18st. **Rep hons:** England (40, SA92, 3t-15pts), A (18, Sp91, 3t-13pts), Barbarians (90-91). **ADPR:** Saracens (1989-91, 22, 8t-32pts), Bath (1991-96, 61, 14t-68pts), Richmond (1996-99, 63, 21t-105pts). Returns to Bath where he enjoyed so much success between 1991 and 1996. Educated at Bishop's Stortford, Clarke originally came to prominence with Saracens before moving to Bath where his career took off. After his debut season with England in 1992 he earned selection with the 1993 British Lions where he was voted player of the series. Uncertainty over his best position in the backrow then saw his place come under threat but by the 1995 World Cup he was a first choice again. Moved the following year, as captain, to Richmond where he did much to inspire their rise in the Premiership before it all went horribly wrong.

COOPER, Gareth James (Scrum-half)
Born Bridgend, 07.05.79. 5′7″, 12st. **ADPR:** Bath (1998-99, 11, 3t-15pts). **Other clubs:** Pencoed, UWIC. Abrasive and hugely competent scrum-half who kept Andy Nicol out in the cold in the latter part of the season. Possessor of a good pass, improving box kick and always dangerous around the base of the scrum, ready to dart through with sniping runs. Wales Under 21 cap and former Wales Schools.

FILIPO, Matthew Tetai (Prop)
Born Otahuhu, New Zealand, 28.10.71. 6′2″, 18st. **ADPR:** Fylde (1997-99, 29). Powerful New Zealand-reared prop who arrives at the Rec after two seasons with Fylde. Formerly with Manawatu Counties.

GARDINER, J. **Angus** (Flanker)
Born England, 06.10.71. 6′1″, 15st. Highly competitive flanker who has played for Canterbury in New Zealand.

DE GLANVILLE, Phillip Ranulph (Centre)
Born Loughborough, 01.10.68. 5′11″, 13st 6lb. **Rep hons:** England (33, SA92, 5t-25pts), A (13, It89, 3t-12pts), Barbarians (93-94). **ADPR:** Bath (1990-99, 122, 24t-116pts). His England place came under increasing pressure throughout a long season, but he still won a cap as a replacement against Australia on the summer tour. That was probably his last bow, though. At club level he stood in as captain for the injured Richard Webster at the start, but the emergence of Mike Tindall and the vast improvement shown by Kevin Maggs meant that, with Jeremy Guscott around as well, first-team places were going to be hard to come by. A dislocated shoulder suffered for England against South Africa did not help his cause but he was still a part of the plans right to the end of the season. Educated at Bryanston and Durham University before winning a Blue from St Catherine's College, Oxford. Represented England, and scored two tries, in their inaugural U21 international against Romania (1989). Made England debut, as a replacement, against South Africa in 1992. Sat on the England bench 21 times before cementing a place in the team. First captained Bath in the 1995 Pilkington Cup final when deputising for the injured John Hall.

EARNSHAW, Russell Dean (Flanker)
Born Billingham, 08.07.75. 6′4″, 15st 3lb. **ADPR:** West Hartlepool (1995-97, 9, 3t-15pts), Bath (1997-99, 39, 8t-40pts). Established himself as a vital member of Bath's backrow. Quick, powerful and defensively sound. Takes ball up well and is developing into a useful flanker with great promise. Educated at Red House School, Norton and Yarm School before studying for a BA in Economics at St John's, Cambridge where he won two Blues. A keen tennis player, he is also Tim Rodber's second cousin.

GUSCOTT, Jeremy Clayton (Centre)
Born Bath, 07.07.65. 6′1″, 13st 10lb. **Rep hons:** England (60, Rom89, 24t, 2dg-113pts), A (3, Aus88), Barbarians (89-90). **ADPR:** Bath (1987-99, 128, 67t, 8c, 1dg-333pts). Critics say he has lost his pace; opponents think differently. Half a dozen tries for his country and a further 14 for his club, making him Bath's leading try-scorer, tell their own tale. If the breaks are less rocket-like he still knows where the line is. Rounded off Bath's season by captaining them to a thunderous victory over London Scottish in which he scored four tries and ensured European rugby into the Millennium. Educated at Ralph Allen CS, a soccer school, learned his rugby with Bath's Mini and Junior sides. Three tries on England debut against Romania; called up by the 89 Lions to replace the injured Will Carling. Key member of England's Grand Slam sides in 1991, 1992 and 1995 and RWC91 and 95 squads. Missed 94 season with a serious pelvic/groin injury. Member of successful 1997 British Lions tour party. Blossoming TV and modelling career. Keen golfer.

HAAG, Stephen **Martin** (Lock)
Born Chelmsford, 28.07.65. 6′5″, 16st 7lb. **Rep hons:** England (2, Arg97), A (6, Sp92, 1t-4pts), Barbarians (94). **ADPR:** Bath (1988-99, 126, 8t-38pts). Underrated lock and sevens specialist and automatic choice for Bath during their campaign to get back into Europe. His consistency and competitive instincts were belatedly rewarded when he was capped in both Tests on England's tour of Argentina in 1997. Educated at Penwith College and was ever-present for England Schools in 1986 before joining Bath.

HATLEY, Steve (Scrum-half)
Born Rhodesia, 16.08.72. 6'1", 14st 6lb. **ADPR:** Bath (1997-99, 19, 3t-15pts). **Other clubs:** Western Province (SA). Former Western Province scrum-half who played against the 1997 Lions. Did not have quite the impact hoped for, not a great passer, built more like a flank forward. Was eventually overtaken by Andy Nicol and then Gareth Cooper.

HORSMAN, Christopher Leslie (Prop)
Born 02.02.77. 6'2", 17st 7lb. **ADPR:** Bath (1996-99, 8). Is making a brave recovery from testicular cancer having shown every sign of picking up where he left off before his illness, as one of England's most promising young props.

JONES, Deiniol Llyr (Lock)
Born Carmarthen, 18.11.77. 6'5", 16st 12lb. **ADPR:** Bath (1997-99, 8). Promising former Wales Schools lock, whose appearances were limited to three.

LONG, Andrew Edward (Hooker)
Born Poole, 02.09.77. 5'11", 15st 8lb. **Rep hons:** England (1, Aus97). **ADPR:** Bath (1996-99, 29, 1t-5pts). **Other clubs:** Bournemouth. Called into the full England team to play against Australia in November 1997 and despite being unceremoniously dropped has clearly recovered and has enjoyed a couple of seasons re-establishing himself in the Bath first team. Has also captained England U21. Educated at St Peter's School, Bournemouth, Andy joined the Bath Academy in 1996 before returning to the Bournemouth club for a short spell on loan. Captained England U21 in Australia in 1997. Has played Minor Counties cricket, as a seam bowler, for Dorset.

LYLE, Daniel Joseph (No 8)
Born San Diego, USA, 28.09.70. 6'5", 17st 12lb. **Rep hons:** USA (22, Ire94, 3t-15pts), Barbarians (97-98). **ADPR:** Bath (1996-99, 33, 7t-35pts). **Other clubs:** OMBAC (USA). Returned to action in December having recovered fully from the anterior cruciate ligament injury suffered the previous March. Possesses superb ball-handling skills, great pace and athleticism. Made his international debut against Ireland in 1994 and was appointed USA captain in the summer of 1996. Has always enjoyed sevens and captained the USA to victory in the Plate competition of the 1997 RWC Sevens. Back in 1992 he was an All-American gridiron representative and was trying out for the Washington Redskins when he switched to rugby.

MAGGS, Kevin Michael (Centre)
Born Bristol, 03.06.74. 5'11", 14st. **Rep hons:** Ireland (19, NZ97, 5t-25pts). **ADPR:** Bristol (1995-98, 53, 6t-30pts), Bath (1998-99, 24, 1t-5pts). One of the most improved players since his move from Bristol. Has developed into a hard-tackling centre with explosive speed, the perfect foil for Jeremy Guscott and Mike Tindall.

MALLETT, John Anthony H. (Prop)
Born Lincoln, 28.05.70. 6'1", 16st. **Rep hons:** England (1, WS95), A (8, Ire94), Barbarians (98-99). **ADPR:** Bath (1991-99, 64, 2t-9pts). Plagued by a recurring back problem the season before last which left him with an uphill struggle to re-establish himself for Bath and England. A product of Millfield School and West London Institute, John finally won a full cap as a replacement against Western Samoa in RWC95 after touring South Africa the previous year with England.

PERRY, Matt Brendan (Full-back)
Born Bath, 21.01.77. 6'1", 13st 7lb. **Rep hons:** England (18, Aus97, 4t-20pts), A (1, Qld96). **ADPR:** Bath (1996-99, 52, 13t, 2c, 4pg-81pts). Enjoyed another fine season for Bath and England, his versatility and attacking skills once more to the fore, but also beginning to prove himself in defence. Capped by England Colts at fly-half, he played centre for Woodward's U21 team in Australia in 1997 but then made his full

England debut at full-back against Australia in November 97. Educated at Millfield School. Before turning professional he worked as a waiter and male model to fund his sporting career.

PETERS, Eric William (Backrow)
Born Glasgow, 28.01.69. 6′5″, 16st 6lb. **Rep hons:** Scotland (29, Can95, 5t-25pts), A (6, WS95, 2t-10pts), Barbarians (92-93). **ADPR:** Bath (1993-99, 60, 13t-65pts). Captained Scotland against Italy and was established in the backrow for club and country until he suffered a broken kneecap in Bath's Premiership victory over Leicester, an injury which put him in plaster for two months and meant he missed Scotland's short, non-Test tour of South Africa. Played his early rugby for Brentwood School and Loughborough University, where he studied Economics, and captained Cambridge University. Played for Saracens before joining Bath in 1993 and opting for Scotland. Made his Scotland debut against Canada in 1995. Impressed during RWC95 and Scotland's tour of New Zealand in 1997.

PRESTON, Jon Paul (Half-back)
Born Dunedin, New Zealand, 15.11.67. 5′10″, 12st 12lb. **Rep hons:** New Zealand (10, USA91, 1t, 4c, 7pg-34pts). **ADPR:** Bath (1998-99, 1, 1pg-3pts). Experienced and versatile All Black half-back who was sidelined last season with an achilles injury. Played for Wellington Hurricanes and Canterbury Crusaders in New Zealand.

REGAN, Mark Peter (Hooker)
Born Bristol, 28.01.72. 5′11″, 16st 2lb. **Rep hons:** England (15, SA95), A (11, Ire95, 2t-10pts). **ADPR:** Bristol (1991-97, 69, 4t-20pts), Bath (1997-99, 40, 5t-25pts). Having struggled in his first season finally made the hooker's berth pretty much his own. Four tries in the Premiership suggested he was growing in confidence and looking to be more of his own man, but he was still unable to break back into the England set-up. Educated at St Brendan's, Bristol and a product of the England age group system.

STURNHAM, Ben (Flanker)
Born St Albans, 06.03.74. 6′5″, 18st 5lb. **Rep hons:** England (3, Aus98), A (1, Ire98, 1t-5pts). **ADPR:** Saracens (1997-98, 12, 2t-10pts), Bath (1998-99, 18, 2t-10pts). **Other clubs:** St Albans. Sent off for allegedly stamping against Bedford but subsequently cleared of the charge and thereafter allowed to concentrate on his game, which needed a lot of attention since he was switched throughout the season from backrow to second row. Scored his two tries from lock. Signed from Saracens in the close season and shows great potential as a ball carrier and handler.

THOMAS, Nathan (Flanker)
Born Bridgend, 22.01.76. 6′3″, 15st 7lb. **Rep hons:** Wales (9, SA96), A (3, Sc97). **ADPR:** Bath (1996-99, 42, 3t-15pts). **Other clubs:** Bridgend. Built on his experience and proved a redoubtable opponent. Rapidly developing flanker who joined Bath from Bridgend. Represented Wales in the 1996 World Students Cup before being capped at senior level.

TINDALL, Michael James (Centre)
Born Wakefield, 18.10.78. 6′2″, 14st 7lb. **ADPR:** Bath (1997-99, 10, 3t-15pts). One of the most exciting talents to emerge since Guscott. He looks to have the lot – pace, power and intelligence, great hands and a fantastic eye for the angle, and is sound, sometimes spectacular, in defence. Made it into England's squad for the brief summer tour of Australia and came on as replacement for Guscott against Queensland.

UBOGU, Victor Eriakpo (Prop)
Born Lagos, Nigeria, 08.09.64. 5′9″, 17st. **Rep hons:** England (24, Can92, 1t-5pts), A (14, Aus90, 5t-21pts). **ADPR:** Richmond (1987-88, 3), Bath (1988-99, 125, 13t-61pts). The grand old man goes on and on. Resuscitated his England career against all odds and expectations, coming on as replacement for Darren Garforth against France and

then Wales. Selected in Woodward's squad for the trip Down Under where he came on as replacement in the Test and the match against Queensland which preceded it, scoring a try in the latter match. Still able to hold his own in the Bath side. Involved in a bizarre incident in Cardiff in an Anglo-Welsh match when he was sent off for allegedly using foul and abusive language to the referee. At a subsequent hearing he was cleared of the charge. The old dynamism was back and the enthusiasm for the game has never waned. He has lived in England since he was 13 and was educated at West Buckland School, Devon, Birmingham University and Oxford. Numbers Richmond and Moseley among his previous clubs and made his senior England debut against Canada at Wembley in 1992.

WAUGH, Warwick William (Lock)
Born Canberra, Australia, 17.09.68. 6'8", 19st 4lb. **Rep hons:** Australia (8, SA93, 1t-5pts). Hugely powerful Australian lock who has fallen out of international contention. Educated at Scots College and has played for the big states – Queensland, New South Wales and Queensland.

REVIEW

It was touch and go for much of the season as to whether they would qualify for Europe. The 12-try rout of London Scottish in the final match settled it, since it left Newcastle with too much to do in their last Premiership game at Saracens and Bath clung on to the sixth, and final, qualifying place. The signing of Jon Preston, the All Black utility half-back, proved a disaster – he played just 27 minutes at Harlequins before suffering the injury that required surgery on an Achilles tendon which ended his season in November. Theirs was only a brief flirtation with the Tetley's Bitter Cup. Kevin Yates left for New Zealand where he will play for Wellington, Nigel Redman retired to take up the reins at Basingstoke, Andy Nicol returned to Scotland and Tony Swift resigned as non-executive chairman.

BATH in Premiership One 1998-99

Sep	5	H	Wasps	Won	36	27	J.Guscott (2T) E.Peters (T) M.Catt (3C, 5P)
	12	A	Newcastle Falcons	Lost	17	19	A.Adebayo (T) M.Catt (4P)
	19	H	Richmond	Won	36	14	J.Guscott (2T) A.Nicol (T) A.Adebayo (T) M.Catt (2C, 4P)
	26	H	Gloucester	Won	21	16	A.Adebayo (T) A.Long (T) M.Catt (C, 3P)
Oct	3	H	Bedford	Won	57	19	J.Guscott (2T) R.Webster (2T) S.Hatley (T) M.Perry (T) I.Balshaw (T) M.Catt (5C, 4P)
	10	H	London Irish	Won	23	20	B.Sturnham (2T) I.Balshaw (T) M.Catt (C, 2P)
	17	A	West Hartlepool	Won	50	20	S.Hatley (2T) J.Guscott (2T) I.Balshaw (T) M.Catt (T, 6C, P) R.Earnshaw (T)
	24	H	Manchester Sale	Won	27	3	Penalty (T) R.Webster (T) A.Nicol (T) M.Catt (3C, 2P)
	31	A	London Scottish	Lost	11	13	A.Nicol (T) M.Catt (2P)
Nov	7	A	Leicester Tigers	Lost	13	36	J.Guscott (T) M.Catt (C, 2P)

21	A	Harlequins	Lost	31	43	M.Regan (T) A.Nicol (T) I.Balshaw (T) J.Preston (P) J.Callard (2C, 3P)
Dec 12	H	Northampton Saints	Lost	9	15	M.Catt (3P)
19	H	Saracens	Lost	11	19	I.Balshaw (T) M.Catt (2P)
Jan 2	A	Gloucester	Lost	7	23	A.Adebayo (T) J.Callard (C)
5	A	Manchester Sale	Won	32	30	M.Catt (T, 3C) D.Hilton (T) J.Guscott (T) A.Adebayo (T) M.Perry (2P)
16	H	Newcastle Falcons	Won	16	11	M.Catt (T, C, 3P)
23	A	Bedford	Won	30	17	I.Balshaw (T) Penalty (T) A.Adebayo (T) M.Catt (3C, 3P)
Feb 7	A	Wasps	Lost	0	35	
Mar 13	A	Richmond	Won	30	23	A.Adebayo (T) M.Perry (T) M.Catt (C, 6P)
28	A	Saracens	Won	33	14	I.Balshaw (3T) E.Peters (T) G.Cooper (T) M.Catt (4C)
Apr 3	H	Leicester Tigers	Won	24	16	Penalty (T) I.Balshaw (T) M.Catt (C, 4P)
17	A	London Irish	Lost	22	47	M.Tindall (T) M.Catt (T, 2C, P) M.Regan (T)
24	H	West Hartlepool	Won	56	24	I.Balshaw (2T) M.Perry (2T) K.Maggs (T) M.Tindall (T) M.Regan (T) G.Cooper (T) M.Catt (5C, 2P)
May 1	A	Northampton Saints	Lost	17	40	M.Tindall (T) M.Catt (T) R.Earnshaw (T) M.Perry (C)
8	H	Harlequins	Lost	13	17	R.Earnshaw (T) M.Perry (C, 2P)
15	H	London Scottish	Won	76	13	J.Guscott (4T) M.Perry (2T) M.Catt (2T, 8C) M.Regan (T) G.Cooper (T) D.Hilton (T) I.Balshaw (T)

Summary of Premiership scorers:

294 M.Catt (7T, 50C, 53P); 70 J.Guscott (14T); 65 I.Balshaw (13T); 46 M.Perry (6T, 2C, 4P); 35 A.Adebayo (7T); 20 M.Regan (4T), A.Nicol (4T); 15 Penalty (3T), R.Webster (3T), M.Tindall (3T), S.Hatley (3T), R.Earnshaw (3T), G.Cooper (3T), J.Callard (3C, 3P); 10 B.Sturnham (2T), E.Peters (2T), D.Hilton (2T); 5 K.Maggs (T), A.Long (T); 3 J.Preston (P).

Summary of Premiership appearances:

25 I.Balshaw (+1); 24 V.Ubogu (+1), K.Maggs (+3), M.Catt; 22 D.Hilton (+1), R.Earnshaw (+10); 21 M.Regan (+5), A.Adebayo; 20 M.Perry (+1); 19 R.Webster (+2), M.Haag, J.Guscott; 18 B.Sturnham (+6); 17 K.Yates (+12); 16 E.Peters (+2); 15 N.Thomas (+1), A.Long (+5); 14 D.Lyle, S.Hatley (+1), S.Borthwick; 13 A.Nicol (+10); 12 N.Redman; 11 J.Mallett (+8), I.Evans (+2), P.De Glanville

(+5), G.Cooper (+1); 8 M.Tindall; 4 R.Bryan (+2), T.Adebayo (+3); 3 D.Jones (+3), J.Fallon (+1), J.Callard (+2); 2 A.Gomarsall (+2); 1 J.Preston, L.Mears (+1), C.Horsman (+1).

BEDFORD

Formation of club: 1886
Ground: Goldington Road, Bedford MK42 3DN
Tel: 01234 347980
Capacity: 7,500 (Seated 4,400)
Colours: Navy, royal blue and sky blue hoops
Honours: Cup Winners (1) – 1974-75, Premiership Two Champions – 1997-98, Division Three Champions – 1994-95
Best League finish: 12th in Division One 1989-90
Last season: Premiership One – 13th. Tetley's Bitter Cup – 4th round (lost 22-29 to Henley Hawks). Cheltenham & Gloucester Cup – losing finalists
Owners: Jefferson Lloyd International
Chief executive: Doug Braddock
Director of coaching: Paul Turner
Captain: TBC

ASHFORTH, Robert William (Fly-half/centre)
Born Dewsbury, 01.05.76. 6′, 13st 7lb. **ADPR:** Rotherham (1996-98, 8, 5c, 2pg-16pts), Bedford (1998-99, 3), Wakefield (1998-99, 8, 1t, 4c, 13pg-52pts). **Other clubs:** Cambridge University, Cleckheaton.

BOWEN, Gareth (Fly-half)
Born 20.06.79. 5′10″, 11st 8lb. Arrives from Bridgend where he won Wales U21 honour.

CANO, Christian Jared (Prop)
Born Hitchin, 25.01.77. 5′10″, 16st 5lb. **ADPR:** Bedford (1998-99, 3). **Other clubs:** Wasps.

CODLING, Alexander John (Lock)
Born Lewisham, 25.09.73. 6′6″, 18st 3lb. **ADPR:** Blackheath (1994-96, 25, 1t-5pts), Richmond (1996-99, 25, 1t-5pts), Bedford (1998-99, 5). **Other clubs:** Wasps.

CRABB, Simon John (Scrum-half)
Born Hamilton, New Zealand, 04.04.69. 5′6″, 13st. **ADPR:** Bedford (1997-99, 11, 3t-15pts), Leeds (1998-99, 5). **Other clubs:** Waikato Chiefs. Voted New Zealand's most promising player in 1993, Simon was badly hindered by injury the season before last. Educated at Waikato University and a qualified accountant, he is a former New Zealand U21 and New Zealand B representative who has played Super 12 rugby for Waikato Chiefs. Made just a handful of appearances last season and very little impact.

DAVIS, Aaron Christopher (Hooker)
Born Luton, 10.11.78. **ADPR:** Bedford (1997-99, 6, 1t-5pts).

DEANS, Matthew Willis (Flanker)
Born Zimbabwe, 27.05.71. 6′3″, 18st. **ADPR:** Bedford (1992-99, 60, 8t-40pts). A long-serving club stalwart, Matt is a strong-running, tough-tackling powerhouse in the pack, and takes a 20″ shirt collar. Educated at King's School, Ely and De Montfort University he played for London U21 and numbers Cambridge City among his previous clubs. His hobbies include cricket and golf and his father played local rugby.

DUKE, Andrew Richard (Lock)
Born Southampton, 28.01.74. 6'7", 17st 2lb. **ADPR:** Newbury (1996-98, 39, 5t-25pts), Bedford (1998-99, 9). **Other clubs:** Paris University.

ELLIOTT, Richard John (Scrum-half)
Born Durham, 05.01.74. 5'8", 12st 1lb. **Rep hons:** Barbarians (97-98). **ADPR:** Rugby Lions (1993-95, 5), Bedford (1998-99, 11, 1t-5pts). Made his debut when coming on as a replacement against London Irish, thereafter the Cambridge Blue provided plenty of competition for Charlie Harrison. Graduate of Loughborough University.

ELPHICK, Philip Andrew (Flanker)
Born Bedford, 31.10.78. **ADPR:** Bedford (1998-99, 4)

GOMARSALL, Andrew Charles Thomas (Scrum-half)
Born Durham, 24.07.74. 5'10", 13st 8lb. **Rep hons:** England (6, It96, 4t-20pts), A (10, S.95, 6t-30pts), Barbarians (94-95). **ADPR:** Wasps (1994-99, 64, 12t-60pts), Bath (1998-99, 2). Talented former England scrum-half who lost form and confidence after a serious back operation and was considered surplus to requirements by Wasps at the end of last season. Educated at the local Bedford School and the Brookes College Oxford, Andy is a former England Schools captain and led them to a grand slam in 1992.

HARRIS, Daniel David (Centre)
Born High Wycombe, 17.05.77. 5'10", 13st 12lb. **ADPR:** Moseley (1996-98, 34, 7t-35pts), Bedford (1998-99, 14). **Other clubs:** Chinnor.

HARRISON, Charles Leslie (Scrum-half)
Born Chippenham, 06.09.75. 5'10", 13st. **ADPR:** Bath (1995-98, 14, 1t, 2c-9pts), Orrell (1997-98, 11, 3t-15pts), Bedford (1998-99, 20, 1t-5pts). Always seemed to get overlooked at Bath, but more established at Bedford, although now facing stern competition from Elliott. Former captain with Mount St Mary's School near Sheffield.

HARTLAND, Virgil Cain (Prop)
Born Cinderford, 23.04.77. 5'10", 15st 12lb. **ADPR:** West Hartlepool (1996-98, 11), Coventry (1997-98, 8), Bedford (1998-99, 14). Powerful scrummager and a useful acquisition from Coventry in the previous close season.

HOWARD, Samuel David (Fly-half)
Born Gravesend, 31.07.74. 6', 13st 7lb. **ADPR:** Blackheath (1993-97, 56, 6t, 31c, 75pg, 9dg-344pts), Bedford (1997-99, 21, 4t, 28c, 20pg, 1dg-139pts). Talented former England Students and England U21 fly-half who established himself at full-back after Rayer's departure. Possesses a good kick and scored 134 points last season.

JONES, Derwyn (Lock)
Born Carmarthen,Wales, 14.11.70. 6'10", 19st. **Rep hons:** Wales (19, SA94), A (3, Ire94). One of the tallest locks in the league, Derwyn joins from Cardiff after a difficult couple of seasons which have seen him drop out of the Welsh national side. Educated at Loughborough University.

McLEAN, Alastair Robert (Wing)
Born Dumfries, Scotland, 17.04.76. 5'10", 13st 5lb. Scotland U21 representative who has played for Boroughmuir and Edinburgh Reivers.

MITCHELL, Simon John (Hooker)
Born Saltburn, 23.11.65. 5'10", 16st. **Rep hons:** England A (1, Sc96), Barbarians (94). **ADPR:** West Hartlepool (1987-95, 82, 6t-28pts), Harlequins (1994-96, 14, 1t-5pts), Wasps (1996-99, 41, 4t-20pts). Much travelled hooker who gives value for money wherever he plays. Educated at Sacred Heart Comprehensive, Redcar.

MURDOCH, Alistair Richard (Centre)
Born Sydney, Australia, 09.05.67. 6'1", 14st 6lb. **Rep hons:** Australia (2, Fr93, 1t-5pts). **ADPR:** Bedford (1997-99, 41, 11t-55pts). **Other clubs:** NSW (Australia). Underrated former Australia centre who also holds an English passport. Spent six years in the New South Wales side and once again had a tremendous influence at Bedford. His try in the second leg of the play-off against Rotherham guaranteed Premiership One rugby this season, Bedford scraping through on the tries countback system.

OLVER, Adrian Michael (Prop)
Born London, 02.06.69. 6', 15st 7lb. **ADPR:** Saracens (1996-99, 36, 2t-10pts), Bedford (1998-99, 8, 1t-5pts). Signed from Saracens and his experience should prove invaluable. Made too few appearances last season to make much difference on the pitch.

OZDEMIR, Altan Mustafa (Prop)
Born Cyprus, 03.09.74. 5'9", 16st. **ADPR:** Bristol (1994-95, 7), Harlequins (1996-98, 8), Bedford (1998-99, 10). A powerhouse of a prop who looked happier at Bedford than he had at his previous clubs.

REES, Gareth Lloyd (Utility back)
Born Duncan, Canada, 30.06.67. 6', 15st. **Rep hons**: Canada (49, USA86, 6t, 38c, 96pg, 7dg-413pts), Barbarians (92-93). **ADPR**: Wasps (1996-99, 49, 5t, 81c, 126pg, 3dg-574pts). Much travelled Canadian who should, barring injury, arrive at Goldington Road, after competing in his fourth World Cup. Educated at Harrow and won Oxford Blues in 1993 and 1994. Has played for Oak Bay Castaways in Canada, Mergnac in France, Newport in Wales and finally Wasps in the Premiership before transferring to Bedford in the summer.

RICHARDS, Chris (Utility back)
Useful goal-kicking utility back who arrives from Jedforest.

ROSSIGNEUX, Florent Pierre (Flanker)
Born Clichy, France, 17.02.70. 6'2", 15st 2lb. **ADPR:** Wasps (1998-99, 4, 1t-5pts). Experienced flanker who has played for RCF, Stade Francais and PUC in France but failed to nail down a place in the Wasps starting line up last season

WINTERS, Royston Anthony (Flanker/lock)
Born Cuckfield, 13.12.75. 6'4", 16st. **Rep hons:** England A (3, NZ97). **ADPR:** Bedford (1996-99, 63, 5t-25pts). Superb all-purpose back five forward who was a key player throughout a turbulent season, winning the admiration and respect of everyone he played against. He played for England A against the All Blacks in 1997. Educated at Haywards Heath and Loughborough University, Roy also won England Schools and Colts caps and was the outstanding forward for England U21 in Australia in the summer of 1997.

REVIEW

A season that seemed to centre around the law courts with Mike Rayer winning his case to be freed to move to Cardiff, then Bedford finding themselves embroiled in owner Frank Warren's legal battle with American boxing promoter Don King. Warren's assets – Bedford included – were frozen, creating wages problems. Coach Paul Turner left, Geoff Cooke resigned. Warren sold out to Jefferson Lloyd International for £1 million. They failed to persuade the Home Office to grant coach Rudi Straeuli a revised work permit; lost Scott Murray to Saracens and Rory Underwood to retirement; and finally came through a tricky play-off against Rotherham to retain their Premiership One status. Reached the final of the Cheltenham & Gloucester Cup for the second year running where, once again, they lost to Gloucester.

BEDFORD in Premiership One 1998-99

Sep	12	A	Manchester Sale	Lost	21	39	D.O'Mahony (T) S.Howard (T, C, 3P)
	19	H	London Scottish	Won	24	16	R.Underwood (T) T.Yapp (T, D) S.Howard (C, 3P)
	26	H	Leicester Tigers	Lost	23	32	J.Forster (T) A.Murdoch (T) S.Howard (2C, 3P)
Oct	3	A	Bath	Lost	19	57	S.Howard (T, 2C) R.Underwood (T) D.O'Mahony (T)
	10	H	Harlequins	Won	35	33	J.Ewens (2T) D.O'Mahony (2T) S.Howard (3C, 2P) T.Yapp (D)
	17	A	Northampton Saints	Lost	29	34	R.Underwood (2T) J.Ewens (T) J.Cockle (T) S.Howard (3C, P)
	21	A	Wasps	Lost	19	35	J.Forster (T) T.Yapp (D) S.Howard (C, 3P)
	24	H	Newcastle Falcons	Lost	22	29	J.Paramore (T) T.Yapp (C, 5P)
Nov	1	A	Richmond	Lost	32	38	D.O'Mahony (3T) J.Paramore (T) S.Howard (3C, 2P)
	7	A	Gloucester	Lost	21	31	T.Yapp (T) J.Forster (T) D.Zaltzman (T) S.Howard (3C)
	15	H	Saracens	Lost	20	25	R.Underwood (T) J.Paramore (T) S.Howard (2C, 2P)
	21	A	London Irish	Lost	19	30	J.Ewens (T) R.Underwood (T) B.Whetstone (T) S.Howard (2C)
Dec	12	H	West Hartlepool	Lost	10	23	S.Howard (T) J.Ewens (T)
	26	A	Leicester Tigers	Lost	0	26	
Jan	3	A	Saracens	Lost	13	44	J.Paramore (T) T.Yapp (C, 2P)
	5	A	Newcastle Falcons	Lost	23	34	R.Underwood (2T) J.Forster (T) T.Yapp (C, P, D)
	23	H	Bath	Lost	17	30	A.Murdoch (T) D.Zaltzman (T) R.Elliott (T) S.Howard (C)
Feb	13	H	Wasps	Won	25	23	J.Richards (T) R.Underwood (T) S.Stewart (T) S.Howard (2C, P, D)
	27	H	Manchester Sale	Lost	7	18	J.Paramore (T) S.Howard (C)
Mar	13	A	London Scottish	Won	24	15	J.Forster (T) R.Underwood (T) T.Yapp (C, 4P)
	27	H	Gloucester	Won	19	15	A.Davis (T) T.Yapp (C, 4P)
Apr	17	A	Harlequins	Lost	16	29	R.Underwood (T) T.Yapp (C, 3P)
	24	H	Northampton Saints	Lost	31	42	J.Forster (T) D.O'Mahony (T) A.Olver (T) A.Murdoch (T) J.Ewens (T) S.Stewart (C) T.Yapp (2C)
May	2	A	West Hartlepool	Won	39	0	D.O'Mahony (3T) D.Zaltzman (T) J.Ewens (T) T.Yapp (4C, P, D)
	8	H	London Irish	Lost	21	36	R.Underwood (T) C.Harrison (T) T.Yapp (T, 3C)

16	H	Richmond	Lost	12	106	M.Cook (2T) S.Howard (C)
Play-offs:						
20	A	Rotherham	Lost	11	19	J.Forster (T) T.Yapp (2P)
23	H	Rotherham	Won	27	19	J.Forster (T) D.O'Mahony (T) A.Murdoch (T) T.Yapp (3C, P, D)

Summary of Premiership scorers:

138 T.Yapp (3T, 18C, 23P, 6D); 134 S.Howard (3T, 28C, 20P, D); 60 R.Underwood (12T), D.O'Mahony (12T); 40 J.Forster (8T); 35 J.Ewens (7T); 25 J.Paramore (5T); 20 A.Murdoch (4T); 15 D.Zaltzman (3T); 10 M.Cook (2T); 7 S.Stewart (T, C); 5 B.Whetstone (T), J.Richards (T), A.Olver (T), C.Harrison (T), R.Elliott (T), A.Davis (T), J.Cockle (T).

Summary of Premiership appearances:

27 J.Richards; 26 A.Murdoch, J.Forster; 25 D.O'Mahony, C.Boyd (+2); 24 T.Yapp, R.Underwood (+6), J.Cockle (+7); 22 S.Murray; 21 D.Zaltzman (+3), R.Winters (+4); 20 C.Harrison (+5); 19 S.Howard (+3); 18 B.Whetstone (+2), J.Ewens (+4); 15 J.Paramore; 14 V.Hartland (+4), D.Harris (+1); 11 R.Elliott (+2); 10 S.Stewart, A.Ozdemir (+4); 9 N.Hatley, A.Duke (+4); 8 A.Olver (+1); 6 R.Straeuli (+2); 5 A.Codling (+1); 4 P.Elphick (+1), A.Davis (+3), S.Crabb, J.Beardshaw (+1); 3 M.Deans (+2), C.Cano (+2), R.Ashforth (+1); 2 R.Ward, P.Hewitt (+1); 1 T.Wood (+1), J.Wells, D.Watts (+1), M.Mainwaring (+1), M.Kirkby, J.Hinkins, L.Gibbons (+1), M.Cook, R.Candlin, S.Burton (+1), J.Abrahams.

BRISTOL

Formation of club: 1888
Ground: Bristol Rugby Limited, The Memorial Ground, Filton Avenue, Horfield, Bristol BS7 0AQ
Capacity: 10,780 (Seated 1,780)
Colours: Navy blue and white
Honours: Cup Winners (1) – 1983. Premiership Two Champions – 1998-99.
Best League finish: 4th in Division One 1993-94
Last season: Premiership Two – Champions. Tetley's Bitter Cup – 4th round (lost 19-43 to London Irish)
Owner: Malcolm Pearce (Millionaire tycoon)
Chief executive: Nick de Scossa
Director of rugby: Bob Dwyer
Coaches: Daryl Jones, Dave Egerton
Captain: TBC

ARCHER, Garath Stuart (Lock)
Born South Shields, 15.12.74. 6'6", 18st 7lb. **Rep hons:** England (14, Sc96), A (14, Ir95). **ADPR:** Newcastle (1993-95, 19, 2t-10pts), Bristol (1994-96, 16, 1t-5pts), Newcastle (1996-99, 62, 11t-55pts). **Other clubs:** Westoe, Durham City. Dean Ryan persuaded him the move back to Bristol was worth it. He began the season with England, was overlooked for the Five Nations, but back in the squad which headed Down Under in the summer, proof that he was not out of Woodward's thoughts.

Whether his return to Bristol will do him any good is another matter. He is an aggressive lock who had rejoined Newcastle from Bristol at the end of 1995-96. Son of former Gosforth wing Stuart Archer, educated at Biddick School and Durham School and a member of the England Schools 18 Group Grand Slam team in 1992. Toured Australia and Fiji with England A in 1995, made senior debut against Scotland the following year.

BABER, Gareth Colin (Scrum-half)
Born Cardiff, 23.05.72. 5′10″, 12st 2lb. **ADPR:** Bristol (1997-99, 33, 11t-55pts). **Other clubs:** Aberavon, Cardiff, Llanelli. Versatile former Aberavon scrum-half, who has also played fly-half for Bristol. Hard to stop from close in and nine tries tells a great deal about his approach.

BACK, Matthew J. (Full-back)
Born Pontypridd, 05.04.70. 6′, 14st 7lb. **Rep hons:** Wales (4, Fr95), A (6, Jap93, 2t-10pts), Barbarians (94). Talented former Swansea and Wales full-back looking to revive his international career after a lean couple of seasons.

BARLOW, Timothy Alexander (Wing)
Born York, 12.01.77. 6′, 14st. **ADPR:** Leicester (1997-98, 3, 1t-5pts), Bristol (1998-99, 5, 1t-5pts).

BARNARD, Andre (Centre)
Born South Africa, 07.04.71. 5′11″, 14st. **Rep hons:** Barbarians (97-98). **ADPR:** Bristol (1998-99, 7, 1t-5pts). **Other clubs:** Natal (South Africa), Pontypridd.

BOOYSE, Ockert (Lock)
Born 25.10.73. 6′8″, 20st. Powerful lock who joins from Newport.

BREEZE, Benjamin George (Wing)
Born Exeter, 08.04.74. 5′10″, 13st. **ADPR:** Bristol (1995-99, 59, 10t-50pts). Appears to have recovered fully from the serious knee injury he suffered a while back. Represented England in the World Students Cup in South Africa in 1996.

BROWN, Spencer Paul (Wing)
Born Eton, 11.07.73. 5′11″, 13st 5lb. **Rep hons:** England (2, Aus98), A (5, NZ97, 1t-5pts). **ADPR:** Richmond (1994-99, 47, 24t-120pts). **Other clubs:** Deal Wanderers. A deadly finisher and a fearsome tackler. Played in two Tests on England's tour to Australia in 1998 and recalled to England A last season. Educated at Weavers School, Wellingborough. Former Royal Marines bandsman who played the French horn at the Marines School of Music in Deal where he played rugby for Deal RFC.

BROWNRIGG, James (Lock/flanker)
Born Chichester, 04.06.77. 6′6″, 15st. **ADPR:** Bristol (1996-99, 37, 2t-10pts). His athleticism and line-out skills were once more to the fore in Bristol's successful season. Has not yet graduated to England A despite playing for the Under 21 squad in the Six Nations tournament in Cape Town in 1998.

CHARRON, Alan John (Backrow)
Born Ottawa, Canada, 27.07.66. 6′6″, 17st 7lb. **Rep hons:** Canada (48, WalB89, 5t-24pts), Barbarians (94). **ADPR:** Moseley (1996-98, 18, 3t-15pts), Bristol (1997-99, 25, 3t-15pts). Powerful and versatile back five forward, who moved from troubled Moseley the season before. A veteran of two World Cups with the Canadian national side.

CROMPTON, Darren Edward (Prop)
Born Exeter, 12.09.72. 6′1″, 17st. **Rep hons:** England A (4, SAus95, 1t-5pts). **ADPR:** Bath (1993-96, 6), Richmond (1996-99, 62, 1t-5pts). A victim of the Richmond debacle, did not stay in international favour after winning a place on England's summer tour in 1998. Educated at Exeter College, he captained England 18 Group in

1991 and is a former Schools and Under 21 captain. Represented England in the 1992 World Students Cup, toured Australia and Fiji with England A in 1995. Had moved to Richmond from Bath in 1996.

DEWDNEY, Dean Edmond (Scrum-half)
Born Zimbabwe, 05.11.74. 5′10″, 11st. **ADPR:** Clifton (1994-95, 7), Bristol (1995-99, 19, 4t-20pts).

EAGLE, Chad Donald (Lock)
Born New Zealand, 24.08.71. 6′5″, 18st. **ADPR:** Bristol (1996-99, 57, 4t-20pts). Strong-scrummaging New Zealand-reared lock.

EVANS, Christian Scott (Backrow)
Born Bridgend, 27.12.69. 6′4″, 14st 2lb. **ADPR:** Bristol (1998-99, 22, 4t-20pts). **Other clubs:** Bayonne (France), UWIC, Maesteg.

EVANS, Jonathan William (Hooker)
Born Swansea, 05.04.72. 5′10″, 15st. **Rep hons:** Barbarians (98-99). **ADPR:** Bristol (1998-99, 21, 4t-20pts). **Other clubs:** Neath, Pontypridd, UWIC. Dynamic player. Former Wales Schools and Welsh Youth captain. Gained a Cambridge Blue while at Homerton in 1995. Educated at Neath Tertiary and Emmanuel GS in Swansea.

EVES, Derek John (Flanker)
Born Bristol, 07.01.66. 5′10″, 15st 5lb. **Rep hons:** England A (2, SAus95, 2t-10pts), Barbarians (93-94). **ADPR:** Bristol (1987-95, 87, 17t-80pts), Coventry (1995-99, 70, 17t-85pts), Bristol (1998-99, 6). Former captain of Bristol before his move to Coventry as player-coach in 1995. Replaced at Coundon Road by Keith Richardson, he decided on a return to his roots.

FENN, Simon Paul (Flanker)
Born Manly, Australia, 24.04.71. 6′2″, 16st. **ADPR:** London Scottish (1997-99, 35, 2t-10pts). **Other clubs:** Manly (Australia). Formerly with London Scottish until the takeover by London Irish. Powerful flanker who will be remembered not so much for his playing as for the little piece of himself that he left in a small corner of England – his left ear, bitten off in a Cup match at Bath. Solid performer and canny signing.

GABEY, Mark Laurence (Lock/flanker)
Born Proserpine, Australia, 27.07.73. 6′4″, 17st. **ADPR:** Bristol (1998-99, 22, 9t-45pts). **Other clubs:** Queensland, Australian Barbarians, Western Districts (Australia). Involved in an unpleasant set-to at Coventry when he claimed he was a victim of racial abuse in a Premiership match at Coundon Road. A Coventry player was later punished.

HASSAN, Carlos Alexander (Centre)
Born Auckland, New Zealand, 22.01.71. 6′2″, 13st 6lb. **ADPR:** Rotherham (1998-99, 10, 1t-5pts), Bristol (1998-99, 6, 2t, 1c-12pts). **Other clubs:** Counties (New Zealand), Bradford Bulls RL.

HONIBALL, Henry William (Fly-half)
Born Estcourt, South Africa, 01.12.65. 6′3″, 13st 5lb. **Rep hons:** South Africa (33, Aus93, 1t, 37c, 22pg-145pts). **Other clubs:** Natal (South Africa). Possibly the coup of the summer, a versatile player who has played in the centre for his country. Made his South Africa debut against Australia in Sydney in 1993. Plays for Natal and The Sharks in the Super 12 series. Runs a sheep and cattle farm not far from Durban.

HORAK, Michael John (Full-back)
Born Johannesburg, South Africa, 03.06.77. 6′2″, 14st 6lb. **ADPR:** Leicester (1997-99, 25, 8t, 2c, 2pg-50pts), Bristol (1998-99, 3, 5c, 4pg-22pts). **Other clubs:** Perth Western Reds RL. Former Free State Under 21 and Perth Reds full-back who has played for England Under 21s. Made just half a dozen appearances for Leicester last season and failed to get on the scoresheet. Follows Bob Dwyer out west to try his luck.

HULL, Paul Anthony (Full-back)
Born Lambeth, 17.05.68. 5′10″, 13st 2lb. **Rep hons:** England (4, SA94), A (19, Fiji89, 6t, 6c, 3pg-50pts), Barbarians (94). **ADPR:** Bristol (1987-99, 154, 29t, 40c, 39pg-335pts). Leading scorer, passing 600 points for the club during the season when supporters saw a return to the sort of form that won him England recognition in 1994 in South Africa where he had an outstanding tour. Unlucky to be dropped after getting injured against Canada. Captained England A on tour of Australia and Fiji in 1995. Had soccer trials with Southampton FC before converting to rugby.

JOHNSTONE, Paul David (Prop)
Born Bulawayo, Zimbabwe, 16.10.70. 6′, 17st 5lb. **Rep hons:** Zimbabwe (35). **ADPR:** Clifton (1996-97, 5, 1t-5pts), London Scottish (1996-99, 58, 5t-25pts). Powerful Zimbabwean who is now seeking Scottish international honours.

LEAUPEPE, George Edward (Centre)
Born Apia, Western Samoa, 27.04.75. 5′10″, 14st 2lb. **Rep hons:** Manu Samoa (20). **ADPR:** Bristol (1998-99, 9, 1t-5pts). **Other clubs:** Papakura, Counties (New Zealand). Classy centre who starred for Western Samoa in the 1995 World Cup.

LEMOINE, Pablo Adrian (Prop)
Born Montevideo, Uruguay, 01.03.75. 6′1″, 20st 6lb. **Rep hons:** Uruguay (14). **ADPR:** Bristol (1998-99, 13, 3t-15pts). **Other clubs:** Montevideo CC (Uruguay). Immensely powerful prop and key member of Uruguay's World Cup squad.

McCONNELL, Barry Robert (Hooker/prop)
Born Garvagh, Northern Ireland, 31.07.75. 5′10″, 15st 10lb. **ADPR:** Bristol (1995-99, 12). Versatile front row forward who went on Ireland's short tour of New Zealand in 1997. Has recovered from a serious knee injury but still made precious few appearances last season.

MacDONALD, Magnus Francis Adam (Prop)
Born Lund, Sweden, 16.03.71. 6′1″, 18st. **ADPR:** London Scottish (1997-99, 13). Formerly with Chesham.

MARSDEN, Sean Fagan Duckworth (Full-back)
Born Stirling, 17.01.80. 6′, 12st 8lb. **ADPR:** Bristol (1998-99, 10, 5t-25pts). **Other clubs:** Clifton, Gloucester.

MARTIN, Simon Andrew (Centre)
Born Thornbury, Bristol, 24.01.75. 5′10″, 13st 8lb. **ADPR:** Bristol (1995-99, 41, 6t, 5c, 2pg-46pts). Former Bristol Colts captain who can kick as well as score tries. Forced his way into the side and there should be more to come from him.

MAYER, Michael James MacKenzie 'Jamie' (Centre)
Born Edinburgh, 16.04.77. 5′10″, 14st 6lb. **Rep hons:** Scotland (1, SA98), A (3, Eng99, 1t-5pts). Enormously strong young centre, formerly with Edinburgh Reivers. Educated at Merchiston Castle.

NABARO, Luke (Wing)
Born Taulia, Fiji, 24.04.76. 6′, 14st 2lb. **Rep hons:** Hong Kong. **ADPR:** Bristol (1998-99, 6, 13t-65pts). Free-running Fijian who played international rugby for Fiji before travelling to England.

PICHOT, Agustin (Scrum-half)
Born Buenos Aires, Argentina, 22.08.74. 5′9″, 12st 5lb. **Rep hons:** Argentina (19, Aus95, 6t-30pts), Barbarians (95-96). **ADPR:** Richmond (1997-99, 25, 7t-35pts). Talented scrum-half who joined Richmond in 1995 from the San Isidro club in Argentina. Sure to play a key part in Argentina's World Cup this autumn before joining his new colleagues at the Memorial Ground.

PRITCHARD, Jonathan Andrew (Centre)
Born Bristol, 20.03.78. 6′, 14st. **ADPR:** Bath (1997-98, 4), Bristol (1998-99, 23, 3t-15pts). Talented former Colston's schoolboy from where he won England Schools honours.

ROBINSON, Mark Powell (Centre)
Born Stratford, New Zealand, 17.01.74. 6′1″, 14st 2lb. **Rep hons:** Barbarians (97-98). **ADPR:** Bristol (1998-99, 6, 4t-20pts). Cambridge Blue 1998.

RUDHAM, Damien Peter (Prop)
Born Barrow-in-Furness, 15.02.76. **ADPR:** London Scottish (1998-99, 20). **Other clubs:** Blackrock (Ireland).

RYAN, Dean (No 8/lock)
Born Tuxford, Nottingham, 22.06.66. 6′6″, 17st. **Rep hons:** England (4, Arg90, 1t-4pts), A (9, Aus88, 3t-13pts), Barbarians (88-89). **ADPR:** Saracens (1987-89, 12), Wasps (1989-96, 69, 13t-61pts), Newcastle (1995-99, 54, 16t-80pts). A second incarnation at Bristol, this time though as player-coach. An immensely forceful No 8, his season was cut short by a serious neck injury which required surgery. During his convalescence he decided to head west again.

SHARP, Alan Victor (Prop)
Born Bristol, 07.10.68. 5′10″, 17st 4lb. **Rep hons:** Scotland (6, Eng94), A (3, Sp89), Barbarians (96-97). **ADPR:** Bristol (1987-90, 16), Coventry (1989-90, 1), Bristol (1990-97, 61, 2t-10pts), Clifton (1991-92, 1t-4pts), Coventry (1996-99, 27), Bristol (1998-99, 8). Home again, the formidable scrummager with the short fuse. He left Coventry with Derek Eves.

SHORT, Craig Lee (Flanker)
Born Kingswood, 26.06.75. 6′1″, 14st 2lb. **ADPR:** Bristol (1996-99, 30, 2t-10pts). Useful openside flanker with bags of pace and aggression.

TAMATI, Dawson (Hooker)
Born New Zealand, 06.04.71. 5′11″, 16st 9lb. **ADPR:** Bristol (1998-99, 13, 1t-5pts). **Other clubs:** Taranaki (New Zealand).

VANDER, Adam John (Flanker)
Born Turners Hill, Sussex, 27.01.74. 6′2″, 15st 7lb. **Rep hons:** England A (3, Sc99, 1t-5pts). **ADPR:** Rosslyn Park (1994-96, 18, 5t-25pts), Richmond (1996-99, 43, 12t-60pts). **Other clubs:** Haywards Heath, Bath. Another Richmond victim, forced out of a team that was beginning to go places thanks to their backrow. Aggressive openside who put in plenty of eye-catching performances last season and could yet make it to the top.

VILE, Steven Jeremy (Fly-half)
Born Waratah, Australia, 16.07.70. 5′11″, 13st. **ADPR:** West Hartlepool (1997-99, 40, 13t, 61c, 95pg, 3dg-481pts). Australian-born utility back who did a fine job in adversity for West Hartlepool last season. Formerly with Ponsonby in New Zealand and Castres in France.

WILLIAMS, Barry Hugh (Hooker)
Born Carmarthen, 06.01.74. 6′, 16st 6lb. **Rep hons:** Wales (12, Fr96, 2t-10pts), A (9, Ire94). **ADPR:** Richmond (1997-99, 44, 6t-30pts). **Other clubs:** Neath. Mobile hooker, good hands and great ball carrier. Won a record 13 caps for Wales Youth before making his Wales debut against France in September 1996 and scoring a try within two minutes.

REVIEW

It was probably no coincidence that Worcester were breathing down their necks when owner Malcolm Pearce proposed the takeover of London Scottish. Bristol retained their option until gaining rightful and honourable re-entry to Premiership One as Second Division champions. They finally dropped letters from their shirts and adopted numbers. Australian fly-half David Knox proved a handful and made a public apology after being sent off against Worcester, Bob Dwyer, the director of rugby, claiming that Knox had been provoked. Former captain Derek Eves and prop Alan Sharp returned from Coventry, as did Garath Archer from Newcastle. Dean Ryan also left the Geordies to take up the post of player-coach.

BRISTOL in Premiership Two 1998-99

Sep	5	A	Exeter	Won	22	15	A.Charron (T) J.Evans (T) B.Breeze (T) P.Hull (2C, P)
	12	H	Fylde	Won	55	14	S.Marsden (3T) P.Hull (T, 5C) A.Charron (T) J.Brownrigg (T) C.Evans (T) D.Dewdney (T) A.Adams (T)
	19	A	Rugby Lions	Won	30	20	D.Dewdney (2T) M.Bennett (T) J.Pritchard (T) P.Hull (2C, 2P)
	26	H	London Welsh	Won	37	3	B.Breeze (T) P.Hull (T, 4C, 3P) T.Barlow (T) A.Larkin (T)
Oct	3	A	Blackheath	Won	41	9	A.Larkin (3T) S.Martin (T) C.Eagle (T) J.Wring (T) P.Hull (4C, P)
	10	H	Orrell	Won	29	19	M.Misson (T) S.Marsden (T) D.Dewdney (T) P.Hull (2P) S.Martin (C, 2P)
	17	A	Leeds Tykes	Won	16	13	M.Gabey (T) P.Hull (C, 3P)
	24	A	Rotherham	Lost	5	16	S.Martin (T)
	30	H	Coventry	Won	14	12	A.Larkin (T) D.Knox (3P)
Nov	7	A	Wakefield	Won	46	15	B.Breeze (2T) A.Larkin (2T) J.Wring (T) C.Evans (T) M.Misson (T) D.Knox (4C, P)
	22	H	Moseley	Won	58	18	M.Misson (2T) M.Gabey (T) G.Baber (T) A.Barnard (T) B.Breeze (T) G.Giles (T) C.Short (T) A.Larkin (T, C) D.Knox (4C, P)
Dec	13	A	Worcester	Lost	9	20	P.Hull (3P)
	19	H	Waterloo Drummers	Won	36	8	A.Larkin (2T) P.Hull (T) C.Hassan (T) M.Gabey (T) M.Bennett (T) S.Martin (3C)
Jan	2	A	Moseley	Won	43	6	A.Larkin (2T) M.Misson (2T) S.Martin (T, C) G.Baber (T) S.Marsden (T) P.Hull (3C)
	16	H	Wakefield	Won	35	19	P.Lemoine (T) Penalty (T) M.Gabey (T) G.Baber (T) D.Knox (3C, 3P)

Feb	6	H	Rotherham	Lost	31	36	J.Pritchard (T) G.Baber (T) M.Gabey (T) Penalty (T) D.Knox (4C, P)
	13	H	Leeds Tykes	Won	20	5	J.Evans (T) D.Knox (3P, D) P.Hull (P)
	21	A	Coventry	Lost	19	22	M.Misson (T) M.Gabey (T) Penalty (T) D.Knox (2C)
	27	A	Orrell	Won	34	32	P.Lemoine (2T) S.Lines (T) G.Baber (T) J.Evans (T) D.Knox (3C, P)
Mar	13	H	Blackheath	Won	50	17	L.Nabaro (5T) D.Tamati (T) C.Hassan (T, C) M.Gabey (T) P.Hull (4C)
	27	A	London Welsh	Won	25	6	L.Nabaro (2T) M.Robinson (T) P.Hull(2C, 2P)
Apr	3	H	Rugby Lions	Won	49	13	L.Nabaro (3T) G.Baber (2T) M.Gabey (T) A.Charron (T) P.Hull (T, 3C, P)
	17	A	Fylde	Won	43	39	M.Robinson (2T) L.Nabaro (2T) P.Hull (T, C, 2P) M.Misson (T) C.Evans (T)
	24	H	Exeter	Won	36	17	C.Eagle (T) M.Robinson (T) A.Larkin (T) J.Pritchard (T) G.Leaupepe (T) G.Baber (T) P.Hull (3C)
May	1	A	Waterloo Drummers	Won	44	13	M.Bennett (T) M.Gabey (T) J.Evans (T) L.Nabaro (T) G.Baber (T) P.Hull (C, 2P) M.Horak (4C, P)
	9	H	Worcester	Won	21	11	C.Eagle (T) C.Evans (T) M.Horak (C, 3P)

Summary of Premiership scorers:

164 P.Hull (5T, 35C, 23P); 82 D.Knox (20C, 13P, D); 67 A.Larkin (13T, C); 65 L.Nabaro (13T); 45 M.Gabey (9T), G.Baber (9T); 40 M.Misson (8T); 31 S.Martin (3T, 5C, 2P); 25 S.Marsden (5T), B.Breeze (5T); 22 M.Horak (5C, 4P); 20 M.Robinson (4T), C.Evans (4T), J.Evans (4T), D.Dewdney (4T); 15 Penalty (3T), J.Pritchard (3T), P.Lemoine (3T), C.Eagle (3T), A.Charron (3T), M.Bennett (3T); 12 C.Hassan (2T, C); 10 J.Wring (2T); 5 D.Tamati (T), C.Short (T), S.Lines (T), G.Leaupepe (T), G.Giles (T), J.Brownrigg (T), A.Barnard (T), T.Barlow (T), A.Adams (T).

Summary of Premiership appearances:

26 M.Bennett; 24 C.Eagle (+2); 23 J.Pritchard (+4); 22 M.Gabey (+2), C.Evans (+6); 21 P.Hull, J.Evans (+9), B.Breeze (+5), G.Baber (+2); 20 A.Charron; 18 M.Misson (+1); 17 J.Wring (+5), S.Emms (+3), J.Brownrigg (+12); 15 S.Martin (+4), A.Larkin (+1); 14 D.Dewdney (+7); 13 D.Tamati, P.Lemoine (+4); 11 D.Hinkins (+4), G.Giles (+1); 10 S.Marsden (+5); 9 G.Leaupepe, D.Knox; 8 A.Sharp; 7 A.Barnard; 6 N.Watkins (+1), M.Robinson, L.Nabaro, C.Hassan

(+1), D.Eves (+5); 5 C.Short (+5), S.Lines (+1), T.Barlow (+2); 4 B.McConnell (+4); 3 M.Horak, K.Dunn (+1); 2 P.Whittaker, S.Morgan (+2), C.Higgs, R.Blake (+1); 1 D.Yapp (+1), T.Tapsell (+1), J.Probyn, J.Evans, A.Adams (+1).

GLOUCESTER

Formation of club: 1873
Ground: Kingsholm, Kingsholm Road, Gloucester GL1 3AX
Tel: 01452 381087
Capacity: 10,800 (Seated 1,498)
Colours: Cherry and white hoops and dark blue trim
Honours: Cup Winners (3) – 1972, 1978, 1982
Best League finish: 2nd in Division One 1988-89, 1989-90
Last season: Premiership One – 10th. Tetley's Bitter Cup – SF (lost 21-35 to Wasps). Cheltenham & Gloucester Cup – Winners
Owner: Tom Walkinshaw (Arrows F1 partner)
Chief executive: Hamish Brown
Director of rugby: Philippe Saint-Andre
Assistants: John Brain, Dave Pointon
Club Captain: TBC

BECK, Laurie John Henry (Scrum-half)
Born Cheltenham, 02.01.71. 5′10″, 13st 2lb. **ADPR:** Gloucester (1990-99, 22). Experienced back-up scrum-half, formerly with Cheltenham. Keen water-polo player.

BEIM, Thomas David (Wing)
Born Frimley, 11.12.75. 5′11″, 13st 9lb. **Rep hons:** England (2, NZ98, 1t-5pts), Barbarians (97). **ADPR:** Gloucester (1995-96, 2, 1t-5pts), Sale (1996-99, 46, 31t-155pts), Gloucester (1998-99, 7, 3t-15pts). **Other clubs:** Hamiltons (South Africa). Managed just eight matches for Sale last season and still scored four tries. But his own unhappiness and inability to settle in the north-west saw him put on the transfer list at his own request. In seven appearances for Gloucester, the club he had left three years before, he scored a further three tries. Opted for England in 1997 when he toured Australia with Clive Woodward's U21 squad. Deservedly earned selection for the senior tour of Australia, New Zealand and South Africa in 1998. Former Cheltenham College schoolboy who has played hockey for Wales U18 and professional polo.

CATLING, Christopher Edward (Full-back)
Born Coulsdon, 17.06.76. 6′2″, 14st 2lb. **Rep hons:** England A (8, SA96, 1t-5pts). **ADPR:** Exeter (1995-96, 6, 1t-5pts), Gloucester (1996-99, 60, 12t, 1dg-63pts). One of the most exciting counter-attacking full-backs around as his eight tries last season bear witness and now looks to have added a bit of beef and nous to his defensive game. Educated at Whitgift School in Croydon, Chris was ever-present in the England Schools grand slam team of 1994 captained by Gloucester's Phil Greening, before moving to Exeter University. Signed from Exeter RFC in the summer of 1996, was a member of England's World Students Cup squad in South Africa in 1996; toured with England U21 in Australia in 1997.

CORNWELL, Mark John (Lock)
Born Gloucester, 22.02.73. 6′7″, 17st 4lb. **Rep hons:** England A (5, Ire98). **ADPR:** Gloucester (1994-99, 42, 2t-10pts). **Other clubs:** Old Richians. Established himself as a first-team regular last season, taking part in a three-man rota in the second row. Hard, aggressive and a reliable ball-winner. Revealed a fair share of mobility in the loose. Clearly benefited from time spent with Hamilton's club in South Africa.

DEACON, Andrew (Prop)
Born Gloucester, 31.07.65. 6′2″, 17st. **ADPR:** Gloucester (1991-99, 94, 5t-25pts). **Other clubs:** Longlevens. Vastly experienced and underrated prop who has added some serious power up front.

EUSTACE, Adam Robert (Utility forward)
Born Gloucester, 09.01.79. 6′5″, 16st. **ADPR:** Gloucester (1998-99, 5, 1t-5pts). **Other clubs:** Coney Hill. Emerged strongly at the end of last season.

EWENS, Joseph Alexander (Centre)
Born Bristol, 16.12.77. 6′, 13st. **Rep hons:** England A (4, Arg96, 1t 5pts). **ADPR:** Bath (1996-98, 2), Bedford (1997-99, 25, 10t-50pts). England U21 cap who has an impressive strike rate and for someone so young shows a degree of maturity against his elders and betters. Won nine England 18 Group caps, captaining the side in 1995-96. Also helped Colston's Collegiate win two consecutive Daily Mail U18 Cup titles.

FANOLUA, Terry Laauli (Utility back)
Born Motoutua, Western Samoa, 03.07.74. 6′, 13st 9lb. **Rep hons:** Manu Samoa (16). **ADPR:** Gloucester (1997-99, 39, 9t, 1pg-48pts). **Other clubs:** Otahuhu (New Zealand). Delayed his return from the World Cup qualifying matches for Western Samoa and got into hot water with the club, then was found guilty of an assault charge and fined £1,000. Quickly into his stride, though, making 17 appearances and scoring a couple of tries. The former Western Samoan sevens captain has proved a major force in Gloucester's revamped backline, showing great strength in the tackle and real pace on the outside.

FIDLER, Robert John (Lock)
Born Cheltenham, 21.09.74. 6′5″, 17st 9lb. **Rep hons:** England (2, NZ98), A (10, SA96, 1t-5pts). **ADPR:** Gloucester (1994-99, 71, 6t-30pts). **Other clubs:** Cheltenham. Deservedly won England recognition, playing in the second Test against New Zealand in 1998 and in the next match against South Africa. Athletic lock with good hands and has the pace and power to trouble defences when in the loose. With Mark Cornwell formed one of the strongest second row pairings in the Premiership. Played for the ERP XV against New Zealand at Ashton Gate the season before last. Son of former Gloucester and England lock John Fidler. Educated at Cheltenham College.

FORTEY, Christopher Paul (Hooker)
Born Gloucester, 25.08.75. 6′, 16st 8lb. **ADPR:** Gloucester (1996-99, 36, 2t-10pts). **Other clubs:** Gordon League. Has gone from being a promising young hooker who rose to the occasion during Phil Greening's absences, to an established first-team player. Twin brother Lee is a former England U21 prop.

GLANVILLE, Peter Neil (Flanker)
Born Gloucester, 10.06.71. 6′2″, 16st. **ADPR:** Gloucester (1992-99, 70, 3t-15pts). Started with Longlevens, came to prominence playing for the South West in the CIS Divisional championship in 1995. Formerly a sales manager for his father's tyre firm before turning professional. Former Gloucester club captain.

HAZELL, Andrew Robert (Flanker)
Born Gloucester, 25.04.78. 6′, 14st 6lb. **ADPR:** Gloucester (1997-99, 11). **Other clubs:** Gloucester OB.

HINKINS, David John (Prop)
Born Exeter, 20.10.66. 6′1″, 18st 5lb. **ADPR:** Bristol (1989-97, 103), Bedford (1997-98, 12, 1t-5pts), Bristol (1998-99, 11), Gloucester (1998-99, 2). Signed from Bristol, a solid prop with a surprising amount of mobility. Played for England in the 1988 World Students Cup.

JEWELL, Robert James (Wing)
Born Bromsgrove, 11.10.78. 6', 15st 2lb. **ADPR:** Gloucester (1997-99, 11, 1t-5pts). Promising wing who joined from Gordon League. Capped by England Colts the season before last and made his senior debut against Fylde in December 1997.

JOHNSON, Brian Gareth William (Wing)
Born Wegberg, West Germany, 27.07.72. 5'11", 13st 4lb. **Rep hons:** England A (4, SA96), Barbarians (96-97). **ADPR:** Newbury (1996-98, 20, 35t-175pts), Gloucester (1997-99, 28, 6t-30pts). Disappointing season with just one Premiership try to his name in 15 appearances. Has searing pace. An army captain, he is studying at RMCS Shrivenham.

JONES, Ian Donald (Lock)
Born Whangerei, New Zealand, 17.04.67. 6'6", 16st 5lb. **Rep Hons:** New Zealand (77, Sc90). One of the most athletic second row forwards in the world, he conquered frontiers no other lock had dared approach. Even in the twilight of his career he should prove a formidable addition to Gloucester's forward strength. His father-in-law being Irish, he will not fall foul of the overseas player ruling. Early season availability depends on whether he makes the New Zealand World Cup squad.

JONES, Phillip **Kingsley** Brian (Flanker)
Born Bedwellty, 19.06.69. 6', 14st 10lb. **Rep hons:** Wales (10, Barb96), A (1, Eng98). **ADPR:** Gloucester (1998-99, 3). **Other clubs:** Ebbw Vale. Sidelined by an Achilles tendon problem but aiming to fight his way back. Earmarked for great things with the club. A classy flanker, fast and a good ball-handler. Sound defensively.

KIMBER, Martin Jon (Fly-half)
Born Auckland, New Zealand, 20.09.68. 6', 13st 10lb. **ADPR:** Gloucester (1994-99, 39, 1t, 2c, 4pg, 12dg-57pts). Has never quite established himself as a regular first-team player. Will continue to fill a stand-in role.

LUMSDEN, Audley Emmanuel (Wing/full-back)
Born London, 06.06.67. 6', 14st 10lb. **Rep hons:** England A (1, Fr89, 1t-4pts). **ADPR:** Bath (1987-96, 45, 18t-86pts), Gloucester (1996-99, 36, 9t-45pts). Evergreen former Bath utility back who may have lost the blazing pace of his youth but remains an accomplished performer at full-back and on the wing. A graduate of both Bath and Oxford Universities, where he won a Blue in 1992, Audley is now a physics teacher at Millfield School. Remarkably has continued at the top level despite suffering a serious broken neck in 1989.

McCARTHY, Neil (Hooker)
Born Slough, 29.11.74. 5'10", 16st. **Rep hons:** England (1, Ire99), Barbarians (96-97). **ADPR:** Bath (1996-97, 2), Bedford (1996-97, 7), Gloucester (1997-99, 29, 1t-5pts). Made his England debut against Ireland, coming on as a temporary replacement for Cockerill and was then selected to go on England's brief tour of Australia. Now established as a regular first-teamer at Kingsholm. Hard, uncompromising player with good technique. Joined from Bath in 1997, having spent much of the 1996-97 season on loan to Bedford. Represented England Colts for a record three years at prop, captaining the side in his last season, but has switched to hooker with success.

MANNIX, Simon James (Fly-half)
Born Lower Hutt, New Zealand, 10.08.71. 5'9", 13st 2lb. **Rep hons:** New Zealand (1, Fr94), Barbarians (96-97). **ADPR:** Sale (1996-98, 22, 8t, 25c, 35pg, 1dg-198pts), Gloucester (1998-99, 19, 2t, 14c, 20pg-98pts). Saint-Andre has made no secret of the fact that he regards the Kiwi as his first choice fly-half. And no wonder. He does everything and does it well. Superb playmaker at outside half who fell out spectacularly with Sale midway through the previous season and was reduced to a touchline spectator thereafter. Completed three years residency in November 1998 and has declared his intention of challenging for an England Test spot. Played for the Petone club in New Zealand and also spent two seasons with Tarvisium in Italy.

MONCRIEFF, Elton A. (Scrum-half)
Born 08.06.72. 5′7″, 12st 8lb. Nuggety and experienced scrum-half who has played for New South Wales and Wellington Crusaders.

OJOMOH, Stephen Oziegbe (Backrow)
Born Benin City, Nigeria, 25.05.70. 6′3″, 16st 9lb. **Rep hons:** England (12, Ire94), A (19, NOtago92, 3t-12pts), Barbarians (94). **ADPR:** Bath (1990-97, 61, 4t-20pts), Gloucester (1997-99, 39, 5t-25pts). Back to his outstanding best last season. Schoolboy decathlete of note who attended West Buckland School and the West of England University. Steve joined Bath from Rosslyn Park and toured New Zealand and Canada with England A before winning his first cap against Ireland. Outstanding for England in South Africa (1994) and a member of England's RWC95 squad.

PARAMORE, Peter **Junior** (Backrow)
Born Apia, Western Samoa, 18.11.68. 6′3″, 17st. **Rep hons:** Manu Samoa (16). **ADPR:** Bedford (1996-99, 50, 18t-90pts). **Other clubs:** Hunter Mariners RL, Castleford RL. Snapped up, after months of chasing, from troubled Bedford where he was player of the year when they won promotion the season before last. A Western Samoan international, with the superb handling skills you always associate with their sevens experts. Fiercely competitive in the tackle, Junior played his early rugby with Manurewa in New Zealand and after RWC95 turned professional with Castleford and Hunter Mariners RL.

PEARCE, Edward (Flanker)
Born Bristol, 02.09.75. 6′5″, 18st 8lb. **ADPR:** Bath (1994-96, 2), Gloucester (1996-99, 29). Beginning to establish himself as a backrow player of quality. Proud owner of size 16 boots. Educated at Clifton College and has developed into an exceptional age group international. Performed well in Bath's cross-code game against Wigan at Twickenham before moving to Kingsholm in August 1996.

POWLES, Adrian (Prop)
Born Coleford, 14.03.67. 5′11″, 17st 2lb. **ADPR:** Gloucester (1994-99, 27). Former Berry Hill front row man who provides valuable front row back-up.

SAINT-ANDRE, Philippe Georges (Wing)
Born Romans, France, 19.04.67. 5′11″, 14st 6lb. **Rep hons:** France (69, Rom90, 32t-152pts), Barbarians (90-91). **ADPR:** Gloucester (1997-99, 31, 14t-70pts). Recovered fully from a quadriceps muscle injury suffered during the previous season and showed some of his old scoring touch with eight Premiership tries in 18 appearances. Now has greater responsibility after taking over the coaching duties from Richard Hill. Philippe, who joined Gloucester in May 1997, has been one of the world's great try-scoring wings and also captained France for 29 successive games. Originally joined Montferrand from his home club Romans in 1988. First capped against Romania in 1990, an inauspicious day as France slipped to a 12-6 defeat. Scored that sensational try at Twickenham in 1991 when France counter-attacked from behind their own line. In 1994 became the first wing to captain France since Christian Darrouy (1967) and went on to become France's most successful captain in history. Owns an Irish pub in Montferrand.

SANCHEZ, Stephane (Prop)
Born Lavelanet, France, 02.01.73. 5′9″, 16st 8lb. Emerging young prop who joins from Montferrand, the old club of Gloucester player-coach Philippe Saint-Andre.

SANDERS, Ian (Scrum-half)
Born Penzance, 22.01.71. 5′9″, 13st 10lb. **Rep hons:** Barbarians (98-99). **ADPR:** Bath (1990-97, 34, 4t-20pts), Gloucester (1997-99, 16). A quick-witted player and a real scrapper of a scrum-half who made a useful contribution to the Gloucester cause. A Cornishman who moved to Gloucester from Bath in 1997. Educated at St Ives School and Penwith College; made his Bath debut in 1990 as a replacement against London Scottish.

TOMBS, Richard Craig (Centre)
Born Te Kuiti, New Zealand, 04.01.68. 6′, 14st 10lb. **Rep hons:** Australia (5, Sc92). **ADPR:** Gloucester (1997-99, 46, 11t-55pts). **Other clubs:** NSW (Australia). Former Australia centre whose experience and mature play contributed much to Gloucester's best performances. Fabulous defence, lethal in attack and scorer of seven tries last season. His name is pronounced to rhyme with 'bombs' and he certainly can explode out of the tackle. Toured England with Ricky Stuart's Australian Schools squad in 1986; member of Australia's World Cup winning squad in 1991.

VICKERY, Philip John (Prop)
Born Barnstaple, 14.03.76. 6′3″, 19st 9lb. **Rep hons:** England (5, Wal98), A (1, NZ97). **ADPR:** Gloucester (1996-99, 27, 1t-5pts). His initial comeback just before Christmas from a career-threatening neck injury lasted just 15 minutes. But finally the England tighthead was ready and reappeared in the Gloucester front row in April. A powerful front row tyro who made an immediate impression on his senior England debut, helping Clive Woodward's side to a record 60-26 win over Wales in 1998. He was subsequently cited for punching an opponent and initially banned for a month, though this was quashed on appeal. Learned his rugby playing for Bude and Redruth before joining Gloucester. Capped at Schools and Colts level.

WARD, Richard Corin (Lock)
Born Munster, Germany, 26.11.70. 6′6″, 18st 8lb. **ADPR:** Havant (1993-96, 41, 2t-10pts), Gloucester (1996-99, 9). Bedford (1998-99, 2). **Other clubs:** Harlequins.

WOODMAN, Trevor James (Prop)
Born Plymouth, 04.08.76. 5′11″, 18st. **Rep hons:** England A (4, Sc99). **ADPR:** Gloucester (1996-99, 25, 1t-5pts). **Other clubs:** Bath. Earned senior England recognition when selected for the short summer tour to Australia after appearing in all four of England A's Five Nations fixtures. With youth on his side, plus plenty of technical know-how, has the potential to break into the full England side before too long.

YATES, Christian Jude (Wing/centre)
Born Otahuhu, New Zealand, 13.05.71. 6′1″, 16st. **ADPR:** Sale (1994-99, 69, 19t, 2dg-101pts). **Other clubs:** Old Aldwinians. Powerful Anglo-Kiwi wing who was a regular in the Sale team last season scoring five tries. Unsettled up north, though, and followed Tom Beim to Kingsholm. Represented England in the 1995 Hong Kong Sevens.

REVIEW

In a season when the trend was for club owners to jump ship, Tom Walkinshaw made an even bigger commitment by increasing his stake in the club to 98 per cent after overwhelming support from members at a special meeting in July. He unveiled plans to increase Kingsholm's capacity to 20,000. Unfortunately no amount of money was able to cure Gloucester of their chronic travel sickness. Yet again their away form cost them dear. Richard Hill was sacked as coach, but his successor Philippe Saint-Andre fared no better. They did win the Cheltenham & Gloucester Cup in a repeat of last year's final against Bedford and reached the semi-final of the Tetley's Bitter Cup. But there were other losses: Keith Richardson returned as forwards coach but lasted just 53 days; hooker Phil Greening went to Sale; then in the summer Mark Mapletoft joined Saracens and Scott Benton joined Leeds.

GLOUCESTER in Premiership One 1998-99

Sep	5	H	London Irish	Won	29	22	Penalty (T) M.Mapletoft (T, 2C, 5P)
	12	A	Richmond	Won	25	22	M.Mapletoft (2T, 2C, 2P) P.Saint-Andre (T)

20	H	West Hartlepool	Won	36	3	R.Tombs (2T) C.Catling (T) S.Ojomoh (T) P.Saint-Andre (T) M.Mapletoft (4C, P)
26	A	Bath	Lost	16	21	S.Mannix (T) P.Saint-Andre (T) M.Mapletoft (P, D)
Oct 3	H	Wasps	Lost	12	13	M.Mapletoft (4P)
17	H	Newcastle Falcons	Won	41	32	C.Catling (3T) P.Saint-Andre (T) A.Lumsden (T) S.Mannix (2C, 4P)
20	A	Harlequins	Lost	7	39	Penalty (T) S.Mannix (C)
25	H	London Scottish	Won	29	16	P.Saint-Andre (T) A.Dawling (T) S.Mannix (2C, 5P)
31	A	Northampton Saints	Lost	8	22	A.Lumsden (T) S.Mannix (P)
Nov 7	H	Bedford	Won	31	21	C.Fortey (T) S.Ojomoh (T) C.Catling (T) M.Mapletoft (2C, 4P)
21	H	Saracens	Won	28	27	R.Tombs (2T) T.Fanolua (T) S.Mannix (2C, 3P)
Dec 12	A	Manchester Sale	Lost	10	26	P.Saint-Andre (T) S.Mannix (C, P)
19	H	Leicester Tigers	Lost	18	23	B.Johnson (T) M.Mapletoft (T, C, 2P)
27	A	Wasps	Lost	9	23	M.Mapletoft (2P) T.Fanolua (P)
Jan 2	H	Bath	Won	23	7	C.Catling (2T) T.Fanolua (T) M.Mapletoft (C, 2P)
5	A	London Scottish	Lost	13	24	M.Mapletoft (T, C, 2P)
16	H	Richmond	Drew	24	24	Penalty (T) S.Benton (T) M.Mapletoft (C, 4P)
23	A	Leicester Tigers	Lost	16	23	R.Tombs (T) M.Mapletoft (C, 3P)
Feb 7	A	London Irish	Lost	20	42	N.Carter (T) P.Saint-Andre (T) S.Benton (T) M.Mapletoft (C, P)
13	H	Harlequins	Lost	20	31	T.Beim (T) Penalty (T) M.Mapletoft (2C, 2P)
Mar 14	A	West Hartlepool	Lost	32	33	N.Carter (T) T.Beim (T) Penalty (T) S.Ojomoh (T) M.Mapletoft (T, 2C, P)
27	A	Bedford	Lost	15	19	M.Cornwell (T) P.Saint-Andre (T) S.Mannix (C, P)
Apr 25	A	Newcastle Falcons	Lost	15	39	M.Davies (T) T.Beim (T) S.Mannix (C) M.Mapletoft (P)
May 1	H	Manchester Sale	Lost	24	34	T.Woodman (T) R.Tombs (T) M.Mapletoft (C, 4P)
7	A	Saracens	Lost	10	26	A.Eustace (T) S.Ward (C, P)
16	H	Northampton Saints	Won	43	31	C.Catling (T) N.Carter (T) S.Mannix (T, 4C, 5P) R.Tombs (T)

Summary of Premiership scorers:

198 M.Mapletoft (6T, 21C, 41P, D); 98 S.Mannix (2T, 14C, 20P); 40 P.Saint-Andre (8T), C.Catling (8T); 35 R.Tombs (7T); 25 Penalty (5T); 15 S.Ojomoh (3T), N.Carter (3T), T.Beim (3T); 13 T.Fanolua (2T, P); 10 A.Lumsden (2T), S.Benton

(2T); 5 T.Woodman (T), S.Ward (C, P), B.Johnson (T), C.Fortey (T), A.Eustace (T), A.Dawling (T), M.Davies (T), M.Cornwell (T).

Summary of Premiership appearances:

26 S.Ojomoh (+1); 25 N.Carter (+3); 24 R.Tombs; 21 T.Woodman (+5), C.Catling (+1); 20 C.Fortey (+10), M.Cornwell (+6); 19 D.Sims (+5), N.McCarthy (+6), S.Mannix (+2), R.Fidler (+1); 18 P.Saint-Andre (+1), M.Mapletoft (+3), A.Deacon (+1); 17 E.Pearce (+1), T.Fanolua, S.Benton (+3); 15 B.Johnson (+1); 14 T.Windo (+3), I.Sanders (+2); 13 A.Lumsden (+2); 11 R.Greenslade-Jones (+5); 10 A.Hazell (+8); 9 S.Devereux (+2); 8 R.Ward (+2); 7 T.Beim (+1); 6 P.Vickery, A.Powles (+4), R.Jewell (+1); 5 A.Eustace (+2); 4 M.Kimber (+3); 3 K.Jones (+1), P.Greening; 2 D.Hinkins (+2), P.Glanville (+2), M.Davies; 1 S.Ward, R.Stott (+1), A.Dawling, N.Cane (+1), L.Beck (+1).

NEC HARLEQUINS

Formation of club: 1866
Ground: Stoop Memorial Ground, Craneford Way, Twickenham TW2 7SX
Club Call Hotline: 0839 664414
Capacity: 9,750 (All seated)
Colours: Light blue, magenta, chocolate, french grey, black and light green
Honours: Cup Winners (2) – 1988, 1991
Best League finish: 3rd in Division One 1987-88, 1990-91, 1995-96, 1996-97
Last season: Premiership One – 4th. Tetley's Bitter Cup – QF (lost 13-15 to Gloucester)
Owner: NEC Electronics
Chief executive: Huw Morgan
Director of rugby: John Gallagher.
Coach: Zinzan Brooke
Assistants: Bernie McCahill, Andrew Skeggs
Captain: Zinzan Brooke

BARNES, David Michael (Prop)
Born Leicester, 12.07.76. 6', 17st 10lb. **ADPR:** West Hartlepool (1996-97, 10, 1t-5pts), Harlequins (1998-99, 15). **Other clubs:** Kendal, Newcastle.

BIBBY, Alexander Guy (Flanker)
Born Leicester, 20.05.74. 6'4", 16st. **ADPR:** Nottingham (1996-97, 5), Orrell (1997-98, 8), Harlequins (1998-99, 1). **Other clubs:** Leicester.

BROOKE, Zinzan Valentine (No 8)
Born Waiuku, New Zealand, 14.02.65. 6'3", 18st. **Rep hons:** New Zealand (58, Arg87, 17t, 3dg-89pts). **ADPR:** Harlequins (1998-99, 18, 1t-5pts). Hugely skilled and versatile former All Black who took on the dual role of player-coach last season. Moulded them into a steelier outfit and saw them into Europe at his first attempt. Was instrumental in persuading Carling to resurrect his career last season. Started as a sevens expert with New Zealand and developed into one of their most accomplished backrow forwards in history. Also proved a popular and effective captain of Auckland. Famed for his outrageous touch kicks and drop goals – he landed one from 40 metres against England in the 1995 World Cup and kicked two others, against South Africa and Wales, in international rugby.

CARLING, William David Charles (Centre)
Born Bradford-on-Avon, 12.12.65. 5′11″, 14st 2lb. **Rep hons:** England (72, Fr88, 12t-54pts), A (1, Fr87), Barbarians (86-87). **ADPR:** Harlequins (1987-99, 104, 20t, 27c, 6pg-162pts). Persuaded by Zinzan Brooke and John Gallagher to kick-start his career with the club 13 months after walking out of rugby. Made a handful of appearances and little impact. Offer on table to carry on into the Millennium but said to be having second thoughts during the summer. Former England captain, who led them to back-to-back Grand Slams in 1991 and 1992 and again in 1995. Holds the record for most tests as a captain, 59, after his appointment in 1988 under Geoff Cooke.

DANIEL, Brendon Wiremu (Wing)
Born New Zealand, 19.07.77. 6′1″, 14st 4lb. **ADPR:** Saracens (1997-99, 36, 16t-80pts). **Other clubs:** Bay of Plenty. Discarded by Saracens late last season despite finishing up as their top try-scorer with 12. Powerful young wing with an excellent pedigree having been a member of New Zealand's U19 and Academy sides and a member of the All Blacks' renowned sevens squad. Caught Saracens' eye when starring for the Barbarians in the 1997 Middlesex Sevens and did well in his first season of senior rugby. English qualified after his marriage to an Englishwoman.

HARRIES, Huw John (Scrum-half)
Born Cardiff, 21.02.73. 5′11″, 13st 7lb. **Rep hons:** Wales A (2, Ire97). **ADPR:** Harlequins (1996-99, 50, 12t-60pts). **Other clubs:** Llanelli. Had the edge on his closest rival for the scrum-half shirt, Nick Walshe. Razor-sharp around the fringes and scorer of three tries in the Premiership. A star product of the Wales age group system, the Welsh-speaking Harries has captained every Welsh side he has represented. Educated at Ysgol Glantaf, New College, Cardiff and Cardiff University. A qualified pharmacist.

JENKINS, Rory Harry John (Flanker)
Born Leicester, 29.06.70. 6′2″, 15st 12lb. **Rep hons:** England A (16, It94, 1t-5pts). **ADPR:** London Irish (1993-94, 15, 1t-5pts), Harlequins (1994-99, 92, 6t-30pts). Ever-present in the Harlequins backrow from where he scored three tries. A powerful and destructive flanker. The son of former Leicester and Cambridge University lock John Jenkins, he was educated at Oundle and Cambridge University where he won Blues in rugby, cricket and athletics. Formerly with Brixham, he joined London Irish and played against the 1993 All Blacks for London before joining Harlequins. Toured Argentina with England 1997 but failed to make the breakthrough at full England level. Qualified solicitor.

KEYTER, Jason Christopher (Centre/wing)
Born Port Elizabeth, South Africa, 20.12.73. 5′11″, 14st 2lb. **Rep hons:** England A (2, Vic95). **ADPR:** Harlequins (1993-95, 12, 5t-25pts), Bristol (1995-96, 9), Harlequins (1996-99, 45, 10t-50pts). Talented utility back and one of Harlequins' more consistent performers behind the scrum last season when he scored four tries. Arrived in England in 1986 and played his junior rugby with Weston-super-Mare. Joined Harlequins as a Colt and made rapid progress before quitting the club and joining Bristol midway through 1994-95 season. Toured Australia and Fiji with England A in 1995 and rejoined Quins from Bristol last season.

LEACH, Adam Charles (No 8)
Born Corowa, NSW, Australia, 24.11.71. 6′2″, 15st 6lb. **ADPR:** Harlequins (1997-99, 39, 2t-10pts). **Other clubs:** NSW (Australia). Former New South Wales backrow forward who signed for Harlequins after advertising his services on the Internet.

LEONARD, Jason (Prop)
Born Barking, 14.08.68. 5′10″, 17st 2lb. **Rep hons:** England (72, Arg90, 1t-5pts), A (2, Fiji89), Barbarians (96). **ADPR:** Saracens (1988-90, 19, 1t-4pts), Harlequins (1990-99, 114, 2t-9pts). A huge improvement on the previous season and looked immoveable as England's loosehead prop. The records continue to fall. He played in all eight

Tests in the domestic season without once being replaced, then achieved the same feat when he played against Queensland and the one-off Test against Australia on the short summer tour. His strength and stamina, not to say appetite for the game at the highest level, remains undiminished and he is still very much a clubman, giving his all to the Harlequins cause. Easy to forget that he probably should not be playing at all after undergoing complicated surgery to his neck which required a bone graft from his hip. Educated at Warren Comprehensive School, Chadwell Heath, Jason joined Barking RFC before moving to Saracens and on to Harlequins.

LILEY, Robert James (Fly-half)
Born Wakefield, 03.04.70. 6′1″, 12st 8lb. **Rep hons:** England A (2, Qld96, 2c, 1pg-7pts), Barbarians (96-97). **ADPR:** Wakefield (1991-94, 23, 3t, 23c, 51pg, 2dg-219pts), Sale (1994-96, 25, 3t, 28c, 44pg, 2dg-209pts), Leicester (1996-97, 13, 3t, 7c, 5pg-44pts), Harlequins (1997-99, 15, 3t, 24c, 10pg-93pts). **Other clubs:** Sandal, Cahors (France). His star looked to be on the wane with just two appearances in the first team, but he still scored 18 points in them. Rob is the younger brother of John and shares many of his footballing skills. Made Yorkshire debut against Cumbria in 1992. Enjoys classical guitar.

LLEWELLYN, Gareth Owen (Lock)
Born Cardiff, 27.02.69. 6′6″, 17st 10lb. **Rep hons:** Wales (62, NZ89, 5t-24pts), A (6, Can89, 1t-5pts), Barbarians (89-90). **ADPR:** Harlequins (1996-99, 61, 4t-20pts). Fought his way back into the Wales set-up, getting on the summer tour to Argentina, after a satisfactory season in the Premiership. He joined Harlequins from Neath after captaining the Welsh All Blacks to the Heineken League championship in 1995-96 and a SWALEC Cup final appearance against Pontypridd. The most capped Welsh lock in history, he has also captained his country against Zimbabwe and Namibia on tour and against France (twice), Italy and South Africa. Gareth was educated at Bryntiron Comprehensive and won Youth and U19 honours from Llanharan before moving to the Gnoll. Switched briefly, without conspicuous success, to blindside flanker during RWC95.

MENSAH, Peter (Centre)
Born Ghana, 10.11.66. 6′, 13st 8lb. **Rep hons:** England A (10, SAus95, 4t-20pts). **ADPR:** Harlequins (1994-99, 69, 19t-95pts). Whole-hearted team performer, occasionally let down by poor hands. Peter came to the senior game late when he joined from Old Millhillians in 1994; has slotted in well at the Stoop and has also earned England A honours. Scored three tries for an England Select XV against a Springbok Veteran XV in a fundraising game for Max Brito in Ghana in May 96.

MORGAN, Garrick Jay (Lock)
Born Sydney, Australia, 25.01.70. 6′7″, 18st 12lb. **Rep hons:** Australia (24, NZ92, 3t-15pts). **ADPR:** Harlequins (1998-99, 22, 2t-10pts). **Other clubs:** Souths, Brisbane (Australia). Made a big impression in his first season of English club rugby with a couple of tries and a solid appearance record. Added beef and nous to the second row and some shuddering defensive work to the side.

MURPHY, Thomas Desmond (Hooker)
Born Longreach, Australia, 25.04.72. 5′11″, 15st 7lb. **Rep hons:** Barbarians (98-99). **ADPR:** Rotherham (1997-98, 3), Harlequins (1998-99, 11, 1t-5pts). A more than useful stand-in for Keith Wood when the Irishman was injured or on international squad duty. Captained Cambridge University in the 1997 Varsity match and took over the mantle of leadership in a number of games for Quins.

NEBBETT, Ricky J. (Prop)
Born Kingston, 16.08.77. 5′11″, 17st. **ADPR:** Harlequins (1997-99, 18, 1t-5pts). Powerful former England Schools prop who gained valuable first-team experience later in the season as Harlequins struggled with injury. Educated at John Fisher School in Purley.

NEPIA, Kevin T. (Prop)
Born New Zealand, 27.12.67. 6′3″, 18st 12lb. New Zealand prop who has played Super 12 rugby for Canterbury Crusaders and for Brive in France.

NGAUAMO, Johnny Fotu (Centre)
Born Nuku'Alofa, Tonga, 20.07.69. 6′1″, 14st. **Rep hons:** Tonga. **ADPR:** Harlequins (1997-99, 17, 4t-20pts). **Other clubs:** Auckland (New Zealand).

OFFICER, David Gordon (Centre)
Born Aberdeen, 09.05.73. 6′2″, 14st 4lb. **Rep hons:** Scotland A (6, Fr98, 2t-10pts). **ADPR:** Harlequins (1998-99, 16, 1t-5pts). **Other clubs:** Currie, Heriot's FP, Edinburgh Univ. Solid performer during his first season with Quins. Moved to Harlequins from the Currie club having played in Europe the previous season with Caledonia. Previously played club rugby for Montrose.

O'LEARY, Daren Stephen (Wing)
Born Harold Wood, Essex, 27.06.73. 6′, 13st 10lb. **ADPR:** Saracens (1992-93, 10, 3t-15pts), Harlequins (1993-99, 104, 58t, 1dg-293pts). Try-poacher par excellence, Daren scored eight League tries last season, finishing second to Dan Luger. Educated at Campion School and West London Institute, Daren developed his try-scoring habits at Saracens before moving to Harlequins in 1993, making his debut that September against Lansdowne. Was called into the England training squad for the 1993 Five Nations and was deservedly recalled for England's visit to Argentina in 1997.

PEARS, David (Fly-half/full-back)
Born Workington, 06.12.62. 5′10″, 12st 7lb. **Rep hons:** England (4, Arg90), A (14, Aus88, 1t, 7c, 24pg, 2dg-96pts), Barbarians (91-92). **ADPR:** Sale (1988-89, 8, 3t, 3c, 26pg, 2dg-102pts), Harlequins (1989-99, 41, 7t, 56c, 83pg, 14dg-431pts), Wharfedale (1998-99, 5t, 24c, 50pg, 4dg-235pts). Turned out for Quins to solve an injury crisis for the home match against Leicester, which Quins lost. The Londoners hoped to persuade the authorities to let him play on a little for them but he was needed at Wharfedale. Now he is attempting to resurrect a career that has been cruelly dogged by injury.

RIDGWAY, Colin John (Hooker)
Born Strood, 22.04.72. 5′11″, 16st 3lb. **ADPR:** Blackheath (1993-98, 79, 12t-60pts), Harlequins (1998-99, 14, 1t-5pts). Came through his first season in the top flight well having stepped up from Blackheath. Technically able and mobile.

SANDERSON, Patrick Harold (Flanker)
Born Chester, 06.09.77. 6′3″, 16st 5lb. **Rep hons:** England (3, NZ98), A (3, NZ97). **ADPR:** Manchester Sale (1996-99, 39, 7t-35pts). Promising young flanker who fell into dispute with Sale last season after returning from England's tour of Australasia in 1998. Educated at Kirkham GS and an England Schools cap who has also played for Littleborough and Preston Grasshoppers.

SCHUSTER, Nesetorio **Johnny** (Centre)
Born Apia, Western Samoa, 17.01.64. 6′, 15st. **Rep hons:** New Zealand (10, Aus88, 1t-4pts), Manu Samoa (2, Ton99, 1c, 5pg-17pts). **ADPR:** Blackheath (1997-98, 4, 1t, 4c, 9pg-40pts), Harlequins (1998-99, 22, 5t, 36c, 77pg, 1dg-331pts). **Other clubs:** Halifax RL. One of the finest strikers of a ball in the game at the moment, be it out of hand or off the ground. His ability to slot crucial penalties from almost anywhere from 60 metres out, regardless of the awkwardness of the angle or conditions, saw him set an Allied Dunbar Premiership record of 331 points. Having won 10 New Zealand caps, the former All Black is now aiming to represent his native Western Samoa in the 1999 World Cup.

SHEASBY, Christopher Mark Andrew (Flanker)
Born Windsor, 30.11.66. 6′3″, 16st. **Rep hons:** England (7, It96, 1t-5pts), A (8, It94, 5t-25pts), Barbarians (89-90). **ADPR:** Harlequins (1987-96, 63, 8t-39pts), Wasps

(1996-98, 27, 8t-40pts), Harlequins (1997-99, 24, 3t-15pts). Having returned to the club in February 1998 after a spell at Wasps where he finally won England recognition, he seemed far happier on his old stamping ground, England recognition or not. Brought back from Wasps the consistency he had lacked in his earlier incarnation at Harlequins. Educated at Radley, London University and Hughes Hall, Cambridge where he gained two Blues (90, 91), Chris is a maths teacher at Pangbourne College. Still enjoys sevens and represented England at the Hong Kong tournament in 1996 and 1997 and captained his country at the 1998 Commonwealth Games.

WILLIAMS, Jamie (Wing/full-back)
Born Marton, New Zealand, 16.03.76. 6′1″, 13st 9lb. **Rep hons:** England A (2, Sc99, 1t-5pts). **ADPR:** Harlequins (1996-99, 35, 10t-50pts). **Other clubs:** Wimbledon. Versatile young New Zealander who has rarely let Quins down since making his debut against London Irish in September 1995. Has real pace when released on the outside. Potent striker who scored five tries last season. Educated at St Patrick's College, Wellington and Surrey University.

WRIGHT, Christopher David (Scrum-half)
Born Heswall, 08.02.68. 5′6″, 11st 10lb. **ADPR:** Orrell (1987-90, 24, 6t-24pts), Wasps (1990-94, 10, 1t-4pts), Harlequins (1994-98, 21, 2t-10pts), London Scottish (1997-98, 8), Harlequins (1998-99, 17, 2t-10pts). You cannot keep a good man down. In his second spell with Harlequins Wright proved he has lost none of his attacking flair, nor his amazing ability to adapt to any position in the backs from scrum-half to full-back. He has played them all, the T-shirt has holes in it, the video is a Betamax.

REVIEW

There were some memorable moments, most of which overshadowed Will Carling's reincarnation 13 months after he had supposedly turned his back on the game. He played half a dozen times without making the sort of impact he might have wanted. In the latter half of the season they assured themselves of a place in Europe, victories such as those at Gloucester, Saracens and Bath (against whom they completed a double) revealing a steelier side to the Fancy Dans of rugby. They wrapped up the season with a convincing win against Wasps and finally showed they had the stamina to sustain a serious campaign. There were other more forgettable happenings, such as three defeats on the trot at the Stoop and a high-scoring draw at home to Richmond. The Tetley's Bitter Cup ended at Kingsholm when they lost by a couple of points to Gloucester. Scrum-half Nick Walshe left them for Saracens as did Thierry Lacroix. At least they kept John Schuster who scored a record-breaking 331 points in the Premiership.

NEC HARLEQUINS in Premiership One 1998-99

Sep	5	A	Leicester Tigers	Lost	15	49	J.Schuster (5P)
	12	A	Northampton Saints	Lost	6	25	J.Schuster (2P)
	26	A	Manchester Sale	Lost	34	44	D.Luger (2T) C.Ridgway (T) J.Schuster (2C, 5P)
Oct	3	H	London Scottish	Won	22	20	D.Luger (T) J.Schuster (C, 5P)
	10	A	Bedford	Lost	33	35	J.Schuster (T, 3C, 4P) R.Jenkins (T) D.Luger (T)

	17	H	Saracens	Won	41	28	J.Williams (T) R.Jenkins (T) K.Wood (T) D.O'Leary (T) J.Schuster (3C, 5P)
	20	H	Gloucester	Won	39	7	D.O'Leary (2T) C.Wright (T) D.Luger (T) J.Schuster (2C, 5P)
	24	H	West Hartlepool	Won	25	10	H.Harries (T) J.Ngauamo (T) D.Luger(T) J.Schuster(2C, 2P)
Nov	1	A	Wasps	Won	22	21	D.Officer (T) J.Schuster (C, 4P, D)
	7	H	Newcastle Falcons	Won	25	20	D.Luger (T) J.Schuster (C, 6P)
	21	H	Bath	Won	43	31	J.Keyter (2T) J.Schuster (2T, 3C, 4P) G.Morgan (T)
Dec	19	A	London Irish	Lost	16	20	K.Wood (T) J.Schuster (C, 3P)
	27	H	Manchester Sale	Won	17	15	J.Williams (T) J.Schuster (4P)
Jan	2	A	London Scottish	Won	35	24	H.Harries (T) Z.Brooke (T) G.Halpin (T) J.Schuster (C, 6P)
	16	H	Northampton Saints	Lost	17	24	J.Schuster (T, 2C) Penalty (T) K.Wood (D)
	23	H	London Irish	Lost	17	22	D.O'Leary (T) P.Mensah (T) J.Schuster (2C, P)
Feb	6	H	Leicester Tigers	Lost	9	34	J.Schuster (3P)
	13	A	Gloucester	Won	31	20	D.O'Leary (T) C.Wright (T) G.O.Llewellyn (T) J.Schuster (2C, 4P)
Mar	27	H	Richmond	Drew	32	32	T.Lacroix (2T) G.Halpin (T) J.Schuster (T, 3C, 2P)
Apr	17	H	Bedford	Won	29	16	D.Luger (T) D.O'Leary (T) J.Williams (T) J.Schuster (C, 4P)
	21	A	West Hartlepool	Won	47	37	R.Liley (T, P) R.Jenkins (T) D.Luger (T) D.O'Leary (T) P.Mensah (T) J.Schuster (5C, 3P)
	25	A	Saracens	Won	38	30	D.Luger (T) D.O'Leary (T) T.Murphy (T) C.Sheasby (T) R.Liley (2C, 2P) T.Lacroix (C, 2P)
May	3	A	Richmond	Won	30	23	T.Lacroix (T, 3C, 2P, D) G.Morgan (T) J.Keyter (T)
	8	A	Bath	Won	17	13	D.Luger (T) P.Mensah (T) J.Williams (T) J.Schuster (C)
	11	A	Newcastle Falcons	Lost	23	33	J.Keyter (T) J.Williams (T) T.Lacroix (2C, 2P, D)
	19	H	Wasps	Won	27	20	H.Harries (T) T.Lacroix (T, 3C, P, D) C.Sheasby (T)

Summary of Premiership scorers:

331 J.Schuster (5T, 36C, 77P, D); 68 T.Lacroix (4T, 9C, 7P, 3D); 55 D.Luger (11T); 40 D.O'Leary (8T); 25 J.Williams (5T); 20 J.Keyter (4T); 18 R.Liley (T, 2C, 3P); 15 P.Mensah (3T), R.Jenkins (3T), H.Harries (3T); 13 K.Wood (2T, D);

10 C.Wright (2T), C.Sheasby (2T), G.Morgan (2T), G.Halpin (2T); 5 Penalty (T), C.Ridgway (T), D.Officer (T), J.Ngauamo (T), T.Murphy (T), G.O.Llewellyn (T), Z.Brooke (T).

Summary of Premiership appearances:

25 R.Jenkins (+3); 24 D.O'Leary (+2), G.O.Llewellyn (+1), A.Leach (+9); 23 D.Luger, G.Halpin (+7); 22 J.Schuster, G.Morgan (+1); 21 J.Leonard (+2), T.Lacroix (+1); 20 P.Mensah (+8); 19 K.Wood (+4), J.Williams (+1), H.Harries, B.Davison (+10); 18 C.Sheasby (+1), J.Keyter (+7), Z.Brooke (+2); 17 C.Wright (+14); 16 D.Officer (+5); 15 D.Barnes (+8); 14 C.Ridgway (+10); 13 N.Walshe (+7); 11 T.Murphy (+4); 10 A.Yates (+5); 9 R.Nebbett (+4); 7 W.Carling (+1); 6 T.Collier (+1); 3 S.Power, V.Going (+3); 2 S.White-Cooper (+1), S.Stewart (+1), J.Ngauamo, R.Liley; 1 D.Pears, G.Bibby.

LEICESTER TIGERS

Formation of club: 1880
Ground: Welford Road Stadium, Aylestone Road, Leicester LE2 7TR
Ticket office: 0116 254 0505
Capacity: 16,250 (Seated 12,500)
Colours: Red, green and white hoops
Honours: Cup Winners (5) – 1979, 1980, 1981, 1993, 1996. League Champions (3) – 1987-88, 1994-95, 1998-99
Last season: Premiership One – Champions. Tetley's Bitter Cup – QF (lost 13-15 to Richmond)
Owner: Members
Chief executive: Peter Wheeler
Rugby manager: Dean Richards
Coaches: John Wells, Joel Stransky
Captain: Martin Johnson

BACK, Neil Antony (Flanker)
Born Coventry, 16.01.69. 5'10", 14st. **Rep hons:** England (21, Sc94, 7t-35pts), A (26, Aus90, 10t-45pts), Barbarians (90-91). **ADPR:** Nottingham (1988-90, 7, 2t-8pts), Leicester (1990-99, 123, 40t-199pts). One of England's players of the season, turning out in every one of the matches from the World Cup qualifiers through to the end of the Five Nations. Then he went on the short summer tour and played in the Test against Australia. Became the darling of punters at Welford Road when bookmakers, who had set up in the ground early season, were offering generous odds on him scoring the first try. He obliged so often that when the bookies departed, they were out of pocket. His 16 tries in the Premiership were unsurpassed by anyone. Educated at Woodlands School, Coventry; played for Earlsdon and Barker's Butts before moving to Nottingham, then to Welford Road. Toured New Zealand and Canada with England A, made his full international debut against Scotland (1994). Treated with mistrust by various England regimes until Clive Woodward made him the side's pivotal player. Outstanding Lions tour to South Africa in 1997.

BALDING, Adam Lee (No 8)
Born Coventry, 07.12.79. 6'3", 16st 5lb. **ADPR:** Leicester (1998-99, 2). Outstanding backrow prospect from Caludon Castle School, ever-present in England Schools 18 Group, playing a prominent role in their successful tour of Australia in 1997. Went with England Colts to Argentina in 1998.

COCKERILL, Richard (Hooker)
Born Rugby, 16.12.70. 5′10″, 17st. **Rep hons:** England (22, Arg97, 3t-15pts), A (6, It95), Barbarians (94). **ADPR:** Coventry (1991-92, 12), Leicester (1992-99, 116, 7t-35pts). A fixture in the England front row having come of age internationally the previous season, initially against New Zealand and then in the Five Nations. Won his first cap as a replacement for great rival Phil Greening in England's first Test against Argentina in May 1997. Voluble character who has become a favourite at Leicester. Formerly an antiques restorer, he is now a full-time professional. Educated at Harris Church of England School, he played for Newbold-on-Avon and Coventry before joining Leicester.

CORRY, Martin Edward (Backrow)
Born Birmingham, 12.10.73. 6′5″, 16st 1lb. **Rep hons:** England (7, Arg97, 1t-5pts), A (10, Vic95), Barbarians (98). **ADPR:** Newcastle (1993-95, 25, 7t-35pts), Bristol (1995-97, 32, 8t-40pts), Leicester (1997-99, 41, 4t-20pts). Outstanding performer in tight and loose. Has stepped into Dean Richards' boots and filled them. Deservedly went on tour to Australia and Lawrence Dallaglio's misfortune could well be the making of Corry at international level, where he had already made his mark only to fall out of favour in 1998 after a generally disappointing season. Educated at Tunbridge Wells GS and Newcastle Polytechnic; played lock for the England Schools grand slam side in 1992. Toured Australia and Fiji with England A in 1995.

CRITCHLEY, Jason (Centre/wing)
Born St Helens, 07.12.70. 6′2″, 14st 10lb. Convert from Rugby League where he played for Castleford, Keighley and Salford. Also represented England and Wales and toured New Zealand with the 1997 British Lions PL team.

EZULIKE, Nnamdi Chuckwudinna (Wing)
Born Enugu, Nigeria, 16.02.77. 6′, 13st 6lb. **ADPR:** Leicester (1996-99, 14, 4t-20pts). Electrifying pace – needs to tighten up in defence, but poses a serious threat to opposing defences.

FERRIS, James Thomas (Scrum-half)
Born Naas, Ireland, 07.11.77. 5′10″, 13st 3lb. **ADPR:** Leicester (1997-99, 1). **Other clubs:** Naas (Ireland).

FLETCHER, Neil Robert (Lock)
Born Walsall, 04.06.76. 6′6″, 17st 10lb. **ADPR:** Moseley (1995-96, 8), Leicester (1996-99, 21, 1t-5pts). **Other clubs:** King Country (New Zealand).

FOURIE, Kenneth Ashley (Prop)
Born Johannesburg, South Africa, 14.02.77. 6′2″, 19st 2lb. **ADPR:** West Hartlepool (1998-99, 9, 2t-10pts). **Other clubs:** Natal, College Rovers (South Africa). Played for South Africa under-19s at the FIRA World Junior Cup in 1995.

FRESHWATER, Perry Thomas (Prop)
Born Wellington, New Zealand, 27.07.73. 6′, 17st 8lb. **Rep hons:** Barbarians (96-97). **ADPR:** Leicester (1995-99, 22). **Other clubs:** Wellington (New Zealand).

GARFORTH, Darren James (Prop)
Born Coventry, 09.04.66. 5′10″, 18st 9lb. **Rep hons:** England (20, Wal97), A (17, Sp93, 3t-15pts), Barbarians (94). **ADPR:** Nuneaton (1988-89, 1t-4pts), Leicester (1991-99, 144, 5t-24pts). **Other clubs:** Coventry Saracens. Got over the disappointment of missing out on England's summer tour of 1998 and made the tighthead berth his own at Test level last season. Played against Australia in the one-off Test on the short summer tour. Ruggedly built prop with a surprising turn of speed, which explains why he was a striker when he played soccer in his formative years. Made his senior England debut as a replacement against Wales in March 1997, and commanded a place in the starting line-up in Argentina in 1997. Educated at Binley Park School, Coventry, he played for Nuneaton before moving to Leicester in 1991-92.

GREENWOOD, William John Heaton (Centre)
Born Blackburn, 20.10.72. 6′4″, 15st 12lb. **Rep hons:** England (10, Aus97, 3t-15pts), A (13, SAus95, 6t-30pts), Barbarians (95-96). **ADPR:** Waterloo (1991-94, 4, 1t-5pts), Harlequins (1994-96, 25, 6t, 1c, 5pg-47pts), Leicester (1996-99, 35, 16t-80pts). Played in England's World Cup qualifiers – scoring a try in each – then suffered an ankle injury followed by a groin injury. The latter hampered him so much that he was eventually forced to sit out the remainder of the season. Managed four Premiership games for Tigers and scored a couple of tries. Had already missed the previous summer's tour to have a much-needed shoulder operation, legacy of his bad knock against Free State, playing for the Lions in 1997. Formerly with Preston Grasshoppers and Waterloo, signed from Harlequins in June 1996, Will comes from the same Sedbergh/Durham University stable as former Quins colleague Will Carling. He toured Australia with England U21 (1993), and scored a hat-trick for England A against Western Samoa in December 1995. His father Dick played for England.

GUSTARD, Paul Simon Keith (Flanker)
Born Newcastle-upon-Tyne, 02.02.76. 6′4″, 17st. **ADPR:** Leicester (1997-99, 35, 9t-45pts). **Other clubs:** Newcastle-Gosforth, Blaydon. Dynamic young flanker who has improved to a point where he is difficult to ignore. Became more of a fixture in the first XV last season. Dad was full-back for Gosforth.

HAMILTON, James Garth (Scrum-half)
Born Guildford, 01.07.70. 5′9″, 12st 7lb. **ADPR:** Leicester (1990-96, 15, 1t-5pts), London Scottish (1996-97, 7, 1t-5pts), Leicester (1997-99, 24, 2t-10pts). **Other clubs:** Linwood (New Zealand), Lincoln. Fast and aggressive around the base of the scrum, made a welcome return from London Scottish the season before. More than just a stand-in for Austin Healey. Deserves to make it on his own recognisance.

HEALEY, Austin Sean (Scrum-half)
Born Wallasey, 26.10.73. 5′10″, 14st 4lb. **Rep hons:** England (18, Ire97, 3t-15pts), A (3, NSW96, 1t-5pts), Barbarians (95-96). **ADPR:** Waterloo (1992-94, 20, 3t, 1dg-18pts), Orrell (1994-96, 33, 4t, 2c, 1pg-27pts), Leicester (1996-99, 57, 11t-55pts). **Other clubs:** Birkenhead Park. Always seems to have to start each season afresh, needing to prove himself once again to whoever is in charge of England. Having made the decision to accept whatever position his club and his country might select him in, he began at scrum-half for Leicester, but on the wing for England. Nevertheless soon fell out of favour. Suspended for three weeks by Leicester after being found guilty of stamping on London Irish scrum-half Kevin Putt, that ban was extended by an RFU disciplinary committee to eight weeks. His speed off the mark and around the base causes all sorts of problems for defenders and he scored a further six tries last season. Transferred from Orrell after switching from wing to scrum-half in 1995-96. Educated at St Anselm's College, he first joined Birkenhead Park and came to national prominence when helping Waterloo to a third-round Pilkington Cup victory over Bath. Would have been called Jensen had he been born a girl!

HOWARD, Patrick William (Centre)
Born Brisbane, Australia, 14.11.73. 5′10″, 13st 9lb. **Rep hons:** Australia (20, NZ93, 2t-10pts), Barbarians (94). **ADPR:** Leicester (1998-99, 22, 1t, 1c-7pts). **Other clubs:** Queensland, ACT, Brumbies (Australia). Can play at centre or outside half. One of the fiercest tacklers around and suffered a fractured jaw in the match against London Irish, although the injury was not detected until after the match. As hard as he plays he has a delicate touch and a good boot. Passes and handles well and has pace off the mark.

JELLEY, Derek Arthur (Prop)
Born Nuneaton, 04.03.72. 6′, 17st 8lb. **ADPR:** Leicester (1992-99, 36, 1t-5pts). **Other clubs:** Market Bosworth. Became a more regular member of the ABC club – the players still wear letters on their shorts – having begun the season at loosehead in

place of Rowntree. Once the latter had won back his place, Jelley would come on as replacement on either side of the front row, revealing an all-round competence in the art of scrummaging.

JOHNSON, Martin Osborne (Lock)
Born Solihull, 09.03.70. 6'6", 18st 7lb. **Rep hons:** England (46, Fr93, 1t-5pts), A (8, Fr92, 1t-5pts), Barbarians (91-92). **ADPR:** Leicester (1988-99, 131, 4t-20pts). **Other clubs:** Wigston College OB (New Zealand). Having enjoyed a summer off from England duties to undergo a second groin operation in 1998, Johnson emerged to play his part in a turbulent season at international level. Began by captaining England in Lawrence Dallaglio's enforced absence from the World Cup qualifiers and having played in every one of the eight Tests, ended up by being appointed captain for the tour and the World Cup after serious allegations were made in a newspaper about Dallaglio and drug abuse. His leadership qualities were not found wanting at club level. He has grown into the job. His personal discipline was called into question with the odd white card being shown but the general conclusion was that he presented too easy a target because of his size and because he is always to be found at the coal-face of the game. Has been an immense force for England since making his debut against France in 1993 as a last-minute call-up in place of Wade Dooley. Was touring Canada with an England XV in May 93 when he was again called on to replace Dooley, this time for the Lions in New Zealand, immediately winning Test selection. Captained the British Lions on their successful 1997 tour to South Africa. Educated at Welland Park and Robert Smythe Upper School, Market Harborough, Martin had already represented England Schools when he travelled to New Zealand to play for King Country and subsequently toured Australia with New Zealand Colts (U21).

JOHNSON, William Warwick (Flanker)
Born Solihull, 18.03.74. 6'4", 17st 2lb. **ADPR:** Leicester (1995-99, 30, 1t-5pts). **Other clubs:** Wigston, Kibworth, Linwood (New Zealand). Hard-grafting flanker, younger brother of club captain Martin Johnson, with plenty of power to add to the pack.

JOINER, Craig Alexander (Wing/centre)
Born Glasgow, 21.04.74. 5'10", 14st 1lb. **Rep hons:** Scotland (21, Arg94, 3t-15pts), A (5, SA94). **ADPR:** Leicester (1996-99, 36, 11t-55pts). **Other clubs:** Melrose, Eastern Suburbs (Australia). Played on the wing and in the centre in what was probably not the most satisfying of seasons for him. The Scottish wing who joined Leicester from Melrose has plenty of competition in both positions. Was educated at Dunfermline HS and Merchiston Castle School, where he was a national schools sprint champion and won 10 schools rugby caps. Craig was ever-present throughout Scotland's RWC95 campaign. Toured Australia and Fiji in summer 1998.

KAY, Benedict James (Flanker)
Born Liverpool, 14.12.75. 6'6", 17st 10lb. **ADPR:** Waterloo (1994-99, 69, 1t-5pts). Son of Waterloo president and High Court judge John Kay and inevitably nicknamed M'lud. Educated at Merchant Taylor's, Crosby and Loughborough University. Represented England at the 1996 World Students Cup in South Africa.

LLOYD, Leon David (Wing)
Born Coventry, 22.09.77. 6'4", 14st 9lb. **Rep hons:** England A (2, Sc99), Barbarians (97). **ADPR:** Leicester (1996-99, 50, 12t-60pts). **Other clubs:** Barker's Butts. Strong-running England Colts wing who has finally made it in senior rugby. Began the season in great form, scoring tries as if they were going out of fashion – they did, for him at least. But he stuck at it and was rewarded with a place on England's tour to Australia in the summer, when he scored two tries in the warm-up match against Queensland. Was unlucky to be left out for the Test the following week.

LOUGHEED, David Cameron (Wing/centre)
Born Toronto, Canada, 11.04.68. 6'2", 14st 9lb. **Rep hons:** Canada (26, Arg90 6t-30pts), Barbarians (95-96). **ADPR:** Leicester (1998-99, 16, 8t-40pts). **Other clubs:**

Toronto Balmy Beach. A powerful hard-tackling wing, with pace over a distance. Practically unstoppable when he is running at full tilt.

MOODY, Lewis Walton (Flanker)
Born Berkshire, 12.06.78. 6′4″, 15st 12lb. **ADPR:** Leicester (1996-99, 37, 2t-10pts). They have been singing the praises of this strong-driving openside flanker for some time now. He finally looks to have come of age and played for England Under 21 last season, having toured Australia with the squad when Clive Woodward was in charge in 1997. Educated at Oakham School.

MURPHY, Geordan Edward Andrew (Full-back)
Born Dublin, Ireland, 19.04.78. 6′, 12st 7lb. **ADPR:** Leicester (1997-99, 17, 5t, 3c, 5pg-46pts). **Other clubs:** Naas (Ireland). An exciting, attacking full-back who has also played at fly-half for the Tigers, filling each position with accomplished performances. Looks to have a promising future, certainly has a prodigious boot on him when he chooses to kick.

POTTER, Stuart (Centre)
Born Lichfield, 11.11.67. 5′11″, 14st 9lb. **Rep hons:** England (1, Aus98), A (18, It93, 5t-25pts), Barbarians (93-94). **ADPR:** Nottingham (1989-92, 30, 5t-20pts), Leicester (1992-99, 97, 17t-85pts). **Other clubs:** Lichfield. Powerful centre hampered by a neck injury last season.

READ, Mitchell Stephen (Wing)
Born Leicester, 07.08.76. 5′10″, 13st 12lb. **ADPR:** Leicester Tigers (1997-98, 1). Promising young centre who has recently recovered from a badly broken thigh in the Barbarians game in February 1998.

ROWNTREE, Graham Christopher (Prop)
Born Stockton-on-Tees, 18.04.71. 6′, 17st. **Rep hons:** England (21, Sc95), A (6, BCol93), Barbarians (93-94). **ADPR:** Leicester (1990-99, 125, 2t-10pts). **Other clubs:** Nuneaton. Battled his way back into the Tigers line-up but unable to keep Jason Leonard out of the England side, so had to watch his Leicester front row colleagues Richard Cockerill and Darren Garforth picking up caps and forming a union with an outsider. Missed out on a tour place to Australia as well, but likely to be in the World Cup reckoning. Educated at Hastings HS and John Cleveland College in Hinckley, Graham emerged from the Nuneaton club and was an outstanding age group international. He toured Canada with an England XV in 1993 playing in both 'Tests'.

SHORT, Peter Thomas (No 8)
Born Liverpool, 20.06.79. 6′5″, 18st. **ADPR:** Moseley (1997-99, 18). Formerly with Newport and UWIC.

STIMPSON, Timothy Richard George (Full-back)
Born Liverpool, 10.09.73. 6′3″, 15st 12lb. **Rep hons:** England (11, It96, 1t, 2c, 2pg-15pts), A (7, Vic95, 2t, 15c, 14pg-82pts), Barbarians (96-97). **ADPR:** Wakefield (1992-93, 1), West Hartlepool (1994-96, 23, 7t, 21c, 42pg-203pts), Newcastle (1996-98, 25, 14t, 29c, 4pg-140pts), Leicester (1998-99, 22, 2t, 14c, 38pg-152pts). Remarkably given that the kicking duties did not fall to him until shortly before Christmas, Stimpson scored 161 points, second only to first-choice kicker Joel Stransky. His defensive game improved greatly in the season, enough to convince England coach Clive Woodward that he was good enough to take on tour to Australia in the summer, suggesting that a World Cup squad place was in the offing. The powerful, long-striding full-back performed wonders with West Hartlepool in 1995-96 before moving to Newcastle. Educated at Silcoates School, Wakefield, Stimpson earned England Schools caps at 16 and 18 Group and then moved to Durham University where he obtained a BA in Anthropology. Toured Australia with the England U21 team in 1993, became an A team regular in 1995-96 and moved to Newcastle in May 1996.

STRANSKY, Joel Theodore (Fly-half)
Born Pietermaritzburg, South Africa, 16.07.67. 5′10″, 13st 7lb. **Rep hons:** South Africa (23, Aus93, 6t, 30c, 47pg, 3dg-240pts), Barbarians (96-97). **ADPR:** Leicester (1996-99, 47, 14t, 81c, 105pg, 3dg-556pts). Combined playing and coaching duties admirably. Suffered a knee injury early in December, returned for a handful of games before aggravating the condition. Played the final match against West Hartlepool and still managed to score more than 200 points in the Premiership. Will forever be remembered as the man who delivered the dream for the rainbow nation in 1995 when the goal he dropped in extra-time clinched victory for South Africa against the All Blacks in the World Cup. Had made his international debut two years earlier against Australia in Sydney when the Springboks won 19-12. Has also played for Natal and Western Province.

VAN HEERDEN, Frederick Johannes 'Fritz' (Lock)
Born Roodepoort, South Africa, 29.06.70. 6′6″, 17st 8lb. **Rep hons:** South Africa (13, Eng94, 1t-5pts). **ADPR:** Leicester (1997-99, 37, 3t-15pts). **Other clubs:** Western Province (South Africa). Athletic Springbok forward who gave up a place in the national squad to play for Leicester. Formerly with Western Province. Hard line-out forward with a great deal of mobility.

WEST, Dorian Edward (Hooker)
Born Wrexham, 05.10.67. 5′11″, 15st 12lb. **Rep hons:** England (2, Fr98), A (2, Otago97), Barbarians (98). **ADPR:** Nottingham (1990-95, 41, 6t-30pts), Leicester (1995-99, 41, 1t-5pts). Has the unenviable task of playing understudy to Richard Cockerill, but with the clubs agreeing to play throughout the World Cup will have plenty of opportunities to make his mark. Educated at Ibstock and Ashby GS; a former captain of Nottingham. Made his England debut as a replacement against France the season before last.

REVIEW

Given their injury list at any one time of the season, their achievement in winning the Allied Dunbar Premiership was all the more remarkable and praiseworthy. Once they got to the top of the table they were never deposed and eventually proved uncatchable. They had to play for much of the time without Joel Stransky, who suffered a knee injury, and centre Will Greenwood, whose season was written off before Christmas by a groin injury. They still ended the season with a flourish, whipping West Hartlepool in a 12-try rout. The Tetley's Bitter Cup ended prematurely in many people's minds with unexpected defeat at Reading against Richmond. Off the field their attempt to suspend Austin Healey for three weeks for stamping on Kevin Putt came to naught, the RFU adding a further five weeks to the sentence. Michael Horak left for Bristol.

LEICESTER TIGERS in Premiership One 1998-99

Sep	5	H	Harlequins	Won	49	15	L.Lloyd (2T) N.Ezulike (T) A.Healey (T) R.Cockerill (T) N.Back (T) J.Stransky (T, 4C, 2P)
	12	A	London Scottish	Won	38	3	J.Stransky (T, 3C, 4P) N.Ezulike (T) T.Stimpson (T) P.Gustard (T)
	19	H	Northampton Saints	Won	35	25	N.Ezulike (T) A.Healey (T) T.Stimpson (T) N.Back (T) J.Stransky (3C, 3P)

	26	A	Bedford	Won	32	23	N.Ezulike (T) S.Potter (T) Penalty (T) N.Back (T) J.Stransky (2C, P) T.Stimpson (C, P)
Oct	11	A	Saracens	Lost	10	22	L.Lloyd (T) J.Stransky (C, P)
	17	H	Manchester Sale	Won	31	15	N.Back (2T) P.Gustard (T) J.Stransky (2C, 4P)
	20	A	London Irish	Lost	23	24	L.Lloyd (T) A.Healey (T) J.Stransky (2C, 3P)
	24	H	Richmond	Won	27	0	N.Back (T) D.Garforth (T) J.Stransky (T, 3C, 2P)
Nov	1	A	West Hartlepool	Won	45	15	G.Murphy (2T, P) J.Overend (2T) J.Stransky (T, 4C, 3P)
	7	H	Bath	Won	36	13	W.Greenwood (2T) J.Overend (T) P.Gustard (T) J.Stransky (T, 4C, P)
	15	A	Wasps	Lost	17	45	G.Murphy (T) P.Gustard (T) J.Stransky (2C, P)
Dec	12	H	Newcastle Falcons	Won	31	18	N.Back (2T) J.Stuart (T) G.Murphy (2C, 2P) T.Stimpson (2P)
	19	A	Gloucester	Won	23	18	D.Lougheed (T) T.Stimpson (6P)
	26	H	Bedford	Won	26	0	N.Back (T) R.Cockerill (T) D.Lougheed (T) T.Stimpson (C, 3P)
Jan	16	H	London Scottish	Won	24	12	F.Van Heerden (2T) L.Lloyd (T) G.Murphy (2P) T.Stimpson (P)
	23	H	Gloucester	Won	23	16	D.Lougheed (2T) J.Stransky (T) T.Stimpson (C, 2P)
	26	A	Richmond	Won	23	11	D.Lougheed (T) M.Johnson (T) D.Jelley (T) T.Stimpson (2P) J.Stransky (C)
Feb	6	A	Harlequins	Won	34	9	L.Lloyd (2T) L.Moody (T) N.Back (T) J.Stransky (T, 3C, P)
	13	H	London Irish	Won	31	10	D.Lougheed (T) L.Lloyd (T) J.Stransky (7P)
Mar	13	A	Northampton Saints	Won	22	15	C.Joiner (T) M.Corry (T) Penalty (T) T.Stimpson (2C, P)
	27	H	Wasps	Won	16	6	N.Back (T) T.Stimpson (C, 3P)
Apr	3	A	Bath	Lost	16	24	Penalty (T) T.Stimpson (3P) P.Howard (C)
	17	H	Saracens	Won	25	18	M.Corry (T) T.Stimpson (C, 6P)
	24	A	Manchester Sale	Won	41	17	N.Back (2T) A.Healey (T) D.Lougheed (T) M.Corry (T) T.Stimpson (2C, 4P)
May	2	A	Newcastle Falcons	Won	21	12	T.Stimpson (7P)
	16	H	West Hartlepool	Won	72	37	N.Back (3T) A.Healey (2T) G.Murphy (2T, C) C.Joiner (T) P.Howard (T) D.Lougheed (T) M.Corry (T) P.Gustard (T) T.Stimpson (5C)

Summary of Premiership scorers:

202 J.Stransky (7T, 34C, 33P); 161 T.Stimpson (2T, 14C, 41P); 80 N.Back (16T); 46 G.Murphy (5T, 3C, 5P); 40 D.Lougheed (8T), L.Lloyd (8T); 30 A.Healey (6T); 25 P.Gustard (5T); 20 N.Ezulike (4T), M.Corry (4T); 15 Penalty (3T), J.Overend (3T); 10 F.Van Heerden (2T), C.Joiner (2T), W.Greenwood (2T), R.Cockerill (2T); 7 P.Howard (T, C); 5 J.Stuart (T), S.Potter (T), L.Moody (T), M.Johnson (T), D.Jelley (T), D.Garforth (T).

Summary of Premiership appearances:

25 L.Lloyd, D.Jelley (+12), D.Garforth; 24 M.Johnson, M.Corry; 23 R.Cockerill, N.Back (+1); 22 F.Van Heerden, T.Stimpson (+2), P.Howard; 21 D.West (+18), A.Healey (+1); 20 G.Rowntree (+7), L.Moody (+5); 18 P.Gustard (+4); 17 J.Stransky; 16 J.Stuart (+8), D.Lougheed (+1); 14 G.Murphy (+4); 13 N.Ezulike (+2); 12 C.Joiner (+2), J.Hamilton (+6); 10 S.Potter, W.Johnson (+7); 9 N.Fletcher (+5); 6 M.Horak (+5); 5 J.Overend (+1), P.Freshwater (+5); 4 W.Greenwood (+1); 2 H.Toews (+1), A.Balding (+2); 1 O.Wingham, B.Smith (+1), M.Poole (+1), A.Goode (+1), J.Ferris (+1), G.Becconsall (+1), J.Aldwinckle (+1), D.Addison.

LONDON IRISH

Formation of club: 1898 (Super club 1999)
Ground: Stoop Memorial Ground, Craneford Way, Twickenham TW2 7SX
Tel: 01932 783034
Capacity: 9,750 (All seated)
Colours: Emerald green and white
Best League Finish: 7th in Division One 1992-93, 1998-99
Best Cup run: Losing finalist 1979-80
Last season: Premiership One – 7th. Tetley's Bitter Cup – QF (lost 3-19 to Wasps)
Owner: Consortium of Members
Chief Executive: Geoff Huckstep
Director of rugby: Dick Best
Coaches: Andy Keast, John McFarland.
Captain: Conor O'Shea.

BACHOP, Stephen John (Fly-half)
Born Lyttelton, New Zealand, 02.04.66. 5'10", 14st 2lb. **Rep hons:** New Zealand (5, Fr94), Barbarians (95-96). **ADPR:** London Irish (1998-99, 18, 4t, 1dg-23pts). **Other clubs:** Otago (New Zealand). Brought his vast experience and cunning as a dual international for Western Samoa and New Zealand to a side that was largely in its formative season and brought them on no end. Ever-dangerous on the break with a stunning turn of speed off the mark. Great passer, pinpoint accuracy with kicking. He combined well with Putt and linked perfectly with Venter outside him. Represented Western Samoa in the 1991 World Cup before switching allegiance to New Zealand. Played provincial rugby for Otago. Younger brother Graeme is a former All Black scrum-half who now plays for Japan. The brothers combined at half-back in New Zealand's three-match series against South Africa in 1994.

BISHOP, Justin Patrick (Wing)
Born Crawley, 08.11.74. 6'1", 15st 5lb. **Rep hons:** Ireland (12, SA98, 3t-15pts), A (1, Can97). **ADPR:** London Irish (1994-99, 91, 19t-95pts). Established member of the Ireland team and went on the tour Down Under, playing in both Tests against

Australia, scoring a try in the second match. Has improved his defensive game, while possessing searing pace which opens up rival defences and if not letting him in, presents him with an opportunity to send others over. Arrived at London Irish from East Grinstead RFC; helped Ireland U21 to victory over England at Northampton in 1995-96 before declaring for England and playing centre for England U21 against Italy. Considered the nationality issue once again the following season, finally decided he was Irish and accompanied the Development XV on their demanding tour of New Zealand. Educated at Sackville College and the West of England University in Bristol.

BOER, Francois Jacobus **'Jake'** (Flanker)
Born Cape Town, South Africa, 01.11.73. 6′2″, 16st 4lb. **ADPR:** London Irish (1998-99, 21, 2t-10pts). **Other clubs:** Villager (South Africa), Leicester. Arguably the Exiles' player of the season. Dynamic flanker, always quick to the breakdown. Great hands, although over-confidence sometimes caused him to snatch at the ball. Is qualified to play for the Netherlands if he so wishes.

BROWN, James Ian Stuart (Fly-half)
Born Solihull, 08.12.77. 5′8″, 12st 8lb. **ADPR:** Coventry (1996-98, 16, 14c, 23pg, 1dg-100pts), London Irish (1998-99, 10). Former Millfield schoolboy who has played representative rugby for England at Schools and U21 level. Toured Australia with England U21 in 1997.

CAMPBELL, Kieran Patrick (Scrum-half)
Born Hillingdon, 06.07.79. 5′8″, 11st 11lb. **ADPR:** London Irish (1997-99, 12, 1t-5pts). Exciting young talent who helped Ireland to victory in the Youth World Cup in Toulouse in April 1998.

CUNNINGHAM, Jarrod Brent (Full-back)
Born Hastings, New Zealand, 07.09.68. 5′11″, 14st 2lb. **ADPR:** London Irish (1998-99, 12, 2t, 23c, 29pg-143pts). **Other clubs:** Hawkes Bay, Wellington (New Zealand). Outstanding goal-kicker, who proved to be a fine attacking full-back and provided captain Conor O'Shea with plenty of competition. Good reader of the game and fine defensively.

DAWSON, Kieron (Flanker)
Born Bangor, Northern Ireland, 29.01.75. 6′1″, 15st 6lb. **Rep hons:** Ireland (3, NZ97), A (5, Wal97). **ADPR:** London Irish (1996-99, 52, 3t-15pts). Another outstanding backrow forward with an impressive workrate although hampered by injury last season. Resourceful defender, hard tackler. A product of the strong Ulster Schools system, Kieron played for Ireland Schools, U21 and the national sevens team at Hong Kong before making his senior debut against the All Blacks in November 1997. Moved to London Irish from the Bangor club. Educated at Bangor GS and Queen's University, Belfast.

FEA'UNATI, Isaac M. (Backrow)
Born Western Samoa, 23.07.73. 6′1″, 16st 11lb. **Rep hons:** Manu Samoa (4). **ADPR:** London Irish (1997-99, 26, 6t-30pts). **Other clubs:** Canterbury (New Zealand). Injured knee ligaments in the final play-off game against Rotherham the season before and therefore made a delayed start to the 1998-99 campaign. A favourite with the Sunbury crowd, typical South Sea Islander attitude to tackling and being tackled – the ball is always available for the support in the latter instance. Born in Western Samoa but learned his rugby in Auckland and with the Canterbury Crusaders before moving to England. Another player to benefit from his love of sevens, being a regular with Western Samoa in Hong Kong.

FULLMAN, Kristyan Paul (Prop)
Born Gloucester, 07.12.72. 5′11″, 17st. **ADPR:** Bristol (1995-98, 43), London Irish (1998-99, 26). A mainstay of the Exiles front row last season. Played for England in the 1996 World Students Cup in South Africa.

GALLACHER, Robert Peter (Flanker)
Born Wigan, 10.04.69. 6′3″, 16st 4lb. **ADPR:** Rugby Lions (1996-97, 4, 1t-5pts), London Irish (1998-99, 23, 3t-15pts). **Other clubs:** Manly (Australia). An ever-present, comfortable at blindside or at No 8, both positions which he filled for Irish. A ball-winner of the highest calibre and another tough tackler. Played for Australia Under 21 and a sevens specialist – no surprise given his power and pace – with New South Wales and the Australian Barbarians.

HARVEY, Nicholas Andrew (Lock/No 8)
Born New South Wales, Australia, 21.10.74. 6′6″, 17st 13lb. **ADPR:** London Irish (1997-99, 33, 5t-25pts). **Other clubs:** NSW, ACT (Australia). Raw-boned Australian who, having made an immediate impact both as a forward and leader when cleared to play after Christmas 1998, carried on the good work last season. Has also represented the Australian Barbarians.

HATLEY, Neal (Prop)
Born Chorley, 23.12.69. 6′, 19st 2lb. **Rep hons:** England A (1, Ire99). **ADPR:** Bedford (1997-99, 26, 2t-10pts), London Irish (1998-99, 18, 1t-5pts). Joined from Bedford after the start of the season but went straight in at loosehead where his superior scrummaging technique earned immediate dividends and kept all his rivals at bay. Played much of his senior rugby for Natal and Western Province and has also played for South Africa Students.

HOWE, Michael John (Hooker)
Born Opotiki, New Zealand, 06.11.73. 6′, 16st 8lb. **ADPR:** London Irish (1998-99, 13). **Other clubs:** Bay of Plenty (New Zealand), Hawick (Scotland).

KIRKE, Richard Paull (Hooker)
Born Fairlie, New Zealand, 16.11.71. 6′, 16st 7lb. **Rep hons:** England A (1, Ire99). **ADPR:** Bedford (1997-98, 12, 1t-5pts), London Irish (1998-99, 26, 5t-25pts). **Other clubs:** Canterbury, Auckland (New Zealand). Brought much experience to the Exiles front row. Explosive in the loose and scorer of five tries for them. Had joined Bedford in June 1997 before moving on last summer to Sunbury. Former Waikato Under 21 captain who has played provincial rugby for Auckland and Canterbury. A BSc graduate from Waikato and former corrosion consultant.

O'SHEA, Conor Michael Patrick (Full-back)
Born Limerick, 21.10.70. 6′2″, 15st 12lb. **Rep hons:** Ireland (20, Rom93, 4t, 1c, 3pg, 1dg-34pts), A (7, Wal95, 4t, 3pg-29pts). **ADPR:** London Irish (1995-99, 81, 35t, 9c, 12pg, 2dg-235pts). **Other clubs:** Lansdowne (Ireland). Probably the outstanding captain in the Premiership last season. His exhilarating counter-attacking style brought him nine tries, but also helped set up others, notably Justin Bishop and Niall Woods. Went on Ireland's tour to Australia and broke his jaw in the first Test defeat in Brisbane. Adventurous, pacy full-back who joined the Exiles from Lansdowne in 1995. Conor was educated at Terenure College and University College, Dublin, and represented Ireland in the World Students Cup in 1992. Made his international debut against Romania in 1993 and played in 10 consecutive internationals before losing out to his friend and rival, Jim Staples, against France in March 1995.

PUTT, Kevin Barry (Fly-half)
Born Cambridge, New Zealand, 28.07.64. 5′10″, 12st 4lb. **ADPR:** London Irish (1998-99, 12). **Other clubs:** Natal (South Africa). Another astute signing by Dick Best, Putt linked up instantly with Bachop and proved an all-round asset at scrum-half. Was stamped on by Leicester's Austin Healey in a Premiership match for which Healey was cited and subsequently banned for eight weeks. Born in New Zealand, but played most of his serious senior rugby in South Africa. Made it into the South Africa squad and toured Britain in 1994, then Argentina and France with the 1996 Springboks.

RICHARDS, Peter Charles (Scrum-half)
Born Portsmouth, 10.03.78. 5′10″, 13st 2lb. **Rep hons:** England A (2, Sc98). **ADPR:** London Irish (1996-99, 30, 4t-20pts). With competition for the No 9 shirt so fierce, patience must be the watchword. Little chance last season to display his talents but he has the ideal person the guide him in Putt. Peter was selected for the tour of Australia, New Zealand and South Africa in 1998. A powerful runner and fierce competitor, Peter has been capped by England at every level from U16 to England A.

STRUDWICK, Ryan Cameron (Lock)
Born Pietermaritzburg, South Africa, 03.08.73. 6′5″, 16st 12lb. **ADPR:** Harlequins (1997-98, 4), London Irish (1998-99, 16). **Other clubs:** Natal (South Africa). Athletic and fiercely competitive lock who can also help out in the backrow.

TODD, Robert Brett (Wing)
Born Auckland, New Zealand, 19.04.71. 5′11″, 15st 3lb. **ADPR:** London Scottish (1997-98, 9, 2t-10pts), London Irish (1998-99, 17, 4t-20pts). **Other clubs:** ACT (Australia). Explosive wing or centre with pace and real power to allow him to burst through tackles. Runs good angles and is a fearless tackler.

VENTER, Brendan (Centre)
Born Johannesburg, South Africa, 29.12.69. 6′1″, 13st 7lb. **Rep hons:** South Africa (14, Eng94, 1t-5pts). **ADPR:** London Irish (1997-99, 37, 4t-20pts). **Other clubs:** Free State (South Africa). Dick Best could not praise him enough. Can compute the progress of a game on his feet in the thick of things and spot the way through a defence, or see the angle for someone else whom he will then put through. Great hands, fine rugby brain, fearless physical competitor. The stylish former Springbok centre has brought a high degree of professionalism and expertise to the Exiles – not to mention confidence. Losing is not something he endured on a regular basis with either Free State or South Africa. A qualified doctor, Brendan was a member of South Africa's 1995 World Cup-winning squad.

WHETSTONE, Benjamin Marcus (Centre/wing)
Born Holbeach, 29.06.70. 5′11″, 14st 7lb. **ADPR:** Bedford (1992-99, 112, 48t, 1dg-243pts). **Other clubs:** Ely. Scored only one try in a frustrating season when he just could not seem to get going. His versatility in the threequarter line gives him added scope for his blistering pace and usually lethal finishing. He converted from soccer to rugby at 18 and joined Ely where he played from 1988-91. Spent the summer of 1994 playing for the Belfast club in Christchurch, New Zealand.

WOODS, Niall Kevin Patrick John (Wing)
Born Dublin, 21.06.71. 6′, 12st 13lb. **Rep hons:** Ireland (8, Aus94, 1t-5pts), A (16, Sc92, 5t, 5c, 10pg-65pts), Barbarians (93-94). **ADPR:** London Irish (1996-99, 64, 29t, 62c, 92pg-545pts). An outstanding goal-kicker, Niall is also an elusive runner and scored 12 tries last season for a Premiership haul of 215 points. Sadly he only won one Ireland cap, although that was in the victory over Wales at Wembley. Looks a world-beater on his day but is prone to lapses in concentration and form. Educated at Blackrock College, he moved to the Blackrock club and was soon a regular with Ireland U21. Toured Southern Africa with Ireland (1993) scoring three tries in their 53-15 win over South Africa Provinces.

WORSLEY, Michael Anthony (Prop)
Born Warrington, 01.12.76. 6′1″, 16st 11lb. **ADPR:** Orrell (1996-97, 17, 1t-5pts), Bristol (1997-98, 9), London Irish (1998-99, 13). **Other clubs:** West Park. England Under 21 prop who shows great promise, but lost out last season once Neal Hatley joined the staff.

REVIEW

They met their target in the Premiership, finishing in the seventh place that director of rugby Dick Best had set for them, but the way they played throughout the season suggested they were capable of better. They lacked consistency – beating Newcastle, Harlequins and Northampton away is admirable, as was the stirring win at Sunbury over Leicester, but all were rendered worthless when set against home defeats to the likes of Sale and Richmond. After their superb away victory over Northampton in the fifth round of the Tetley's Bitter Cup great thing were expected at Wasps. Sadly the quarter-final tie was a non-event. The end of the season was dominated by talk of the takeover of struggling neighbours Richmond and London Scottish, putting even the switch of all future matches from Sunbury to Harlequins' Stoop Memorial Ground in the shade.

LONDON IRISH in Premiership One 1998-99

Sep	5	A	Gloucester	Lost	22	29	M.Jones (T) N.Woods (C, 5P)
	13	A	West Hartlepool	Won	44	20	P.Richards (T) J.Bishop (T) N.Woods (T, 5C, 3P) B.Venter (T) C.O'Shea (T)
	19	H	Wasps	Lost	24	36	N.Woods (T, C, 3P) B.Venter (T) C.O'Shea (P)
	27	A	Newcastle Falcons	Won	23	21	K.Campbell (T) C.O'Shea (T, C, 2P) N.Woods (C, P)
Oct	3	H	Richmond	Lost	29	33	M.O'Kelly (T) R.Todd (T) N.Woods (2C, 5P)
	10	A	Bath	Lost	20	23	N.Woods (2T, C, P) C.O'Shea (T)
	20	H	Leicester Tigers	Won	24	23	C.O'Shea (T, D) N.Harvey (T) N.Woods (C, 3P)
	24	H	Northampton Saints	Lost	10	26	N.Woods (T, C, P)
Nov	7	H	Manchester Sale	Lost	25	31	N.Burrows (2T) N.Harvey (T) N.Woods (2C, 2P)
	14	A	London Scottish	Won	23	17	S.Bachop (T) N.Woods (T, C, 2P) J.Cunningham (C, P)
	21	H	Bedford	Won	30	19	N.Burrows (2T) S.Berridge (T) J.Cunningham (2C, 2P) N.Woods (C, P)
Dec	13	A	Saracens	Lost	26	40	J.Boer (T) R.Kirke (T) J.Cunningham (2C, 4P)
	19	H	Harlequins	Won	20	16	S.Bachop (T) Penalty (T) J.Cunningham (2C, 2P)
	26	A	Richmond	Won	25	13	R.Gallacher (T) J.Cunningham (C, 6P)
Jan	2	H	Newcastle Falcons	Won	16	14	J.Bishop (T) J.Cunningham (C, 3P)
	5	A	Northampton Saints	Won	32	8	N.Woods (4T, 2C, P) N.Burrows (T)

16	H	West Hartlepool	Won	43	21	R.Kirke (3T) N.Burrows (2T) J.Boer (T) S.Bachop (T) J.Cunningham (4C)
23	A	Harlequins	Won	22	17	C.O'Shea (2T) J.Bishop (T) N.Woods (2C, P)
Feb 7	H	Gloucester	Won	42	20	S.Berridge (2T) N.Woods (T, C) I.Fea'unati (T) J.Cunningham (T, 2C, P) N.Hatley (T) S.Bachop (D)
13	A	Leicester Tigers	Lost	10	31	B.Venter (T) N.Woods (C, P)
Mar 14	A	Wasps	Lost	27	38	N.Burrows (T) B.Venter (T) J.Bishop (T) N.Woods (C, 2P) J.Cunningham (2C)
27	H	London Scottish	Won	35	12	R.Gallacher (T) R.Kirke (T) J.Cunningham (C, 4P) C.O'Shea (C, 3P)
Apr 3	A	Manchester Sale	Lost	27	30	N.Harvey (T) R.Gallacher (T) C.O'Shea (T) J.Cunningham (3C, 2P)
17	H	Bath	Won	47	22	R.Todd (3T) C.O'Shea (T, 3C, 2P) R.Hardwick (T) S.Berridge (T) N.Burrows (T)
May 1	H	Saracens	Lost	21	26	K.Dawson (T) N.Harvey (T) N.Woods (C, 3P)
8	A	Bedford	Won	36	21	J.Cunningham (T, 2C, 4P) N.Woods (T) C.O'Shea (T) S.Bachop (T)

Summary of Premiership scorers:

215 N.Woods (12T, 25C, 35P); 143 J.Cunningham (2T, 23C, 29P); 82 C.O'Shea (9T, 5C, 8P, D); 45 N.Burrows (9T); 25 R.Kirke (5T); 23 S.Bachop (4T, D); 20 B.Venter (4T), R.Todd (4T), N.Harvey (4T), J.Bishop (4T), S.Berridge (4T); 15 R.Gallacher (3T); 10 J.Boer (2T); 5 Penalty (T), P.Richards (T), M.O'Kelly (T), M.Jones (T), R.Hardwick (T), N.Hatley (T), I.Fea'unati (T), K.Dawson (T), K.Campbell (T).

Summary of Premiership appearances:

26 B.Venter, R.Kirke (+6), K.Fullman (+15); 23 C.O'Shea, R.Gallacher (+4); 21 N.Woods (+3), R.Hardwick (+6), N.Burrows (+3), J.Boer; 20 N.Harvey (+1); 19 K.Dawson, J.Bishop (+1); 18 N.Hatley (+5), S.Bachop; 17 R.Todd (+7); 16 R.Strudwick (+1); 15 M.O'Kelly; 14 K.Spicer (+4); 13 M.Worsley (+6), P.Richards (+5), M.Howe (+7), I.Fea'unati (+4); 12 K.Putt, J.Cunningham (+1); 11 K.Campbell (+5); 10 J.Brown (+7); 9 P.Rogers (+3); 8 S.Berridge (+2); 7 M.Jones (+2), M.Bird (+4); 2 M.Jarvis (+2).

LONDON SCOTTISH

London Scottish, so proud to have won promotion just 12 months earlier, paid the ultimate price for attempting to become a full-time professional club in the Premiership by being forced into a merger with London Irish and Richmond at the end of the season. Though the amateur club lives on in name, London Scottish as a senior club no longer exists, an extraordinarily high price to pay.

In retrospect it is easy to see why it all ended in tears, though all credit is due to a small playing staff who proved flinty competitors throughout and deservedly avoided relegation, as if that is any consolation. In playing terms there can be little wrong with the heart and spirit of a side who managed victory over the three outstanding sides of the previous season – European champions Bath, Allied Dunbar Premiership champions Newcastle and Tetley's Bitter Cup winners Saracens. Former Springbok Jannie de Beer was a calming influence at fly-half, scrum-half Guy Easterby one of the most underrated players in the Premiership and wing Conan Sharman had real pace. Zimbabwean prop Paul Johnston and Simon Holmes were trojans up front, as were Mick Watson and Paul Burnell, the latter winning yet another Scotland recall.

In an attempt to attract bigger crowds and possibly woo the corporate sponsors they so desperately needed, London Scottish moved from their traditional home at the Recreation Ground, Richmond to Harlequins' Stoop Memorial Ground just down the A316. Alas the spectators did not follow, nor did the money men. Scottish, effectively, were trying to run a professional club on average crowds of well under 1,800 by the end of the season. Majority shareholder Tony Tiarks was right to wonder, as the club slipped into extinction, where all the big Scottish interests in London were when they were needed. At least one prominent Scottish company hired a box for Harlequins' home games yet spurned their countrymen.

Soon after Christmas, with their slender playing squad continuing to work wonders on the pitch, the club were facing closure when Matthew Pearce, the Bristol owner, bought a 26.1 per cent holding as an insurance policy should his side, then in Division One, fail to win promotion as of right. The idea was that had Bristol been denied they would take over London Scottish, claim their place in the Premiership and then field a side in the First Division. It is probably just as well that this rather flawed plan was never called into action but the immediate effect was that at least the London Scottish wage bill was paid, by Pearce, for the remainder of the season. However, when Bristol won promotion, it virtually sealed London Scottish's fate and negotiations with neighbouring London Irish and ailing co-tenants Richmond were immediately started.

LONDON SCOTTISH in Premiership One 1998-99

Sep	5	H	Manchester Sale	Won	25	20	K.Milligan (T) I.McAusland (C, 6P)
	12	H	Leicester Tigers	Lost	3	38	I.McAusland (P)
	19	A	Bedford	Lost	16	24	C.Sharman (T) I.McAusland (C, 3P)
	26	H	Saracens	Lost	20	58	K.Milligan (2T) J.Bonney (T) I.McAusland (C, P)
Oct	3	A	Harlequins	Lost	20	22	E.Jones (T) I.McAusland (5P)
	10	H	Northampton Saints	Lost	22	33	E.Jones (T) I.McAusland (C, 5P)
	25	A	Gloucester	Lost	16	29	S.Holmes (T) I.McAusland (C, 3P)
	31	H	Bath	Won	13	11	C.Sharman (T) I.McAusland (C, 2P)
Nov	14	H	London Irish	Lost	17	23	S.Holmes (T) G.Easterby (T) J. De Beer (2C, P)
	22	A	West Hartlepool	Won	37	7	R.Hunter (2T) S.Forrest (T) G.Easterby (T) S.Fenn (T) J.De Beer (3C, 2P)
Dec	12	H	Wasps	Lost	9	17	J.De Beer (3P)

	19	H	Richmond	Lost	16	28	G.Easterby (T) J.De Beer (C, 3P)
	27	A	Saracens	Won	24	7	K.Milligan (T) B.Irving (T) M.Watson (T) I.McAusland (3C, P)
Jan	2	H	Harlequins	Lost	24	35	K.Milligan (T) R.Hunter (T) S.Forrest (C, P) I.McAusland (3P)
	5	H	Gloucester	Won	24	13	G.Easterby (T) P.Johnstone (T) J.De Beer (C, 3P, D)
	16	A	Leicester Tigers	Lost	12	24	J.De Beer (3P, D)
	23	A	Richmond	Lost	22	40	R.Hunter (T) J.De Beer (4P, D) I.McAusland (C)
Feb	6	A	Manchester Sale	Won	23	7	T.Davies (T) G.Easterby (T) J.De Beer (2C, 3P)
	13	H	Newcastle Falcons	Won	27	17	S.Fenn (T) P.Johnstone (T) G.Easterby (T) S.Holmes (T) J.De Beer (2C, P)
Mar	13	H	Bedford	Lost	15	24	J.Bonney (T) M.Watson (T) J.De Beer (C, P)
	27	A	London Irish	Lost	12	35	J.De Beer (3P, D)
	31	A	Newcastle Falcons	Lost	20	43	J.De Beer (T, 2C, P, D) G.Easterby (T)
Apr	17	A	Northampton Saints	Lost	13	44	I.McAusland (T) J.De Beer (C, 2P)
May	2	A	Wasps	Lost	22	45	C.Sharman (T) J.De Beer (P, D) I.McAusland (C, 3P)
	8	H	West Hartlepool	Won	26	14	C.Sharman (2T) J.De Beer (2C, 4P)
	15	A	Bath	Lost	13	76	S.Holmes (T) I.McAusland (C) J.De Beer (2P)

Summary of Premiership scorers:

168 J.De Beer (T, 17C, 37P, 6D); 128 I.McAusland (T, 12C, 33P); 35 G.Easterby (7T); 25 C.Sharman (5T), K.Milligan (5T); 20 R.Hunter (4T), S.Holmes (4T); 10 M.Watson (2T), P.Johnstone (2T), E.Jones (2T), S.Forrest (T, C, P), S.Fenn (2T), J.Bonney (2T); 5 B.Irving (T), T.Davies (T).

Summary of Premiership appearances:

25 P.Johnstone, S.Holmes (+1); 24 M.Watson, R.Hunter (+1), S.Fenn, G.Easterby (+1), P.Burnell (+1); 23 K.Milligan, E.Jones (+2); 22 C.Sharman (+1), J.Bonney (+3); 21 R.Eriksson (+3); 20 D.Rudham (+6), I.McAusland (+3), R.Davies (+8); 17 G.Manson-Bishop (+9), S.Binns (+5); 16 J.De Beer, D.Cummins (+8); 14 T.Davies (+11); 10 M.MacDonald (+6), M.McAtamney (+9); 9 S.Forrest (+4); 7 D.Lee (+3); 6 C.Tarbuck (+4); 5 S.Cook (+4); 4 P.Robertson (+2), J.McLellan (+2), C.Johnston (+4); 3 R.Smith (+1), J.Philip (+1); 2 C.Mulraine, D.Millard (+2), B.Irving; 1 G.Phillip (+1), D.McFadyen (+1), B.Hepi, L.Goodwin, J.Cameron, R.Bijl (+1).

LONDON WASPS

Formation of club: 1867
Ground: Loftus Road Stadium, South Africa Road, Shepherd's Bush, London W12 7PA
Tel: 0181 743 0262
Capacity: 19,000 (all seated)
Colours: Black with gold wasp
Honours: Cup Winners – 1999. League Champions (2) – 1989-90, 1996-97
Last season: Premiership One – 5th. Tetley's Bitter Cup – Winners
Owner: Chris Wright (Chrysalis Records)
Director of rugby: Nigel Melville
Coach: John Mitchell
Captain: Lawrence Dallaglio (tbc)

ALEXOPOULOS, Dinos (Hooker)
Born Manchester, 02.12.76. 6'1", 17st 4lb. **Rep hons:** Barbarians (97). **ADPR:** Wasps (1997-99, 7, 1t-5pts). Powerful young prop who learned his rugby at Millfield School. Formerly with Penryn and Harlequins.

BEARDSHAW, Joseph John (Lock)
Born Norwich, 30.10.76. 6'5", 17st. **ADPR:** Wasps (1997-99, 4), Bedford (1998-99, 4). An outstanding prospect, this former England Schools lock started his career at North Walsham and played on loan at Bedford last season.

BLACK, Adam (Prop)
Born 24.05.75. 6'1", 17st. **ADPR:** Wasps (1997-99, 17, 1t-5pts).

DALLAGLIO, Lawrence Bruno Nero (Flanker)
Born Shepherds Bush, 10.08.72. 6'4", 15st 7lb. **Rep hons:** England (26, SA95, 5t-25pts), A (4, Fr94), Barbarians (95-96). **ADPR:** Wasps (1993-99, 104, 18t-90pts). A hitherto golden career was derailed during the summer when Dallaglio had to resign as England captain to fight newspaper allegations of drug abuse and dealing. At the time of going to print he had been recalled into the England squad pending the result of an independent inquiry. Just a week before the story broke he had helped Wasps to the Tetley's Bitter Cup, while a mixed season with England had included a memorable victory over South Africa but a disappointing defeat against Wales at Wembley when the Grand Slam was at stake. Educated at Ampleforth College, where he played in their outstanding sevens team that won the Festival and Open titles at Rosslyn Park in 1989, Dallaglio missed out on an England Schools cap but soon played for England Colts and U21 and was a prominent member of the England team that won the 1993 World Sevens championship. After touring Australia with England U21 in 1993 he travelled to South Africa with the senior England squad in 1994 but failed to make the Test side. Overlooked for the 1995 World Cup, he made his international debut later the same year as a replacement against South Africa and won a starting place against Western Samoa in the next game. Enjoyed an outstanding tour of South Africa in 1997 for the British Lions, playing in all three Tests, and was confirmed as England captain later that year. Led Wasps to the Premiership title in 1996-97.

DENNEY, Mark Christian Alexander (Centre)
Born Epping Forest, 25.07.75. 5'11", 15st 11lb. **Rep hons:** Barbarians (97-98). **ADPR:** Bedford (1992-93, 2), Bristol (1993-98, 40, 4t-20pts), Wasps (1997-99, 15, 2t-10pts). Made an immediate impact after coming down from Cambridge University in the New Year, so much so that he won a starting place in the Tetley's Bitter Cup final. Educated at Bedford Modern, Mark spent two years in the England Schools 18 Group side, the last as captain, before studying at Bristol University when he lined up

alongside future Wasps colleagues Alex King, Josh Lewsey and Fraser Waters. Played for Bristol in the Premiership but joined Wasps on moving to Cambridge University where he won two Blues, in 1997 and 98.

DUNSTON, Ian Charles 'Paddy' (Prop)
Born Forest Gate, Essex, 11.06.68. 5′11″, 17st. **ADPR:** Wasps (1988-99, 59, 4t-18pts). Reliable back-up prop. 'Paddy' is a product of Romford RFC and Gidea Park.

FRIDAY, Michael John (Scrum-half)
Born Chichester, 25.04.72. 5′9″, 12st 1lb. **ADPR:** Blackheath (1993-97, 64, 19t-95pts), Wasps (1997-99, 30, 6t-30pts). Lively character at scrum-half who represented England in the Commonwealth Games Sevens tournament in Kuala Lumpur in September 1998. Formerly with Bromley.

GREEN, William Robert (Prop)
Born Littlehampton, 25.10.73. 5′11″, 17st 4lb. **Rep hons:** England (2, Aus97), A (4, Wal98). **ADPR:** Wasps (1995-99, 63, 5t-25pts). Underrated prop who has never let Wasps or England down. Educated at Eastbourne College, where he was a more than useful schoolboy cricketer, before studying at Oxford Brookes University. England Schools and U21 international before gaining senior honours.

HENDERSON, Robert Alexander James (Centre)
Born Dover, 27.10.72. 6′1″, 15st 4lb. **Rep hons:** Ireland (11, WS96), A (3, Wal96, 1t-5pts), Barbarians (96-97). **ADPR:** London Irish (1993-97, 56, 22t-110pts), Wasps (1996-99, 40, 6t-30pts). Powerful centre who mysteriously fell out of favour with Ireland last season. Educated at Tiffin School and St Mary's, Teddington, Henderson was originally a promising footballer and only turned to rugby when asked to make up the numbers at the Kingston club. Is also qualified to play for Scotland through his father but opted for Ireland.

IONS, Jonathan Alexis (Flanker)
Born Wakefield, 12.12.76. 6′2″, 15st. **ADPR:** West Hartlepool (1995-97, 23, 4t-20pts), Wasps (1997-99, 5, 2t-10pts). Former Bradford GS and England Schools captain who joined Wasps from Wakefield.

KING, Alexander David (Fly-half)
Born Brighton, 17.01.75. 6′, 13st 4lb. **Rep hons:** England (2, Arg97, 1t-5pts), A (9, WS95, 1t, 12c, 16pg, 2dg-83pts), Barbarians (95-96). **ADPR:** Rosslyn Park (1993-96, 7, 2t, 9c, 14pg-70pts), Wasps (1996-99, 54, 8t, 11c, 16pg, 8dg-134pts). Recovered superbly from a disastrous tour of Australia and New Zealand in 1998 when, hampered by a knee injury, his form totally deserted him. King was educated at Brighton College and first came to prominence when, as an unheralded Bristol University student, he was called into the South West side to contest the Divisional championship. On graduating from university he resisted the offers of Bristol and Bath to move to Wasps and complete his accountancy exams. Damaged his knee in the autumn of 1997 and aggravated the injury by rushing back for a European Cup tie against Brive.

LE CHEVALIER, Andrew John (Prop)
Born Epping, 05.11.75. 6′2″, 17st 9lb. **ADPR:** Wasps (1998-99, 6, 1t-5pts). Formerly with Saracens and Harlequins.

LEOTA, Trevor H. (Hooker)
Born Western Samoa, 08.02.75. 5′10″, 17st 4lb. **Rep hons:** Manu Samoa (9). **ADPR:** Wasps (1997-99, 38, 8t-40pts). Big-hitting Western Samoan who has quickly become a crowd favourite at Loftus Road for his clattering tackles. Encountered disciplinary trouble in the summer when he was sent off for a high tackle playing for Western Samoa against France in Apia. Played for New Zealand Colts, as a prop, and Auckland before moving to Britain. Noted for his garish hairstyles.

LEWSEY, Owen **Joshua** (Full-back/wing)
Born Bromley, 30.11.76. 5′10″, 12st 7lb. **Rep hons:** England (3, NZ98), A (2, Sc98, 1t-5pts). **ADPR:** Bristol (1996-98, 27, 7t, 1c, 3pg-46pts), Wasps (1998-99, 21, 4t-20pts). Another who has recovered well from England's disastrous tour of Australia and New Zealand in 1998, Lewsey's outstanding pace and strength in the tackle were finding full employment on the wing by the end of last season, though he can also play full-back and fly-half. Formerly a student at Bristol University, he played for England Colts and U21 and Bristol in the Premiership before moving to Wasps in June 1998.

LOGAN, Kenneth McKerrow (Wing)
Born Stirling, 03.04.72. 6′1″, 14st 8lb. **Rep hons:** Scotland (39, Aus92, 8t, 14c, 8pg-92pts), A (8, Sp92, 4t-20pts), Barbarians (94-95). **ADPR:** Wasps (1996-99, 43, 23t, 36c, 51pg-340pts). Enjoyed an outstanding 1998-99 season for club and country, not least as a goal-kicker. Educated at Wallace HS and formerly with Stirling County before moving to Wasps. Ever-present during the 1995 World Cup for Scotland and a key performer in last season's Five Nations championship-winning side.

MACER, Dugald Scott (Hooker)
Born 03.06.72. 6′1″, 16st 5lb. **ADPR:** Wasps (1995-99, 21). Combative hooker who joined Wasps from Old Verulamians.

MOLLOY, Darren (Prop)
Born Middlesex, 31.08.72. 6′2″, 17st. **Rep hons:** England A (1, Fr98). **ADPR:** Wasps (1991-99, 91, 2t-10pts). **Other clubs:** Old Gaytonians, London Irish. Toured Australia with England U21 in 1993.

REED, Andrew Ian (Lock)
Born St Austell, 04.05.69. 6′7″, 17st 10lb. **Rep hons:** Scotland (17, Ire93), A (1, Ire92). **ADPR:** Camborne (1988-89, 11, 2t-8pts), Plymouth Albion (1989-90, 10), Bath (1990-95, 24), Wasps (1996-99, 49, 3t-15pts). A stalwart performer at lock where he finally shrugged off long-term back problems last season. Educated at Bodmin CS, Bristol Polytechnic and Cheshire College of Agriculture. A member of Cornwall's famous County Championship-winning side in 1991 and a former Cornish Schools goalkeeper, he toured New Zealand with the 1993 British Lions.

ROISER, Shane Maurice (Wing)
Born London, 07.06.73. 5′9″, 13st. **ADPR:** Rosslyn Park (1992-94, 26, 10t-50pts), Wasps (1994-99, 77, 24t-120pts). Lightning-quick wing who continues to trouble the best defences. Educated at Trinity Whitgift School.

ROLLITT, Eben David (Backrow)
Born Bristol, 23.11.72. 6′3″, 16st 5lb. **ADPR:** Richmond (1992-95, 2), Bristol (1995-98, 53, 6t-30pts), Wasps (1998-99, 13, 1t-5pts). Versatile and reliable backrow back-up. Won England Schools honours from St Paul's and a Cambridge Blue in 1994 while studying at Magdalene College.

SAMPSON, Paul Christian (Full-back/wing)
Born Wakefield, 12.07.77. 5′10″, 11st 10lb. **Rep hons:** England (1, SA98), A (2, Arg96), Barbarians (97-98). **ADPR:** Otley (1995-96, 2), Wasps (1996-99, 33, 12t-60pts). Finally beginning to fulfil his vast potential after nailing down a starting place on the wing in the second half of last season – he had started late after breaking a leg in the summer. A product of Woodhouse Grove School, Paul played for England Schools in two successive seasons, appearing in their famous 30-3 win over Australia at Kingsholm in 1995. The following summer he posted a startling 10.48secs to beat Dwaine Chambers and win the England Schools 100m title.

SCRASE, Laurence William (Wing/centre)
Born Dubai, UAE, 19.09.72. 6′, 12st 7lb. **ADPR:** Wasps (1992-99, 50, 9t-45pts). Joined Wasps as a Colt in 1990. Pole vaulter and 200m runner of some note. Formerly with Datchworth.

SCRIVENER, Peter (Backrow)
Born 27.10.73. 6′5″, 16st. **Rep hons:** Barbarians (97). **ADPR:** Wasps (1993-99, 53, 13t-65pts). Outstanding young forward who has returned to his best after a series of serious shoulder injuries. Educated at Coopers Coburn School and a graduate of Brunel University, Scrivener was a member of the 1992 England Schools team that achieved a grand slam and has also represented England at sevens.

SHAW, Simon Dalton (Lock)
Born Nairobi, Kenya, 01.09.73. 6′9″, 19st. **Rep hons:** England (8, It96), A (7, Ire95), Barbarians (94-95). **ADPR:** Bristol (1992-97, 58, 3t-15pts), Wasps (1997-99, 42, 2t-10pts). **Other clubs:** Pirates (New Zealand), Cranleigh. Back to his best form last season after a miserable couple of injury-prone years. At 6′8″ and 18st 4lb Shaw was England's biggest-ever Schools international when he played against Ireland at Thomond Park in 1991. Capped at Colts and U21 level before appearing as a replacement in the England squad that toured South Africa in 1994. Returned to South Africa in 1997 as a member of the victorious British Lions squad. Educated at St Peters, Huntingdon and Godalming Sixth Form College.

UFTON, Jonathan Derek Giles (Full-back)
Born Dulwich, 31.01.74. 6′1″, 12st 7lb. **Rep hons:** Barbarians (98). **ADPR:** Wasps (1994-99, 60, 9t, 11c, 4pg, 2dg-85pts). Fine footballer but dogged by injury in recent seasons. Member of the England Schools team that won the Grand Slam in 1992. Surrey Schoolboy cricketer and fencer, father Derek was a distinguished former Charlton Athletic and England footballer who also kept wicket for Kent. Educated at Trinity Whitgift.

VOLLEY, Paul (Flanker)
Born 02.11.71. 6′1″, 15st 6lb. **Rep hons:** England A (1, Wal99). **ADPR:** Wasps (1996-99, 25, 7t-35pts). **Other clubs:** Chinnor. No-nonsense, in-your-face openside, Volley emerged as a key figure in Wasps' backrow last season.

WATERS, Fraser Henry Hamilton (Centre)
Born Cape Town, South Africa, 31.03.76. 6′, 13st 9lb. **Rep hons:** England A (1, Wal99), Barbarians (96-97). **ADPR:** Bath (1995-96, 1, 1t-5pts), Bristol (1996-98, 18, 2t-10pts), Wasps (1998-99, 10, 1t-5pts). Has overcome a career-threatening groin injury. This powerful former England Schools and Bristol University centre enjoyed a fine end of the season in tandem with Mark Denney at centre. Educated at Harrow.

WEEDON, Mark (Lock)
Born Tauranga, New Zealand, 31.07.68. 6′6″, 18st 8lb. **ADPR:** Wasps (1997-99, 39, 5t-25pts). **Other clubs:** North Harbour, Canterbury Crusaders (New Zealand). Emerged as a strong character last season when, under his leadership, Wasps won the Tetley's Bitter Cup and qualified for Europe. Former All Black triallist.

WOOD, Martyn Benjamin (Scrum-half)
Born Harrogate, 25.04.77. 5′9″, 13st. **ADPR:** Wasps (1996-99, 22, 5t-25pts). Pacy former England Schools cap who disputed the starting position at scrum-half last season with Michael Friday.

WORSLEY, Joseph Paul Richard (Backrow)
Born Redbridge, Hants, 14.06.77. 6′5″, 17st. **Rep hons:** Barbarians (97-98). **ADPR:** Wasps (1995-99, 39, 2t-10pts). A conspicuous presence in Wasps' backrow last season, Worsley subsequently gained a place in England's training party in Australia. Educated at Hitchin Boys HS, he played his early rugby at Welwyn RFC and was an outstanding member of the England Schools team that won the Grand Slam in 1995. Talented saxophone player.

REVIEW

A season of solid achievement for Wasps culminating in their first ever Tetley's Bitter Trophy after four previous disappointments at Twickenham. A strong finish in the League also ensured a top-six spot and a place in the forthcoming European Cup. Individually the emergence of Kenny Logan as a top-class goal-kicker proved a bonus – and ironically hastened the end-of-season departure of Gareth Rees, who joined Bedford. Paul Volley, Peter Scrivener and Joe Worsley remain fine prospects in the backrow, Alex King and Simon Shaw were back to their best form at fly-half and lock respectively, and Lawrence Dallaglio, as ever, played with as much commitment and passion for his club as he does for England.

LONDON WASPS in Premiership One 1998-99

Sep	5	A	Bath	Lost	27	36	K.Logan (T) T.Leota (T) J.Worsley (T) G.Rees (4P)
	19	A	London Irish	Won	36	24	L.Scrase (T) P.Volley (T) S.Roiser (T) K.Logan (T, 2C, 4P)
	27	H	West Hartlepool	Won	71	14	S.Roiser (2T) P.Volley (2T) J.Worsley (T) A.King (T) L.Dallaglio (T) S.Shaw (T) K.Logan (T, 6C, 3P) N.Greenstock (T)
Oct	3	A	Gloucester	Won	13	12	W.Green (T) K.Logan (C, 2P)
	11	A	Newcastle Falcons	Lost	19	27	L.Dallaglio (T) S.Roiser (T) T.Leota (T) K.Logan (2C)
	18	H	Richmond	Lost	22	27	T.Leota (T) K.Logan (C, 5P)
	21	H	Bedford	Won	35	19	F.Rossigneux (T) L.Dallaglio (T) M.Friday (T) K.Logan (C, 6P)
	25	A	Saracens	Won	31	17	K.Logan (T, C, 3P) A.King (T) R.Henderson (T) J.Lewsey (T)
Nov	1	H	Harlequins	Lost	21	22	L.Scrase (T) N.Greenstock (T) K.Logan (C, 3P)
	7	A	Northampton Saints	Lost	21	26	P.Volley (T) K.Logan (T, C, 3P)
	15	H	Leicester Tigers	Won	45	17	T.Leota (2T) P.Volley (2T) S.Roiser (T) K.Logan (T, 3C, 3P)
	22	H	Manchester Sale	Won	32	19	S.Roiser (T) E.Rollitt (T) M.Weedon (T) T.Leota (T) A.King (3C, P, D)
Dec	12	A	London Scottish	Won	17	9	Penalty (T) J.Lewsey (T) K.Logan (2C, P)
	27	H	Gloucester	Won	23	9	P.Sampson (T) A.Le Chevalier (T) K.Logan (2C, 3P)
Jan	3	A	West Hartlepool	Lost	17	21	P.Scrivener (T) D.Alexopoulos (T) N.Greenstock (T) K.Logan (C)
	6	H	Saracens	Drew	15	15	K.Logan (5P)
Feb	7	H	Bath	Won	35	0	P.Scrivener (2T) M.Wood (2T) M.Weedon (T) A.King (2C, 2P)

13	A	Bedford	Lost	23	25	A.Reed (T) P.Sampson (T) A.King (T, C, 2P) L.Dallaglio (T)
Mar 14	H	London Irish	Won	38	27	P.Scrivener (2T) P.Sampson (T) M.Weedon (T) K.Logan (3C, 4P)
27	A	Leicester Tigers	Lost	6	16	A.King (D) K.Logan (P)
Apr 13	H	Northampton Saints	Lost	15	24	A.King (5P)
18	H	Newcastle Falcons	Won	34	33	J.Lewsey (T) M.Wood (T) D.Molloy (T) A.King (2C, 4P, D)
25	A	Richmond	Won	29	5	J.Ufton (T) M.Denney (T) P.Sampson (T) K.Logan (T) A.King (C, P) K.Logan (2C)
May 2	H	London Scottish	Won	45	22	P.Sampson (T) J.Lewsey (T) P.Volley (T) F.Waters (T) M.Denney (T) Penalty (T) K.Logan (3C, 3P)
8	A	Manchester Sale	Won	27	13	L.Dallaglio (T) K.Logan (T, 3C, 2P) P.Sampson (T)
19	A	Harlequins	Lost	20	27	R.Henderson (T) G.Rees (T, 2C, 2P)

Summary of Premiership scorers:

263 K.Logan (8T, 35C, 51P); 87 A.King (3T, 9C, 5P, 3D); 35 P.Volley (7T); 30 P.Sampson (6T), S.Roiser (6T), T.Leota (6T); 27 G.Rees (T, 2C, 6P); 25 P.Scrivener (5T), L.Dallaglio (5T); 20 J.Lewsey (4T); 15 M.Wood (3T), M.Weedon (3T), N.Greenstock (3T); 10 Penalty (2T), J.Worsley (2T), L.Scrase (2T), R.Henderson (2T), M.Denney (2T); 5 F.Waters (T), J.Ufton (T), S.Shaw (T), E.Rollitt (T), F.Rossigneux (T), A.Reed (T), D.Molloy (T), A.Le Chevalier (T), W.Green (T), M.Friday (T), D.Alexopoulos (T).

Summary of Premiership appearances:

25 J.Worsley (+4); 24 M.Weedon, D.Molloy (+1); 23 S.Shaw (+9); 22 A.King (+2), W.Green, L.Dallaglio; 21 P.Volley (+1), J.Lewsey; 20 K.Logan, T.Leota (+2); 18 R.Henderson (+3), M.Friday (+10); 17 S.Roiser, A.Reed (+5); 16 L.Scrase (+2); 15 A.Gomarsall (+6); 13 E.Rollitt (+8), N.Greenstock (+7); 12 P.Sampson (+1); 10 F.Waters, P.Scrivener (+3); 9 M.Wood, J.Ufton (+3), D.Macer (+4), M.Denney; 8 G.Rees (+1), A.Black (+4); 6 A.Le Chevalier (+5); 5 S.Mitchell (+4), D.Alexopoulos (+3); 4 F.Rossigneux (+1); 3 J.Beardshaw (+1); 2 I.Dunston; 1 J.Ions (+1).

MANCHESTER SALE

Formation of club: 1861
Ground: Heywood Road, Sale, Cheshire M33 3WB
Tel: 0161 283 1861
Capacity: 5,500 (Seated 3,200)
Colours: Royal blue and white
Honours: Division Two Champions – 1993-94
Best League finish: 4th in Division One 1994-95

Best Cup run: Losing finalist 1996-97
Last season: Premiership One – 11th. Tetley's Bitter Cup – 4th round (lost 31-47 to Northampton Saints)
Owner: Tourney Events Group
Chief executive: Graham Walker
Rugby manager: Adrian Hadley
Captain: Jim Mallinder

ANGLESEA, Peter (Flanker)
Born Blackrod, Bolton, 30.10.71. 6'3", 16st 2lb. **ADPR:** Orrell (1995-97, 27, 5t-25pts), Bedford (1997-98, 4), Sale (1997-99, 29, 1t-5pts). **Other clubs:** Aspull. Former England A squad flanker who returned to the north-west after a spell at Bedford last season and settled down to become a regular in the side.

BALDWIN, David Neil (Lock)
Born Ilkley, 03.09.65. 6'6", 18st 5lb. **Rep hons:** England A (5, Rus89), Barbarians (94). **ADPR:** Wakefield (1987-89, 14, 2t-8pts), Sale (1988-99, 151, 14t-68pts). A much-respected and vastly experienced front-of-line jumper, this former Bramley and Wakefield lock made his Yorkshire county debut against Northumberland in 1985. Toured New Zealand with England B in 1992. Passed the landmark of 150 League appearances last season.

BAXENDELL, Joshua John Neill (Centre)
Born Manchester, 03.12.72. 6', 14st 4lb. **Rep hons:** England (2, NZ98), A (2, SA96). **ADPR:** Sheffield (1992-94, 14, 2t-10pts), Sale (1993-99, 103, 19t-95pts). Overlooked for any England representation last season after playing two Tests for England on their Australasian tour in 1998. Fared well with Sale, appearing in the bulk of their Premiership matches. Educated at King's, Macclesfield, Jos played first with Wilmslow and then moved to Heywood Road from Sheffield where he studied at the local university. Dextrous with the ball in hand as befits a keen basketball player. A qualified surveyor.

BELL, Duncan Stuart Crampton (Prop)
Born King's Lynn, 01.10.74. 6'2", 18st 8lb. **ADPR:** Sale (1997-99, 42, 2t-10pts). **Other clubs:** Bath, Harlequins, London Irish, Ebbw Vale. Former England Schools and Bath Colts lock who has switched to the front row with marked success. Was a fixture there last season. Won a place on England's summer tour of the southern hemisphere the season before last.

DAVIDSON, Steven William (Centre)
Born Whitehaven, 25.04.76. 6'2", 16st. **ADPR:** Aspatria (1995-98, 39, 8t, 1c, 1pg-45pts), Sale (1997-99, 20, 4t, 6c, 3pg-41pts). Began to establish himself in the first team with 14 appearances.

DE BEER, Jan Hendrik (Fly-half)
Born Welkom, South Africa, 22.04.71. 6', 13st 9lb. **Rep hons:** South Africa (7, BI97, 2t, 15c, 11pg, 2dg-79pts). **ADPR:** London Scottish (1998-99, 16, 1t, 19c, 37pg, 6dg-172pts). Free State stalwart who made his Springbok debut in the third and final Test against the British Lions in 1997. Educated at Wessel Maree School in the Free State. Joins from London Scottish.

DIAMOND, Steve (Hooker)
Born Manchester, 03.02.68. 5'9", 14st 10lb. **Rep hons:** Barbarians (97-98). **ADPR:** Sale (1990-99, 117, 4t-20pts). Durable hooker who toured Argentina with England in 1997. Spent five years with the Metrovick club before joining Sale. Joker in the pack but an upbeat and inspiring character. Former captain of the North Division. Fully qualified RFU coach who helps out with Sale's coaching.

GERAGHTY, Damien Peter (Hooker)
Born Wellington, New Zealand, 29.03.68. 6', 15st 10lb. **ADPR:** Moseley (1996-98, 28, 1t-5pts), Sale (1998-99, 8). **Other clubs:** Marist St Pats (New Zealand).

GREENING, Philip Bradley Thomas (Hooker)
Born Gloucester, 03.10.75. 6′, 17st. **Rep hons:** England (6, It96), A (4, WS95, 1t-5pts). **ADPR:** Gloucester (1994-99, 40, 2t-10pts), Sale (1998-99, 15, 1t-5pts). Had to reinvent himself after leaving Gloucester and appears to have come through with flying colours. Made it on to England's tour to Australia and came on in the Test and the warm-up as a replacement. His chief rival for an England squad place was, ironically, Neil McCarthy at his old club Gloucester. Made his international debut as a replacement against Italy. Captained England Schools and Colts and earned England A selection during his first season of senior rugby in 1995-96. Educated at Kingsholm Junior, Chosen Hill and Gloucester College and joined Gloucester from a local hotbed of talent, Spartans.

HANLEY, Steven Melvyn (Wing)
Born Whitehaven, 11.06.79. 6′4″, 16st 7lb. **Rep hons:** England (1, Wal99, 1t-5pts), A (2, Sc99). **ADPR:** Aspatria (1997-98, 20, 19t-95pts), Sale (1998-99, 12, 12t-60pts). A memorable season beginning quietly and building to a personal high. His try-scoring feats for Sale quickly caught the eye and Hanley was called up for England A v Scotland A. Played the next game against Ireland A before finding himself in the full England team to face Wales at Wembley. Even if it did end in defeat, for Hanley it was a stunning climax to the season. He then went on England's tour to Australia. Sadly he suffered a dislocated left shoulder in training and therefore missed a chance to cement a place in the team.

MALLINDER, David **James** (Full-back)
Born Halifax, 16.03.66. 6′3″, 16st. **Rep hons:** England (2, Arg97), A (3, Qld96, 3t-15pts), Barbarians (97-98). **ADPR:** Sale (1989-99, 152, 37t, 2dg-179pts). After the upheaval caused by John Mitchell's departure Mallinder emerged in the role of assistant coach, a role he will combine with playing this season. Long-striding full-back who narrowly missed out on selection for the 1997 British Lions. Educated at Porter GS, Halifax and Carnegie College. Formerly with Old Crossleyans and Roundhay. Plays squash and has swum for Yorkshire.

MATHER, Barrie-Jon (Centre)
Born Wigan, 15.01.73. 6′7″, 16st 4lb. **Rep hons:** England (1, Wal99), A (2, Sc99). **ADPR:** Sale (1998-99, 18, 4t-20pts). Made a very successful transition from league to union – so successful that he made his England debut, along with Steve Hanley, in the ill-fated match against Wales at Wembley, and went too on the short Australian tour. Joined Sale from Castleford when his RL contract expired last autumn. The tallest centre in Premiership rugby, he was a former England Schools lock. His Christian name derives from his father's admiration for Wales fly-half Barry John.

MOORE, Matthew Thomas (Wing)
Born Frimley, 02.04.76. 5′11″, 13st 6lb. **ADPR:** Sale (1996-99, 33, 16t-80pts). Good finisher and unlucky to be in the same club as two England wings, Rees and Hanley. In fact played more than his fair share of Premiership matches, scoring 10 tries in his 20 appearances, an impressive strike rate. Went on England's disastrous southern hemisphere tour of 1998 and, while looking to have got over the mental misery, was not even considered for an England A place. Played his early representative rugby for Sussex and currently a student at Manchester Metropolitan University.

MORRIS, Andrew James (Flanker)
Born Blackburn, 01.09.71. 6′, 15st. **ADPR:** Sheffield (1992-93, 2t-10pts), Nottingham (1993-94, 5), Sale (1995-99, 27, 1t-5pts).

MURPHY, Christopher Ian (Lock)
Born Hull, 02.02.76. 6′8″, 18st. **Rep hons:** England A (2, Ire96). **ADPR:** West Hartlepool (1994-97, 37), Sale (1997-99, 35, 1t-5pts). Giant young former England Schools lock who attended Hymer's School in Hull, and who last season established himself firmly in the first XV set-up. Made a great contribution to the Sale line-out cause.

REES, David Llewellyn (Wing)
Born London, 15.10.74. 5'9", 13st 7lb. **Rep hons:** England (11, Aus97, 3t-15pts), A (1, Otago97). **ADPR:** Sale (1995-99, 44, 11t-55pts). Exciting, scuttling runner who broke into the senior England ranks under Clive Woodward before he became yet another Sale player to succumb to a groin injury. Rapidly building a reputation as a fearless tackler. Suffered with injuries throughout the season, though, and ended up on England's tour and the Sale transfer list. A graphic design and advertising student at Manchester Metropolitan University, he represented England in the World Students Cup in 1996. Educated at Gosforth HS and RGS Newcastle. A sporting all-rounder, David has played soccer for Newcastle Boys, was a Northumberland schools sprint champion and county tennis player and a nationally ranked table tennis junior. Represented Northumberland in the 1995 CIS County final against Warwickshire.

SANDERSON, Alex (Flanker)
Born Chester, 07.10.79. 6'2", 15st. **ADPR:** Sale (1998-99, 18, 1t-5pts). A fine season – as expected – culminating in being appointed captain of the England Under 21 side for the SANZA tournament in Buenos Aires, having led the side in the Five Nations. Devastatingly quick openside flanker who starred for England Schools during their triumphant tour of Australia in 1997 and then captained the Schools side throughout last season. Like older brother Pat, educated at Kirkham HS and headed straight for top honours.

SMITH, Andrew George (Prop)
Born Nantwich, 28.03.69. 6'1", 17st 6lb. **ADPR:** Sale (1990-99, 85, 1t-5pts). Educated at Rossall School and member of Chester RFC before joining Sale. Toured South Africa with North (1994). Good ball-handler and sound scrummager. Twin brother of Paul.

SMITH, Paul Leslie (Prop)
Born Nantwich, 28.03.69. 6'1", 17st 4lb. **ADPR:** Sale (1989-99, 52). **Other clubs:** Chester. Twin brother of Andrew and equally uncompromising in the front row. Also educated at Rossall, Paul was another to fight against injury last season, being impeded with a sore back.

THERON, David Francois **'Dawie'** (Prop)
Born Bloemfontein, South Africa, 15.09.66. 6'3", 18st 12lb. **Rep hons:** South Africa (13, Aus96). **ADPR:** Sale (1998-99, 9). **Other clubs:** Griqualand West. A useful acquisition whose experience will prove invaluable. Dawie Theron was on the bench for the first two Tests against the British Lions in 1997 and brought into the side that beat them in the third Test. Later that year he toured France and England with the Springboks. Made his South Africa debut against Australia in 1996. His preferred position is tighthead prop but he can play loosehead.

WILLIAMSON, Daniel (Prop)
Born Stockport, 23.09.71. 6'2", 17st 7lb. **ADPR:** Manchester (1996-97, 4), Sale (1997-99, 18).

WINSTANLEY, Philip (Prop)
Born Orrell, 16.09.68. 5'11", 16st 10lb. **ADPR:** Orrell (1988-96, 39, 3t, 1pg-17pts), Sale (1996-99, 44, 6t-30pts). Goal-kicking prop who graduated into senior rugby via Orrell Colts having spent his early years playing in the backrow or even on the wing. Remains extremely mobile and established himself as a first choice last season.

REVIEW

A turbulent season which saw the departure of chief executive Howard Thomas, coach John Mitchell, assistant coach Graham Dawe and leading playmaker Shane Howarth. Mitchell's exit was triggered by a players' vote of no confidence – his England duties apparently encroaching too much on his club commitments. Adrian

Hadley and Jim Mallinder took over but were unable to prevent the club finishing 10th, their lowest position since reaching the top division in 1995. Steve Hanley's emergence on the wing and his England debut was a major plus in a season that ended with a raft of players being put on the transfer market in an effort to cut the wage bill. They made an early exit in the Tetley's Bitter Cup, but did reach the semi-finals of the Cheltenham & Gloucester Cup.

MANCHESTER SALE in Premiership One 1998-99

Sep	5	A	London Scottish	Lost	20	25	R.Smith (2T) M.Moore (T) S.Howarth (C, P)
	12	H	Bedford	Won	39	21	M.Moore (2T) J.Machacek (T) T.Beim (T) C.Yates (T) S.Howarth (4C, 2P)
	20	A	Saracens	Lost	26	43	M.Moore (T) T.Beim (T) R.Smith (T) J.Machacek (T) S.Howarth (3C)
	26	H	Harlequins	Won	44	34	P.Winstanley (T) C.Yates (T) R.Smith (T) T.Beim (T) S.Howarth (3C, 6P)
Oct	3	A	Northampton Saints	Lost	17	37	J.Machacek (T) S.Howarth (T, 2C, P)
	17	A	Leicester Tigers	Lost	15	31	S.Howarth (T, C, P) R.Smith (T)
	24	A	Bath	Lost	3	27	S.Howarth (P)
	28	H	Richmond	Lost	10	39	P.Sanderson (T) S.Howarth (C, P)
Nov	7	A	London Irish	Won	31	25	D.O'Cuinneagain (T) Penalty (T) T.Beim (T) S.Howarth (2C, 4P)
	13	H	West Hartlepool	Won	42	26	K.Ellis (2T) S.Davidson (T, 4C, 3P) Penalty (T) D.Baldwin (T)
	22	A	Wasps	Lost	19	32	S.Davidson (2T, 2C) C.Yates (T)
Dec	12	H	Gloucester	Won	26	10	S.Hanley (2T) S.Howarth (T, 3C) J.Mallinder (T)
	20	A	Newcastle Falcons	Lost	15	30	S.Hanley (T) S.Howarth (T, C, P)
	27	A	Harlequins	Lost	15	17	C.Yates (T) S.Hanley (T) S.Howarth (C, P)
Jan	2	H	Northampton Saints	Lost	24	39	S.Hanley (2T) J.Machacek (T) M.Moore (T) S.Howarth (2C)
	5	H	Bath	Lost	30	32	M.Moore (2T) S.Hanley (T) A.Sanderson (T) S.Howarth (2C, 2P)
	23	H	Newcastle Falcons	Lost	20	28	S.Hanley (T) S.Davidson (T) D.O'Cuinneagain (T) S.Howarth (C, P)
Feb	6	H	London Scottish	Lost	7	23	B-J.Mather (T) J.Shaw (C)
	14	A	Richmond	Lost	24	29	S.Hanley (2T) S.Howarth (T, 2C) B-J.Mather (T)
	27	A	Bedford	Won	18	7	S.Hanley (2T) S.Howarth (C, 2P)
Mar	13	H	Saracens	Won	32	24	J.Baxendell (T) C.Yates (T) S.Raiwalui (T) S.Howarth (C, 5P)

	28	A	West Hartlepool	Drew	33	33	J.Baxendell (T) M.Moore (T) D.O'Cuinneagain (T) S.Howarth (3C, 4P)
Apr	3	H	London Irish	Won	30	27	K.Ellis (T) S.Howarth (T, 3C, 2P, D) P.Greening (T)
	24	H	Leicester Tigers	Lost	17	41	J.Baxendell (T) S.Howarth (T, C) B-J.Mather (T)
May	1	A	Gloucester	Won	34	24	S.Howarth (2T, 4C, P, D) R.Smith (T) M.Moore (T)
	8	H	Wasps	Lost	13	27	M.Moore (T) B-J.Mather (T) S.Howarth (P)

Summary of Premiership scorers:

246 S.Howarth (9T, 42C, 37P, 2D); 60 S.Hanley (12T); 50 M.Moore (10T); 41 S.Davidson (4T, 6C, 3P); 30 R.Smith (6T); 25 C.Yates (5T); 20 B-J.Mather (4T), J.Machacek (4T), T.Beim (4T); 15 J.Baxendell (3T), D.O'Cuinneagain (3T), K.Ellis (3T); 10 Penalty (2T); 5 P.Winstanley (T), A.Sanderson (T), P.Sanderson (T), S.Raiwalui (T), J.Mallinder (T), P.Greening (T), D.Baldwin (T); 2 J.Shaw (C).

Summary of Premiership appearances:

26 D.Bell (+3); 23 C.Murphy (+3), S.Howarth, P.Anglesea (+2); 22 C.Yates (+2), R.Smith (+5); 21 S.Raiwalui, J.Baxendell (+2); 20 M.Moore (+1), J.Mallinder (+2); 19 P.Sanderson (+3), D.Baldwin (+7); 18 A.Sanderson (+5), B-J.Mather (+4); 17 D.O'Cuinneagain (+2), K.Ellis (+8); 16 P.Winstanley (+4); 15 P.Greening (+3); 14 S.Davidson (+1); 13 S.Diamond (+4); 12 S.Hanley (+1); 11 J.Machacek (+1); 9 D.Williamson (+8), D.Theron; 8 D.Geraghty (+4), T.Beim (+1); 7 D.Rees (+2), J.Devereux (+3); 6 A.Smith (+1); 4 A.Morris (+1); 2 M.Tetlow, P.Smith, G.Dawe (+1); 1 A.Whittle (+1), J.Shaw (+1), S.Mills (+1), P.Knight (+1).

NEWCASTLE FALCONS

Founded: 1995 (Gosforth formed in 1877)
Ground: Kingston Park, Brunton Road, Kenton Bank Foot, Newcastle, NE13 8AF
Ticket Office: 0191 496 1166
Capacity: 8,000 (Seated 3,200)
Colours: Black and white
Honours: Cup Winners (2) – 1976, 1977 (when Gosforth RFC). Premiership Champions – 1997-98. Division Two Champions – 1992-93
Last season: Premiership One – 8th. Tetley's Bitter Cup – losing finalists
Chief executive: Ken Nottage
Director of rugby: Rob Andrew
Coach: Steve Bates
Captain: TBC

ANDREW, Christopher **Robert** (Fly-half)
Born Richmond, Yorks, 18.02.63. 5'9", 12st 8lb. **Rep hons:** England (71, Rom85, 2t, 33c, 86pg, 21dg-396pts), Barbarians (85-86). **ADPR:** Wasps (1987-96, 77, 16t, 82c, 161pg, 11dg-748pts), Newcastle (1995-99, 68, 13t, 152c, 65pg, 2dg-570pts). **Other**

clubs: Nottingham, Gordon (Australia), Toulouse. World Cup calls on Jonny Wilkinson see Rob carry on for a little longer. It might give him another chance of bowing out on a high note. He had planned on the Tetley's Bitter Cup final being his swansong, but suffered a dislocated left shoulder in April against Wasps and so was ruled out. His signing as director of rugby in October 1995 heralded the beginning of modern professionalism. Educated at Barnard Castle School, Durham and Cambridge University where he won rugby and cricket Blues. First capped against Romania in 1985 when he scored 24 points in a 54-3 win, he won 69 of his 71 caps at fly-half, a world record. He also holds the world record for drop goals in internationals with 22, including two for the British Lions. Other individual highlights include a 30-point haul against Canada (December 94), with a 12 out of 12 kicking record, and 27 points against South Africa in Pretoria (94). A member of England's three World Cup squads, he shared in three Grand Slam triumphs and was a Lion in 1989 and 1993.

ARMSTRONG, Gary (Scrum-half)
Born Edinburgh, 30.09.66. 5'8", 13st 8lb. **Rep hons:** Scotland (45, Aus88, 4t-16pts), A (3, It92), Barbarians (89-90). **ADPR:** Newcastle (1995-99, 69, 50t-250pts). Led Scotland to emphatic victories over Wales, Ireland and France and was as combative as ever for club and country. With the World Cup in mind he went on the short summer tour to South Africa as captain. Enjoyed a good season with the Falcons, scoring a dozen tries to make him the club's joint leading try-scorer with Va'aiga Tuigamala. He was educated at Jedburgh GS and Dunfermline HS and won Scotland recognition out of the Jedburgh club where he succeeded Roy Laidlaw at scrum-half. Made his international debut against Australia in 1988. Played a massive part in Scotland's 1990 Grand Slam triumph and produced possibly the best rugby of his career the following year during RWC91. A British Lion in 1989.

ARNOLD, Richard Karl (Backrow)
Born Taranaki, New Zealand, 16.08.65. 6'4", 15st 12lb. **Rep hons:** Wales A (4, Sc99, 1t-5pts). **ADPR:** Newcastle (1991-99, 115, 16t-74pts). **Other clubs:** Eltham (New Zealand), Taranaki (New Zealand). Abrasive Kiwi forward who has played for Newcastle since before the professional era after arriving from New Zealand where he was a member of the Eltham club. A stalwart in the backrow, he also made his Wales A debut last season.

BEATTIE, Ross Scott (No 8)
Born Sittingbourne, 15.11.77. 6'5", 17st 7lb. **ADPR:** Newcastle (1997-99, 22, 2t-10pts). Began to show his immense talent. Ever-present in the side, revealing a hardness that belies his youth. Shone successively for England Schools, Colts and U21. Educated at Hymer's College, Hull, Ross is also qualified for Scotland.

CARTMELL, William **James** Studholme (Flanker)
Born Carlisle, 08.01.77. 6', 13st 7lb. **ADPR:** Newcastle (1998-99, 10, 3t-15pts). **Other clubs:** Wigton.

CHARLTON, Hall Christopher (Scrum-half)
Born Durham, 25.10.79. 5'11", 13st 2lb. **ADPR:** Newcastle (1998-99, 3, 2t-10pts). **Other clubs:** Durham City. Local product who learned his rugby at Durham School.

GRAHAM, George (Prop)
Born Stirling, Scotland, 19.01.66. 5'7", 17st. **Rep hons:** Scotland (6, Aus97), A (6, Ire89, 1t-5pts). **ADPR:** Newcastle (1996-99, 55, 11t-55pts). **Other clubs:** London Scottish, Stirling County. Remained in the Scotland reckoning, coming on as a replacement in the win over France in Paris and then going on the short summer tour of South Africa. Ever-present in the formidable Falcons front row and proved a handful in the loose as well. Joined Newcastle in 1996, signing from Carlisle RL. Toured Zimbabwe with Scotland back in 1988 and was finally capped, as a replacement, against Australia in November 1997. Also a Scotland RL representative.

GRIMES, Stuart Brian (Lock)
Born Aberdeen, 04.04.74. 6′5″, 16st 7lb. **Rep hons:** Scotland (13, Aus97, 1t-5pts), A (6, SA96, 1t-5pts), Barbarians (98-99). **Other clubs:** Watsonians, Glasgow Caledonians. Enjoyed an outstanding Five Nations for Scotland and was snapped up from Glasgow Caledonians in the close season. Went off to South Africa on Scotland's non-Test tour. Great prospect.

HORTON, Richard Lee (Hooker)
Born Middlesbrough, 22.06.76. 5′10″, 15st. **ADPR:** Newcastle (1997-99, 9, 1t-5pts). **Other clubs:** Middlesbrough. Locally developed talent who has won a place in the England U21 squad.

HURTER, Marius Hofmeyer (Prop)
Born Potchefstroom, South Africa, 08.10.70. 6′2″, 17st 13lb. **Rep hons:** South Africa (13, Rom95). **ADPR:** Newcastle (1998-99, 16). **Other clubs:** Blue Bulls, Western Stormers (South Africa). This powerhouse of a prop, like a lot of the Springboks, looks as comfortable tucking a ball under his arm as he does when doing the same with opposition players. His considerable presence added a formidable element to the front row.

LEGG, Stuart James (Full-back)
Born Solihull, 27.09.75. 6′1″, 14st. **ADPR:** Birmingham/Solihull (1995-96, 2, 2t-10pts), Newcastle (1997-99, 42, 12t, 7c-74pts). **Other clubs:** Durham Univ, Toronto Nomads. Former England Colt who was a stalwart of the championship-winning side at full-back. The circumstances of his selection the previous season, above Tim Stimpson, were not of his making – he simply grabbed his opportunity with both hands. Welsh-qualified.

MASSEY, Peter Martin (Full-back)
Born Pontefract, 03.04.75. 5′11″, 13st 7lb. **ADPR:** Wakefield (1996-97, 22, 7t-35pts), Moseley (1997-98, 12, 3t-15pts), Newcastle (1998-99, 14).

MAY, Tom Alexander (Centre)
Born London, 05.02.79. 5′10″, 14st 7lb. **ADPR:** Newcastle (1998-99, 4). **Other clubs:** Richmond.

NAYLOR, James Richard (Wing)
Born Halifax, 06.02.74. 5′11″, 15st 1lb. **Rep hons:** England A (6, SAus95, 3t-15pts). **ADPR:** Orrell (1993-97, 60, 17t-85pts), Newcastle (1997-99, 40, 14t-70pts). Proved a major success after transferring from Orrell. Scored four tries in four matches for England Colts in 1993 before graduating to the England U21 squad and then making an England A debut against Fiji in 1995. Educated at Crossley Heath School and Wigan Tech and played his early rugby for Crossley Heath RFC. Also Welsh qualified.

NESDALE, Ross Patrick (Hooker)
Born Feilding, New Zealand, 30.07.68. 5′10″, 16st 2lb. **Rep hons:** Ireland (11, Wal97), A (2, Fr97). **ADPR:** Newcastle (1996-99, 66, 13t-65pts). **Other clubs:** Auckland (New Zealand). Enjoyed a fiercely competitive time with Keith Wood vying for an Ireland place. Power, technical skill and streetwise approach made him a permanent fixture in the Falcons front row. The Irish connection is real enough – Tom Nesdale, a cousin of his father's, played for Ireland in 1961. Educated at St Patrick's College, Silverstream and Waikato Polytechnic, Ross played for Auckland University and then spent four years as Sean Fitzpatrick's understudy with the provincial side.

O'NEILL, Stephan (Flanker)
Born Blaydon, 10.10.72. 6′1″, 16st 7lb. **ADPR:** Newcastle (1996-99, 35, 4t, 1pg-23pts). **Other clubs:** Blaydon. Powerfully built flanker, developed locally.

PEEL, Ian (Prop)
Born Otley, 24.01.76. 6′, 17st. **ADPR:** Wharfedale (1994-97, 61, 2t-10pts), Newcastle (1998-99, 14).

SHAW, Martin (Wing)
Born Bishop Auckland, 02.09.75. 5′11″, 14st. **Rep hons:** England A (1, Sc98), Barbarians (98). **ADPR:** Newcastle (1996-99, 37, 8t-40pts). **Other clubs:** Durham City, Hartlepool. Quickly established himself this season as a sharp wing who can score. Educated at Durham School and Northumbria University, Martin represented England Colts and U21 before making his England A debut, as a replacement, against Scotland in March 1998.

TUIGAMALA,Va'aiga Lealuga (Wing/centre)
Born Faleasiu, Western Samoa, 04.09.69. 5′10″, 17st 4lb. **Rep hons:** New Zealand (19, USA91, 5t-21pts), Manu Samoa (8, Ire96, 1t-5pts). **ADPR:** Wasps (1996-97, 8, 3t-15pts), Newcastle (1996-99, 50, 27t, 1c-137pts). **Other clubs:** Ponsonby, Wigan RL. The ultimate professional on and off the field. No one could have been more disappointed at the Cup final failure. His contribution in the Premiership could not be faulted, 12 tries made him top scorer with Gary Armstrong. Returned to union after a successful spell in RL with Wigan. Although born in Western Samoa, Va'aiga was brought up in Auckland and first came to the attention of the All Black selectors when he scored five tries against Mid Canterbury in 1989. Made his full international debut against USA in the 1991 World Cup. Last capped for New Zealand when defeated by England in 1993. Now fully committed to the Western Samoan cause.

UNDERWOOD, Tony (Wing)
Born Ipoh, Malaysia, 17.02.69. 5′9″, 13st 7lb. **Rep hons:** England (27, Can92, 13t-65pts), A (19, Fr89, 16t-68pts), Barbarians (89-90). **ADPR:** Leicester (1988-95, 42, 24t-111pts), Newcastle (1995-99, 47, 26t-130pts). After a season of more injury woe the year before, he finally got back on track scoring eight tries in 16 appearances and reawakening England interest in him. Tony was educated at Barnard Castle School and Cambridge University (Blues in 1990 and 91) and played for England in the World Students Cup (1988) before touring Argentina with England (1990) when another knee injury again restricted his effectiveness. After an outstanding season for England B in 1992, he won his first senior cap against Canada at Wembley later that year. Shared in England's Grand Slam (95) and played in four games during RWC95.

VYVYAN, Hugh Donnithorne (Lock)
Born Guildford, 08.09.76. 6′6″, 16st. **ADPR:** Newcastle (1996-99, 12, 1t-5pts). **Other clubs:** Northumberland, Northern. Developing young lock, one of seven rugby-playing brothers headed by former Sale and England No 8 Charlie Vyvyan.

WALTON, Peter (Flanker)
Born Alnwick, 03.06.69. 6′3″, 18st. **Rep hons:** Scotland (19, Eng94, 3t-15pts), A (9, It93, 1t-5pts), Barbarians (95-96). **ADPR:** Newcastle (1991-92, 11, 10t-40pts), Northampton (1992-95, 31, 2t-10pts), Newcastle (1995-99, 56, 11t-55pts). Peter's power and strength have become an integral part of the Falcons' strategy. Anglo-Scot who played club rugby for Alnwick, Gosforth, Northampton before rejoining the newly constituted Newcastle Gosforth club. Educated at Merchiston Castle School and the Royal Agricultural College, Cirencester.

WEIR, George Wilson (Lock)
Born Edinburgh, 04.07.70. 6′6″, 17st 7lb. **Rep hons:** Scotland (52, Arg90, 4t-19pts), A (7, Ire89, 2t-10pts), Barbarians (92-93). **ADPR:** London Scottish (1989-91, 5, 1t-4pts), Newcastle (1995-99, 69, 8t-40pts). **Other clubs:** Stewart's Melville, Melrose. A busy season for club and country, sadly culminating in injury on tour with Scotland in the summer. He suffered a knee injury against Mpumalanga on the same ground in Witbank where he suffered the injury that ended his Lions tour two years ago. Should be fine for the World Cup though. Versatile, experienced and much-travelled Scottish forward who moved to Newcastle from Melrose where he was a

member of five championship-winning teams. Doddie was educated at Stewart's Melville College and toured New Zealand with Scottish Schools in 1988 when he played in seven of the eight games. Has subsequently toured New Zealand, North America, Australia and the South Pacific with the full Scottish squad. Father played for Gala, as does brother Tom. Keen horse rider (one-day eventing) and enjoys clay pigeon shooting.

WILKINSON, Jonathan Peter (Fly-half)
Born Frimley, 25.05.79. 5′10″, 13st 7lb. **Rep hons:** England (8, Ire98, 7c, 17pg-65pts). **ADPR:** Newcastle (1997-99, 36, 9t, 51c, 53pg-306pts). **Other clubs:** Farnham. Outstanding international and club season. Scored 306 points for Falcons including nine tries. Equalled Rob Andrew's and Simon Hodgkinson's record of kicking seven penalties in a match when England beat France. Played at centre throughout the Five Nations but at fly-half against Australia in the one-off Test in Sydney. Became England's youngest capped international for 71 years when he came on as a replacement against Ireland in March 1998 aged 18 years 301 days. Jonny has been content to bide his time at Newcastle where Rob Andrew has been playing as well as ever. Clive Woodward, however, had no hesitation in asking him to start at outside half against Australia in the opening game of their summer tour, having played centre for England Schools against Australia just 12 months earlier. Wilkinson had also accumulated 38 points from fly-half for England 18 Group the previous winter when they claimed the junior Grand Slam. Educated at Lord Wandsworth School in Hampshire.

WOOD, Michael Denis (Wing)
Born Stockton-on-Tees, 15.07.76. 5′11″, 12st 2lb. **ADPR:** West Hartlepool (1995-97, 23, 6t-30pts), Bath (1997-98, 1), West Hartlepool (1997-98, 11, 3t-15pts), Newcastle (1998-99, 9, 1t-5pts). Promising wing who has won England U21 caps.

REVIEW

There were some worried clubs around when it was first announced that Sir John Hall had decided to sell up. He had been the first owner and if he had decided to go, then what chance everyone else? But the wobbles settled and Newcastle were bought up by businessman David Thompson, with Rob Andrew taken on to the board. They were already resigned to the loss of captain Dean Ryan through injury, but his departure for Bristol in the New Year was still a setback, as was that of England lock Garath Archer who joined Bristol at the end of the season. Their defence of the Allied Dunbar Premiership title was a disappointment and they even missed out on a place in Europe. Andrew was injured and so missed what was expected to be his swansong, the Tetley's Bitter Cup final at Twickenham, where Wasps won comfortably.

NEWCASTLE FALCONS in Premiership One 1998-99

Sep	5	A	Richmond	Lost	29	41	J.Naylor (T) P.Walton (T) V.Tuigamala (T) G.Weir (T) R.Andrew (2C) J.Wilkinson (C, P)
	12	H	Bath	Won	19	17	D.Ryan (T) J.Wilkinson (C, 4P)
	27	H	London Irish	Lost	21	23	T.Underwood (T) Penalty (T) J.Wilkinson (C, 3P)
Oct	4	A	West Hartlepool	Won	24	19	V.Tuigamala (T) P.Walton (T) G.Weir (T) J.Wilkinson (3C, P)
	11	H	Wasps	Won	27	19	T.Underwood (T) G.Armstrong (T) J.Wilkinson (C, 5P)

17	A	Gloucester	Lost	32	41	P.Walton (T) G.Weir (T) J.Naylor (T) J.Wilkinson (T, 3C, 2P)
24	A	Bedford	Won	29	22	T.Underwood (T) J.Naylor (T) V.Tuigamala (T) G.Armstrong (T) R.Andrew (2C) J.Wilkinson (C, P)
31	H	Saracens	Won	43	12	T.Underwood (3T) R.Horton (T) G.Armstrong (T) M.Shaw (T) J.Wilkinson (4C, P) R.Andrew (C)
Nov 7	A	Harlequins	Lost	20	25	T.Underwood (T) J.Naylor (T) G.Armstrong (T) J.Wilkinson (C, P)
15	H	Northampton Saints	Won	45	35	J.Wilkinson (2T, 6C, P) G.Armstrong (T) V.Tuigamala (T) P.Walton (T) R.Arnold (T)
Dec 12	A	Leicester Tigers	Lost	18	31	S.Legg (T) R.Andrew (T) J.Wilkinson (C, 2P)
20	H	Manchester Sale	Won	30	15	S.Legg (2T) G.Armstrong (T) M.Shaw (T) G.Archer (T) J.Wilkinson (C, P)
27	H	West Hartlepool	Won	29	13	J.Wilkinson (T, 3C, P) R.Beattie (T) V.Tuigamala (T) H.Charlton (T)
Jan 2	A	London Irish	Lost	14	16	V.Tuigamala (T) G.Armstrong (T) J.Wilkinson (2C)
5	H	Bedford	Won	34	23	V.Tuigamala (2T) J.Cartmell (T) M.Shaw (T) J.Wilkinson (T, 3C, P)
16	A	Bath	Lost	11	16	J.Naylor (T) J.Wilkinson (2P)
23	A	Manchester Sale	Won	28	20	G.Graham (T) T.Underwood (T) H.Vyvyan (T) J.Wilkinson (2C, 3P)
Feb 13	A	London Scottish	Lost	17	27	M.Shaw (T) S.Legg (T) J.Wilkinson (2C, P)
Mar 27	A	Northampton Saints	Lost	16	57	H.Charlton (T) R.Andrew (C, 3P)
31	H	London Scottish	Won	43	20	G.Graham (T) S.Legg (T) P.Walton (T) J.Wilkinson (T, 3C, 4P) J.Cartmell (T)
Apr 18	A	Wasps	Lost	33	34	V.Tuigamala (2T) J.Wilkinson (T, 3C, 4P)
21	H	Richmond	Won	47	14	G.Armstrong (3T) J.Wilkinson (T) R.Beattie (T) G.Graham (T) J.Naylor (T) S.Legg (6C)
25	H	Gloucester	Won	39	15	G.Armstrong (2T) M.Wood (T) S.Legg (T) G.Graham (T) J.Wilkinson (4C, 2P)
May 2	H	Leicester Tigers	Lost	12	21	J.Wilkinson (4P)
11	H	Harlequins	Won	33	23	V.Tuigamala (2T) J.Cartmell (T) J.Wilkinson (3C, 4P)
20	A	Saracens	Lost	26	40	J.Wilkinson (T, 2C, 4P) M.Shaw (T)

Summary of Premiership scorers:

306 J.Wilkinson (9T, 51C, 53P); 60 V.Tuigamala (12T), G.Armstrong (12T); 42 S.Legg (6T, 6C); 40 T.Underwood (8T); 30 J.Naylor (6T); 26 R.Andrew (T, 6C, 3P); 25 P.Walton (5T), M.Shaw (5T); 20 G.Graham (4T); 15 G.Weir (3T), J.Cartmell (3T); 10 H.Charlton (2T), R.Beattie (2T); 5 Penalty (T), M.Wood (T), H.Vyvyan (T), D.Ryan (T), R.Horton (T), R.Arnold (T), G.Archer (T).

Summary of Premiership appearances:

25 J.Wilkinson, P.Walton (+6), R.Nesdale (+1); 24 G.Weir, G.Graham (+3), G.Archer (+1); 23 V.Tuigamala, G.Armstrong; 22 J.Naylor (+4), R.Beattie (+4); 21 S.Legg (+2), R.Andrew; 20 M.Shaw (+1), R.Arnold (+1); 17 S.O'Neill (+8); 16 T.Underwood (+3), M.Hurter; 14 I.Peel (+5), P.Massey (+7); 10 J.Cartmell (+4); 9 M.Wood (+2), H.Vyvyan (+6), D.Ryan; 7 R.Horton (+5); 6 N.Popplewell; 4 T.May; 3 H.Charlton, S.Best (+3); 2 A.Chilten (+2); 1 J.Rule (+1), N.Frankland (+1).

NORTHAMPTON SAINTS

Formation of club: 1880
Ground: Franklin's Gardens, Weedon Road, Northampton NN5 5BG
Ticket Office: (Sixfields) 01604 588338
Capacity: 9,800 (Seated 6,500)
Colours: Black, gold and green cross bands
Honours: Division Two Champions – 1989-90, 1995-96
Best League finish: 2nd in Division One 1998-99
Best Cup run: Losing finalist 1990-91
Last season: Premiership One – Runners-up. Tetley's Bitter Cup – 5th round (lost 6-21 to London Irish)
Owner, chairman & chief executive: Keith Barwell
Director of rugby: John Steele
Captain: Tim Rodber

ALLAN, Colin John (Flanker)
Born Inverness, 01.04.73. 5′9″, 15st 9lb. **ADPR:** Northampton (1998-99, 4, 1t-5pts). **Other clubs:** Loughborough Univ.

ALLEN, Christopher John (Prop)
Born Wellingborough, 12.10.69. **ADPR:** Northampton (1991-99, 29, 1t-5pts).

ALLEN, Matt Charles (Centre)
Born Farnborough, 28.02.74. 6′2″, 15st 2lb. **Rep hons:** England A (6, Otago97, 1t-5pts), Barbarians (96-97). **ADPR:** Northampton (1994-99, 86, 35t-175pts). **Other clubs:** Loughborough Univ. A solid centre whose midfield defence improves with each succeeding season. Also knows how to score tries, witness his League record of 35 in 86 appearances. Educated at St Dunstan's and Loughborough University, Matt toured Argentina with England in 1997 and returned there at the end of last season with the Barbarians.

BATEMAN, Allan Glen (Centre)
Born Maesteg, 06.03.65. 5′9″, 14st. **Rep hons:** Wales (19, Sc90, 6t-30pts), A (1, Fr89), Barbarians (96-97). **ADPR:** Richmond (1996-99, 55, 26t-130pts). Sees angles that only Pythagoras would spot. Remains a potent midfield player and a canny signing

from the now defunct Richmond, where he was the fulcrum of the backline in his three seasons with them. Still in the Wales set-up, enjoyed the successful tour of Argentina and was also a member of the team which recorded the historic win over South Africa in the Millennium Stadium in June. May have lost a little bit of an edge to his pace, but still a threat. He had joined Richmond from Cronulla, where he had been playing rugby league in Australia for two seasons. Began his career at Maesteg in 1985, moved to Neath in 1988 and helped them to a Welsh championship and two Welsh Cup wins. Capped four times by Wales before turning pro with Warrington RL, playing 142 games and enjoying Regal Cup success and club championship triumph. Went on the British Lions tour to South Africa in 1997, when he came on as a replacement in the third Test.

BEAL, Nicholas David (Full-back/wing)
Born York, 02.12.70. 6'2", 13st 8lb. **Rep hons:** England (10, Arg96, 2t-10pts), A (10, Ire93, 2t-10pts), Barbarians (94). **ADPR:** Northampton (1992-99, 100, 23t, 11c, 12pg, 1dg-176pts). Enjoyed an injury-free season and became more of a fixture in the England squad, playing during the Five Nations then being selected for the short tour of Australia. On the club front his exhilarating bursts into the line brought a fistful of tries and gave all opposing sides a real headache. Sevens expert who represented England in the RWC Sevens in 1993 and Hong Kong (1996). Nick won his first senior cap against Argentina in December 1996, his versatility also helping him win a place on the Lions tour to South Africa in 1997. Nick was educated at RGS High Wycombe and 'discovered' playing for High Wycombe.

BLYTH, Andrew Awburn (Centre/wing)
Born Hexham, 02.10.75. 6', 13st 9lb. **Rep hons:** England A (4, WS95, 1t-5pts). **ADPR:** West Hartlepool (1995-96, 10, 2t-10pts), Newcastle (1996-97, 13, 5t-25pts), Northampton (1997-99, 13, 1t, 1c-7pts). **Other clubs:** Harlequins. A powerful utility back who was signed a couple of seasons ago from Newcastle. Sound midfield defence and capable of bursting out of tackles. Made his England A debut in 1995 against Western Samoa. Began his senior career with West Hartlepool. Enjoys salmon fishing.

COHEN, Ben Christopher (Wing)
Born Northampton, 14.09.78. 6'3", 15st. **ADPR:** Northampton (1996-99, 27, 4t-20pts). A real speed merchant who has improved immeasurably. With youth on his side is definitely going places. Made the most of limited opportunities last season. Has appeared for England Colts and England U21 in successive seasons, playing for the latter in the SANZA tournament in Argentina. Educated at King's Thorpe Upper School, he represented East Midlands Colts in their three championship-winning years, 1995-97. Nephew of England 1966 World Cup soccer star George Cohen.

DAWSON, Matthew James Sutherland (Scrum-half)
Born Birkenhead, 31.10.72. 5'11", 12st 10lb. **Rep hons:** England (22, WS95, 5t, 2c, 3pg-38pts), A (11, Fr93, 7t-35pts), Barbarians (94). **ADPR:** Northampton (1991-99, 112, 29t, 23c, 24pg, 1dg-265pts). Put the trauma of captaining England on their disastrous Antipodean tour of 1998 behind him and although he was replaced by Lawrence Dallaglio as captain, managed to make the scrum-half berth his own for much of the Five Nations campaign, before ceding his place to Kyran Bracken. Got back in when Bracken was injured against France. The duel between the two continued on the short tour Down Under where the Saracen got the nod for the one-off Test, only to be replaced after half-time by Dawson. Dawson's kicking was outstanding. He showed he has the nerves for the job in the win over South Africa and although Jonny Wilkinson took over the duties, Saints benefited to the tune of 17 conversions and eight penalties when Grayson was laid up. A member of the triumphant 1997 British Lions team after recovering from knee surgery to make the trip, playing in all three Tests and scoring two tries. Played junior rugby for Marlow and represented England U21 at centre before reverting to scrum-half. Useful wicketkeeper; played soccer for Chelsea Boys.

GRAYSON, Paul James (Fly-half)
Born Chorley, 30.05.71. 6′, 12st 7lb. **Rep hons:** England (19, WS95, 1t, 40c, 51pg, 6dg-256pts), A (9, BCol93, 16c, 26pg, 3dg-119pts). **ADPR:** Waterloo (1992-93, 10, 1t, 8c, 29pg, 6dg-126pts), Northampton (1993-99, 94, 12t, 157c, 206pg, 13dg-1031pts). The back end of his season was written off by a pelvic stress fracture, although by then he had certainly done his bit for club and country. Kicked an England record 15 conversions in the defeat of the Netherlands in the World Cup qualifier, missing just one kick at goal in the match. A knee injury robbed him of a cap against South Africa but he battled back to face Ireland, though thereafter he lost out to Mike Catt. Will face a tougher challenge for his England spot this season from Jonny Wilkinson. A convert from soccer, made his debut for England in 1995-96. Educated at Parklands High in Chorley and Dr Tuson College, Preston, Paul arrived at Northampton via Preston Grasshoppers and Waterloo for whom he starred in their famous Pilkington Cup victory over Bath in 1992. Useful club cricketer.

HEPHER, Alastair Mark (Fly-half)
Born Yardley Gobian, 03.10.74. 6′2″, 14st. **Rep hons:** Barbarians (97). **ADPR:** Northampton (1994-99, 24, 4t, 30c, 47pg, 2dg-227pts). Grabbed his opportunities as international calls and injury sidelined Grayson. This promising young fly-half, who has had to show a lot of patience with first Gregor Townsend then Grayson ahead of him, appeared in half the Premiership programme and slotted more than 100 points. Captained East Midlands in their CIS U21 County Championship final at Twickenham in 1996.

HEPHER, Simon Anthony (No 8)
Born Ashington, 10.06.77. **ADPR:** Northampton (1998-99, 6, 2t-10pts). Younger brother of Alastair.

HYNES, Martin Peter (Prop)
Born Wigan, 23.08.68. 5′9″, 16st. **Rep hons:** England A (10, NOtago92). **ADPR:** Orrell (1988-94, 65, 1t-4pts), Northampton (1994-99, 62). A tough scrummager, Martin was educated at Wigan Tech and moved to Northampton from Orrell. Played in the inaugural U21 international when England beat Romania 54-13 in Bucharest. Was a bench reserve for England throughout the 1992 Five Nations.

JOHNSON, Christopher Andrew Philip (Hooker)
Born Oldham, 23.05.73. 5′11″, 15st 7lb. **ADPR:** Leicester (1993-96, 7, 1t-5pts), Northampton (1996-99, 30, 2t-10pts). **Other clubs:** Old Veseians. Experienced former England Students captain who has had to play second fiddle, first to Alan Clarke then to Freddy Mendez.

LAM, Patrick Richard (Backrow)
Born Auckland, New Zealand, 29.09.68. 6′2″, 16st. **Rep hons:** Manu Samoa (35). **ADPR:** Newcastle (1996-98, 33, 22t-110pts), Northampton (1998-99, 23, 14t-70pts). Was his usual explosive self, an inspiration to a hugely talented backrow. Experienced Western Samoa captain who helped his country to both the 1991 and 1995 World Cup quarter-finals. Played against Wales, Argentina and Scotland in 1991 and was ever-present four years later. Learned his rugby with Auckland and represented New Zealand Colts and the national seven at Hong Kong but his first allegiance has always been Manu Samoa.

MACKINNON, Don Charles (Flanker)
Born Sydney, Australia, 27.03.71. 6′3″, 15st 7lb. **ADPR:** Northampton (1996-99, 31, 3t-15pts). Athletic Australian who provides useful backrow cover.

MALONE, Dominic James (Scrum-half)
Born Bedford, 12.12.74. 6′, 15st. **ADPR:** Northampton (1996-99, 11, 5t-25pts). Useful as cover for Matt Dawson, dangerous around the fringes and from close in. Scored five tries in just eight appearances.

MENDEZ, Federico Eduardo (Hooker)
Born Ciudad de Mendoza, Argentina, 02.08.72. 6', 18st. **Rep hons:** Argentina (36, Ire90, 2t-10pts), Barbarians (96-97). **ADPR:** Bath (1996-98, 18, 7t-35pts), Northampton (1998-99, 19, 3t-15pts). **Other clubs:** Natal (South Africa), Mendoza (Argentina). Will have to sit out the early stages of the season after tearing an Achilles tendon playing touch rugby in training early in July. Will forever be remembered as the teenager who had the temerity to create England rugby's first sleeping policeman, when he punched Paul Ackford in a Test at Twickenham in 1990. But after last season what will live long in the memory was his ball-handling, adroit running, passing and general potency. No wonder they pulled out all the stops to dissuade him from calling it a day because of homesickness. Undoubtedly the player of the season at Franklin's Gardens. A veteran of the 1991 and 1995 World Cups, he played for Natal in 1996, helping them to the Currie Cup. Had an unhappy season with Bath the following year before moving to the Midlands. Scored three tries and set up no end of others.

METCALFE, Richard (Lock)
Born Leeds, 21.11.73. 7'1", 19st. **Rep hons:** England A (2, Vic95, 1t-5pts), Scotland A (5, Fr98). **ADPR:** Newcastle (1993-98, 42, 3t-15pts), Northampton (1998-99, 18, 2t-10pts). The only senior player in Britain currently topping 7ft, Richard is a talented all-round forward who proved a valuable asset in Saints' push for honours last season after quitting Newcastle and heading south. He switched allegiance the season before last and was immediately rewarded with a Scotland A cap and a place on their summer tour of Fiji and Australia. Educated at Rodillian School, Wakefield.

MOIR, Craig Calder (Wing)
Born Aberdeen, 25.09.73. 5'10", 14st 10lb. **Rep hons:** Scotland A (4, Wal99). **ADPR:** Northampton (1993-99, 63, 15t-75pts). Speedster who played his early rugby for Milford Haven and Llanelli, in 1991-92, before attending Nene College and joining Saints. Has dual qualification and represented the Welsh seven in Taipei and Uruguay, spent much of the 1996 summer playing and coaching at Sciotto Valley in Columbus, Ohio. But last year finally plumped for Scotland and won four caps with the A team. Missed just one Premiership game last season.

NORTHEY, Andrew John (Centre)
Born St Helens, 17.02.72. 6', 16st. **ADPR:** Waterloo (1991-95, 14, 2t-9pts), Northampton (1997-99, 28). **Other clubs:** St Helens RL.

PAGEL, Garry Louis (Prop)
Born King William's Town, South Africa, 17.09.66. 6'4", 17st. **Rep hons**: South Africa (5, Aus95). **ADPR:** Northampton (1997-99, 38, 7t-35pts). Gifted and mobile front row forward who is also a powerful scrummager. Scored five tries in the Premiership and hardly missed a match since arriving from Western Province midway through the 1997-98 season. Also appeared for Eastern Province before breaking into the Springbok side in 1995. Had previously achieved notoriety in 1993 when involved in an incident with Jeff Tordo that resulted in the France captain requiring over 50 stitches in a cut face.

PHILLIPS, Jon-Lee (Lock)
Born Peterborough, 16.08.72. 6'6", 17st. **Rep hons:** Barbarians (98). **ADPR:** Northampton (1991-99, 111, 6t-30pts). A hard, but honourable, utility forward who came of age on the England U21 tour of Australia in 1993 when he forced his way into the Test side. Accused, but ultimately cleared, of attacking the referee in a Cheltenham & Gloucester Cup tie last November. Went on to enjoy a fruitful season. Appears to be coping with the greater degree of responsibility that has been piled on him following the retirement of Martin Bayfield. Many still believe his best position would be blindside wing forward.

POUNTNEY, Anthony Charles 'Budge' (Flanker)
Born Southampton, 13.11.73. 6'2", 15st. **Rep hons:** Scotland (6, SA98), A (2, Ire98). **ADPR:** Northampton (1994-99, 85, 22t-110pts). Tireless scavenging flanker in the old-fashioned style, Budge's consistent form has seen him establish himself in the Scotland backrow, where there is a raft of talent challenging for a place. He qualifies for Scotland because a grandparent was born in the Channel Islands. A former member of Winchester (1989-91) and attended King's School, Winchester before studying for a BA in European Studies at Bedford University and joining Northampton. Member of England's squad in the 1996 World Students Cup.

RODBER,Timothy Andrew Keith (Backrow/lock)
Born Richmond, Yorks, 02.07.69. 6'6", 16st 7lb. **Rep hons:** England (41, Sc92, 5t-25pts), A (6, Fr90, 2t-8pts), Barbarians (92-93). **ADPR:** Northampton (1989-99, 117, 17t-82pts). Made the switch from backrow to lock for club and country with a degree of success. It was a steep learning curve and he was not perfect, but he assimilated a huge amount very quickly. Has always had line-out ability and his mobility added an extra dimension when he switched to second row. Went to Australia last summer on the short tour with England. Educated at Churchers, Hampshire and Oxford Polytechnic, he played for Petersfield and Oxford Old Boys before joining Northampton. Developed rapidly under the tutelage of All Black Wayne Shelford, made his England debut against Scotland in 1992 and was a member of England 1993 RWC Sevens-winning team. Performed wonderfully well in South Africa during England's 1994 tour, but career suffered a blip when dismissed for punching against Eastern Province at Port Elizabeth. Played throughout England's RWC95 campaign.

SEELY, Grant Lionel (Backrow)
Born Aylesbury, 07.01.74. 6'4", 16st 2lb. **Rep hons:** England A (1, Ire99). **ADPR:** Northampton (1994-99, 76, 29t-145pts). An integral member of one of the most feared backrows. Destructive in defence, taking opposition attacks apart, while proving a prolific try-scorer himself. Has developed out of all recognition since joining Northampton from Aylesbury in 1991. Former England U21 captain.

SLEIGHTHOLME, Jonathan Mark (Wing)
Born Malton, 05.08.72. 5'10", 13st 5lb. **Rep hons:** England (12, Fr96, 4t-20pts), A (9, Ire95, 3t-15pts), Barbarians (92-93). **ADPR:** Wakefield (1991-94, 38, 27t-127pts), Bath (1994-98, 39, 22t-110pts), Northampton (1997-99, 25, 2t-10pts). Dogged by injuries in recent years but determined to renew his international career. Educated at Whitgift School, Grimsby, and Chester College, John played for Grimsby and Hull Ionians before moving to Wakefield, where he scored 42 tries in 60 appearances. Gradually became established at Bath, made England A debut against Ireland in January 1995 and full debut at Parc des Princes in February 96.

STEWART, Matthew James (Prop)
Born Dartford, 18.05.73. 5'11", 17st. **Rep hons:** Scotland (12, It96), A (1, Wal99). **ADPR:** Blackheath (1993-96, 41, 2t-10pts), Northampton (1996-99, 40). Has developed into a fine scrummager and played his part in a successful season. Grandfather came from Dunfermline. Lance Corporal Mattie Stewart is a PT instructor with the Princess of Wales Regiment and came to rugby late, only taking the game up when he entered the Army, aged 16. Immediately showed promise, joined the Blackheath club and broke into the Scotland Development XV in 1995 before making his senior debut against Italy in 1996. Keen boxer.

VOLLAND, Matthew James (Prop)
Born Peterborough, 30.06.74. 6', 16st 7lb. **Rep hons:** England A (2, SA96). **ADPR:** Northampton (1993-99, 65). **Other clubs:** Peterborough. Powerful young prop still learning his trade. Worked as a scaffolder before turning professional.

WALTER, Stephen (Hooker)
Born Hemel Hempstead, 15.07.78. 6′2″, 17st 7lb. **ADPR:** Northampton (1998-99, 4). Enormously powerful young hooker who represented England U21 in the SANZA tournament in Argentina.

REVIEW

The departure of Ian McGeechan after their most successful season in the top flight was cruelly ironic. Just as the team was beginning to produce the brand of rugby that McGeechan has always believed in and aimed for, so he leaves. It was the only job he would have left for – coach of Scotland. But it is a shame that he will not be there to mastermind their debut season in the European Cup. Their performance in the Allied Dunbar Premiership was impressive, the backrow proving to be one of the most effective in the division, accounting for 32 of their 80-odd tries and yet maintaining an outstanding defensive reputation. Saints came unstuck with defeats at home to Saracens and Leicester in February which allowed the Tigers to open up a substantial gap. Saints' subsequent run of six victories, including a second over Bath, was enough to confirm them in second place, but they blotted their copybook by losing their last match at Gloucester. Their Tetley's Bitter Cup campaign faltered at the second hurdle at home to London Irish. The back end of the season saw England fly-half Paul Grayson sidelined with a pelvis injury.

NORTHAMPTON SAINTS in Premiership One 1998-99

Sep	6	A	Saracens	Lost	7	34	M.Dawson (T) P.Grayson (C)
	12	H	Harlequins	Won	25	6	G.Seely (2T) D.Dantiacq (T) A.Pountney (T) P.Grayson (C, P)
	19	A	Leicester Tigers	Lost	25	35	A.Pountney (T) A.Hepher (C) P.Grayson (6P)
Oct	3	H	Manchester Sale	Won	37	17	D.Dantiacq (T) Penalty (T) C.Moir (T) M.Allen (T) P.Grayson (4C, 3P)
	10	A	London Scottish	Won	33	22	M.Allen (T) D.Mackinnon (T) P.Lam (T) A.Hepher (T) P.Grayson (2C, 3P)
	17	H	Bedford	Won	34	29	J.Sleightholme (T) P.Lam (T) N.Beal (T) G.Pagel (T) P.Grayson (2P) A.Hepher (C, 2P)
	24	A	London Irish	Won	26	10	A.Hepher (T, C, 3P) A.Pountney (T) P.Lam (T)
	31	H	Gloucester	Won	22	8	Penalty (T) A.Hepher (C, 4P) P.Grayson(P)
Nov	7	H	Wasps	Won	26	21	D.Mackinnon (T) N.Beal (T) P.Grayson (2C, 4P)
	15	A	Newcastle Falcons	Lost	35	45	G.Pagel (2T) R.Metcalfe (T) D.Malone (T) A.Hepher (3C, 3P)
	21	H	Richmond	Won	44	27	Penalty (T) C.Allan (T) G.Pagel (T) M.Allen (T) G.Seely (T) A.Hepher (4C, 3P) A.Blyth(C)
Dec	12	A	Bath	Won	15	9	M.Dawson (T) A.Pountney (T) P.Grayson (C, P)

	20	A	West Hartlepool	Won	33	9	M.Dawson (2T) P.Lam (2T) A.Pountney (T) P.Grayson (4C)
Jan	2	A	Manchester Sale	Won	39	24	P.Lam (3T) M.Allen (T) D.Malone (T) P.Grayson (4C, 2P)
	5	H	London Irish	Lost	8	32	A.Blyth (T) P.Grayson (P)
	16	A	Harlequins	Won	24	17	P.Grayson (T, 3C, P) G.Pagel (T) P.Lam (T)
	23	H	West Hartlepool	Won	19	14	P.Lam (T) P.Grayson (C, 4P)
Feb	6	H	Saracens	Lost	18	21	P.Grayson (6P)
Mar	13	H	Leicester Tigers	Lost	15	22	M.Dawson (5P)
	27	H	Newcastle Falcons	Won	57	16	B.Cohen (2T) F.Mendez (2T) R.Metcalfe (T) M.Allen (T) M.Dawson (T, 6C) A.Pountney (T) N.Beal (T)
Apr	13	A	Wasps	Won	24	15	N.Beal (T) P.Lam (T) A.Hepher (C, 4P)
	17	H	London Scottish	Won	44	13	A.Pountney (2T) N.Beal (T) C.Moir (T) P.Lam (T) M.Dawson (T) A.Hepher (4C, 2P)
	24	A	Bedford	Won	42	31	P.Lam (2T) Penalty (T) B.Cohen (T) G.Seely (T) A.Hepher (4C, 3P)
May	1	H	Bath	Won	40	17	G.Seely (2T) A.Pountney (T) F.Mendez (T) A.Hepher (2P) M.Dawson (4C, 2P)
	8	A	Richmond	Won	31	19	D.Malone (2T) J.Phillips (T) G.Seely (T) M.Dawson (4C, P)
	16	A	Gloucester	Lost	31	43	S.Hepher (2T) D.Malone (T) D.Dantiacq (T) C.Moir (T) M.Dawson (3C)

Summary of Premiership scorers:

156 P.Grayson (T, 23C, 35P); 128 A.Hepher (2T, 20C, 26P); 88 M.Dawson (6T, 17C, 8P); 70 P.Lam (14T); 45 A.Pountney (9T); 35 G.Seely (7T); 25 G.Pagel (5T), D.Malone (5T), N.Beal (5T), M.Allen (5T); 20 Penalty (4T); 15 C.Moir (3T), F.Mendez (3T), D.Dantiacq (3T), B.Cohen (3T); 10 R.Metcalfe (2T), D.Mackinnon (2T), S.Hepher (2T); 7 A.Blyth (T, C); 5 J.Sleightholme (T), J.Phillips (T), C.Allan (T).

Summary of Premiership appearances:

25 C.Moir; 24 N.Beal; 23 G.Seely (+8), J.Phillips (+9), P.Lam; 22 A.Pountney, G.Pagel, M.Dawson; 20 M.Allen (+2); 19 F.Mendez; 18 R.Metcalfe (+1), M.Hynes (+6); 17 T.Rodber; 16 D.Dantiacq (+3); 15 P.Grayson (+1); 14 M.Stewart (+1), A.Hepher (+4), B.Cohen; 13 M.Volland (+8), A.Blyth (+4); 12 A.Northey (+2), D.Mackinnon (+1); 11 J.Sleightholme, C.Johnson (+5); 8 D.Malone (+3); 6 S.Hepher (+5); 4 S.Walter (+2), J.Chandler, C.Allan (+2), C.Allen; 3 H.Thorneycroft (+1), A.Newman; 2 S.Foale (+2), J.Bramhall (+1).

RICHMOND

No story more painfully and acutely sums up the challenge and the pitfalls of the professional era than Richmond's – one of England's oldest and most historic of clubs which suffered a slow and torturous death last season. Put into administration in March with debts of over £700,000, no single backer could be found for the club and eventually, reluctantly, they had no option but to become part of the South West London Super club which has resulted from their takeover, and that of London Scottish, by London Irish.

What an extraordinary state of affairs for a club founded in 1861, fully ten years before the RFU itself. The amateur section of the club will continue and, who knows, may yet rise from the ashes. But don't bet on it – only the strong and wealthy survive these days. Richmond's ascent from the lower reaches of the old Division Three was almost entirely down to the financial contribution of majority shareholder Ashley Levett who reportedly poured some £8m into the club in four years. The money began to run out in 1997-98 – Levett repeatedly signalled that he needed somebody to share the financial burden – but no helping hand was offered and by last August Richmond were forced to go for broke. They moved to the Madjeski Stadium in Reading in the hope of attracting regular 10,000-plus crowds but alas they rarely achieved that target figure – the appalling access to the stadium not helping.

Early last season their decision to allow Scott Quinnell to return to Llanelli had the alarm bells ringing for many – why were an apparently ambitious club allowing such a high-profile player to leave at such a crucial stage of the season? In truth they badly needed the transfer fee that was paid. A brave Tetley's Bitter Cup run, which only ended in the semi-finals when they were defeated by Newcastle, hinted at the potential of a playing squad that also suffered badly all season with injuries. A Twickenham final might possibly have saved them – a potential sponsor was more likely to pay attention – but after the defeat against the Falcons Richmond suffered a slow and horrible death. Their squad was cut to the bare minimum and the remaining League games were played out as if in a nightmare. The redundancies continued, rumours abounded and gradually all hope disappeared. EFDR threatened to invoke a clause and close them down unless a solution could be found, a late bid by a consortium called the Richmond Heavies was rejected and eventually, albeit with no great enthusiasm, the London Irish deal was put together.

So near but so far. Behind the scenes Richmond believed they had every reason to hope for a prosperous future. Their U21 squad emerged as national champions, the nursery system was in place, they were a club going places. It all left a bad taste. This is not how a once-famous club should have departed from the scene. The only positive is that perhaps others may learn the lessons.

RICHMOND in Premiership One 1998-99

Sep	5	H	Newcastle Falcons	Won	41	29	R.Hutton (2T) B.Clarke (T) A.Pichot (T) A.Bateman (T) S.Brown (T) A.Davies (4C, P)
	12	H	Gloucester	Lost	22	25	A.Bateman (T) C.Quinnell (T) A.Cuthbert (T) A.Davies (2C, P)
	19	A	Bath	Lost	14	36	B.Williams (T) M.Deane (T) A.Davies (2C)
Oct	3	A	London Irish	Won	33	29	S.Brown (2T) S.Quinnell (T) E.Va'a (T, 2C, P) A.Davies (P) M.Pini (P)
	10	H	West Hartlepool	Won	41	23	S.Quinnell (2T) A.Pichot (2T) L.Best (2T) N.Walne (T) E.Va'a (3C)

	18	A	Wasps	Won	27 22	M.Pini (T, P) S.Brown (T) E.Va'a (T, 2C) B.Clarke (T)
Oct	24	A	Leicester Tigers	Lost	0 27	
	28	A	Manchester Sale	Won	39 10	S.Quinnell (T) C.Quinnell (T) A.Bateman (T) B.Clarke (T) A.Pichot (T) S.Brown (T) E.Va'a (3C, P)
Nov	1	H	Bedford	Won	38 32	C.Quinnell (2T) E.Va'a (T, 2C, 3P) B.Williams (T) A.Vander (T)
	8	A	Saracens	Lost	17 33	Penalty (T) E.Va'a (T) R Butland (2C, P)
	21	A	Northampton Saints	Lost	27 44	N.Walne (2T) S.Brown (T) E.Va'a (T, 2C, P)
Dec	19	A	London Scottish	Won	28 16	A.Vander (2T) E.Va'a (T, 2C, 3P)
	26	H	London Irish	Lost	13 25	A.Pichot (T) M.Pini (T) E.Va'a (P)
Jan	16	A	Gloucester	Drew	24 24	B.Clarke (T) S.Brown (T) E.Va'a (C, 4P)
	23	H	London Scottish	Won	40 22	A.Bateman (2T) N.Walne (T) C.Quinnell (T) A.Vander (T) R.Hutton (T) E.Va'a (3C) M.Pini (2C)
	26	H	Leicester Tigers	Lost	11 23	N.Walne (T) E.Va'a (2P)
Feb	14	H	Manchester Sale	Won	29 24	A.Pichot (T) B.Clarke (T) S.Brown (T) E.Va'a (C, 4P)
Mar	13	H	Bath	Lost	23 30	A.Vander (T) R.Hutton (T) E.Va'a (2C, 3P)
	27	A	Harlequins	Drew	32 32	R.Hutton (T) E.Va'a (T, 3C, 2P) B.Clarke (T) M.Dixon (T)
Apr	18	A	West Hartlepool	Won	36 35	J.Wright (T) L.Best (T) B.Williams (T) E.Va'a (3C, 5P)
	21	A	Newcastle Falcons	Lost	14 47	B.Williams (T) R.Butland (3P)
	25	H	Wasps	Lost	5 29	A.Pichot (T)
May	3	H	Harlequins	Lost	23 30	A Bateman (2T) B Clarke (T) N.Walne (T) E.Va'a (P)
	8	H	Northampton Saints	Lost	19 31	A.Vander (2T) C.Quinnell (T) E.Va'a (2C)
	12	H	Saracens	Lost	18 25	E.Va'a (T, C, 2P) J.Wright(T)
	16	A	Bedford	Won	106 12	B.Cusack (3T) M.Deane (3T) C.Quinnell (2T) J.Wright (2T) A.Vander (T) A.Bateman (T) B.Williams (T) N.Walne (T) T.Whitford (T) B.Shelbourne (T) R.Butland (13C)

Summary of Premiership scorers:

203 E.Va'a (8T, 32C, 33P); 42 R.Butland (15C, 4P); 40 A.Vander (8T), C.Quinnell (8T), S.Brown (8T), A.Bateman (8T); 35 N.Walne (7T), A.Pichot (7T), B.Clarke (7T); 25 B.Williams (5T), R.Hutton (5T), A.Davies (8C, 3P); 20 J.Wright (4T),

S.Quinnell (4T), M.Pini (2T, 2C, 2P), M.Deane (4T); 15 B.Cusack (3T), L.Best (3T); 5 Penalty (T), T.Whitford (T), B.Shelbourne (T), M.Dixon (T), A.Cuthbert (T).

Summary of Premiership appearances:

25 C.Gillies; 24 N.Walne (+1); 23 B.Williams, D.McFarland (+1); 22 D.Crompton (+1); 21 A.Vander, E.Va'a (+2), M.Pini (+1); 20 B.Clarke, S.Brown; 18 R.Hutton (+4), A.Bateman; 17 A.Pichot, M.Deane (+4), B.Cusack (+7); 16 C.Quinnell; 15 J.Wright (+2); 14 M.Dixon (+3); 12 A.Cuthbert (+8); 11 J.Davies (+4), L.Cabannes (+6); 10 A.Moore (+1); 9 L.Best (+4); 7 J.Barfoot (+4); 6 M.Swift (+2), A.Sheridan (+3); 5 T.Whitford (+5), S.Quinnell, A.Davies (+1), D.Chapman, R.Butland; 4 G.Powell (+2), A.Codling (+3); 3 C.Palmer (+3), M.Fitzgerald (+3); 2 B.Shelbourne (+2), D.Quinn; 1 J.Smith (+1), J.Hamilton-Smith (+1).

SARACENS

Formation of club: 1876
Ground: Vicarage Road, Watford, Herts WD1 8ER
Ticket Office: 01923 496009
Capacity: 22,000 (all seated)
Colours: Black, red star and crescent
Honours: Cup Winners – 1998. Division Two Champions – 1988-89, 1994-95
Best League finish: 2nd in Premiership One 1997-98
Last season: Premiership One – 3rd. Tetley's Bitter Cup – QF (lost 0-15 to Newcastle)
Owner: Nigel Wray (leisure entrepreneur)
Director of rugby: Mark Evans
Player-coach/Captain: Francois Pienaar

BRACKEN, Kyran Paul Patrick (Scrum-half)
Born Dublin, 22.11.71. 5′11″, 13st 3lb. **Rep hons:** England (23, NZ93, 2t-10pts), A (6, BCol93, 3t-15pts), Barbarians (94). **ADPR:** Bristol (1991-96, 47, 7t-35pts), Saracens (1996-99, 50, 7t-35pts). Some injury problems again last season, including his by now obligatory concussion, but not enough to prevent him making an impact at club and international level. Re-established himself in the England No 9 shirt, although facing great competition from Matt Dawson. Burst on to the international scene with a courageous performance against New Zealand in 1993 when he overcame a painful ankle injury courtesy of Jamie Joseph's reckless stamp. A regular for England throughout the 1995 Five Nations, he lost his place to Dewi Morris in RWC95 and then lost out to Matt Dawson in 1995-96 after playing against South Africa in November. Educated at Stonyhurst, Lancashire, and originally capped by England 16 Group at fly-half.

CAIRNS, Matthew Ian (Hooker)
Born Birkenhead, 31.03.79. 5′10″, 14st. **ADPR:** Saracens (1998-99, 2). **Other clubs:** Wirral.

CHESNEY, Kristian John (Wing/lock)
Born Ilford, 02.03.74. 6′6″, 18st. **ADPR:** Saracens (1995-98, 20, 5t-25pts), Bristol (1997-98, 5, 2t-10pts), Saracens (1998-99, 14). A powerhouse who has not quite fulfilled his potential. Moved out of the scrum on to the wing a few years ago where he was prematurely described as an English Jonah Lomu. Fell a little short of that mark but more at home these days back in the pack and still has plenty to contribute.

CHUTER, George (Hooker)
Born Greenwich, 09.07.76. 5′10″, 15st 4lb. **Rep hons:** England A (7, Fr98, 1t-5pts). **ADPR:** Saracens (1997-99, 47, 3t-15pts). Tough young Londoner who enjoyed a marvellous debut season with Saracens, establishing himself as first-choice hooker and winning a summer tour place with England in 1998. Consolidated his England A status, appearing in three out of the four Five Nations A games. Played more matches than anyone else for Saracens in the Premiership. Educated at Trinity School, Croydon, George missed out on schoolboy honours but was capped by England Colts. Joined Saracens from his junior club, Old Mid-Whitgiftians.

COLE, Benedict Luke (Flanker)
Born 31.08.75. 6′3″, 15st 3lb. **ADPR:** Saracens (1997-99, 8, 1t-5pts). **Other clubs:** Torquay, Bath.

CONSTABLE, Ryan (Centre/wing)
Born Durban, South Africa, 20.10.71. 6′, 13st. **Rep hons:** Australia (1, Ire94). **ADPR:** Saracens (1997-99, 43, 8t-40pts). Former Australia Sevens captain with a devastating burst of pace who made an immediate impact with Saracens during his first two seasons. Australia must be very strong indeed to ignore his blossoming talent. South African-born, the family moved to Australia when he was 12. Studying for a Bachelor of Business degree in Marketing.

DAVISON, William Richard (No 8)
Born Kitwe, Zambia, 08.04.69. 6′6″, 16st 8lb. **Rep hons:** England A (2, Arg96). **ADPR:** Richmond (1990-91, 1), Rosslyn Park (1991-94, 23, 2t-10pts), Harlequins (1994-99, 71, 4t-20pts). **Other clubs:** Cobham, Sheffield, Hawke's Bay (New Zealand). Much-travelled and ultra-reliable utility forward who retained his reputation of being Harlequins' most reliable man up front. Educated at Hinchlewood School, Esher Sixth Form College and Sheffield Polytechnic. Played for Hawke's Bay in 1993 when they defeated the British Lions.

DIPROSE, Anthony James (Backrow)
Born Orsett, 22.09.72. 6′5″, 17st 8lb. **Rep hons:** England (10, Arg97, 1t-5pts), A (24, Ire94, 6t-30pts). **ADPR:** Saracens (1992-99, 125, 23t-115pts). Still in the England reckoning, toured Australia in the summer a year after having to captain the side in the humiliating defeat Down Under when he took over from the injured Matt Dawson. Played his fair share of Premiership rugby last season, but lost the captaincy to Pienaar midway through. Educated at Campion School, Hornchurch, he graduated from Loughborough University with a BSc in PE and Recreation Management and made his England A debut against Ireland in 1994, being voted the RFU Young Player of the Year that season. Toured Australia with England U21 in 1993 and captained England A to an unbeaten season in 1995-96.

FLATMAN, David Luke (Prop)
Born Maidstone, 20.01.80. 6′, 17st 7lb. **ADPR:** Saracens (1998-99, 11, 1t-5pts). **Other clubs:** Dulwich College. Outstanding prospect. Burst through and although still only a teenager plays like a man 10 years his senior. Technically superb scrummager but also mobile, a great pair of hands.

GRAU, Roberto Diego (Prop)
Born Buenos Aires, Argentina, 16.07.70. 5′11″, 17st. **Rep hons:** Argentina (21, Jap90, 2t-10pts). **ADPR:** Saracens (1997-99, 31, 1t-5pts). **Other clubs:** Gauteng (South Africa), Liceo Naval (Argentina), Brive. One of the game's most respected scrummagers. Toured England with Argentina in 1996, helping the squad win five of their seven games and playing in the Test team beaten 20-18 by England. His late brother was captain of the Argentina Youth team 1992 and an Argentinian reserve later that year. Roberto missed out on the 1995 World Cup, when Argentina's front row was universally recognised as the best in the tournament, but looks a certainty for RWC99.

GREWCOCK, Daniel Jonathan (Lock)
Born Coventry, 07.11.72. 6′6″, 17st 7lb. **Rep hons:** England (10, Arg97, 1t-5pts), A (1, SA96), Barbarians (96-97). **ADPR:** Coventry (1994-97, 33, 3t-15pts), Saracens (1997-99, 39, 3t-15pts). Influential line-out presence and athletic performer in the loose. Established himself in the England squad last season and then went to Australia, getting on as a replacement in the one-off Test. A highly combative lock who has improved immensely since getting into the top flight, building on an already promising career forged at Coventry from where he won his first England cap during their tour of Argentina in 1997. Educated at Woodlands School and Crewe & Alsager College, Danny was at Barker's Butts for five years before moving to Coventry.

HILL, Richard Anthony (Flanker)
Born Dormansland, 23.05.73. 6′3″, 15st 8lb. **Rep hons:** England (20, Sc97, 4t-20pts), A (8, It95, 3t-15pts), Barbarians (94). **ADPR:** Saracens (1993-99, 88, 17t-85pts). **Other clubs:** Salisbury. Switched to blindside for England as Clive Woodward fielded his ideal backrow of Hill, Back and Dallaglio. One of England's players of the season last year. Clever, constructive and hard-tackling flanker, who played a conspicuous part in the 1997 British Lions success in South Africa. Richard was educated at Stratford Castle Primary and Bishop Wordsworth School. An outstanding Schools international, he completed his education at Brunel University. Represented England A against Western Samoa in December 1995 and New South Wales in January 1996 before finally receiving the call at senior level in 1997.

JONES, Adam Windsor (Wing/full-back)
Born Basingstoke, 07.11.74. 5′11″, 12st 7lb. **ADPR:** Harlequins (1995-96, 1), Richmond (1996-97, 2), London Welsh (1997-99, 20, 10t-50pts).

LACROIX, Thierry (Fly-half)
Born Nogaro, France, 02.03.67. 5′11″, 13st 12lb. **Rep hons:** France (43, Aus89, 6t, 32c, 89pg, 2dg-367pts). **ADPR:** Harlequins (1996-99, 48, 9t, 64c, 72pg, 8dg-413pts). **Other clubs:** Dax. A canny signing for Harlequins where he enjoyed another good season and stayed pretty well injury-free. His experience and playmaking ability will be very welcome at Saracens. Lacroix, a lifelong member of Dax before joining Harlequins, made his international debut as a replacement against Australia in 1989 and subsequently scored 367 points in his 43 international appearances. Appeared at fly-half in France's unsuccessful 1991 World Cup campaign but thereafter switched to centre. Enjoyed his finest moment in the 1995 World Cup when he emerged as the tournament's top scorer with 116 points in six games. He stayed on in South Africa that summer and his goal-kicking helped Natal to victory in the Currie Cup.

LUGER, Daniel Darko (Wing)
Born Chiswick, 11.01.75. 6′1″, 14st. **Rep hons:** England (8, Neth98, 4t-20pts), A (4, Arg96, 2t-10pts). **ADPR:** Richmond (1994-96, 20, 5t-25pts), Orrell (1995-96, 5, 1t-5pts), Harlequins (1996-99, 43, 21t-105pts). Proved an irresistible force, improving on his try-scoring feats of the previous season by a long way. He ran in 11 touchdowns for Harlequins and more importantly carved out a niche in the England team, for whom he scored on his debut against the Netherlands and continued the good work in the other World Cup qualifier and then in the Five Nations. Underwent surgery to a serious knee injury the year before last but has completely recovered. Had joined Quins from Orrell, having formerly been with Richmond. Played for London U21 against NZ U21 in 1994 and appeared for England Students and U21 in 1995-96. A member of England's squad in the World Students Cup in South Africa in 1996.

MAPLETOFT, Mark Sterland (Fly-half)
Born Mansfield, 25.12.71. 5′7″, 13st 2lb. **Rep hons:** England (1, Arg97, 1pg-3pts), A (11, SA96, 4t, 17c, 21pg, 1dg-120pts). ADPR: Rugby Lions (1989-94, 41, 7t, 14c, 45pg, 3dg-205pts), Gloucester (1994-99, 75, 19t, 90c, 179pg, 8dg-836pts). Prolific

points-scorer and darling of the Shed, but forced out of Gloucester by pressure on him to play out of position at full-back. Happy to compete with the likes of Lacroix for the fly-half spot. Though he broke many goal-kicking records at Gloucester, he occasionally failed to launch their potent back division and needs to extend his fly-half skills if he is to succeed at Saracens. Educated at Bawnmore Middle and Lawrence Sheriff School in Rugby and Loughborough University, he starred for England 18 Group before the first of two serious knee injuries. Recovered in time to make an outstanding contribution on England's U21 tour of Australia (1993) but after joining Gloucester he again injured knee ligaments, against West Hartlepool. Represented Coventry City Reserves as a schoolboy.

MURRAY, Scott (Lock)
Born Musselburgh, 15.01.76. 6′6″, 16st 7lb. **Rep hons:** Scotland (12, Aus97, 2t-10pts), A (8, It96), Barbarians (95-96). **ADPR:** Bedford (1996-99, 61, 7t-35pts). **Other clubs:** Preston Lodge, Edinburgh Academicals. A great signing from Bedford. Athletic lock who survived a traumatic international debut against Australia in November 1997 – when he scored Scotland's only try in a 37-8 defeat – to bounce back, recovering his form in time to make the Scotland tour party for Fiji and Australia. Has since taken the international world by storm and will no doubt do likewise for Saracens. He enjoyed a spell playing rugby in Perth, Western Australia, and is a former Scottish Schools basketball international. Educated at Morgan Academy in Dundee and a former animal technician before turning professional. Learned his rugby with Preston Lodge before moving to Edinburgh Accies.

OGILVIE, Philip John Maxwell (No 8)
Born Hitchin, 08.12.77. 6′6″, 17st 2lb. **ADPR:** Saracens (1996-99, 14, 1t-5pts). Former England Schools cap.

OLSEN, Marcus James (Scrum-half)
Born Salisbury, 23.06.72. 5′7″, 11st 11lb. **ADPR:** Bath (1993-95, 4), Saracens (1996-99, 15, 5t-25pts). Deputises well for Kyran Bracken when called upon. A practising aromatherapist, Marcus learned his rugby with the Salisbury club and has represented England Colts and U21. Played for Llandovery and Welsh Universities while studying at Cardiff Institute of Higher Education.

O'MAHONY, Darragh William (Wing)
Born Cork, 18.08.72. 5′9″, 11st. **Rep hons:** Ireland (4, It95, 2t-10pts), A (10, Eng95, 6t-30pts). **ADPR:** Moseley (1996-98, 33, 32t-160pts), Bedford (1998-99, 25, 12t-60pts). **Other clubs:** Lansdowne, UCD (Ireland). Electrifying pace, lethal finisher, but perhaps lacks the defensive abilities which are vital if he is to make it at the very top. An exciting signing from Bedford by Saracens.

PIENAAR, Jacobus **Francois** (Flanker)
Born Vereeniging, South Africa, 02.01.67. 6′4″, 17st. **Rep hons:** South Africa (29, Fr93, 3t-15pts). **ADPR:** Saracens (1996-99, 47, 13t-65pts). **Other clubs:** Transvaal. Took over the captaincy from Diprose halfway through and once it was all over assumed the mantle of director of coaching after Mark Evans was shunted into an administrative post. Still put in his share of the hard yards in what was ultimately a disappointing season for him, with no silverware to show for a lot of effort. Captained Transvaal to successive Currie Cup wins in 1993 and 1994 and also led them to victory in the 1993 Super Ten and an excellent 24-21 win over England the following year. Captained South Africa on his debut in 1993 against France in Durban, becoming only the third Springbok to be honoured in such a way – the others being Basil Kenyon and Des van Jaarsveld – and famously led the rainbow nation to the 1995 World Cup at Ellis Park. Unceremoniously dumped later the following year by Andre Markgraaff.

POWELL, Matthew James (Scrum-half)
Born Abergavenny, 08.05.78. 5′10″, 13st 8lb. **ADPR:** Saracens (1997-99, 6). **Other clubs:** Christchurch HSOB (New Zealand), Brecon.

RAVENSCROFT, Stephen Charles Wood (Centre)
Born Bradford, 02.11.70. 5′11″, 14st 2lb. **Rep hons:** England (2, Aus98), A (2, Fr98). **ADPR:** Saracens (1990-99, 113, 15t-75pts). Blossomed under the influence of Philippe Sella and Michael Lynagh – so much so that he was called into the England tour party and named in their side to play Australia in their opening Test, then coming on as a replacement in the second Test against New Zealand on the ill-fated tour. Educated at Bradford GS, Steve previously played for Otley and Bradford & Bingley before joining Saracens. Played provincial U21 rugby for North Harbour during a prolonged stay in New Zealand and represented England in the 1992 World Students Cup.

ROCQUES, Anthony William Seymour (Flanker)
Born Bromley, 07.09.78. 6′2″, 14st. **ADPR:** Saracens (1997-99, 5). Educated at Sevenoaks School and a former captain of England Schools, for whom he starred during their 1997 tour of Australia. Still not getting as much opportunity as he would no doubt like.

RUSSELL, Robert Reid (Hooker)
Born Brisbane, Australia, 01.05.76. 5′10″, 14st 6lb. **Rep hons:** Scotland A (3, Eng99). Rapidly emerging Australian-born Scot who made a big impact on Scotland's short tour of South Africa in the summer. Has also played for Queensland and joins Saracens from Edinburgh Reivers.

SHANKLIN, Tomos (Centre)
Born Harrow, 24.11.79. **ADPR:** London Welsh (1998-99, 4, 3t-15pts).

SORRELL, Kevin James (Centre)
Born Harold Wood, 06.03.77. 6′, 13st 4lb. **ADPR:** Saracens (1996-99, 18, 4t-20pts). Another product of Campion School, Kevin played his early club rugby for Upminster. Formerly a member of school barbershop singing group.

THIRLBY, Robert Graham (Wing)
Born Penzance, 02.03.79. 5′11″, 13st. **ADPR:** Redruth (1997-98, 23, 17t, 48c, 25pg-256pts), Saracens (1998-99, 9, 1t, 4c, 3pg-22pts). Slightly built, deceptively strong and quick runner. Outstanding member of the England U21 squad at the SANZA tournament in Argentina this summer.

THOMSON, Jeremy Roy David (Centre)
Born Pietermaritzburg, South Africa, 24.06.67. 5′10″, 13st 9lb. **ADPR:** Saracens (1998-99, 17, 1t-5pts). **Other clubs:** Natal (South Africa). Called into the England training squad early last season, but went no further. His mother comes from Watford, now Saracens' home base. Powerful runner, astute tactical brain and can slice open defences with some clever angles.

WALLACE, Paul Stephen (Prop)
Born Cork, 30.12.71. 6′, 16st 12lb. **Rep hons:** Ireland (29, Jap95, 3t-15pts), A (4, Eng95, 1t-5pts). **ADPR:** Saracens (1996-99, 59, 8t-40pts). **Other clubs:** Blackrock. An immense figure for Saracens and Ireland as usual last season. Technically acknowledged as one of the best tightheads around and proved it time and again. Educated at Crescent College, Limerick, Paul was an exceptional schools international in 1989 and 90 and has made smooth progress towards a place in the full Ireland side. Made his senior debut against Japan in RWC95 and has grown in stature ever since. Brother of Ireland wing Richard and promising Ireland A flanker David Wallace.

WALSHE, Nicholas Patrick James (Scrum-half)
Born Chiswick, 01.11.73. 5′11″, 13st 4lb. **Rep hons:** England A (4, Arg96). **ADPR:** Rosslyn Park (1993-95, 25, 2t-10pts), Harlequins (1995-99, 40, 7t, 2c-39pts). Feisty scrum-half who just could not seem to get ahead of Huw Harries. Will have to content himself with being understudy to Bracken, unless and until he knocks him off his perch. Formerly at Rosslyn Park, Nick impressed at full-back for London U21 v NZ U21 in 1994, but then switched to scrum-half and continued to press Harries hard for the starting spot last season. Educated at Worth Abbey.

WHITE, Julian (Prop)
Born 14.05.73. 6′1″, 19st. England qualified prop who arrives with a big reputation from Bridgend.

REVIEW

The year began on a high note with the news that they had doubled season ticket sales, a staggering achievement since they were breaking new ground at Watford. The genius behind their marketing drive, Peter Deakin, unfortunately left them for his first love, rugby league, only a couple of months after being offered a lucrative five-year contract. Troy Coker also left, with a few stinging remarks about the standard of club rugby in England. Mark Evans was moved into more of an administrative role leaving Francois Pienaar in sole charge of things. The former Springbok captain relieved Tony Diprose of the captaincy and took it on himself. They finished in Europe, but out of contention for the title. Their quarter-final appearance in the Tetley's Bitter Cup was a disappointment. They discarded a number of players but signed a few as well, including Dan Luger, Thierry Lacroix and Nick Walshe from Harlequins, Mark Mapletoft from Gloucester and former Queensland hooker Robbie Russell. They also lost to Penguins in the Middlesex Sevens final.

SARACENS in Premiership One 1998-99

Sep	6	H	Northampton Saints	Won	34	7	A.Penaud (T) T.Coker (T) J.Thomson (T) G.Johnson (T, 4C, 2P)
	20	H	Manchester Sale	Won	43	26	B.Daniel (2T) Penalty (T) R.Constable (T) M.Singer (T) G.Johnson (3C, 4P)
	26	A	London Scottish	Won	58	20	G.Johnson (2T, 6C, 2P) B.Daniel (2T) R.Constable (T) P.Wallace (T) M.Singer (T) G.Chuter (T)
Oct	11	H	Leicester Tigers	Won	22	10	R.Constable (T) G.Johnson (C, 3P) A.Penaud (2P)
	17	A	Harlequins	Lost	28	41	B.Daniel (T) A.Penaud (T, 4C) S.Ravenscroft (T) P.Wallace (T)
	20	A	West Hartlepool	Won	52	3	F.Pienaar (T) Penalty (T) T.Diprose (T) R.Wallace (T) K.Bracken (T) R.Hill (T) K.Sorrell (T) A.Penaud (3C, 3P) A.Lee (C)
	25	H	Wasps	Lost	17	31	B.Daniel (T) G.Johnson (T, 2C, P)
	31	A	Newcastle Falcons	Lost	12	43	G.Johnson (T, C) R.Hill (T)
Nov	8	H	Richmond	Won	33	17	S.Ravenscroft (2T) G.Johnson (T, 3C, 4P)
	15	A	Bedford	Won	25	20	T.Coker (T) W.De Jonge (T) R.Wallace (T) G.Johnson (2C, 2P)
	21	A	Gloucester	Lost	27	28	K.Sorrell (T) P.Ogilvie (T) S.Ravenscroft (T) G.Johnson (3C, 2P)

Dec	13	H	London Irish	Won	40	26	F.Pienaar (2T) B.Free (T) D.Flatman (T) G.Johnson (4C, 4P)
	19	A	Bath	Won	19	11	S.Ravenscroft (T) G.Johnson (C, 3P) A.Penaud (D)
	27	H	London Scottish	Lost	7	24	B.Daniel (T) G.Johnson (C)
Jan	3	H	Bedford	Won	44	13	D.Grewcock (2T) R.Wallace (T) P.Johns (T) B.Daniel (T) M.Olsen (T) G.Johnson (4C, 2P)
	6	A	Wasps	Drew	15	15	G.Johnson (5P)
Feb	6	A	Northampton Saints	Won	21	18	B.Daniel (T) S.Ravenscroft (T) G.Johnson (C, 3P)
	14	H	West Hartlepool	Won	48	27	T.Diprose (3T) A.Penaud (T) K.Bracken (T) R.Thirlby (T, C) D.Grewcock (T) G.Johnson (4C, P)
Mar	13	A	Manchester Sale	Lost	24	32	R.Hill (T) A.Penaud (T, D) R.Thirlby (C, 3P)
	28	H	Bath	Lost	14	33	R.Hill (T) R.Grau (T) R.Thirlby (2C)
Apr	17	A	Leicester Tigers	Lost	18	25	G.Johnson (6P)
	25	H	Harlequins	Lost	30	38	B.Daniel (2T) Penalty (T) G.Johnson (3C, 3P)
May	1	A	London Irish	Won	26	21	G.Johnson (T, 2C, 3P) T.Diprose (T) A.Penaud (D)
	7	H	Gloucester	Won	26	10	K.Bracken (T) B.Cole (T) B.Daniel (T) G.Johnson (C, 3P)
	12	A	Richmond	Won	25	18	G.Johnson (T, 2C, 2P) A.Penaud (T) K.Sorrell (T)
	20	H	Newcastle Falcons	Won	40	26	K.Bracken (T) G.Chuter (T) R.Constable (T) T.Diprose (T) G.Johnson (4C, 3P) A.Penaud (D)

Summary of Premiership scorers:

318 G.Johnson (8T, 52C, 58P); 66 A.Penaud (5T, 7C, 5P, 4D); 60 B.Daniel (12T); 30 S.Ravenscroft (6T), T.Diprose (6T); 22 R.Thirlby (T, 4C, 3P); 20 R.Hill (4T), R.Constable (4T), K.Bracken (4T); 15 Penalty (3T), R.Wallace (3T), K.Sorrell (3T), F.Pienaar (3T), D.Grewcock (3T); 10 P.Wallace (2T), M.Singer (2T), T.Coker (2T), G.Chuter (2T); 5 J.Thomson (T), M.Olsen (T), P.Ogilvie (T), P.Johns (T), R.Grau (T), B.Free (T), D.Flatman (T), W.De Jonge (T), B.Cole (T); 2 A.Lee (C).

Summary of Premiership appearances:

26 G.Chuter; 25 T.Diprose; 24 A.Penaud; 23 G.Johnson (+1); 22 R.Hill (+1); 21 S.Ravenscroft (+7), B.Daniel (+1), R.Constable; 19 P.Johns (+3); 18 D.Grewcock; 17 P.Wallace (+1), J.Thomson (+3), F.Pienaar (+3), K.Bracken; 16 B.Reidy (+6); 15 M.Singer (+6), R.Grau (+1); 14 T.Coker (+1), K.Chesney (+7); 13 K.Sorrell (+3), P.Ogilvie (+10); 12 C.Yandell (+2), R.Wallace (+1); 11 A.Olver (+8), D.Flatman (+4); 9 R.Thirlby (+2); 8 B.Cole (+5); 7 B.Free (+4); 6 M.Olsen (+1); 5 G.Botterman (+5); 4 B.Taylor (+1), M.Powell (+3); 3 W.De Jonge (+1); 2 M.Cairns (+2); 1 P.Turner (+1), B.Stanley (+1), T.Rocques (+1), K.Roche (+1), B.Lea, A.Lee (+1).

ALLIED DUNBAR PREMIERSHIP

Premiership Two

COVENTRY

Formation of club: 1874
Ground: Coundon Road, Barker Butts Lane, Coventry CV6 1DU
Capacity: 9,900 (Seated 900)
Colours: Navy blue and white
Honours: Cup winners (2) – 1972-73, 1973-74. Division Three champions – 1993-94, 1995-96
Best League finish: 11th in Division One 1987-88
Last season: Premiership Two – 7th. Tetley's Bitter Cup – 3rd round (lost 26-36 to Worcester)
Owners: Coventry Ventures Limited (consortium)
Chairman: Keith Fairbrother
Director of rugby: TBC
Coach: Ralph Knibbs.
Captain: TBC

ADDLETON, David James (Hooker)
Born Coventry, 30.03.67. 5′9″, 14st 8lb. **ADPR**: Coventry (1989-99, 134, 4t-20pts). Stalwart hooker who arrived at Coventry from the Barker's Butts club. Has also represented Irish Exiles. Educated at Woodlands and a water engineer by profession.

CANE, Nigel John (Scrum-half)
Born Plymouth, 19.09.77. 6′, 13st 5lb. **ADPR**: Plymouth Albion (1995-96, 2, 1t-5pts), Gloucester (1997-99, 1).

CRANE, Mark Richard (Prop)
Born Bristol, 17.11.67. 6′3″, 19st. **ADPR**: Bath (1988-92, 5, 1t-4pts), Clifton (1995-96, 11, 5t-25pts), Coventry (1996-97, 21, 3t-15pts), Worcester (1997-98, 10, 1t-5pts), Coventry (1998-99, 22, 2t-10pts). Much-travelled and experienced prop who rejoined Coventry last season and proved a major force in their pack.

CROFTS, Lee Bryan (Flanker)
Born Coventry, 07.09.68. 6′4″, 17st 4lb. **ADPR**: Coventry (1993-99, 89, 11t-55pts). Former British Police heavyweight boxing champion. Learned his rugby at the Broadstreet club, moved from second row to backrow in 1995-96 when he was voted Coventry's most promising player. Played for the Midlands against Argentina in 1996.

CURTIS, Michael Derek (Centre)
Born Coventry, 27.06.72. 5′11″, 16st 6lb. **ADPR**: Coventry (1992-99, 72, 9t-45pts). Powerful centre, son of former Coventry City centre-half Mick Curtis, joined Coventry from the Trinity Guild club.

DALE, Brent (Lock)
Born Newcastle, Australia, 08.01.76. **ADPR**: Coventry (1998-99, 1). Formerly with the Gordon club in Newcastle, Australia.

DAWSON, Anthony Richard (Scrum-half)
Born Crewe, 29.01.75. 5′10″, 11st. **ADPR**: Coventry (1996-99, 60, 10t-50pts). 'Tigger' joined Coventry in January 1996 from the Stourbridge club and made an immediate impact. A teacher, he was educated at Crewe and Alsager College and also played for Whitchurch FC.

EDWARDS, Scott Charles
Born Lydney, 11.01.76. **ADPR**: Gloucester (1996-97, 2), Coventry (1997-99, 3). Joined Coventry from Lydney.

EYRES, Richard Anthony (Lock)
Born St Helens, 07.12.69. **ADPR**: Coventry (1998-99, 5). Joined from Rochdale at the beginning of the 1998-99 season.

FOUNTAINE, Mark Simon (Lock)
Born Leamington Spa, 07.06.67. 6′6″, 17st 4lb. **ADPR**: Bristol (1994-96, 9), Northampton (1996-97, 1), Coventry (1998-99, 24, 1t-5pts). One of Coventry's most reliable forwards last season, played for Birmingham and Solihull before he joined Bristol in 1994.

GALLAGHER, Matthew David (Utility back)
Born Solihull, 21.03.73. 6′1″, 13st. **ADPR**: Nottingham (1993-96, 44, 4t, 8c, 26pg-114pts), Coventry (1996-99, 60, 10t, 9c, 4pg, 5dg-95pts). Member of the Warwickshire County Championship-winning side in 1995. Studied building technology at Sheffield Hallam University.

GOUGH, Stephen Paul (Fly-half)
Born Leigh, 22.04.66. 5′10″, 13st. **ADPR**: Fylde (1987-98, 121, 26t, 85c, 142pg, 6dg-739pts), Sheffield (1988-89, 1t-4pts), Coventry (1998-99, 26, 10t, 48c, 53pg-305pts). An inspired signing from Fylde for troubled Coventry last season, Gough was ever-present and his superb goal-kicking saw him top the Division scoring charts. Learned his rugby at Leigh RFC.

HADFIELD, James David (Prop)
Born 02.02.78. **ADPR**: Coventry (1998-99, 2).

HAYTER, James William (Hooker)
Born Plymouth, 14.08.78. 6′1″, 15st 10lb. **ADPR:** Orrell (1997-99, 15). Summer recruit from Orrell.

HEWLETT, Jason John (Scrum-half)
Born Cardiff, 30.05.74. 5′8″, 12st 10lb. **Rep hons**: Barbarians (97). **ADPR**: Coventry (1997-98, 2, 1t-5pts), London Welsh (1998-99, 2, 3pg-9pts), Coventry (1998-99, 9). Former Wales Schools and U21 cap who played for Cardiff before moving to England. Can play anywhere in the back division.

HORROBIN, Julian Keith (Flanker)
Born Lydney, 17.04.69. 6′2″, 16st 7lb. **ADPR**: Bristol (1990-91, 10, 4t-16pts), Coventry (1993-99, 101, 28t-140pts). Powerful West Country flanker who is a former England U21 and Schools cap. Joined Bristol in 1990 from Berry Hill in the Forest of Dean.

HOUSTON, Carl Rawiri (Flanker)
Born Palmerston North, New Zealand, 28.04.75. 6′0″, 14st 6lb. **ADPR**: Coventry (1998-99, 9, 1t-5pts). Joined Coventry from the South Districts club in Australia.

HYSLOP, Ricky Terence George
Born 21.03.78. **ADPR**: Coventry (1998-99, 3).

KERR, Simon Arthur (Prop)
Born Berrigan, NSW, Australia, 01.04.70. **ADPR**: Coventry (1998-99, 15, 1t-5pts). Experienced Australian who has played for Norths, Manly and Trangie back home.

KERSHAW, Andrew Phillip (Prop)
Born Hammersmith, 10.10.77. 6'1", 18st 12lb. **ADPR**: London Irish (1997-98, 5), Coventry (1998-99, 5).

KILFORD, Wayne Ashley (Full-back)
Born Malvern, 25.09.68. 5'11", 13st 7lb. **ADPR**: Nottingham (1988-92, 20, 1t, 2c, 5pg-23pts), Leicester (1992-96, 22, 4t, 1pg-23pts), Coventry (1996-99, 50, 14t-70pts). Former England Colts and U21 cap, Wayne also represented Nottinghamshire CC in his youth. Educated at Joseph Whitaker School, Notts.

McADAM, Andrew (Wing)
Born Coventry, 29.03.71. 6'1", 14st. **ADPR**: Leicester (1994-96, 6), Coventry (1996-99, 41, 15t-75pts). Former England Colts cap, works as a financial advisor.

MAFI, Mateaki Fonlua Ma'a Tonga (Wing)
Born Tonga, 19.09.72. 6', 15st 10lb. **ADPR**: Coventry (1998-99, 7, 3t-15pts). Powerful Tongan international wing who joined from Warrington RL.

MIKA, Michael Alaifat (Prop)
Born Lower Hutt, New Zealand, 24.07.68. 6'1", 18st. **Rep hons**: Manu Samoa, Barbarians (95-96). **ADPR**: Coventry (1998-99, 8). Western Samoan whose brother Dylan was recently capped at flanker by New Zealand against Western Samoa.

MINSHULL, Jason Stuart (Centre/wing)
Born Leamington Spa, 20.12.67. 5'11", 13st 5lb. **ADPR**: Coventry (1987-99, 73, 12t-54pts). Previously played for Kenilworth and Barker's Butts. Represented Taranaki against Australia in 1990 while staying with the Tukapi club.

MORGAN, Russell James (Prop)
Born Hemel Hempstead, 28.02.73. 5'10", 15st. **ADPR**: Coventry (1994-99, 18). Formerly with Old Coventrians.

ROBINSON, Richard Philip (Centre)
Born Liverpool, 05.07.67. 6'1", 14st. **Rep hons**: Barbarians (96-97). **ADPR**: Leicester (1993-96, 24, 3t-15pts), Coventry (1996-99, 55, 14t-70pts). An accountant who joined Coventry in 1996 having played for Leicester in the Pilkington Cup final that May. Formerly with Blackpool and Market Bosworth.

SALISBURY, Robert Lloyd (No 8)
Born Birmingham, 14.12.76. 6'3", 16st 9lb. **ADPR**: Coventry (1996-98, 8), Blackheath (1998-99, 5), Coventry (1998-99, 13, 1t-5pts). Yet another Coventry player who hails from the nearby Barker's Butts club.

SMALLWOOD, Andrew Mark Charles (Wing)
Born Solihull, 13.08.72. 5'10", 12st 8lb. **ADPR**: Nottingham (1993-96, 47, 11t-55pts), Coventry (1996-99, 60, 37t-185pts). Deadly finisher who snaffled 15 League tries last season. Educated at Solihull School and Nottingham University, and a former player with Birmingham & Solihull and Barker's Butts.

SODEN, Brian Jason (Hooker)
Born Coventry, 17.04.71. 5'11", 16st 7lb. **ADPR**: Coventry (1996-99, 10).

WALLWORK, Martin (Scrum-half)
Born Blackpool, 30.03.78. 5'11", 12st. **ADPR**: Fylde (1997-98, 9), Coventry (1998-99, 6). Educated at Arnold School and Loughborough University.

WATKINS, Neil (Lock)
Born Bridgend, 10.11.75. 6'7", 17st 10lb. **Rep hons**: Wales A (2, Rom97, 1t-5pts). **ADPR**: Bristol (1998-99, 6), Coventry (1998-99, 10, 2t-10pts). Outstanding schoolboy and Wales U21 international who moved to Bristol from Neath in 1998 before joining Coventry last season.

REVIEW

Coventry may have only finished seventh in the League but considering they nearly went out of business last summer, there are few at Coundon Road who will argue with that. Consistency was Coventry's big problem – a side who are good enough to thrash London Welsh 63-19 and defeat Rotherham 22-12 should not be losing 46-21 to Moseley and being defeated by Midlands rivals Rugby Lions. Fly-half Steve Gough was their mainstay, kicking magnificently to garner 305 points while the elusive Andy Smallwood scored 15 tries.

COVENTRY in Premiership Two 1998-99

Sep	5	A	Worcester	Lost	7	22	A.Smallwood (T) S.Gough (C)
	12	H	Waterloo Drummers	Won	21	15	M.Fountaine (T) D.Eves (T) S.Gough (C, 3P)
	19	A	Exeter	Lost	25	31	S.Gough (T, 2C, 2P) D.Eves (T) K.Whitley (T)
	26	H	Fylde	Won	64	9	W.Kilford (3T) A.Smallwood (2T) M.Crane (T) M.Gallagher (T) L.Crofts (T) S.Gough (T, 8C, P)
Oct	4	A	Rugby Lions	Won	20	17	J.Horrobin (T) L.Criscuolo (D) S.Gough (4P)
	10	H	London Welsh	Won	63	19	S.Gough (3T, 5C, 3P) W.Kilford (2T) M.Curtis (T) L.Crofts (T) L.Criscuolo (T, 2C)
	17	A	Blackheath	Won	30	18	R.Robinson (2T) J.Horrobin (T) D.Eves (T) S.Gough (2C, 2P)
	24	H	Orrell	Won	26	14	Penalty (T) R.Robinson (T) S.Gough (2C, 4P)
	30	A	Bristol	Lost	12	14	S.Gough (4P)
Nov	7	H	Rotherham	Won	22	12	A.Smallwood (T) S.Gough (T, 2C, P) M.Gallagher (T)
	22	A	Leeds Tykes	Lost	12	36	R.Robinson (T) A.Smallwood (T) L.Criscuolo (C)
Dec	12	A	Wakefield	Won	18	10	D.Eves (T) J.Minshull (T) S.Gough (C, 2P)
	20	H	Moseley	Lost	21	46	L.Crofts (T) Penalty (T) J.Horrobin (T) S.Gough (3C)
Jan	3	H	Leeds Tykes	Lost	27	33	M.Mafi (2T) Penalty (T) S.Gough (3C, 2P)
	16	A	Rotherham	Lost	12	19	S.Gough (4P)
Feb	6	A	Orrell	Lost	0	31	
	13	H	Blackheath	Won	35	8	K.Whitley (T) M.Gallagher (T, 3C, 2P) A.Smallwood (T) N.Watkins (T) L.Criscuolo (D)
	21	H	Bristol	Won	22	19	K.Whitley (T) R.Robinson (T) S.Gough (T, 2C, P)

27	A	London Welsh	Lost	34	42	A.Smallwood (T) D.Addleton (T) J.Horrobin (T) S.Gough (2C, 4P) L.Criscuolo (D)
Mar 13	H	Rugby Lions	Lost	19	21	S.Gough (T, C, 4P)
27	A	Fylde	Lost	22	27	S.Kerr (T) S.Gough (T, 2C, P) A.Smallwood (T)
Apr 3	H	Exeter	Won	20	13	M.Curtis (T) L.Crofts (T) S.Gough (2C, 2P)
17	A	Waterloo Drummers	Won	25	24	A.Smallwood (T) S.Gough (T, 2C, 2P) T.Dawson (T)
24	H	Worcester	Won	26	17	A.Smallwood (2T) S.Gough (2C, 4P)
May 1	A	Moseley	Lost	29	30	J.Horrobin (T) M.Crane (T) N.Watkins (T) R.Salisbury (T) S.Gough (3C, P)
8	H	Wakefield	Won	40	13	A.Smallwood (4T) M.Mafi (T) C.Houston (T) S.Gough (2C, 2P)

Summary of Premiership scorers:

305 S.Gough (10T, 48C, 53P); 75 A.Smallwood (15T); 27 M.Gallagher (3T, 3C, 2P); 25 R.Robinson (5T), W.Kilford (5T), J.Horrobin (5T); 20 D.Eves (4T), L.Criscuolo (T, 3C, 3D), L.Crofts (4T); 15 Penalty (3T), K.Whitley (3T), M.Mafi (3T); 10 N.Watkins (2T), M.Curtis (2T), M.Crane (2T); 5 R.Salisbury (T), J.Minshull (T), S.Kerr (T), C.Houston (T), M.Fountaine (T), T.Dawson (T), D.Addleton (T).

Summary of Premiership appearances:

26 S.Gough (+1), D.Addleton (+3); 25 L.Crofts; 24 K.Whitley, M.Fountaine (+4); 23 J.Horrobin; 22 A.Smallwood (+2), T.Dawson (+3), M.Curtis (+3), M.Crane (+5); 20 R.Robinson (+7), L.Criscuolo (+3); 19 J.Minshull (+1); 18 M.Gallagher (+2); 17 D.Eves (+1); 16 W.Kilford (+3); 15 A.Sharp, S.Kerr (+6); 13 R.Salisbury (+8); 11 A.McAdam (+4);10 N.Watkins (+4); 9 C.Houston, J.Hewlett (+4); 8 R.Morgan(+5), M.Mika (+1); 7 M.Mafi (+1); 6 M.Wallwork (+3), J.Soden(+3); 5 A.Kershaw (+4), R.Eyres (+5); 3 R.Hyslop (+2); 2 J.Hadfield (+2), S.Edwards; 1 B.Dale (+1).

EXETER CHIEFS

Formation of club: 1872
Ground: County Ground, Church Road, St Thomas, Exeter EX2 9BQ
Capacity: 5,200 (Seated 700)
Colours: Black and white with Cambridge blue
Honours: Division Four Champions – 1995-96. Division Three Champions – 1996-97
Best League Finish: 5th in Premiership Two 1998-99
Best Cup run: QF 1992-93, 1994-95
Last season: Premiership Two – 5th. Tetley's Bitter Cup – 5th round (lost 10-37 to Richmond)
Owner: Members
Rugby manager/coach: Ian Bremner
Captain: Rob Baxter

ALVIS, James Nicholas (Prop)
Born Clifton, 19.12.70. 5′11″, 18st 10lb. **ADPR**: Exeter (1997-99, 44, 12t-60pts). Remarkably mobile try-scoring prop who is a schoolteacher at Blundells. Formerly with Newport, Pontypridd and Cardiff.

ARMSTRONG, Robert William (Backrow)
Born Liverpool, 17.08.67. 6′4″, 18st. **ADPR:** Plymouth Albion (1990-92, 17, 2t-8pts), Bristol (1992-96, 40), Exeter (1996-99, 59, 14t-70pts). Royal Marines officer and former Inter-Services super-heavyweight boxing champion. Played for the Combined Services against the 1993 All Blacks.

BARROW, Craig Anthony (Backrow)
Born Leicester, 26.02.69. 6′6″, 16st 7lb. **ADPR:** Exeter (1990-91, 6), Bristol (1991-97, 61, 3t-14pts), Exeter (1997-99, 42, 4t-20pts). Athletic operator at No 8 who also enjoys sevens. Formerly at Exeter University, Craig also represented England Students.

BAXTER, Richard John (Flanker)
Born Exeter, 23.06.78. **ADPR:** Exeter (1997-99, 30, 5t-25pts). Powerful blindside wing forward who has also played for Upper Clapton and Loughborough University.

BAXTER, Robert Edward (Lock)
Born Tavistock, 10.03.71. 6′5″, 16st 7lb. **ADPR:** Exeter (1989-99, 132, 9t-44pts). Former England Colt who has spent his entire rugby career at the County Ground save for a short spell at Gloucester. Club captain who missed just one League game last season. Rob is a farmer and son of Exeter chairman John Baxter.

BEATTIE, Andrew James (No 8)
Born London, 06.09.78. **ADPR:** Exeter (1998-99, 14, 2t-10pts). Outstanding former England Schools cap who made an immediate impression last season after joining from Richmond.

CROSS, Derek Lionel (Lock)
Born Watford, 05.08.71. **ADPR:** Exeter (1996-99, 35, 2t-10pts). Reliable second row who joined from Devonport Services.

DOYLE, Sean Michael (Full-back/wing)
Born Exeter, 21.08.74. 6′, 14st 10lb. **ADPR:** Exeter (1992-99, 81, 18t-90pts). Strong-running wing who originally joined from the Tiverton club. Works for SW Telecoms.

EASSON, Bryan Robert (Fly-half)
Born St Andrews, Scotland, 08.10.73. 5′8″, 13st. **ADPR:** Exeter (1998-99, 26, 2t, 39c, 51pg-241pts). Influential Scottish fly-half who had an immediate impact when moving south of the border last season. Formerly with Boroughmuir and Caledonia Reds.

FABIAN, Jon Geoffrey (Full-back)
Born Plymouth, 18.09.76. 6′3″, 14st 7lb. **ADPR:** Exeter (1996-99, 49, 9t, 23c, 50pg-241pts). Exeter University student and former England U21 cap. Formerly with Plymouth Albion.

FOOTE, Blair M. (Flanker)
Born New Zealand, 08.05.73. 6′3″, 14st 2lb. Has played for Waikato and North Harbour in New Zealand.

GIBBINS, Richard John (Prop)
Born 06.08.67. **ADPR:** Exeter (1987-99, 147, 5t-25pts). Loyal club man who remains a permanent fixture in the Exeter front row.

GREENAWAY, Phillip Christopher (Full-back)
Born Exeter, 01.09.78. **ADPR:** Exeter (1997-99, 10). Young full-back who has already had spells at Clifton, Bristol and Moseley.

HARGREAVES, Paul Austin (Wing)
Born Bury, 07.01.78. **ADPR:** Exeter (1998-99, 3, 1t-5pts). Joined from Crediton at the beginning of the 1998-99 season.

HUTCHINSON, Roger Anthony (Flanker)
Born Singapore, 21.11.69. 6′, 14st 7lb. **ADPR:** Exeter (1991-99, 95, 12t-60pts). Another key player in the pack, Roger is a former England Students cap.

JOHN, Phillip (Hooker)
Born Merthyr Tydfil, 05.02.62. 5′9″, 14st. **Rep hons:** Wales A (1, Fr89), Barbarians (88-89). **ADPR:** Exeter (1998-99, 21, 1t-5pts). Immensely powerful and experienced former Pontypridd hooker who was a key figure in Ponty's success stories during the 90s.

JOHN, Richard Simon (Scrum-half)
Born Exeter, 30.05.74. 5′10″, 13st. **ADPR:** Exeter (1995-99, 50, 6t-30pts). Educated at Sealehayne Agricultural College and works as a conservationist. Joined from Crediton.

LAITY, Colin (Centre)
Born Helston, 19.06.65. 5′11″, 14st 3lb. **ADPR:** Exeter (1998-99, 12, 2t-10pts). Cornishman who made his name alongside John Devereux in the South Glamorgan Institute side of 1985. Subsequently played for Neath, Aberavon and Cardiff and was even included in the Welsh squad before returning to the West Country.

PELLOW, Ricky (Scrum-half/centre)
Born Helston, 19.02.78. 5′8″, 11st 7lb. **ADPR:** Bath (1997-98, 5), Exeter (1998-99, 16). Former Colston's Collegiate and England Schools scrum-half who relished regular first-team rugby last season after moving from Bath.

REED, Wayne (Prop)
Born Tiverton, 27.10.71. 5′10″, 17st 6lb. **ADPR:** Exeter (1995-99, 47, 6t-30pts).

ROSE, Mark Antony (Full-back/wing)
Born 17.03.71. 5′11″, 14st 1lb. **ADPR:** Exeter (1998-99, 15, 2t-10pts).

SLUMAN, Philip John (Prop)
Born Exeter, 15.03.67. 6′, 17st. **ADPR:** Exeter (1989-99, 94, 4t-19pts).

THOMAS, Jason Paul (Centre)
Born Aberdare, 02.03.71. 5′9″, 11st 7lb. **ADPR:** Exeter (1994-99, 75, 12t, 1dg-63pts). Formerly with Paignton.

TURNER, Andrew Keith (Centre)
Born Saddleworth, 27.11.70. 6′1″, 14st. **ADPR:** Exeter (1989-99, 107, 12t-60pts). Manufacturer of pharmaceutical products.

WALL, Christopher (Wing)
Born Bath, 14.02.76. **ADPR:** Exeter (1998-99, 10, 4t-20pts). Strong wing who has also played for UWIC.

WEBBER, Lee Robert (Centre)
Born Plymouth, 25.10.75. 5′10″, 13st 2lb. **ADPR:** Exeter (1997-99, 27, 4t-20pts). Formerly with Tavistock and Northampton.

WESTCOTT, Shaun
Born 15.04.71. **ADPR:** Exeter (1994-99, 13).

WILLIS, Gary (Flanker)
Born Billingham, 07.10.68. **ADPR:** Exeter (1997-99, 28, 5t-25pts). Formerly with Torquay and Bristol.

WOODMAN, Mark Charles (Wing)
Born Exeter, 18.09.70. 6′, 15st. **ADPR:** Bath (1993-94, 1, 1t-5pts), Exeter (1995-99, 80, 29t-145pts). Prolific try-scorer, formerly with Crediton and Bath.

WOOLTORTON, Martyn John (Hooker)
Born Leeds, 03.03.67. 5′10″, 14st. **ADPR:** Exeter (1994-99, 48, 2t-10pts). Royal Marine who numbers Morley, Plymouth, and Huddersfield YMCA among his former clubs.

REVIEW

Could Exeter finally be on the verge of achieving their enormous potential? Under director of rugby Ian Bremner they took giant strides forward to finish fifth last season and now have their sights set firmly on Premiership One rugby. Former Scotland A fly-half Bryan Easson proved an inspired signing, contributing 241 points, while Mark Woodman was the side's most penetrative runner, scoring nine tries. Up front, captain Rob Baxter, prop James Alvis and Royal Marine Rob Armstrong in the backrow were as reliable as ever.

EXETER CHIEFS in Premiership Two 1998-99

Sep	5	H	Bristol	Lost	15	22	B.Easson (5P)
	12	A	Rotherham	Lost	17	28	A.Turner (T) J.Alvis (T) B.Easson (2C, P)
	19	H	Coventry	Won	31	25	J.Alvis (T) B.Easson (T, 2C, 4P) D.Cross (T)
	26	A	Wakefield	Won	27	19	J.Fabian (T) L.Webber (T) B.Armstrong (T) B.Easson (4P)
Oct	3	H	Moseley	Won	20	8	M.Woodman (T) J.Thomas (T) J.Fabian (T) B.Easson (C, P)
	10	A	Worcester	Lost	15	40	J.Alvis (T) P.John (T) B.Easson (C, P)
	17	H	Waterloo Drummers	Won	41	14	J.Fabian (4T) D.Cross (T) C.Wall (T) R.E.Baxter (T) B.Easson (3C)
	25	H	Leeds Tykes	Won	13	11	Penalty (T) B.Easson (C, 2P)
	31	A	Fylde	Drew	26	26	R.Hutchinson (T) J.Alvis (T) B.Easson (2C, 4P)
Nov	7	H	Rugby Lions	Lost	7	23	J.Alvis (T) B.Easson (C)
	21	A	London Welsh	Lost	27	62	W.Reed (T) L.Wilkinson (T) R.John (T) M.Woodman (T) A.Beattie (T) B.Easson (C)
Dec	12	H	Blackheath	Won	26	7	P.Hargreaves (T) P.Sluman (T) R.John (T) B.Easson (C, 3P)
	19	A	Orrell	Won	23	21	L.Wilkinson (T) B.Armstrong (T) B.Easson (2C, 3P)
Jan	2	H	London Welsh	Lost	16	17	M.Woodman (T) B.Easson (C, 3P)

	23	H	Fylde	Won	42	10	R.J.Baxter (3T) C.Laity (T) M.Woodman (T) Penalty (T) B.Easson (3C, 2P)
Feb	7	A	Leeds Tykes	Lost	7	44	C.Barrow (T) B.Easson (C)
	13	A	Waterloo Drummers	Won	13	11	R.E.Baxter (T) B.Easson (C, 2P)
	27	H	Worcester	Won	27	23	L.Webber (T) A.Beattie (T) B.Armstrong (T) B.Easson (3C, 2P)
Mar	13	A	Moseley	Won	15	12	J.Alvis (T) M.Woodman (T) B.Easson (C, P)
	21	A	Rugby Lions	Lost	9	13	B.Easson (3P)
	27	H	Wakefield	Won	37	13	G.Willis (2T) M.Woodman (2T) L.Webber (T) B.Easson (3C, 2P)
Apr	3	A	Coventry	Lost	13	20	M.Rose (T) G.Willis (T) B.Easson (P)
	10	A	Blackheath	Won	41	26	B.Armstrong (T) L.Webber (T) M.Woodman (T) M.Rose (T) P.Sluman (T) R.John (T) B.Easson (T, 3C)
	17	H	Rotherham	Lost	24	35	M.Woodman (T) R.E.Baxter (T) B.Easson (C, 4P)
	24	A	Bristol	Lost	17	36	C.Wall (2T) C.Barrow (T) B.Easson (C)
May	1	H	Orrell	Won	42	32	W.Reed (3T) C.Laity (T) C.Wall (T) B.Easson (4C, 3P)

Summary of Premiership scorers:

241 B.Easson (2T, 39C, 51P); 45 M.Woodman (9T); 30 J.Fabian (6T), J.Alvis (6T); 20 L.Webber (4T), C.Wall (4T), W.Reed (4T), B.Armstrong (4T); 15 G.Willis (3T), R.John (3T), R.E.Baxter (3T) R.J.Baxter (3T); 10 Penalty (2T), L.Wilkinson (2T), P.Sluman (2T), M.Rose (2T), C.Laity (2T), D.Cross (2T), A.Beattie (2T), C.Barrow (2T); 5 A.Turner (T), J.Thomas (T), P.John (T), R.Hutchinson (T), P.Hargreaves (T).

Summary of Premiership appearances:

26 B.Easson; 25 G.Willis (+1), R.E.Baxter; 24 B.Armstrong (+3); 23 D.Cross; 22 J.Alvis (+9); 21 M.Woodman, P.John, R.John (+3), J.Fabian (+3); 20 L.Webber, P.Sluman (+3), W.Reed (+8), C.Barrow (+11); 19 R.Gibbins (+9), R.J.Baxter (+8); 16 R.Pellow (+8), R.Hutchinson (+8); 15 M.Rose (+1); 14 A.Beattie (+7); 12 C.Laity; 11 A.Turner; 10 C.Wall, P.Greenaway (+8); 7 J.Thomas (+1), M.Craig; 6 D.Oxland (+6), S.Doyle (+1); 4 N.Southern (+4), S.Ryan (+1); 3 M.Wooltorton (+1), J.Sussex (+3), P.Hargreaves; 2 N.Osman (+1), L.Ingledon (+2); 1 S.Westcott (+1), S.Shortland, J.Purnell, J.Kindon (+1), B.Goss (+1).

HENLEY HAWKS

Formation of club: 1930
Ground: Dry Leas, Marlow Road, Henley-on-Thames, Oxfordshire RG9 2JA
Capacity: 3,000 (Seated 120)
Colours: Gold with navy and dark green hoops
Honours: Champions South West Two – 1992, South West One – 1994, Jewson One – 1999
Best Cup run: Last 16 1997-98
Last season: Jewson One – Champions. Tetley's Bitter Cup – 5th round (lost 9-31 to Gloucester)
Director of rugby: Tony Macarthur
Coach: Nigel Dudding and Mike Poulson
Captain: TBC

AYRES, Benjamin Matthew (Scrum-half)
Born Crickhowell, 07.05.74. **ADPR:** Reading (1997-98, 9, 2t-10pts), Henley (1998-99, 25, 7t-35pts). Formerly with Bedford and Wasps.

BARNES, Stephen Barry (Flanker)
Born Henley-on-Thames, 29.10.71. **ADPR:** Northampton (1996-98, 9), Henley (1998-99, 22). Learned his rugby at High Wycombe.

CASSIDY, Darren Scott (Hooker)
Born Great Yarmouth, 13.07.67. 5′9″, 14st 4lb. **ADPR:** Henley (1998-99, 5). Feisty hooker who first came to prominence during Bicester's appearances at Twickenham in the Pilkington Shield in the early 80s. Has also enjoyed spells at Northampton and Chinnor.

DAVIES, Peter Allan (Wing)
Born Newport, Gwent, 01.12.75. 5′8″, 12st. **ADPR:** Henley (1998-99, 23, 14t-70pts). Wales Schools, U21 and Universities representative. Joined from UWIC in 1998 and was second highest try-scorer in the Jewson League last season. Works as a teacher.

FULLER, Rowan Hedley (Prop)
Born Wigan, 01.11.72. 5′10″, 16st 7lb. **ADPR:** Newcastle (1991-94, 23, 1t-5pts), Moseley (1994-96, 21,1t-5pts), Reading (1997-98, 8), Henley (1998-99, 15, 1t-5pts). Systems analyst who is a former England Schools cap.

HOBBS, Benjamin Paul (Scrum-half)
Born Bath, 11.04.75. 5′8″, 15st. **ADPR:** Henley (1997-99, 12, 2t-10pts). Company researcher who played all his junior rugby at Bath before studying at Brunel University and joining Saracens. Hampered last season by a shoulder injury.

HOLDER, Dean Marcus (Backrow)
Born Cheltenham, 02.06.69. 6′3″, 16st 4lb. **ADPR:** Newcastle (1995-96, 9, 1t-5pts), Harrogate (1996-98, 27, 8t-40pts). RAF officer who has represented the Combined Services.

LEHNER, Raymond Paul (Prop)
Born Sacramento, USA, 13.03.72. 6′1″, 17st 3lb. **Rep hons:** USA (27, Canada95). **ADPR:** Henley (1998-99, 5). Mature student, an Oxford Blue in 1997, who expects to be available after the World Cup.

MORTIMORE, Alistair (No 8)
Born Okehampton, 12.12.73. 6′2″, 16st. **ADPR:** Bedford (1993-96, 3), Henley (1997-99, 50, 6t-30pts). Major force in the Bedford backrow. Sales manager who joined from Bedford in August 1997.

NOYCE, Andrew Thomas (Wing/centre)
Born Crawley, 19.03.76. 6′, 13st 8lb. **ADPR:** Henley (1998-99, 1). Promising goal-kicker, formerly with Northampton

OSMAN, Philip Scott (Fly-half)
Born Exeter, 18.12.68. 6′, 13st 7lb. **ADPR:** Newbury (1996-97, 5, 4c, 1pg-11pts), Henley (1997-99, 40, 8t, 14c, 10pg, 8dg-122pts). Schoolteacher who has also played for Harlequins and Nottingham.

OSMAN, Russell James (Centre)
Born Southampton, 17.06.72. 6′1″, 13st 8lb. **ADPR:** Harlequins (1994-95, 2), Newbury (1996-98, 32, 11t-55pts), Henley (1998-99, 24, 9t-45pts). Solicitor and brother of Phil.

PARTON, Andrew Richard (Full-back)
Born Coventry, 31.01.68. 6′2″, 14st 7lb. **ADPR:** Coventry (1987-91, 19, 5t-20pts), Harlequins (1992-93, 1), Rosslyn Park (1994-95, 7, 1t, 3c, 6pg-29pts), Henley (1995-99, 48, 17t, 5c, 3pg-104pts). Cambridge Blue in 1990-91 and a member of the England Students team at the 1992 World Students Cup in Italy. Educated at King Henry VIII School, Coventry and St Edmund's House, Cambridge.

PHILLIPS, Willie W. (Utility forward)
Born Paparoa, New Zealand, 16.04.59. 5′10″, 14st 11lb. **ADPR:** Coventry (1993-94, 8, 2t-10pts), Henley (1994-99, 97, 20t-100pts). Represented North Auckland 99 times, mainly as a flanker. Technically a veteran but formidably fit.

RAMUS, Alistair Stewart (Lock/No 8)
Born Harrogate, 16.05.78. 6′5″, 16st 8lb. **ADPR:** West Hartlepool (1996-97, 2), Harrogate (1997-98, 1), Henley (1998-99, 2). Sales executive and former England Colts cap.

ROKE, Duncan John (Centre/fly-half)
Born Mtarfa, Malta, 05.07.74. 6′2″, 13st. **ADPR:** Leicester (1997-98, 1), Henley (1998-99, 13, 6t, 20c, 15pg-115pts). Clinical trials manager. Joined Henley in November after being released by Leicester. Has quickly become a key player.

SAMPSON, Jeremy (Lock)
Born London, 04.06.69. 6′4″, 16st 8lb. **ADPR:** Blackheath (1993-96, 18, 1t-5pts), Henley (1995-99, 68, 5t-25pts). Experienced campaigner who played for Weston-super-Mare before joining Blackheath. Voted clubman of the year last season. Works as a business information analyst.

SHARP, Gavin (Wing/centre)
Born Scarborough, 04.01.75. 5′9″, 13st 11lb. **ADPR:** Bristol (1994-96, 20, 5t-25pts), Henley (1996-99, 59, 35t-175pts). Devastating runner who has scored 35 tries in just 59 League games for Henley. Works as a civilian fireman for the RAF and represented the Combined Services against the All Blacks in 1997. Has also played for Scarborough.

STEBBINGS, Jonathan Peter Carless (Centre/full-back)
Born Wokingham, 28.10.76. 5′11″, 13st 6lb. **ADPR:** Henley (1998-99, 18, 2t, 8c, 12pg-62pts). Student who arrived at Henley from London Irish in 1998. Has played for Irish Exiles and England Students.

VENNER, Mark Richard (Flanker)
Born Weston-super-Mare, 14.04.69. 6′2″, 15st. **ADPR:** Weston-super-Mare (1994-97, 34, 12t-60pts), Henley (1997-99, 50, 24t-120pts). Mobile flanker with an eye for a try. Accountant who joined Henley from Weston-super-Mare in 1997 and top-scored the following season with 11 League tries. Has captained Somerset in the County Championship final and also represented the Barbarians.

WALKER, Giles (Prop)
Born Aylesbury, 07.07.71. 6′1″, 15st. **ADPR:** Henley (1997-99, 17, 3t-15pts). Backrow player who has moved into the front row. Formerly with Cholsey.

WALKER, Robert Charles (Flanker)
Born Aylesbury, 11.05.73. 6'2", 15st 8lb. **ADPR:** Henley (1995-99, 42, 5t-25pts). Talented backrow man and brother of Giles. Works as a chartered accountant. Also from the Cholsey club.

WALSH, Trevor Andrew (Centre)
Born Townsville, Australia, 18.01.72. 6', 14st. **Rep hons:** Barbarians (98-99). **ADPR:** Henley (1997-99, 41, 8t-40pts). Investment banker who won an Oxford Blue in 1996. Has represented Queensland U21 and Australian Universities and played for the Barbarians against Combined Services and East Midlands in 1998-99. Educated at St Joseph's, Brisbane and Keble College, Oxford.

REVIEW

The Henley success story continues. After winning promotion the previous season, Henley stormed into Premiership Two by taking Jewson National League One in some style, four points ahead of second-placed Manchester with Rosslyn Park fully 10 points adrift. Coach Nigel Dudding, who took over after England coach Clive Woodward had put in a six-year spell at Dry Leas, can be proud of his charges. In a strong squad Duncan Roke emerged as top scorer on 115 League points while wing Peter Davies comfortably topped the try-scoring charts with 14.

HENLEY HAWKS in Jewson One 1998-99

Sep	5	H	Harrogate	Lost	5	20	R.Osman (T)
	12	A	Wharfedale	Won	8	6	M.Venner (T) J.Stebbings (P)
	19	H	Manchester	Won	39	20	R.Osman (T) T.Walsh (T) B.Ayres (T) W.Phillips (T) S.Berryman (T) J.Stebbings (4C, P) P.Osman (D)
	26	A	Nottingham	Won	35	6	M.Venner (2T) J.Sampson (T) R.Walker (T) R.Osman (T) J.Stebbings (C, P) M.Maudsley (C) P.Osman (P)
Oct	3	H	Camberley	Won	22	7	J.Stebbings (T, 3P) B.Ayres (T) P.Osman (D)
	10	H	Newbury	Won	44	10	B.Ayres (2T) G.Sharp (2T) M.Maudsley (T, 3C, P) R.Osman (T) P.Davies (T)
	24	A	Morley	Won	13	10	Penalty (T) J.Stebbings (C, 2P)
	31	H	Lydney	Won	23	11	G.Sharp (T) M.Venner (T) J.Stebbings (2C, 3P)
Nov	7	A	Otley	Lost	8	19	M.Maudsley (T) J.Stebbings (P)
	21	H	Reading	Won	25	9	P.Davies (2T) R.Osman (T) D.Roke (2C) M.Maudsley (2P)
	28	A	Rosslyn Park	Won	10	7	P.Davies (T) W.Phillips (T)
Dec	5	H	Birmingham/ Solihull	Won	26	13	G.Sharp (2T) M.Maudsley (T, 3C) Penalty (T)
	12	A	Liverpool St Helens	Won	67	12	G.Sharp (3T) P.Davies (2T) M.Maudsley (T, 7C) P.Osman (T, D) R.Fuller (T) M.Venner (T) Penalty (T)

19	H	Rosslyn Park	Won	18	15	P.Davies (T) R.Osman (T) M.Maudsley (C, 2P)
28	A	Reading	Won	36	6	J.Hendriksz (T) A.Mortimore (T) J.Stebbings (T) M.Venner (T) M.Maudsley (2C, 2P) P.Osman (2D)
Jan 2	H	Otley	Won	5	0	J.Sampson (T)
23	H	Morley	Won	24	13	P.Osman (T) D.Roke (T, 3C, P) J.Sampson (T)
Feb 6	A	Camberley	Won	31	19	D.Roke (2T, 2C, 4P) R.Osman (T)
13	H	Nottingham	Won	43	24	B.Ayres (2T) M.Venner (T) D.Roke (T, 4C) R.Osman (T) P.Osman (T) M.Maudsley (T)
20	A	Newbury	Drew	26	26	P.Davies (2T) D.Roke (T,C, 3P)
27	A	Manchester	Lost	7	13	G.Sharp (T) D.Roke (C)
Mar 13	H	Wharfedale	Won	30	0	P.Davies (T) J.Hendriksz (T) M.Venner (T) P.Osman (T) M.Maudsley (2C) D.Roke (2P)
20	A	Lydney	Won	7	0	J.Hendriksz (T) D.Roke (C)
27	A	Harrogate	Won	31	17	P.Davies (3T) T.Walsh (T) J.Hendriksz (T) D.Roke (3C)
Apr 3	H	Liverpool St Helens	Won	39	8	J.Sampson (T) B.Ayres (T) G.Sharp (T) M.Venner (T) R.Osman (T) D.Roke (T, 2C) P.Davies (T)
17	A	Birmingham/ Solihull	Won	22	8	T.Walsh (T) D.Roke (C, 5P)

Summary of League scorers:

115 D.Roke (6T, 20C, 15P); 84 M.Maudsley (5T, 19C, 7P); 70 P.Davies (14T); 62 J.Stebbings (2T, 8C, 12P); 50 G.Sharp (10T); 45 M.Venner (9T), R.Osman (9T); 38 P.Osman (4T, P, 5D); 35 B.Ayres (7T); 20 J.Sampson (4T), J.Hendriksz (4T); 15 Penalty (3T), T.Walsh (3T); 10 W.Phillips (2T); 5 R.Walker (T), A.Mortimore (T), R.Fuller (T), S.Berryman (T).

LEEDS TYKES

Founded: 1992 by merger of Headingley (founded 1878) and Roundhay (1924)
Address: Headingley Stadium, St Michael's Lane, Headingley, Leeds LS6 3BR
Capacity: 23,000 (Seated 9,000)
Colours: Royal blue, white and gold
Best League finish: 6th in Premiership Two 1998-99
Best Cup run: Last 16 in 1995-96, 1998-99
Last season: Premiership Two – 6th. Tetley's Bitter Cup – 5th round (lost 0-49 to Leicester Tigers)
Owners: Members
Chief executive: Gary Hetherington
Director of rugby: Phil Davies
Captain: Scott Benton

BENSON, Jonathan (Wing)
Born Co. Durham, 11.01.76. 6', 13st. **ADPR:** West Hartlepool (1995-99, 34, 6t, 10c, 10pg-80pts). Former Durham City star who worked hard with West Hartlepool to overcome a serious knee injury. England Schools cap.

BENTON, Scott (Scrum-half)
Born Bradford, 08.09.74. 5'11", 14st 2lb. **Rep hons**: England (1, Aus98), A (6, Otago97, 3t-15pts), Barbarians (97-98). **ADPR:** Morley (1992-96, 23, 6t-30pts), Gloucester (1995-96, 59, 8t, 4pg-52pts). Fell into dispute with Gloucester last season and happily accepted an offer to return to Yorkshire as Leeds captain. Won senior honours on England's ill-starred tour of Australasia in 1998 when he emerged with much honour. A former England Colts captain, he played with Morley before joining Gloucester.

CAWTHORN, Michael (Scrum-half)
Born Bridlington, 15.05.72. 5'10", 13st 10lb. **ADPR:** Wakefield (1993-95, 6), Leeds (1996-99, 61, 15t-75pts).

CLARK, Joseph (Hooker)
Born Bristol, 03.06.77. 5'10", 15st. **ADPR:** Moseley (1997-98, 7), Fylde (1998-99, 14), Leeds (1998-99, 5). Formerly with Bath.

DENHAM, Lee Francis (Flanker)
Born 05.03.74. 6'1", 17st 3lb. **ADPR:** Leeds (1995-99, 48, 9t-45pts). Continued his supersub role as an impact player last season when he came off the bench on no less than 16 occasions. Formerly with Sale. Army and Combined Services representative.

DUNCOMBE, Matthew Nicholas (Fly-half)
Born Leicester, 27.08.75. 6', 13st. **ADPR:** Leeds (1998-99, 3, 1dg-3pts). Loughborough University graduate.

EDWARDS, Diccon (Centre)
Born London, 13.03.73. 5'8", 13st 10lb. **Rep hons:** Wales A (2, Fr95). **ADPR:** Wakefield (1992-94, 23, 2t-10pts), Leicester (1994-95, 15), Leeds (1996-99, 49, 6t-30pts).Represented England Schools, Colts and U21 before opting for Wales in 1995 and winning A caps. Joined Leeds from Leicester in 1997 and has done well since overcoming a persistent knee problem. Formerly with Castleford RL. Educated at Pocklington and Loughborough.

EMMERSON, Craig Anthony (Centre)
Born Halifax, 14.09.71. 5'11", 13st 4lb. **ADPR:** West Hartlepool (1991-92, 1), Morley (1992-96, 37, 5t-25pts), Gloucester (1996-98, 13), Leeds (1998-99, 22, 2t-10pts). Has done well since returning to Yorkshire from Gloucester where his first-team opportunities were limited.

FAULKNER, Robert William (Prop)
Born Alexandria, Scotland, 04.04.77. 6', 18st. **ADPR:** Harrogate (1996-98, 21, 3t-15pts), Leeds (1998-99, 1). Formerly with Bath and Plymouth.

FEELEY, Jonathan Michael (Wing)
Born Bradford, 12.04.79. 6', 13st. **ADPR:** Leeds (1998-99, 8, 4t-20pts). Promising wing, England U21 cap.

FOURIE, Timothy Wayne (No 8)
Born Port Elizabeth, South Africa, 12.03.68. 6'4", 16st. **ADPR:** Leeds (1997-99, 48, 19t-95pts). Powerful South African flanker who has played for the Centurions back home as well as Northern Transvaal.

HUGHES, Adam (Centre)
Born Leeds, 01.10.77. **ADPR:** Leeds (1998-99, 1).

JAMES, Andrew David (Full-back)
Born Neath, 02.03.76. 5′10″, 13st. **ADPR:** Leeds (1998-99, 18, 2t, 10c, 1pg-33pts). Had an excellent first season with the club after joining from Seven Sisters near Swansea.

LANCASTER, William **Stuart** (Flanker)
Born Penrith, 09.10.69. 6′, 14st. **ADPR:** Leeds (1992-99, 59, 6t-30pts). Formerly with Wakefield.

LE BAS, Richard Leslie Joffre (Fly-half)
Born Carterton, New Zealand, 26.07.71. 5′10″, 14st. **ADPR:** Moseley (1996-97, 14, 3t, 27c, 36pg-177pts), Worcester (1997-99, 46, 13t, 86c, 46pg, 1dg-378pts). Big-kicking Kiwi who has also played for Northland and North Auckland.

LUFFMAN, Mark Edward (Hooker)
Born Nottingham, 17.08.71. 6′, 14st 3lb. **ADPR:** Otley (1995-96, 10, 1t-5pts), Leeds (1996-99, 76, 3t-15pts). Durable flanker who has been a key member of the pack since arriving from Otley in 1996. Ever-present last season. Formerly with Ilkley.

MIDDLETON, Simon (Wing)
Born Kellington, 02.02.66. 5′10″, 13st 8lb. **ADPR:** Otley (1996-97, 8, 2t-10pts), Leeds (1997-99, 34, 27t-135pts). Joint top try-scorer last season with 10. Formerly with Castleford RL.

O'HARE, Hefin Bryn (Centre)
Born Wrexham, 02.06.79. 5′10″, 14st. **ADPR:** New Brighton (1997-98, 19, 4t-20pts), Leeds (1998-99, 19, 4t-20pts). Wales U21 representative.

OLIVER, Matthew James (Centre/wing)
Born Northampton, 30.11.76. 6′1″, 13st 7lb. **ADPR:** Bedford (1994-98, 37, 13t-65pts), Orrell (1997-99, 19, 7t-35pts). England U21 centre who impressed at Orrell last season after arriving from Bedford where he struck up a fine centre partnership with Ben Whetstone.

PALMER, Thomas (Flanker)
Born London, 27.03.79. 6′5″, 16st. **ADPR:** Leeds (1998-99, 23, 1t-5pts). Former New Zealand Schools representative. Voted Leeds' Young Player of the Season for 1998-99.

PONTON, James William (Flanker)
Born Hexham, 31.07.74. 6′3″, 14st 7lb. **ADPR:** West Hartlepool (1997-99, 44, 5t-25pts). An outstanding performer for West in their promotion year (97-98) and again last season when things were much more difficult. Formerly with Percy Park and Tynedale.

RADACANU, Christian (Lock)
Born Bucharest, Romania, 02.10.67. 6′6″, 16st 9lb. **Rep hons:** Romania. **ADPR:** Headingley (1990-91, 5), Sale (1991-92, 7, 1t-4pts), Leeds (1994-99, 72, 28t-140pts). Vastly experienced former Romanian international who sought political asylum in this country after their tour in 1989. Has also played for Bradford & Bingley.

RAWLINSON, Robert John (Prop)
Born Littleborough, 23.08.76. 6′, 16st. **ADPR:** Orrell (1995-99, 36). Developing prop who also spent a season with the Pirates club in Johannesburg.

SHELLEY, Michael John (Prop)
Born Leeds, 02.03.74. 6′2″, 18st 4lb. **ADPR:** West Hartlepool (1994-96, 18, 4t-20pts), Leeds (1996-99,74, 13t-65pts). Former England Students representative who will serve as vice-captain this season under Scott Benton.

STEPHENS, Colin John (Fly-half)
Born Morriston, 29.11.69. 5′7″, 13st. **Rep hons:** Wales (4, Ire92, 2pg, 1dg-9pts), A (3, Can89, 1t, 2pg, 1dg-14pts), Barbarians (90-91). **ADPR:** Leeds (1995-99, 55, 17t, 19c,

23pg, 13dg-231pts). Mercurial Welsh fly-half who as a youngster with Llanelli looked destined for great things after a glittering schoolboy career. Duly won four senior caps but the selectors dropped him with indecent haste and serious knee injuries have plagued him in recent years.

SWARBRIGG, Jonathan William Desmond (Scrum-half)
Born 16.09.69. 5′9″, 12st 10lb. **ADPR:** Headingley (1990-91, 9), Leeds (1992-99, 26, 2t-10pts).

SWIFT, Michael (Flanker)
Born Hammersmith, London, 18.10.77. **ADPR:** Richmond (1998-99, 6). Young Ireland qualified backrow man who was pressed into first-team service at Richmond last season.

REVIEW

Ultimately a disappointing season for Leeds who had declared they would be content with nothing less than promotion. Yet Leeds lost three of their first four games and never recovered. Sixth was poor reward for a massive investment in the likes of Australian Rugby League star Wendell Sailor at the club in the autumn – Sailor scored eight tries in just seven League appearances and was sorely missed when he left. Tongan World Cup star Sateki Tuipulotu, the team's goal-kicker, again emerged as top points-scorer with 250 but fell into dispute with the club and left at the end of the season, as did Scotland No 8 Stuart Reid, who departed for Narbonne, and former Ireland scrum-half Chris Saverimutto.

LEEDS TYKES in Premiership Two 1998-99

Sep	6	H	London Welsh	Lost	18	20	M.Cawthorn (T) S.Easterby (T) S.Tuipulotu (C, 2P)
	12	A	Moseley	Lost	22	27	M.Shelley (T) S.Lancaster (T) M.Kirkby (T) S.Tuipulotu (2C, P)
	20	H	Blackheath	Won	60	6	M.Kirkby (2T) J.Feeley (2T) S.Easterby (T) M.Cawthorn (T) S.Reid (T) S.Tuipulotu (T, 6C, P) J.Swarbrigg (T)
	27	A	Worcester	Lost	19	24	Penalty (T) S.Tuipulotu (C, 4P)
Oct	3	A	Orrell	Won	13	11	T.Fourie (T) S.Tuipulotu (C, P) M.Duncombe (D)
	10	A	Waterloo Drummers	Lost	12	13	S.Tuipulotu (4P)
	17	H	Bristol	Lost	13	16	S.Tuipulotu (T, C, 2P)
	25	A	Exeter	Lost	11	13	C.Emmerson (T) S.Tuipulotu (2P)
Nov	1	H	Rotherham	Won	15	10	S.Tuipulotu (5P)
	7	A	Fylde	Won	26	6	W.Sailor (T) T.Fourie (T) H.O'Hare (T) S.Tuipulotu (C, 3P)
	22	H	Coventry	Won	36	12	T.Fourie (2T) D.Edwards (T) W.Sailor (T) S.Tuipulotu (2C, 4P)
Dec	13	A	Rugby Lions	Won	18	9	W.Sailor (T) C.Saverimutto (T) S.Tuipulotu (C, 2P)

	20	H	Wakefield	Won	38	0	W.Sailor (T) S.Tuipulotu (T, 4C) T.Rhodes (T) S.Middleton (T) C.Saverimutto (T) L.Denham (T)
Jan	3	A	Coventry	Won	33	27	C.Saverimutto (T) W.Sailor (T) S.Tuipulotu (C, 7P)
	17	H	Fylde	Won	48	0	W.Sailor (3T) A.James (T, 4C) T.Fourie (T) H.O'Hare (T) M.Shelley (T) J.Scales (T)
	23	A	Rotherham	Lost	10	25	Penalty (T) A.James (C, P)
Feb	7	H	Exeter	Won	44	7	J.Scales (4T) S.Easterby (T) D.Edwards (T) C.Emmerson (T) S.Tuipulotu (2C, P) T.Rhodes (C)
	13	A	Bristol	Lost	5	20	L.Denham (T)
	28	H	Waterloo Drummers	Lost	9	10	S.Tuipulotu (3P)
Mar	14	H	Orrell	Won	20	7	S.Middleton (2T) S.Tuipulotu (2C, 2P)
	28	H	Worcester	Won	24	16	M.Shelley (T) S.Middleton (T) S.Tuipulotu (C, 4P)
Apr	3	A	Blackheath	Won	37	22	S.Easterby (T) S.Middleton (T) A.James (T) T.Fourie (T) J.Scales (T) H.O'Hare (T) S.Tuipulotu (2C, P)
	18	H	Moseley	Won	50	8	S.Easterby (2T) C.Saverimutto (2T) J.Scales (T) T.Fourie (T) S.Middleton (T) L.Denham (T) S.Tuipulotu (5C)
	25	A	London Welsh	Lost	17	24	S.Middleton (T) S.Tuipulotu (4P)
May	2	A	Wakefield	Won	51	13	J.Scales (2T) T.Fourie (2T) M.Shelley (T) P.Jones (T) S.Easterby (T) S.Middleton (T) J.Feeley (T) A.James (3C)
	9	H	Rugby Lions	Won	64	21	S.Middleton (2T) H.O'Hare (T) S.Easterby (T) M.Cawthorn (T) C.Saverimutto (T) P.Jones (T) T.Palmer (T) J.Feeley (T) J.Scales (T) S.Tuipulotu (5C) A.James (2C)

Summary of Premiership scorers:

250 S.Tuipulotu (3T, 38C, 53P); 50 J.Scales (10T), S.Middleton (10T); 45 T.Fourie (9T); 40 W.Sailor (8T), S.Easterby (8T); 33 A.James (2T, 10C, P); 30 C.Saverimutto (6T); 20 M.Shelley (4T), H.O'Hare (4T), J.Feeley (4T); 15 M.Kirkby (3T), L.Denham (3T), M.Cawthorn (3T); 10 Penalty (2T), P.Jones (2T), C.Emmerson (2T), D.Edwards (2T); 7 T.Rhodes (T, C); 5 J.Swarbrigg (T), S.Reid (T), T.Palmer (T), S.Lancaster (T); 3 M.Duncombe (D).

Summary of Premiership appearances:

26 M.Luffman, S.Easterby; 24 H.Thomas (+2), M.Shelley (+2), S.Reid (+3), T.Fourie (+2); 23 T.Palmer (+5), S.Griffiths (+4); 22 S.Tuipulotu, C.Saverimutto (+3), C.Emmerson (+1); 20 M.Beckham (+13); 19 H.O'Hare (+1); 18 A.James (+8),

D.Edwards (+1), L.Denham (+16), M.Cawthorn (+6); 16 T.Rhodes, S.Middleton (+2), P.Jones (+3); 14 S.Lancaster (+7); 10 J.Scales (+3); 8 J.Feeley (+3); 7 W.Sailor (+1), M.Kirkby; 5 C.Stephens (+2), S.Crabb (+3), J.Clark (+5); 4 C.Radacanu (+2); 3 M.Duncombe (+1); 2 J.Swarbrigg (+2); 1 A.Hughes, R.Faulkner.

LONDON WELSH

Formation of club: 1878
Ground: Old Deer Park, Kew Road, Richmond, TW9 2AZ
Capacity: 7,200 (Seated 1,200)
Colours: Scarlet and white
Honours: Division Five South Champions – 1994-95
Best League finish: 4th in Premiership Two 1998-99
Best Cup run: Losing finalist 1984-85
Last season: Premiership Two – 4th. Tetley's Bitter Cup – 3rd round (lost 6-8 to Rotherham)
Owner: Members
General manager: Ron Holley
Director of rugby: Clive Griffiths
Captain: TBC

ALEXANDER, Colin David (Flanker)
Born Johannesburg, South Africa, 31.08.72. **ADPR:** Rugby Lions (1997-98, 19, 3t-15pts), London Welsh (1998-99, 22, 1t-5pts). Formerly with Wanderers in South Africa.

BUCKETT, Ian Martin (Prop)
Born Holywell, 23.12.67. 6′1″, 17st 7lb. **Rep hons:** Wales (3, Ton94), A (9, Holl90), Barbarians (90-91). **ADPR:** London Welsh (1998-99, 25, 1t-5pts). Former Wales prop who immediately strengthened the Exiles front row after joining from Swansea last season. Educated at Holywell HS, and an Oxford Blue in 1992.

CARR, Paul Allan (Lock)
Born London, 25.03.68. 6′7″, 16st. **ADPR:** Fylde (1988-92, 35), Richmond (1992-98, 66, 1t-5pts), London Welsh (1998-99, 23, 1t-5pts).

CURRIER, Andrew Stephen (Centre)
Born Widnes, 08.04.66. 6′4″, 15st 4lb. **ADPR:** London Welsh (1997-99, 47, 28t, 1dg-143pts). Enormously powerful centre who has enjoyed two excellent seasons with the Exiles since switching from Rugby League. Formerly with Widnes and Featherstone, Andy was a GB Rugby League international.

DAWES, Michael Rhodri John (Centre)
Born Walton-on-Thames, 25.01.68. 5′10″, 12st 13lb. **ADPR:** London Welsh (1990-99, 76, 22t, 12c, 8pg-154pts). Reliable utility back, son of former London Welsh and Wales captain John Dawes. Formerly with London Irish.

EDWARDS, Darren (Scrum-half)
Born Maesteg, 25.03.73. 5′8″, 12st 6lb. **ADPR:** Saracens (1996-97, 1), Bedford (1996-97, 5, 3t-15pts), London Welsh (1997-99, 48, 10t-50pts). Feisty scrum-half, sevens specialist.

FITZGERALD, Matthew Francis (Back five forward)
Born London, 07.06.73. 6′4″, 17st. **ADPR:** Richmond (1993-98, 46, 6t-30pts), London Welsh (1998-99, 12).

FRENCH, Gary James (Hooker)
Born St Helens, 02.12.67. 5′11″, 15st. **Rep hons:** England A (1, Arg96). **ADPR:** Liverpool St Helens (1987-92, 9), Orrell (1993-94, 18, 2t-10pts), Bath (1995-98, 4), London Scottish (1997-98, 9, 1t-5pts), London Welsh (1998-99, 21). Educated at Cowley HS where father Ray, the TV commentator and dual international, taught rugby union.

GIRAUD, Martin Pattison (Wing)
Born Essex, 16.11.77. 5′11″, 12st 11lb. **ADPR:** London Welsh (1995-99, 60, 21t-105pts). A speed merchant on the wing, Giraud has a personal best of 10.5sec for 100m. Member of Wales Sevens squad.

GRIFFITHS, Dylan Ellis (Flanker)
Born Ormskirk, 02.09.71. 6′1″, 14st. **ADPR:** London Welsh (1997-99, 13, 3t-15pts). Formerly with Wasps and Richmond.

HOLMES, Garry (Prop)
Born Hampstead, 07.07.65. 5′11″, 17st. **Rep hons:** England A (5, Nam90). **ADPR:** Wasps (1987-95, 62, 2t-9pts), Saracens (1995-97, 13, 1t-5pts), Blackheath (1996-97, 14), London Welsh (1997-99, 47).

JOHANSEN, Ashley David (Lock)
Born Sydney, Australia, 14.03.69. 6′6″, 17st 11lb. **ADPR:** London Welsh (1997-99, 15, 1t-5pts). Former New South Wales lock who played for Eastwood and Gordon.

JONES, Luke Evan (Flanker)
Born Suffolk, 06.11.70. 6′3″, 15st 7lb. **ADPR:** Richmond (1993-97, 39, 6t-30pts), London Welsh (1997-99, 33, 4t-20pts). Formerly with Beccles. Educated at RGS Guildford and St Edmund Hall, Oxford, winning a Blue in 1991.

LANGLEY, Colin James (Lock)
Born Cardiff, 17.10.71. 6′5″, 17st. **ADPR:** London Welsh (1998-99, 23). Experienced lock who began his career at UWIC before joining Cardiff. Has also enjoyed a spell with Stade Francais in Paris. Brother Mark has now left the club.

LEE, Andrew John (Fly-half)
Born Wanstead, 10.11.68. 5′9″, 13st 7lb. **ADPR:** Saracens (1989-99, 67, 8t, 28c, 49pg, 16dg-290pts), London Welsh (1998-99, 15, 1t, 26c, 14pg-99pts). A major success while on loan from Saracens last season. Educated at Chigwell School, Andy is a remarkable all-round sportsman, having represented his country at three sports. He played cricket for England Schools with Graham Thorpe and Nasser Hussain and still plays for Woodford in the Essex League. Played soccer for England Schools and West Ham Youth and finally represented England Schools and Colts rugby sides. Completed his sporting studies at West London Institute.

LURIE, Richard Kirk (Scrum-half)
Born Port Elizabeth, South Africa, 25.09.70. **ADPR:** London Welsh (1998-99, 14, 1t-5pts).

MARDON, Nicholas Robert (Full-back/centre)
Born Dingwall, 24.09.71. **ADPR:** London Welsh (1998-99, 4, 4t-20pts). Formerly with London Broncos.

MILLWARD, Andrew John (Prop)
Born Neath, 01.12.71. 5′10″, 17st. **ADPR:** London Welsh (1997-99, 36, 1t-5pts). A stalwart in the Exiles front row, Andrew played for Penarth and Aberavon after graduating from UWIC.

OLNEY, Charles Brendon (Hooker)
Born Taunton, 11.08.71. 5′11″, 16st 8lb. **ADPR:** Saracens (1993-97, 18), London Welsh (1997-99, 33, 1t-5pts).

PEARCE, Matthew (Fly-half)
Born Bridgend, 03.10.78. **ADPR:** London Welsh (1998-99, 12, 2t, 13c, 13pg-75pts). Formerly with Worcester.

POPE, Stephen Mark (Prop)
Born Harlow, 24.11.73. 5′11″, 17st 2lb. **ADPR:** Blackheath (1995-98, 35), London Welsh (1998-99, 6).

RAYMOND, Richard **Craig** (Fly-half)
Born Llanelli, 30.01.69. 5′11″, 13st 7lb. **ADPR:** London Welsh (1994-99, 82, 22t, 160c, 147pg, 15dg-916pts). Formerly with Bath.

ROSKELL, Scott Thomas (Wing)
Born Gold Coast, Australia, 25.04.70. 6′2″, 15st. **ADPR:** London Welsh (1997-99, 32, 18t-90pts). Formerly with London Broncos.

SAGE, Geoffrey Robert (Lock)
Born Hillingdon, 19.04.68. 6′6″, 17st. **ADPR:** Wasps (1991-92, 1), Richmond (1994-96, 31), London Welsh (1997-99, 14).

SHAW, Peter Daniel Martin (Full-back)
Born Hammersmith, 09.11.73. 5′11″, 13st. **ADPR:** London Welsh (1994-99, 55, 12t-60pts).

STOREY, James Stuart (Wing)
Born Harlow, 26.11.76. 6′3″, 14st. **ADPR:** London Welsh (1997-99, 21, 10t-50pts). Former England Schools cap. Son of GB athlete and BBC commentator Stuart Storey, educated at Haileybury. Formerly with Northampton and Harlequins.

WHITE, Michael Kevin (Flanker)
Born Poole, 30.03.66. 6′1″, 14st 8lb. **Rep hons:** Barbarians (96-97). **ADPR:** Wasps (1987-98, 116, 13t-62pts), London Welsh (1998-99, 21, 7t-35pts). Terrific grafting wing-forward who won championship honours with Wasps before joining London Welsh. Learned his rugby with Swanage & Wareham.

WHITTAKER, Christopher Michael (Lock)
Born Victoria, Canada, 12.09.71. 6′5″, 17st. **Rep hons:** Canada (16, USA93, 1t-5pts). **ADPR:** London Welsh (1997-99, 12, 3t-15pts). Formerly with James Bay in Canada.

WOODARD, Lenny David (Wing)
Born Pontypool, 02.04.76. 6′, 15st. **ADPR:** London Welsh (1998-99, 15, 14t-70pts). Formerly with Ebbw Vale. Toured South Africa with Wales in 1998, scoring a try against Gauteng Falcons.

REVIEW

A season of consolidation for London Welsh who will be content with fourth place. They were never genuine promotion challengers, especially after a run of three consecutive defeats in early autumn, but at their best could produce an exciting brand of running rugby that augurs well for the future. Andy Lee, on loan from Saracens, was their leading points-scorer with a comparatively modest 99 while former GB Rugby League star Andy Currier comfortably headed the try-scoring chart with 15. Currier was ever-present, while stalwarts in the pack included Rowland Phillips, Andrew Millward and Mark Langley.

LONDON WELSH in Premiership Two 1998-99

Sep	6	A	Leeds Tykes	Won	20	18	C.Whittaker (T) A.Currier (T) L.Jones (T) M.Pearce (C, P)
	13	A	Blackheath	Won	20	16	I.Buckett (T) M.Pearce (T, 2C, 2P)
	19	H	Orrell	Won	24	17	P.Shaw (T) M.Pearce (T, C, P) J.Hewlett (2P) A.Currier (D)
	26	A	Bristol	Lost	3	37	J.Hewlett (P)
Oct	3	H	Rotherham	Lost	13	27	P.Shaw (T) M.Pearce (C, 2P)
	10	A	Coventry	Lost	19	63	P.Shaw (T) C.Whittaker (T) M.White (T) S.Pilgrim (C) M.Pearce (C)
	17	H	Wakefield	Won	45	21	M.White (3T) R.Phillips (2T) M.Giraud (T) J.Storey (T) M.Pearce (2C, 2P)
	24	A	Moseley	Won	31	16	J.Storey (T) Penalty (T) R.Phillips (T) P.Shaw (T) M.Pearce (4C, P)
	31	H	Worcester	Lost	14	22	A.Lee (T) M.Pearce (3P)
Nov	7	A	Waterloo Drummers	Lost	10	12	A.Currier (T) M.Pearce (C, P)
	21	H	Exeter	Won	62	27	A.Currier (3T) M.Giraud (2T) T.Shanklin (2T) P.Shaw (T) R.Phillips (T) D.Edwards (T) A.Lee (6C)
Dec	12	H	Fylde	Won	36	15	L.Woodard (3T) R.Phillips (T) D.Edwards (T) A.Currier (T) A.Lee (3C)
	19	H	Rugby Lions	Won	11	7	L.Woodard (T) A.Lee (2P)
Jan	2	A	Exeter	Won	17	16	L.Woodard (T) J.Storey (T) A.Lee (2C, P)
	16	H	Waterloo Drummers	Won	49	17	M.White (2T) A.Jones (2T) J.Storey (2T) D.Edwards (T) L.Woodard (T) A.Lee (3C, P)
	23	A	Worcester	Lost	12	14	S.Roskell (T) A.Currier (T) A.Lee (C)
Feb	6	H	Moseley	Won	26	24	M.Giraud (2T) A.Currier (T) A.Lee (C, 2P) C.Raymond (P)
	13	A	Wakefield	Won	30	16	M.Giraud (T) D.Edwards (T) A.Currier (T) A.Lee (3C, 3P)
	27	H	Coventry	Won	42	34	A.Currier (3T) M.White (T) D.Edwards (T) C.Alexander (T) A.Lee (3C, 2P)
Mar	13	A	Rotherham	Lost	8	28	A.Currier (T) A.Lee (P)
	27	H	Bristol	Lost	6	25	A.Lee (2P)
Apr	3	A	Orrell	Lost	15	18	R.Phillips (T) T.Shanklin (T) R.Lurie (T)

	17	H	Blackheath	Won	71	22	L.Woodard (4T) N.Mardon (3T) J.Storey (T) P.Carr (T) A.Millward (T) A.Currier (T) C.Raymond (8C)
	25	H	Leeds Tykes	Won	24	17	L.Woodard (2T) A.Currier (T) C.Raymond (3C, P)
May	1	A	Rugby Lions	Won	33	12	J.Storey (2T) L.Woodard (2T) Penalty (T) A.Lee (4C)
	8	A	Fylde	Won	21	11	C.Raymond (T, 3C) N.Mardon (T) J.Storey (T)

Summary of Premiership scorers:

99 A.Lee (T, 26C, 14P); 78 A.Currier (15T, D); 75 M.Pearce (2T, 13C, 13P); 70 L.Woodard (14T); 45 J.Storey (9T); 39 C.Raymond (T, 14C, 2P); 35 M.White (7T); 30 R.Phillips (6T), M.Giraud (6T); 25 P.Shaw (5T), D.Edwards (5T); 20 N.Mardon (4T); 15 T.Shanklin (3T); 10 Penalty (2T), C.Whittaker (2T), A.Jones (2T); 9 J.Hewlett (3P); 5 S.Roskell (T), A.Millward (T), R.Lurie (T), L.Jones (T), P.Carr (T), I.Buckett (T), C.Alexander (T); 2 S.Pilgrim (C).

Summary of Premiership appearances:

26 A.Currier; 25 R.Phillips, C.Olney (+6), I.Buckett (+1); 24 A.Millward (+1); 23 C.Langley (+2), P.Carr (+2); 22 D.Edwards (+3), C.Alexander (+3); 21 M.White (+1), G.Holmes (+16), M.Giraud (+1), G.French (+14); 20 J.Storey (+1); 15 L.Woodard, P.Shaw (+4), A.Lee (+2), A.Jones; 14 R.Lurie (+7); 12 S.Roskell (+3), M.Pearce (+4), M.Fitzgerald (+8); 8 G.Sage (+4), M.Dawes (+1); 7 C.Whittaker (+3), L.Jones, D.Griffiths (+5); 6 C.Raymond (+3), S.Pope (+6); 5 A.Johansen (+4); 4 T.Shanklin (+1), N.Mardon; 3 S.Pilgrim (+1), T.Lewsey (+3); 2 G.Peacock (+1), J.Hewlett (+1); 1 T.Mouton (+1), M.Langley, C.Brown (+1).

MANCHESTER

Formation of club: 1860
Ground: Grove Park, Grove Lane, Cheadle Hulme, Cheshire SK8 7NB
Capacity: 4,000 (Seated 250)
Colours: Red and white hoops
Honours: Champions North West Two – 1990, North West One – 1992, North Two – 1993, North One – 1996
Best League finish: 2nd in Jewson One 1998-99
Best Cup run: Last 16 1991-92
Last season: Jewson One – 2nd. Tetley's Bitter Cup – 2nd round (lost 17-20 to Sedgley Park)
Owner: Members
Director of rugby: Alex Keay
Coach: Phil Jee, Guy Parker
Captain: Steve Swindells

BAKER, Simon James (Scrum-half)
Born Coventry, 01.02.75. 5'9", 11st 7lb. **ADPR:** Rugby Lions (1996-98, 29, 4t-20pts), Manchester (1998-99, 24, 2t-10pts). Combative scrum-half who learned his rugby at Barker's Butts and represented Warwickshire.

BARROW, Marcus Paul (Full-back)
Born Bournemouth, 05.12.78. **ADPR:** Manchester (1998-99, 1). Back-up to Steve Swindells. North U21 representative.

BATT, James Thomas (Prop)
Born Barnet, 13.05.75. 6', 17st. **ADPR:** Sale (1996-97, 1), Manchester (1998-99, 23, 1t-5pts). Lancashire representative who played for Macclesfield and Matlock before joining Sale in 1996.

BLOOD, Michael (Wing)
Born Manchester, 06.08.68. 6'2", 15st. **ADPR:** Manchester (1995-99, 61, 28t-140pts). Cheshire county wing who arrived at Manchester from the Lymm club.

BRADSHAW, Richard Neil (Lock)
Born Birkenhead, 24.01.78. **ADPR:** Manchester (1998-99, 2). North U21 representative who joined Manchester from Wirral RFC.

BURGON, Timothy (Flanker)
Born Manchester, 21.09.64. 5'10", 14st 8lb. **ADPR:** Manchester (1995-99, 66, 44t-220pts). Lancashire flanker with an extraordinary try-scoring record, snaffling another 11 last season. Joined Manchester from Stockport and has also represented the Barbarians.

CRADDOCK, David (Lock)
Born Manchester, 06.11.69. 6'6", 15st 10lb. **ADPR:** Manchester (1995-99, 79, 10t-50pts). Cheshire county lock and another Barbarians representative.

CRADDOCK, Peter (Flanker)
Born Manchester, 21.08.71. 6'4", 14st. **ADPR:** Manchester (1995-99, 52, 16t-80pts). Lancashire county representative.

DOBSON, Matthew Patrick (Backrow)
Born Ballymoney, Northern Ireland, 12.06.73. **ADPR:** Sale (1991-97, 17, 1t-5pts), Manchester (1998-99, 13, 3t-15pts). Ireland U21 cap.

DUGGAN, John Joseph (Flanker)
Born Leicester, 16.03.74. 6'4", 16st. **ADPR:** Fylde (1995-98, 26, 3t-15pts), Manchester (1998-99, 12, 1t-5pts). Lancashire flanker who has also played for the Vipers club.

ELLIS, Roderic (Centre)
Born Manchester, 06.06.68. 6'1", 14st. **ADPR:** Manchester (1995-99, 75, 28t, 2c, 3pg, 3dg-162pts). Cheshire centre who has also played for West Park and Bramhope.

FOWLER, John Brian (Lock)
Born Bexley, 06.02.68. 6'7", 17st. **Rep hons:** England A (8, SAus95). **ADPR:** Richmond (1989-91, 20, 1t-4pts), Rosslyn Park (1991-93, 17), Newcastle (1993-95, 15), Sale (1994-97, 43, 5t-25pts), Manchester (1998-99, 9, 2t-10pts). John is beginning to resurrect his career after a knee ligament injury torpedoed his international ambitions – he had been picked to tour Argentina with England in 1997 when injury struck. As well as his considerable experience playing in England, John has enjoyed two spells in New Zealand with King Country and Hawkes Bay, representing the latter against the 1993 British Lions. Toured Australia and Fiji with England A in 1995. Educated at Epsom College.

GERRARD, Gareth Edward (Fly-half/centre)
Born Ashton, 24.08.78. **ADPR:** Manchester (1998-99, 1). Promising Lancashire fly-half, formerly with Broughton Park.

GREEN, Tim John (Scrum-half)
Born Bradford, 02.08.69. 5′9″, 12st 9lb. **ADPR:** Sale (1988-89, 1), Manchester (1997-99, 27, 1t-5pts). Formerly with Winnington Park.

GREENLEES, Jamie (Wing)
Born Stockport, 18.07.76. 5′11″, 14st 4lb. **ADPR:** Manchester (1997-99, 7, 2t-10pts). Cheshire representative who has also played with Bath and Moseley.

GROSS, Lewis (Wing)
Born Manchester, 19.09.74. 6′1″, 13st 6lb. **ADPR:** Manchester (1996-99, 25, 11t-55pts).

HEWSON, Luke (Hooker)
Born Stafford, 06.12.69. 5′11″, 17st. **ADPR:** Sale (1991-97, 14, 1t-5pts), Manchester (1997-99, 44, 4t-20pts). Experienced Cheshire hooker and an important figure in Manchester's recent rise to prominence.

HOSKIN, Matthew (Wing)
Born London, 25.12.68. 6′, 15st 13lb. **Rep hons:** Barbarians (97-98). **ADPR:** Exeter (1988-92, 15, 2t-8pts), Headingley (1991-92, 3t-12pts), Leeds (1992-93, 6, 2t-10pts), Exeter (1992-93, 1, 1t-5pts), Manchester (1995-99, 35, 34t-170pts).

HUGHES, Richard (Centre)
Born Liverpool, 28.01.76. 5′10″, 14st. **ADPR:** Manchester (1998-99, 22, 3t-15pts). Cheshire representative.

JEE, Philip (Fly-half)
Born Manchester, 24.07.62. 5′10″, 14st 2lb. **ADPR:** Sale (1987-94, 44, 2t, 11c, 31pg, 4dg-136pts), Manchester (1996-99, 63, 9t, 6c, 9pg, 1dg-87pts). Player-coach who threatens to retire this season. Former Lancashire stalwart.

KIRKE, Matthew Brian (Flanker)
Born Fairlie, New Zealand, 26.06.73. 6′5″, 17st 4lb. **ADPR:** London Scottish (1996-97, 1), Sale (1997-98, 1), Manchester (1998-99, 24, 3t-15pts). Powerhouse flanker who has also played for the Hakkaido club in Japan.

LANGHORN, Gary (Centre)
Born Manchester, 27.09.70. 6′2″, 15st. **ADPR:** Manchester (1995-99, 72, 14t-70pts). Lancashire flanker who joined from Stockport.

SIMPKINS, Derek (Prop)
Born Mafeking, South Africa, 16.03.69. 6′1″, 17st 5lb. **ADPR:** Manchester (1995-99, 60, 1t-5pts).

SWINDELLS, Stephen Richard (Full-back)
Born Altrincham, 25.10.69. 5′11″, 13st 10lb. **ADPR:** Waterloo (1992-95, 44, 4t, 15c, 88pg-314pts), Manchester (1995-99, 79, 25t, 224c, 199pg-1170pts). Possibly the best goal-kicker playing in England, Steve has been an inspiration at full-back for Manchester and needs just 16 points to score 1500 in all League games, having also enjoyed a spell at Waterloo. A former England U21 international.

WILLIAMS, Stuart (Flanker)
Born Leeds, 06.09.75. 6′5″, 15st. **ADPR:** Liverpool St Helens (1995-97, 11), Manchester (1997-99, 31, 6t-30pts). Cumbrian county player, formerly with Wigton and Liverpool St Helens.

REVIEW

Manchester's amazing climb up through the Leagues continues apace with last season's second place in Jewson One being the sixth time in nine seasons they have won promotion. Under player-coach Phil Jee and captain Steve Swindells they were worthy runners-up to Henley and had the added bonus of beating old rivals Orrell 29-27 to win the Lancashire Cup final. The ever-consistent Swindells again headed the points-scoring charts with 365 League points, having kicked 398 the previous season when they won promotion from Jewson Two. Tim Burgon was the leading try-scorer with 11 – Burgon along with lock Dave Craddock also represented the Barbarians.

MANCHESTER in Jewson One 1998-99

Sep	5	A	Nottingham	Won	29	13	T.Green (T) T.Burgon (T) S.Swindells (2C, 5P)
	12	H	Camberley	Won	72	5	M.Hoskin (5T) M.Dobson (2T) S.Baker (T) D.Craddock (T) J.Greenlees (T) S.Swindells (8C, 2P)
	19	A	Henley Hawks	Lost	20	39	J.Greenlees (T) M.Blood (T) S.Swindells (C, 2P) R.Ellis (C)
	26	H	Morley	Won	29	5	T.Burgon (T) J.Duggan (T) S.Swindells (2C, 5P)
Oct	3	A	Lydney	Won	16	12	T.Burgon (T) S.Swindells (C, 3P)
	10	H	Otley	Won	36	26	T.Burgon (T) P.Craddock (T) P.Jee (T) S.Swindells (3C, 5P)
	24	A	Reading	Won	28	14	T.Burgon (2T) P.Jee (T) S.Swindells (2C, 3P)
	31	H	Rosslyn Park	Won	26	25	R.Ellis (T, D) Penalty (T) S.Swindells (2C, 3P)
Nov	7	A	Birmingham/ Solihull	Won	30	27	Penalty (2T) S.Williams (T) S.Swindells (3C, 3P)
	21	H	Liverpool St Helens	Won	50	5	T.Burgon (2T) S.Swindells (T, 6C, P) M.Blood (T) R.Hughes (T) L.Gross (T) M.Dobson (T)
	28	A	Harrogate	Won	18	10	S.Swindells (6P)
Dec	5	H	Wharfedale	Won	15	3	S.Swindells (5P)
	12	A	Newbury	Lost	14	17	M.Blood (T) S.Swindells (3P)
	19	H	Harrogate	Won	27	0	L.Gross (T) D.Craddock (T) M.Kirke (T) S.Swindells (3C, 2P)
	28	A	Liverpool St Helens	Won	40	15	R.Ellis (T) S.Williams (T) M.Blood (T) S.Swindells (T, 4C, 4P)
Jan	2	H	Birmingham/ Solihull	Won	42	0	R.Ellis (3T) J.Fowler (T) Penalty (T) S.Swindells (4C, 3P)
	16	A	Rosslyn Park	Lost	0	12	
	23	H	Reading	Won	41	0	S.Swindells (2T, 3C) M.Blood (T) R.Ellis (T) D.Simpkins (T) R.Hughes (T) Penalty (T)
	30	A	Otley	Lost	6	20	S.Swindells (P) R.Ellis (D)
Feb	6	H	Lydney	Won	67	0	Penalty (2T) M.Blood (T) R.Ellis (T) P.Jee (T) J.Fowler (T) D.Craddock (T) M.Kirke (T) P.Craddock (T) G.Langhorn (T) S.Swindells (7C, P)

	13	A	Morley	Won	23	17	S.Baker (T) T.Burgon (T) S.Swindells (C, 2P) R.Ellis (C, P)
	27	H	Henley Hawks	Won	13	7	T.Burgon (T) S.Swindells (C, 2P)
Mar	13	A	Camberley	Won	28	22	J.Batt (T) L.Gross (T) R.Hughes (T) S.Swindells (2C, 2P) R.Ellis (D)
	27	H	Nottingham	Won	32	17	G.Langhorn (T) L.Gross (T) M.Kirke (T) T.Burgon (T) P.Jee (3C) R.Ellis (2P)
Apr	3	H	Newbury	Lost	26	31	S.Swindells (T, 2C, 4P) S.Williams (T)
	17	A	Wharfedale	Drew	30	30	S.Swindells (2T, 3C, 3P) L.Hewson (T)

Summary of League scorers:

365 S.Swindells (7T, 60C, 70P); 57 R.Ellis (7T, 2C, 3P, 3D); 55 T.Burgon (11T); 35 Penalty (7T); 30 M.Blood (6T); 25 M.Hoskin (5T); 21 P.Jee (3T, 3C); 20 L.Gross (4T); 15 S.Williams (3T), M.Kirke (3T), M.Dobson (3T), D.Craddock (3T); 10 G.Langhorn (2T), R.Hughes (2T), J.Greenlees (2T), J.Fowler (2T), P.Craddock (2T), S.Baker (2T); 5 D.Simpkins (T), R.Hughes (T), L.Hewson (T), T.Green (T), J.Duggan (T), J.Batt (T).

MOSELEY

Formation of club: 1873
Ground: The Reddings, Reddings Road, Moseley, Birmingham B13 8LW
Capacity: 5,041 (Seated 1,021)
Colours: Red and black
Honours: Cup Winners (1) – 1981-82 (shared with Gloucester)
Best League finish: 7th in Division One 1987-88
Last season: Premiership Two – 10th. Tetley's Bitter Cup – 4th round (lost 24-25 to Lydney)
Owner: Moseley Ventures Limited (consortium)
Managing director: George Walters
Director of rugby: John White.
Coach: TBC
Captain: Mark Chudleigh

ADAMS, Hamish John (Prop)
Born New Zealand, 31.05.69. **ADPR:** Moseley (1998-99, 5). Formerly with Kenilworth and the Tecnico club in Portugal.

AYEB, Yazid (Centre)
Born Belfort, France, 18.07.74. **ADPR:** Moseley (1998-99, 18, 3t-15pts). French centre who had previously played for St Claude, Graulhet and Toulouse.

BEMOND, Scott Kenneth (Scrum-half)
Born Hereford, 21.09.78. **ADPR:** Moseley (1997-99, 14).

BINNS, Andrew Jeremy (Fly-half/full-back)
Born Yorkshire, 29.06.76. 6′2″, 13st. **ADPR:** Moseley (1996-99, 48, 8t, 11c, 17pg, 1dg-116pts). Developing fly-half who learned his rugby at Bradford GS and then Exeter University. Leading points-scorer last season with 88.

BRADING, Simon Don (Centre)
Born Cambridge, 03.07.79. **ADPR:** Bedford (1997-99, 5, 1t-5pts), Moseley (1998-99, 7, 2t-10pts).

BUXTON, Peter George (Flanker)
Born Cheltenham, 21.08.78. 6′4″, 17st. **ADPR:** Moseley (1997-99, 34, 4t-20pts). Former England Colt who has developed quickly since joining from Cheltenham in August 1997.

CHUDLEIGH, Mark Anthony (Scrum-half)
Born Launceston, 31.01.74. **ADPR:** Moseley (1993-94, 2), Bristol (1994-95, 8, 1t-5pts), Moseley (1995-99, 47, 4t-20pts). Cornish-born former England U21 cap who captained the side last season.

COOK, Marcus James Evan (Full-back/wing)
Born Cuckfield, 14.07.75. 6′4″, 15st. **ADPR:** Bedford (1993-97, 38, 5t, 1dg-28pts), Moseley (1998-99, 22, 9t, 1c-47pts). Leading try-scorer with nine last season. Arrived at the Reddings after a spell with Le Creusot and Montchannin in France.

DRAKE-LEE, William Michael (Flanker)
Born Kettering, 09.08.70. 6′, 15st. **ADPR:** Leicester (1991-97, 26, 1t-5pts), Moseley (1997-99, 35, 2t-10pts). Educated at Irwin Academy and de Montfort University. Bill started his career at Kettering RFC before joining Leicester and finally Moseley. Son of former England prop Nick Drake-Lee. Works as an estate agent.

FORTEY, Lee James (Prop)
Born Gloucester, 25.08.75. **ADPR:** Moseley (1997-99, 18). Twin brother of Gloucester hooker Chris Fortey. Formerly with Gordon League and Gloucester.

GREGORY, Geoffrey Walter (Fly-half/wing)
Born Wolverhampton, 08.06.74. **ADPR:** Moseley (1997-99, 22, 3t-15pts). Formerly with Wolverhampton RFC.

HALL, Andrew John Anderson (Lock)
Born Solihull, 05.06.79. **ADPR:** Nottingham (1992-93, 3), Moseley (1998-99, 11).

HAMPTON, Richard Patrick (Hooker)
Born Birmingham, 09.05.70. **ADPR:** Moseley (1991-99, 19). Formerly with Stourbridge and Old Halesonians.

JONES, Philip **Steffan** (Wing/full-back)
Born Llanelli, 09.02.74. 6′2″, 14st. **ADPR:** Bristol (1997-98, 7), Exeter (1997-98, 3), Moseley (1998-99, 19, 2t, 9c, 18pg-82pts). Somerset county cricketer who has also played rugby for Swansea.

LONG, Matthew Robert (Prop)
Born Gloucester, 25.05.73. 6′. **ADPR:** Newcastle (1994-97, 31, 1t-5pts), Moseley (1997-99, 34). Graduate of Newcastle University.

MacKINNON, Stuart Donald (Prop)
Born 06.01.69. 6′, 17st 7lb. **ADPR:** Moseley (1995-99, 37, 6t-30pts).

MARTIN, Roderick Charles Kirk (Wing/centre)
Born Southend, 25.11.75. 6′, 14st. **ADPR:** Moseley (1996-99, 52, 13t-65pts). Product of Moseley's Development squad. Represented England Universities while at Birmingham University.

MELLORS, Jason (Flanker)
Born Birmingham, 30.06.79. **ADPR:** Moseley (1997-99, 12, 4t-20pts).

MITCHELL, Neil John (Lock)
Born Newcastle, 22.06.66. 6′6″, 17st 5lb. **ADPR:** Moseley (1996-99, 45, 5t-25pts). Formerly with Warley and Stourbridge. Toured South Africa with the British Police in 1997.

PATTEN, Ian Stuart (Backrow)
Born Bristol, 31.05.70. 6'5", 16st. **ADPR:** Bristol (1991-96, 36, 3t-15pts), Coventry (1995-98, 47, 10t-50pts), Moseley (1998-99, 25, 2t-10pts). Moseley's most consistent forward last season when he missed just one game. Formerly with Kingsfield and Soundwell.

PROTHEROUGH, Richard David (Hooker)
Born Cheltenham, 09.11.76. 5'9", 14st. **ADPR:** Worcester (1996-97, 2, 1t-5pts), Moseley (1998-99, 23, 2t-10pts). Capped by England at Schools, Colts and U21 level. Son of former Moseley hooker Dave Protherough. Graduate of Loughborough University.

ROBERTS, Martin John (Centre)
Born Gloucester, 26.01.68. 6'3", 15st 2lb. **ADPR:** Gloucester (1990-98, 48, 3t, 6c, 13pg-66pts), Moseley (1998-99, 19, 3t-15pts). Product of the Cheltenham club before moving to Gloucester and then Moseley.

SIMPSON, Nigel Tansie Ashton (Wing)
Born Suva, Fiji, 25.04.75. **ADPR:** Moseley (1998-99, 15, 6t-30pts). Formerly with the Marist club in New Zealand.

SMART, Jonathan (Fly-half)
Born Birmingham, 24.01.75. **ADPR:** Nottingham (1997-98, 21, 3t-15pts), Birmingham/Solihull (1998-99, 2t, 1pg-13pts), Moseley (1998-99, 9, 1t, 10c, 9pg, 3dg-61pts).

WEBBER, Nathan (Prop)
Born Cardiff, 20.06.74. 6'1", 17st. **Rep hons:** England A (1, SA96). **ADPR:** Moseley (1994-99, 73). Educated at Stratford-on-Avon HS.

WHITE, Richard James (Lock)
Born Totnes, 20.09.74. 6'5". **ADPR:** Bedford (1996-97, 7, 1t-5pts), Nottingham (1997-98, 16,1t-5pts), Moseley (1998-99, 8, 1t-5pts).

REVIEW

After the traumas of the previous season it was unrealistic to expect too much from Moseley and ultimately they will have been happy to preserve their League Two status. An early win over Leeds Tykes indicated some potential but thereafter their lack of strength in depth saw them struggle against the top sides though they did achieve a double over Coventry. Among the forwards, Peter Buxton and Ian Patten were stalwart performers and Mark Chudleigh proved again an influential figure at scrum-half.

MOSELEY in Premiership Two 1998-99

Sep	5	H	Wakefield	Lost	32	33	I.Patten (T) Penalty (T) N.Simpson (T) J.Smart (T, 3C, 2P)
	12	H	Leeds Tykes	Won	27	22	B.Eason (T) M.Cook (T) G.Gregory (T) M.Chudleigh (T) A.Binns (2C, P)
	19	A	Worcester	Lost	8	23	N.Simpson (T) A.Binns (P)
	26	H	Waterloo Drummers	Lost	13	15	G.Gregory (T) R.White (T) A.Binns (P)
Oct	3	A	Exeter	Lost	8	20	R.Martin (T) A.Binns (P)

10	H	Fylde	Won	44	22	M.Chudleigh (T) P.Buxton (T) R.Martin (T) N.Simpson (T) Y.Ayeb (T) A.Binns (5C, 3P)
18	A	Rugby Lions	Lost	8	30	J.Mellors (T) A.Binns (P)
24	H	London Welsh	Lost	16	31	P.Buxton (T) J.Smart (C, 3P)
31	A	Blackheath	Won	18	14	M.Cook (T) J.Mellors (T) J.Smart (C, P, D)
Nov 7	H	Orrell	Won	25	3	S.Jones (2T, C, P) J.Mellors (T) M.Cook (T)
22	A	Bristol	Lost	18	58	R.Martin (T) N.Simpson (T) J.Smart (C, P, D)
Dec 12	H	Rotherham	Lost	6	16	S.Jones (2P)
20	A	Coventry	Won	46	21	G.Gregory (T) S.MacKinnon (T) T.Healy (T) N.Mitchell (T) P.Buxton (T) Y.Ayeb (T) S.Jones (5C, 2P)
Jan 2	H	Bristol	Lost	6	43	S.Jones (2P)
16	A	Orrell	Lost	14	20	R.Protherough (T) S.Jones (3P)
23	H	Blackheath	Won	22	16	M.Cook (T) I.Patten (T) N.Simpson (T) J.Smart (2C, P)
Feb 6	A	London Welsh	Lost	24	26	M.Cook (T) N.Mitchell (T) S.Jones (4P) A.Binns (C)
13	H	Rugby Lions	Won	35	20	N.Simpson (T) R.Martin (T) A.Binns (T) J.Mellors (T) S.Jones (3C, 3P)
27	A	Fylde	Lost	8	17	M.Roberts (T) S.Jones (P)
Mar 13	H	Exeter	Lost	12	15	A.Binns (4P)
27	A	Waterloo Drummers	Won	32	8	M.Roberts (2T) R.Protherough (T) M.Cook (T) B.Drake-Lee (T) A.Binns (2C, P)
Apr 3	H	Worcester	Won	18	16	R.Martin (T) S.Brading (T) A.Binns (C, 2P)
18	A	Leeds Tykes	Lost	8	50	S.Brading (T) A.Binns (P)
24	A	Wakefield	Lost	20	38	M.Cook (2T) P.Buxton (T) A.Binns (C, P)
May 1	H	Coventry	Won	30	29	A.Binns (T) Y.Ayeb (T) M.Cook (T) R.Martin (T) J.Smart (2C, P, D)
8	A	Rotherham	Lost	0	27	

Summary of Premiership scorers:

88 A.Binns (2T, 12C, 18P); 82 S.Jones (2T, 9C, 18P); 61 J.Smart (T, 10C, 9P, 3D); 45 M.Cook (9T); 30 N.Simpson (6T), R.Martin (6T); 20 J.Mellors (4T), P.Buxton (4T); 15 M.Roberts (3T), G.Gregory (3T), Y.Ayeb (3T); 10 R.Protherough (2T), I.Patten (2T), N.Mitchell (2T), M.Chudleigh (2T), S.Brading (2T); 5 Penalty (T), R.White (T), S.MacKinnon (T), T.Healy (T), B.Eason (T), B.Drake-Lee (T).

Summary of Premiership appearances:

25 I.Patten, M.Long (+6), P.Buxton; 24 R.Martin (+3), M.Chudleigh (+5); 23 R.Protherough (+6), A.Binns (+1); 22 M.Cook (+1); 21 G.Gregory (+3); 20 N.Mitchell (+3); 19 M.Roberts (+1), S.Jones (+8); 18 T.Healy (+1), Y.Ayeb (+9); 17 B.Drake-Lee (+2); 15 N.Simpson, P.Short (+8); 14 S.Bemond (+7); 13 N.Webber (+1); 12 S.MacKinnon (+5), L.Fortey (+1); 11 A.Hall (+3); 10 J.Mellors (+4), R.Hampton (+2); 9 J.Smart; 8 R.White (+1); 7 S.Brading; 5 H.Adams (+2); 4 C.Hall (+1); 2 A.Hubbleday (+1), B.Eason, C.Colvin; 1 R.Sigley (+1), A.Coniff.

ORRELL

Formation of club: 1927
Ground: Edge Hall Road, Orrell, Wigan, Lancashire WN5 8TL
Capacity: 6,000 (Seated 1,000)
Colours: Amber and black
Best League finish: 2nd in Division One 1991-92
Best Cup run: SF 1973-74, 1986-87, 1990-91, 1993-94
Last season: Premiership Two – 8th. Tetley's Bitter Cup – 4th round (lost 11-18 to Waterloo Drummers)
Owner: Members
Chairman: Ron Pimblett
Rugby manager: Sammy Southern.
Coach: Mike Slemen
Captain: TBC

BAILEY, David Alan (No 8)
Born Whiston, 07.10.74. **ADPR:** Orrell (1997-99, 13).

BELL, Gary Allen (Centre)
Born Leeds, 01.02.75. **ADPR:** Winnington Park (1996-98, 48, 20t, 69c, 53pg-397pts), Orrell (1998-99, 5, 1t, 1c-7pts). Formerly with Sandbach.

BENTLEY, Christopher Charles (Lock)
Born Sunderland, 24.05.79. **ADPR:** New Brighton (1997-98, 6), Orrell (1998-99, 8).

BROWN, Matthew Denis (Flanker)
Born 16.03.76. **ADPR:** Orrell (1998-99, 2, 1t-5pts). Formerly with Macclesfield and Leigh.

CARROLL, Andrew (Prop)
Born Ormskirk, 26.06.74. **ADPR:** Orrell (1998-99, 6).

CUNDICK, Jason Paul (Prop)
Born Manchester, 18.06.71. 6′, 17st. **ADPR:** Orrell (1994-99, 62, 1t-5pts). School-teacher who re-established himself in the front row last season after a back injury. Formerly with Winnington Park and Old Salians.

CUSANI, Charles Dominic (Lock)
Born Wigan, 22.10.65. 6′6″, 17st. **ADPR:** Orrell (1987-99, 121, 1t-5pts). Rugged ball-handling lock who has worked as a chef and as Orrell steward. Played rugby league at school, graduated to the senior Lancashire and North Divisional sides and also enjoyed a spell with Roma in the Italian First Division.

GRAINEY, Ian Michael (Flanker)
Born Leigh, 21.04.78. **ADPR:** Orrell (1998-99, 11, 1t-5pts). Formerly with Leigh RFC.

HAMER, Paul J. (Centre/wing)
Born St Helens, 12.11.66. 6′, 13st 4lb. **ADPR:** Vale of Lune (1987-88, 2t, 1pg-11pts), Liverpool St Helens (1988-89, 5, 1t-4pts), Sale (1989-91, 14, 3t, 1c, 5pg-29pts), Orrell (1992-99, 59, 12t, 9c, 4pg, 2dg-96pts). Utility back who has also represented England Schools and British Police.

HITCHMOUGH, Robert David (Wing)
Born St Helens, 17.12.75. 5′10″, 12st 7lb. **ADPR:** Orrell (1996-97, 19, 3t, 2c, 3pg-28pts), Wakefield (1998-99, 13, 2t-10pts), Orrell (1998-99, 8, 1t-5pts). Product of West Park who has returned to Orrell after an outstanding debut season in 1996-97 when he earned selection in the England A squad.

HOPE, Guy Daniell (Centre)
Born Beverley, 27.10.76. **ADPR:** Orrell (1996-99, 29, 3t-15pts). Formerly with Pocklington.

HUXLEY, Jeffrey Ellis (No 8/lock)
Born Billinge, 28.07.63. 6′3″, 16st 7lb. **ADPR:** Orrell (1994-99, 54, 2t-10pts). Merseyside policeman who has also been helping out with coaching duties.

JOHNSON, Kurt Louis (Wing)
Born Slough, 23.06.77. **ADPR:** Orrell (1998-99, 14, 10t-50pts). Effective try-scorer who arrived from Rotherham at the start of last season.

KELLY, Stephen Joseph (Prop)
Born Manchester, 11.05.72. **ADPR:** Orrell (1997-99, 36, 4t-20pts).

LACEY, Matthew John (Flanker)
Born Merseyside, 10.03.78. **ADPR:** Orrell (1997-99, 25, 2t-10pts).

LIPTROT, Neil Anthony (Wing)
Born Wigan, 14.06.78. **ADPR:** Orrell (1997-99, 7, 5t, 1c-27pts).

LYON, David Geoffrey (Centre/full-back)
Born Wigan, 03.09.65. 6′1″, 14st 8lb. **ADPR:** Orrell (1996-99, 53, 12t-60pts). Former Warrington and St Helens RL centre. Nephew of Billy and Eric Lyon.

MILLACHIP, Peter Charles (Flanker)
Born Bowdon, 01.09.69. **ADPR:** Orrell (1997-99, 22, 1t-5pts). Formerly with Lymm and Middlesbrough

MOFFAT, Alexander Graham (Hooker)
Born Workington, 29.06.68. 5′2″, 13st. **ADPR:** Fylde (1990-94, 22, 3t-13pts), Orrell (1995-99, 55, 1t-5pts).

NEWTON, Paul James (Scrum-half)
Born Penrith, 29.04.78. **ADPR:** Orrell (1996-99, 20, 2t-10pts).

POVALL, Gary Lee (Scrum-half)
Born Great Sutton, Wirral, 03.01.72. 5′8″, 12st 4lb. **ADPR:** Orrell (1993-96, 3), Preston Grasshoppers (1996-97, 4), Orrell (1998-99, 1). Has also played for Waterloo.

REES, Paul Michael (Lock)
Born Dagenham, 10.04.73. 6′6″, 17st. **ADPR:** Orrell (1996-99, 65, 2t-10pts). Police officer who has been an outstanding success in the boilerhouse since arriving from Winnington Park.

RUSSELL, Gareth Mark (Flanker)
Born Rochdale, 30.07.72. 6′, 15st 5lb. **ADPR:** Fylde (1991-98, 99, 10t-50pts), Orrell (1998-99, 6, 2t-10pts).

RYAN, Neil Andrew (Utility back)
Born Wigan, 29.11.73. 5′9″, 13st 4lb. **ADPR:** Waterloo (1993-96, 25, 4t, 5pg, 8dg-59pts), Sale (1995-97, 9, 4t-20pts), Orrell (1997-99, 40, 8t, 3c, 1pg, 3dg-58pts).

Educated at Mount St Mary's and Spinkhill and capped by England 16 Group, 18 Group before winning England U21 honours.

SLEMEN, David Joseph (Fly-half)
Born Liverpool, 12.09.78. 6′2″, 13st 9lb. **ADPR:** Orrell (1998-99, 18, 4t, 2c, 3pg-33pts). Son of Orrell coach and former England wing Mike, David was one of Orrell's most consistent backs last season.

SMITH, Jason Daniel (Wing)
Born 31.01.73. **ADPR:** Waterloo (1989-96, 10, 2t-10pts), Orrell (1996-99, 3).

SOUTHERN, Martin Alan (Fly-half)
Born Wigan, 01.04.73. **ADPR:** Orrell (1998-99, 1). Formerly with Aspull.

TABERNER, Steven (Full-back)
Born Orrell, 15.09.62. 5′10″, 13st. **ADPR:** Orrell (1987-99, 102, 15t, 1dg-70pts). One of the grand old men of Orrell rugby who is still happy to turn out when required. Former club captain who enjoys triathlons and amateur dramatics.

VERBICKAS, Simon John (Wing)
Born Manchester, 22.04.75. 6′1″, 13st 7lb. **ADPR:** Broughton Park (1992-93, 1, 1c-2pts), Sale (1993-97, 26, 20t, 7c, 6pg-132pts), Orrell (1997-99, 40, 25t, 54c, 52pg-389pts). Multi-talented back who was both Orrell's leading try-scorer and goal-kicker last season. Qualified to play for England, Ireland, Germany and Lithuania.

WARR, Mark Kevin (Scrum-half)
Born Birmingham, 24.02.67. 5′9″, 12st 12lb. **ADPR:** Sale (1992-97, 43, 15t-75pts), Orrell (1997-99, 36, 2t-10pts). Product of Barker's Butts, has appeared in three County Championship finals for Warwickshire. Studied Psychology and PE at Birmingham University.

WILKINSON, Nicholas (Prop)
Born Billinge, 03.03.73. **ADPR:** Orrell (1998-99, 12). Formerly with Fylde and Wigan.

WYNN, Ian (Centre)
Born St Helens, 11.08.68. 6′2″, 14st. **ADPR:** Orrell (1989-96, 58, 16t-80pts), Wakefield (1996-97, 22, 3t-15pts), Leeds (1997-98, 17, 4t-20pts), Orrell (1998-99, 23, 6t, 1dg-33pts). Former Scottish Exiles centre enjoying a second spell at Orrell.

REVIEW

A season that started with every likelihood of Orrell going out of business ended with a welcome degree of stability, with their friends at Wigan RL purchasing Edge Hall Road for £500,000 for its training facilities, the pitch being leased back to Orrell. An early-season win over Rotherham proved a false dawn as far as playing prospects were concerned and eighth place just about reflected the side's ability. The versatile Simon Verbickas was their top points-scorer with 224, including 13 tries. In the backs none did better than the experienced Ian Wynn and Mark Warr while young David Slemen, son of coach Mike, is one to look out for.

ORRELL in Premiership Two 1998-99

Sep	5	A	Fylde	Won	20	6	P.Manley (T) N.Liptrot (T) M.Oliver (T) S.Verbickas (C, P)
	12	H	Rugby Lions	Won	32	3	N.Liptrot (T) I.Wynn (T) Penalty (T) M.Oliver (T) S.Verbickas (3C, 2P)

	19	A	London Welsh	Lost	17	24	M.Oliver (T) G.Russell (T) N.Liptrot (C) S.Verbickas (C, P)
	26	H	Blackheath	Won	60	3	D.Lyon (2T) S.Kelly (2T) N.Liptrot (2T) A.Moffat (T) P.Manley (T) P.Hamer (7C, 2P)
Oct	3	H	Leeds Tykes	Lost	11	13	N.Liptrot (T) P.Hamer (2P)
	10	A	Bristol	Lost	19	29	J.Cundick (T) D.Lyon (T) G.Bell (T, C) P.Hamer (C)
	17	H	Rotherham	Won	19	12	G.Russell (T) M.Warr (T) S.Verbickas (2P) N.Ryan (D)
	24	A	Coventry	Lost	14	26	K.Johnson (T) S.Verbickas (3P)
	31	H	Wakefield	Won	24	5	D.Slemen (2T, 3P) D.Lyon (T)
Nov	7	A	Moseley	Lost	3	25	S.Verbickas (P)
	21	H	Worcester	Lost	9	13	S.Verbickas (2P) N.Ryan (D)
Dec	12	A	Waterloo Drummers	Won	17	10	I.Wynn (T) S.Verbickas (3P) N.Ryan (D)
	19	H	Exeter	Lost	21	23	K.Johnson (2T) S.Kelly (T) S.Verbickas (2P)
Jan	2	A	Worcester	Lost	0	17	
	16	H	Moseley	Won	20	14	M.Lacey (T) S.Verbickas (T, C, 2P) D.Slemen (C)
	23	A	Wakefield	Lost	13	25	D.Slemen (T) S.Verbickas (C, 2P)
Feb	6	H	Coventry	Won	31	0	G.Hope (T) I.Wynn (T) D.Slemen (T) S.Verbickas (T, 4C, P)
	13	A	Rotherham	Lost	10	47	K.Johnson (T) G.Hope (T)
	27	H	Bristol	Lost	32	34	K.Johnson (3T) S.Verbickas (T, 3C, 2P)
Mar	14	A	Leeds Tykes	Lost	7	20	S.Verbickas (T, C)
	27	A	Blackheath	Lost	9	15	S.Verbickas (3P)
Apr	3	H	London Welsh	Won	18	15	K.Johnson (T) M.Lacey (T) S.Verbickas (C, 2P)
	17	A	Rugby Lions	Won	41	29	S.Verbickas (2T, 3C) I.Wynn (2T) M.Warr (T) N.Ryan (T) P.Newton (T)
	24	H	Fylde	Won	28	18	S.Verbickas (2T, 2C, 2P) P.Rees (T) I.Wynn (D)
May	1	A	Exeter	Lost	32	42	S.Verbickas (2T, 3C, 2P) P.Newton (T) M.Brown (T)
	8	H	Waterloo Drummers	Won	59	15	S.Verbickas (3T, 6C) K.Johnson (2T) I.Wynn (T) I.Grainey (T) R.Hitchmough (T) S.Kelly (T) D.Slemen (C)

Summary of Premiership scorers:

224 S.Verbickas (13T, 30C, 33P); 50 K.Johnson (10T); 33 I.Wynn (6T, D), D.Slemen (4T, 2C, 3P); 28 P.Hamer (8C, 4P); 27 N.Liptrot (5T, C); 20 D.Lyon (4T), S.Kelly (4T); 15 M.Oliver (3T); 14 N.Ryan (T, 3D); 10 M.Warr (2T), G.Russell (2T),

P.Newton (2T), P.Manley (2T), M.Lacey (2T), G.Hope (2T); 7 G.Bell (T, C); 5 Penalty (T), P.Rees (T), A.Moffat (T), R.Hitchmough (T), I.Grainey (T), J.Cundick (T), M.Brown (T).

Summary of Premiership appearances:

25 P.Rees; 24 G.Hope (+3); 23 I.Wynn, M.Warr (+7), D.Lyon (+2), M.Lacey (+4), S.Kelly (+3), C.Cusani (+1); 22 S.Verbickas; 21 A.Moffat (+6); 19 N.Ryan (+7), J.Cundick; 18 D.Slemen, R.Rawlinson (+3); 17 P.Newton (+7); 14 K.Johnson (+1), J.Hayter (+8); 12 N.Wilkinson (+11), D.Bailey (+5); 11 I.Grainey (+3); 10 S.Turner, J.Huxley; 9 P.Manley; 8 R.Hitchmough (+3), C.Bentley; 6 G.Russell, M.Oliver, N.Liptrot (+2), A.Carroll (+4); 5 P.Millachip (+1), P.Hamer, G.Bell (+5); 4 D.Wright; 2 A.Unsworth (+2), J.Smith (+1), M.Brown (+2); 1 S.Taberner, S.Southern (+1), G.Povall (+1), S.Nicholas (+1), P.Engwell (+1), N.Gregory, M.Glynn.

ROTHERHAM

Formation of club: 1923
Ground: Clifton Lane Sports Ground, Badsley Moor Lane, Rotherham S65 2AA
Capacity: 4,000 (Seated 1,000)
Colours: Maroon, sky blue, navy blue and white
Honours: Champions North East One – 1988-89, North Two – 1989-90, North One – 1991-92, Division Five North – 1993-94, Division Four – 1994-95
Best League finish: 2nd in Premiership Two 1998-99
Best Cup run: Last 16 1996-97
Last season: Premiership Two – 2nd. Tetley's Bitter Cup – 4th round (lost 24-27 to Leeds Tykes)
Owners: Members
Chief executive: Mike Yarlett
Director of rugby: Steve Cousins.
Coaches: Jim Kilfoyle, John Phillips
Captain: Mike Schmid

BINNS, Simon James (Fly-half)
Born Shipley, 20.09.74. 5′11″, 15st. **Rep hons:** Barbarians (97-98). **ADPR:** Moseley (1995-96, 5, 1t, 2c, 2pg, 1dg-18pts), Rotherham (1996-98, 40, 13t, 43c, 45pg, 3dg-295pts), London Scottish (1998-99, 17). Learned his rugby at Bradford GS from where he won England Schools caps. Enjoyed a brief spell with Leicester.

BRAMLEY, Richard Anthony (Lock/flanker)
Born Doncaster, 19.10.71. 6′5″, 17st 5lb. **Rep hons:** Barbarians (97-98). **ADPR:** Wakefield (1990-94, 21, 1t-5pts), Rotherham (1996-99, 15, 1t-5pts). Former England U21 captain. Educated at QEGS Wakefield, won five Blues at Cambridge between 1993-97.

BUNTING, Simon Colin (Prop)
Born Rotherham, 17.09.70. 6′, 16st. **ADPR:** Rotherham (1990-99, 87, 3t-15pts). Star product of the Rotherham Youth system who has been much involved with the club's success story.

BUZZA, Alan Jan (Full-back)
Born Beverley, 03.03.66. 5′11″, 13st. **Rep hons:** England A (7, Fr90, 1t, 2c-9pts), Barbarians (98). **ADPR:** Wasps (1990-94, 31, 4t, 5c, 11pg-62pts), Rotherham (1996-

99, 42, 5t, 1dg-28pts). Pacey former England A full-back. Educated at Redruth CS and Loughborough University. Won Cambridge Blues in 1988 and 89 while at Hughes Hall.

COOK, Daniel James (Lock)
Born Nottingham, 10.09.74. 6′8″, 18st 5lb. **ADPR:** Otley (1994-96, 12), Rotherham (1996-99, 38).

DUDLEY, John Robert (No 8/lock)
Born Sheffield, 16.07.66. 6′, 16st. **ADPR:** Rotherham (1987-99, 169, 40t-191pts). Voted Premiership Two player of the season last year, a loyal one-club man who has served Rotherham mightily over the past 12 seasons.

GARNETT, Terence Ashley (Hooker)
Born Hull, 10.05.67. 6′, 16st 6lb. **ADPR:** Wakefield (1988-98, 133, 17t-77pts), Rotherham (1998-99, 24, 2t-10pts). Long-time Wakefield stalwart who joined Rotherham last season. Former England Schools flanker who switched to the front row. Also won international swimming honours at school and is a black belt at karate. Has represented the Irish Exiles.

GREAVES, Philip Samuel (Centre)
Born Keighley, 16.02.78. 6′, 14st 8lb. **ADPR:** West Hartlepool (1998-99, 13, 2t-10pts). Formerly with Boldon, Bradford & Bingley and Northampton.

HALL, Lee (Prop)
Born Nelson, New Zealand, 12.02.71. **ADPR:** Rotherham (1998-99, 17, 2t-10pts). Formerly with Canterbury in New Zealand.

HANDLEY, Tobias Peter (Scrum-half)
Born Catterick, 14.04.76. 5′9″, 12st 3lb. **ADPR**: West Hartlepool (1997-99, 15, 1t-5pts). Formerly with Durham City and the Pretoria Quins club in South Africa.

HANSON, Richard John (Prop)
Born Whalley, 11.08.75. **ADPR:** Orrell (1996-97, 1), Fylde (1997-98, 17), Rotherham (1998-99, 15). Developing centre who learned the game with Calder Vale RFC.

HARPER, Jonathan Mark (Centre)
Born London, 09.09.74. 6′, 13st 7lb. **ADPR:** Rotherham (1994-99, 75, 20t-100pts). Creative ball-handling centre who joined the club from Sheffield University.

KENWORTHY, Glen Barry (Lock)
Born Dunedin, New Zealand, 15.03.74. **ADPR:** Rotherham (1998-99, 18, 1t-5pts). Key line-out forward who arrived at Rotherham from the Taradale club in New Zealand.

LAX, Dean (Wing)
Born Rotherham, 10.07.74. 6′, 13st 7lb. **ADPR:** Rotherham (1996-99, 51, 25t, 10c, 22pg-211pts). Strong-running wing who was Rotherham's leading try-scorer in the League last season with 19. Joined Rotherham from Dinnington.

McINTYRE, Darron (Scrum-half)
Born Hull, 07.04.69. 5′11″, 13st 7lb. **ADPR:** Rotherham (1995-99, 25, 3t, 1dg-18pts).

MANLEY, Paul Edmund (Backrow)
Born Stockport, 25.01.68. 6′, 15st 7lb. **ADPR:** Orrell (1987-96, 86, 7t-29pts), Wakefield (1996-97, 19, 5t-25pts), Orrell (1997-99, 30, 8t-40pts), Worcester (1998-99, 4). Vastly experienced and tough backrow operator. An RFU qualified coach who enjoyed a spell with the Ngtapa club in New Zealand.

MISSON, Michael Nathan (Wing)
Born Sydney, Australia, 07.05.73. 5′10″, 12st 5lb. **ADPR:** Bristol (1998-99, 18, 8t-40pts). Did well for Bristol last season before moving north to Rotherham. Played for Randwick, Easts and North in Australia.

NIARCHOS, Jason Thomas (Fly-half)
Born Sudbury, 30.10.78. 6′. **ADPR:** Rotherham (1998-99, 18, 1t, 27c, 22pg-125pts). Formerly with Sudbury and now at Loughborough University. Jason became a key member of the squad last year, performing well in the play-off games against Bedford when Doug Trivella was injured.

PARR, Howard Martin (Lock/flanker)
Born York, 01.01.72. 6′4″, 16st. **ADPR:** Orrell (1992-96, 8), Rotherham (1998-99, 16, 3t-15pts). Powerful former Bedford back five forward whose availability is often affected by his duties as an RAF officer.

PINDER, Mark (Flanker)
Born Rotherham, 18.12.70. 6′, 16st 7lb. **ADPR:** Rotherham (1994-99, 37).

SCHMID, Mike (No 8)
Born Canada, 28.11.69. 6′3″, 16st 1lb. **Rep hons:** Canada (15, Uruguay96, 2t-10pts). **ADPR:** Rotherham (1997-99, 40, 13t-65pts). Inspirational captain and the first Rotherham player to be capped. Almost certain to be absent in the early autumn with Canada on World Cup duties.

SCULLY, David Andrew (Scrum-half)
Born Doncaster, 07.08.65. 5′9″, 12st 6lb. **Rep hons:** England A (4, It92, 1t-4pts), Barbarians (96-97). **ADPR:** Wakefield (1987-98, 161, 51t, 6c, 17pg-293pts), Rotherham (1998-99, 24, 6t, 3c, 2pg-42pts). Evergreen former England A scrum-half who has played more League games (185) than any player in England. Toured New Zealand with England A in 1992, captained the North against the All Blacks the following year and was a member of the England Sevens team that won the World Cup Sevens in 1993 and competed in the 1997 tournament in Hong Kong. Has also helped the Barbarians to two Middlesex Sevens titles at Twickenham. Fitness fanatic who works as a firefighter.

SHEPHERD, Jon (Centre)
Born Dewsbury, 31.07.74. 5′9″, 13st. **ADPR:** Morley (1994-97, 63, 18t-90pts), Rotherham (1997-99, 30, 5t-25pts). Former England Schools and Colts representative.

SINCLAIR, James Robert Welch (Centre)
Born Enfield, 14.09.74. 6′, 13st 7lb. **ADPR:** Rotherham (1996-99, 17, 3t-15pts).

SPENCE, Neil Andrew (Flanker)
Born Hull, 30.08.76. 5′10″, 13st. **ADPR:** Rotherham (1996-99, 45, 2t-10pts). Lively openside flanker who started at Hull Ionians and was capped by England Schools before brief spells at Leicester and Gloucester.

THORP, James Milner (Prop)
Born Birmingham, 22.05.75. **ADPR:** Rotherham (1998-99, 5, 1t-5pts). RAF officer who has also played for Sudbury.

TOEWS, Harry (Prop)
Born Alberta, Canada, 07.08.71. 6′, 17st 6lb. **Rep hons:** Canada (4, Jap98). **ADPR:** Leicester (1998-99, 2), Rotherham (1998-99, 10). Experienced international prop who hails from the Abbotsford club in Canada.

TRIVELLA, Douglas Orlando (Full-back)
Born Harare, Zimbabwe, 03.05.74. 6′1″, 15st 2lb. **Rep hons:** Zimbabwe. **ADPR:** Orrell (1997-98, 15, 3t, 1pg-18pts), Rotherham (1998-99, 18, 5t, 28c, 21pg-144pts). Clever play-maker and goal-kicker. Formerly with College Rovers in South Africa.

TURNER, Stuart Charles (Prop)
Born Southport, 22.04.72. **ADPR:** Waterloo (1992-96, 38), Orrell (1996-99, 54, 2t-10pts), Worcester (1998-99, 9, 2t-10pts).

UMAGA, Michael T. (Full-back)
Born Auckland, New Zealand, 19.02.66. 6′, 14st 2lb. **Rep hons:** Manu Samoa (12). **ADPR:** Rotherham (1997-99, 35, 9t-45pts). Combative Western Samoan full-back who seems certain to figure in their World Cup side as he did in 1995. Lined up against his younger brother Tana in June when the latter was playing centre for the All Blacks against Western Samoa.

WADE, Simon **Ben** (Backrow)
Born Leeds, 11.09.74. 6′3″, 15st 7lb. **ADPR:** Morley (1992-97, 54, 22t-110pts), Rotherham (1997-99, 51, 23t-115pts). Former England Schools flanker with an enviable try-scoring record – 45 in 105 League appearances to date.

WEBSTER, Gavin (Lock)
Born Northampton, 11.05.73. 6′5″, 16st 7lb. **ADPR:** Northampton (1993-95, 12), Rotherham (1996-99, 63, 4t-20pts). Loughborough University graduate who joined Rotherham from Northampton in 1996. Represented Ireland in the 1996 World Students Cup.

WEST, Craig John (Flanker)
Born Rotherham, 08.02.64. 6′2″, 16st 7lb. **ADPR:** Rotherham (1988-99, 134, 25t-118pts). Another key figure in Rotherham's rise through the Leagues. Played his early rugby for Deddington RFC.

REVIEW

For the second season in succession Rotherham reached the Premiership play-offs, this time to be denied in the cruellest fashion against Bedford, finishing level on points after the two games but losing by virtue of Bedford's superior (4-3) try count. Another marvellous season, however, though automatic promotion and the League One title were probably squandered in the autumn when they lost four games – after being defeated by Coventry in November they didn't lose again until the final play-off game. Doug Trivella was top points-scorer with 144, John Niarchos was close behind on 128 and Dean Lax scored 19 tries. Veteran lock John Dudley was voted the Division's player of the season.

ROTHERHAM in Premiership Two 1998-99

Sep	5	A	Waterloo Drummers	Lost	7	22	J.Dudley (T) D.Trivella (C)
	12	H	Exeter	Won	28	17	G.Austin (2T) A.Buzza (T) D.Trivella (2C3P)
	26	H	Rugby Lions	Won	44	0	D.Trivella (T, 4C, 2P) M.Schmid (T) C.Hassan (T) B.Wade (T) J.Harper (T) G.Austin (T)
Oct	3	A	London Welsh	Won	27	13	D.Trivella (T, 2C, P) M.Schmid (T) J.Dudley (T) G.Austin (T)
	10	H	Blackheath	Won	46	3	B.Wade (2T) D.Trivella (T, 5C, 2P) M.Schmid (T) D.Lax (T) J.Harper (T)
	17	A	Orrell	Lost	12	19	B.Wade (T) D.Lax (T) D.Trivella (C)
	24	H	Bristol	Won	16	5	D.Trivella (T, C, 3P)

Nov 1	A	Leeds Tykes	Lost	10	15	J.Thorp (T) D.Scully (C, P)
Nov 7	A	Coventry	Lost	12	22	D.Scully (T, C) B.Wade (T)
21	H	Wakefield	Won	34	7	Penalty (T) T.Garnett (T) B.Wade (T) M.Umaga (T) L.Hall (T) D.Scully (C, P) J.Niarchos (2C)
Dec 12	A	Moseley	Won	16	6	G.Austin (T) J.Niarchos (C, 3P)
19	H	Worcester	Won	29	19	G.Austin (2T) M.Walker (T) M.Umaga (T) J.Niarchos (3C, P)
Jan 2	A	Wakefield	Won	40	13	M.Walker (2T) G.Austin (T) D.Scully (T) B.Wade (T) M.Schmid (T) J.Niarchos (2C, 2P)
16	H	Coventry	Won	19	12	J.Harper (T) J.Niarchos (C, 4P)
23	H	Leeds Tykes	Won	25	10	B.Wade (3T) D.Lax (T) H.Parr (T)
Feb 6	A	Bristol	Won	36	31	D.Lax (T) N.Spence (T) B.Wade (T) M.Umaga (T) D.Trivella (2C, 4P)
13	H	Orrell	Won	47	10	D.Lax (4T) J.Dudley (T) D.Scully (T) G.Kenworthy (T) D.Trivella (2C, 2P) J.Niarchos(C)
20	A	Fylde	Won	34	5	M.Schmid (2T) D.Scully (T) B.Wade (T) D.Lax (T) J.Niarchos (3C, P)
28	A	Blackheath	Won	29	19	M.Walker (T) J.Shepherd (T) D.Scully (T) D.Lax (T) M.Umaga (T) J.Niarchos (2C)
Mar 13	H	London Welsh	Won	28	8	B.Wade (T) J.Niarchos (T) J.Dudley (T) D.McIntyre (T) D.Trivella (4C)
27	A	Rugby Lions	Won	33	10	D.Lax (2T) M.Umaga (T) J.Dudley (T) B.Wade (T) D.Trivella (C, 2P)
Apr 3	H	Fylde	Won	43	16	J.Shepherd (T) B.Wade (T) C.West (T) D.Lax (T) M.Schmid (T) H.Parr (T) J.Sinclair (T) J.Niarchos (4C)
17	A	Exeter	Won	35	24	D.Trivella (T, 2C, 2P) B.Wade (T) H.Parr (T) D.Lax (T) M.Umaga (T)
24	H	Waterloo Drummers	Won	44	3	D.Lax (3T) G.Austin (T) J.Dudley (T) C.West (T) L.Hall (T) J.Niarchos (3C, P)
May 1	A	Worcester	Won	35	27	M.Walker (3T) G.Austin (T) J.Niarchos(3C, 3P)
8	H	Moseley	Won	27	0	D.Lax (T) M.Walker (T) G.Webster (T) T.Garnett (T) J.Niarchos (C, P) D.Trivella (C)
Play-offs:						
20	H	Bedford	Won	19	11	M.Umaga (T) J.Niarchos (C, 4P)
23	A	Bedford	Lost	19	27	D.Lax (T) D.Scully (T) J.Niarchos (3P)

Summary of Premiership scorers:

144 D.Trivella (5T, 28C, 21P); 128 J.Niarchos (T, 27C, 23P); 95 D.Lax (19T); 80 B.Wade (16T); 50 G.Austin (10T); 42 D.Scully (6T, 3C, 2P); 40 M.Walker (8T); 35 M.Umaga (7T), M.Schmid (7T); 30 J.Dudley (6T); 15 H.Parr (3T), J.Harper (3T); 10 C.West (2T), J.Shepherd (2T), L.Hall (2T), T.Garnett (2T); 5 Penalty (T), G.Webster (T), J.Thorp (T), N.Spence (T), J.Sinclair (T), D.McIntyre (T), G.Kenworthy (T), C.Hassan (T), A.Buzza (T).

Summary of Premiership appearances:

28 M.Schmid; 27 B.Wade (+1), J.Dudley (+6); 25 G.Austin; 24 M.Umaga, D.Scully, T.Garnett (+1); 23 G.Webster (+9), D.Lax; 21 M.Walker (+2); 20 N.Spence; 19 J.Shepherd (+8), M.Pinder (+6); 18 D.Trivella (+4), J.Niarchos (+4), G.Kenworthy; 17 J.Harper, L.Hall (+8); 16 H.Parr (+10), S.Bunting; 15 R.Hanson (+2); 12 C.West (+8); 11 A.Buzza (+3); 10 H.Toews (+3), C.Hassan; 8 D.McIntyre (+4), D.Cook (+6); 7 J.Sinclair (+4); 5 J.Thorp (+4); 3 S.Wilson (+1), R.Bramley (+2); 2 N.Pattinson (+2).

RUGBY LIONS

Formation of club: 1994 (originally formed in 1873)
Ground: Webb Ellis Road, Rugby, CV22 7AU
Capacity: 3,396 (Seated 240)
Colours: Orange, black and white
Honours: Champions Area League North – 1987-88, Division Two – 1990-91
Best League finish: 11th in Division One 1991-92
Best Cup run: Last 16 1990-91, 1992-93, 1997-98
Last season: Premiership Two – 11th. Tetley's Bitter Cup – 3rd round (lost 7-68 to Leeds Tykes)
Owners: Members
Chief executive: Mike Adnitt
Director of coaching: Geoff Davies
Team manager: Derry Diamond
Captain: Mark Ellis

BAILEY, David Daniel (Scrum-half)
Born Kettering, 28.03.75. **ADPR:** Rugby Lions (1997-99, 24, 3t-15pts). Formerly with Northampton and Kibworth.

BALE, Paul (Wing)
Born Rugby, 20.12.76. **ADPR:** Rugby Lions (1996-99, 59, 20t-100pts). Free-scoring wing, product of Rugby's Youth set up.

BISHOP, David (Scrum-half)
Born Westminster, 05.01.64. 5′10″, 13st 8lb. **ADPR:** Rugby Lions (1987-99, 152, 41t, 1dg-191pts). Former club captain who remains as effective as ever. Educated at Skinners in Tunbridge Wells and Leicester University. Has represented Warwickshire, the Midlands and Irish Exiles. Formerly at Kenilworth.

BURDETT, Robert Leslie (Hooker)
Born Rugby, 26.07.73. 5′11″, 14st 7lb. **ADPR:** Rugby Lions (1993-99, 63, 4t-20pts). Educated at Lawrence Sheriff School and Loughborough University. Now a schoolteacher at Nicholas Chamberlaine School in Bedworth. Warwickshire representative.

CZERPAK, Josef Stefan (Fly-half)
Born Reading, 25.08.75. **ADPR:** Exeter (1994-95, 2, 3pg-9pts), Newbury (1995-96, 5, 3t,1c, 1pg-20pts), Rugby Lions (1997-99, 10, 1t, 4c, 2pg-19pts).

DAVIES, Alwyn John (Flanker)
Born Ammanford, 14.10.75. **ADPR:** Rugby Lions (1998-99, 21, 1t-5pts). Made an immediate impression last season. Formerly with Amman Utd, Swansea and UWIC.

DAVIES, Martyn Lloyd (Utility back)
Born Ammanford, 12.10.73. **ADPR:** Rugby Lions (1997-99, 37, 4t, 33c, 64pg-278pts). Leading points-scorer last season with 189.

DAVIES, Matthew (Hooker)
Born Carmarthen, 23.07.74. **ADPR:** Rugby Lions (1997-99, 14, 1c, 3pg-11pts).

ELLIS, Mark Richard (Flanker)
Born Kirby Muxloe, 23.12.68. 5′11″, 14st 12lb. **ADPR:** Rugby Lions (1988-99, 119, 14t-66pts). Stalwart Rugby servant and fine flanker, Mark joined as a teenager from Hinckley. Educated at Mount Grace High, John Cleveland College and Hinckley College. Works as a builder.

EVANS, Denzil (Full-back)
Born Rugby, 01.12.74. **ADPR:** Rugby Lions (1994-99, 23, 11c, 11pg, 1dg-58pts).

EVANS, Stephen John (Prop)
Born 10.02.75. **ADPR:** Rugby Lions (1995-99, 13, 2t-10pts).

FIELD, Robert John (Lock)
Born Coventry, 22.06.71. 6′7″, 18st. **ADPR:** Coventry (1991-94, 20, 1t-5pts), Leicester (1994-97, 6), Rugby Lions (1997-99, 47, 3t-15pts).

GALLAGHER, Andrew Thomas Martin (Scrum-half)
Born Dungannon, 15.05.73. **ADPR:** Northampton (1994-96, 3), Rugby Lions (1998-99, 16, 1t-5pts).

GILLOOLY, Adrian Michael (Centre)
Born Rugby, 06.04.70. 6′, 14st 1lb. **ADPR:** Rugby Lions (1988-99, 101, 9t-45pts). Educated at Lawrence Sheriff School and Loughborough University and also played for a year with Dundas Valley in Australia. Works as an accountant. Irish Exiles representative.

GLADSTONE, Allan Fergus (Flanker)
Born Stonehaven, 29.03.78. **ADPR:** Rugby Lions (1998-99, 4). Great-grandson of the famous Prime Minister. Loughborough University student, having previously studied at Gordonstoun where he captained the Scottish Schools XV. Has also played for Taupiri in Waikato.

HARDING, Robert Tony Nelson Mantez (Hooker)
Born Hurstpierpoint, 12.03.74. **ADPR:** Rugby Lions (1998-99, 4).

HARRISON, Ben Richard (Wing)
Born Coventry, 08.09.78. **ADPR:** Rugby Lions (1997-99, 9, 2t-10pts).

HARRISON, Thomas John (Wing)
Born Rugby, 25.12.74. **ADPR:** Rugby Lions (1996-99, 15, 3t-15pts).

HOPKINS, Stephen (Fly-half)
Born Carmarthen, 15.02.74. **ADPR:** Rugby Lions (1998-99, 21, 1t, 1c, 2pg-13pts). Much-travelled fly-half who arrived at Rugby after spells at Neath and Swansea in Wales and Old Crescent and Ballina in Ireland.

JASNIKOWSKI, Mark (Centre)
Born Kingston-upon-Thames, 16.01.73. 6′, 14st 4lb. **ADPR:** Leicester (1996-97, 1), Rugby Lions (1998-99, 14).

KINSEY, Richard Mark (Lock)
Born Barnet, 05.02.64. 6′5″, 18st. **Rep hons:** Barbarians (97). **ADPR:** Wasps (1990-97, 75, 4t-20pts), Rugby Lions (1998-99, 22). Former England B lock who won a Premiership title with Wasps. Represented Queensland while playing in Australia.

MILNER, Robert James (Hooker)
Born Coventry, 05.06.68. 5′11″, 14st 9lb. **ADPR:** Nuneaton (1990-91, 1t-4pts), Rugby Lions (1992-99, 63, 7t-35pts). Educated at Nicholas Chamberlaine Senior at Bedworth and Warwickshire College of Agriculture. Works as a farmer.

MORGAN, Jonathan **Dean** (Fly-half)
Born Ammanford, 23.11.71. **ADPR:** Coventry (1989-90, 3), Rugby Lions (1997-99, 48, 8t, 1pg, 4dg-55pts). Began his rugby career with Dunvant and Bonymaen.

PAIN, Benjamin Joseph (No 8)
Born Leicester, 11.05.76. 6′4″, 16st 6lb. **ADPR:** Nottingham (1997-98, 25, 5t-25pts), Rugby Lions (1998-99, 8).

REES, David (Prop)
Born Merthyr Tydfil, 11.04.66. **ADPR:** Rugby Lions (1997-99, 40, 2t-10pts). Formerly with Newbridge and Bridgend.

REVAN, Samuel **Trevor** (Prop)
Born Birmingham, 05.12.63. 6′2″, 17st 7lb. **Rep hons:** England A (1, Ire91). **ADPR:** Rugby Lions (1988-99, 158, 9t-41pts). Immensely powerful prop who has missed just one season of League competition with Rugby, trying his hand with Dijon in France three years ago. Educated at Hatfield Crescent CS and a former member of Birmingham Welsh.

ROBINSON, Richard Andrew James (Flanker)
Born Coventry, 13.06.77. **ADPR:** Rugby Lions (1998-99, 1). Loughborough University student who has also played for Nottingham.

SAUNDERS, Edmund (Wing)
Born Nottingham, 02.11.60. 6′, 12st 7lb. **Rep hons:** Barbarians (95-96). **ADPR:** Rugby Lions (1987-99, 164, 80t-368pts). One of the great men of English rugby, he simply goes on and on. The leading try-scorer in League history with 80, though England honours always eluded him. Sevens specialist who also scored some memorable tries for Coventry – pre Leagues – and enjoyed a spell in New Zealand with the Takapuna club. Won an award from the Rugby Writers Club in 1996 for his services to the game. He threatens to give up ‘one day’.

TARBUCK, Christopher Richard (Backrow)
Born Harlow, 20.08.68. 6′4″, 17st 6lb. **ADPR:** Saracens (1989-93, 44, 3t-12pts), Leicester (1993-96, 18, 4t-20pts), London Scottish (1996-99, 51, 11t-55pts), Rugby Lions (1998-99, 18, 4t-20pts). Ultra-reliable all-purpose backrow forward. Educated at Mark Hall, Marlow and West London Institute, from where he joined the backrow academy at Saracens which also included Eric Peters and Ben Clarke, soon to be followed by Richard Hill and Tony Diprose. Represented England Students in the 1992 World Students Cup and has also played for the Scottish Exiles.

THOMPSON, Paul (No 8)
Born Warwick, 24.09.74. 6′4″, 15st 7lb. **ADPR:** Rugby Lions (1995-99, 41, 5t-25pts).

UNDERHILL, Neil Barry (Lock)
Born Lutterworth, 23.06.72. 6′10″, 17st. **ADPR:** Rugby Lions (1992-99, 61, 6t-30pts). One of the English game’s tallest locks, who also spent a year playing in Canterbury, New Zealand.

VAEGA, To'o Malo (Centre)
Born Moto'otua,Western Samoa, 17.08.65. 5'11", 14st 2lb. **Rep hons:** Manu Samoa. **ADPR:** Rugby Lions (1997-99, 37, 9t-45pts). Marvellously gifted Western Samoan centre who hopes to be appearing in a third World Cup this autumn – was ever-present in Manu Samoa's 1991 and 1995 campaigns. Has also played for Southland in New Zealand. Named one of his sons Cardiff after Western Samoa's famous World Cup win over Wales at the Arms Park in 1991.

WINGHAM, James Michael William (Prop)
Born Portsmouth, 01.06.70. 6', 16st 7lb. **ADPR:** Coventry (1992-93, 1), Leicester (1993-98, 1), Rugby Lions (1998-99, 20, 1t-5pts).

WINGHAM, Oscar John (Flanker)
Born Fareham, 08.03.72. 6'3", 17st 8lb. **ADPR:** Leicester (1993-99, 11).

WITHERS, James Alexander (Flanker)
Born Stratford-upon-Avon, 15.03.75. **ADPR:** Moseley (1995-97, 2), Rugby Lions (1997-99, 26, 4t-20pts).

REVIEW

Stubborn Rugby refuse to give up their place in Premiership One, despite almost overwhelming odds. Under the captaincy of Mark Ellis they finished 11th last season, a full six points ahead of 12th-placed Wakefield. Martin Davies was top points-scorer with 189 and Eddie Saunders again defied the years to finish as the top try-scorer with seven – he has now scored 80 tries in all League games. Elsewhere To'o Vaega proved a constant source of excellence at centre and Wasps and England B lock Richard Kinsey was a useful acquisition.

RUGBY LIONS in Premiership Two 1998-99

Sep	5	H	Blackheath	Won	18	12	J.Withers (T) T.Revan (T) S.Hopkins (C, 2P)
	12	A	Orrell	Lost	3	32	D.Evans (P)
	19	H	Bristol	Lost	20	30	E.Saunders (T) J.Wingham (T) M.L.Davies (2C, 2P)
	26	A	Rotherham	Lost	0	44	
Oct	4	H	Coventry	Lost	17	20	P.Bale (T) M.L.Davies (3P) D.Morgan (D)
	10	A	Wakefield	Won	26	22	P.Bale (T) A.Gillooly (T) P.Thompson (T) M.L.Davies (C, 2P) D.Morgan (D)
	18	H	Moseley	Won	30	8	A.Davies (T) T.Vaega (T) P.Bale (T) M.L.Davies (3C, 3P)
	24	A	Worcester	Lost	6	29	D.Morgan (P, D)
	31	H	Waterloo Drummers	Won	20	9	P.Bale (T) Penalty (T) M.L.Davies (2C, 2P)
Nov	7	A	Exeter	Won	23	7	D.Morgan (2T) E.Saunders (T) M.L.Davies (C, 2P)
	21	H	Fylde	Won	30	16	C.Tarbuck (T) R.Field (T) M.Ellis (T) E.Saunders (T) M.L.Davies (2C, 2P)

Dec	13	H	Leeds Tykes	Lost	9	18	M.L.Davies (3P)
	19	A	London Welsh	Lost	7	11	A.Gallagher (T) M.L.Davies (C)
Jan	2	A	Fylde	Won	14	6	E.Saunders (T) M.L.Davies (3P)
	23	A	Waterloo Drummers	Lost	3	11	M.L.Davies (P)
Feb	6	H	Worcester	Lost	23	36	E.Saunders (T) M.L.Davies (T, 2C, 3P)
	13	A	Moseley	Lost	20	35	E.Saunders (2T) M.Ellis (T) D.Evans (C) M.L.Davies (P)
	27	H	Wakefield	Lost	17	23	R.Field (T) C.Tarbuck (T) M.L.Davies (2C, P)
Mar	13	A	Coventry	Won	21	19	C.Tarbuck (T) S.Hopkins (T) M.L.Davies (C, 3P)
	21	H	Exeter	Won	13	9	R.Milner (T) T.Vaega (T) M.L.Davies (P)
	27	H	Rotherham	Lost	10	33	M.L.Davies (T, C, P)
Apr	3	A	Bristol	Lost	13	49	P.Bale (T) M.L.Davies (C, 2P)
	17	H	Orrell	Lost	29	41	P.Bale (T) T.Vaega (T) M.L.Davies (T, 2C) C.Tarbuck (T) J.Withers (T)
	24	A	Blackheath	Lost	20	43	M.L.Davies (T, 2C, 2P) B.Harrison (T)
May	1	H	London Welsh	Lost	12	33	M.L.Davies (4P)
	9	A	Leeds Tykes	Lost	21	64	D.Docherty (T) S.Evans (T) D.Bailey (T) D.Evans (2C) M.Bedden (C)

Summary of Premiership scorers:

189 M.L.Davies (4T, 23C, 41P); 35 E.Saunders (7T); 30 P.Bale (6T); 22 D.Morgan (2T, P, 3D); 20 C.Tarbuck (4T); 15 T.Vaega (3T); 13 S.Hopkins (T, C, 2P); 10 R.Field (2T), J.Withers (2T), M.Ellis (2T); 9 D.Evans (3C, P); 5 Penalty (T), J.Wingham (T), P.Thompson (T), T.Revan (T), R.Milner (T), B.Harrison (T), A.Gillooly (T), A.Gallagher (T), S.Evans (T), D.Docherty (T), A.Davies (T), D.Bailey (T); 2 M.Bedden (C).

Summary of Premiership appearances:

26 R.Field; 24 T.Revan (+9), M.L.Davies (+1); 23 E.Saunders; 22 D.Morgan (+1), R.Kinsey, M.Ellis; 21 T.Vaega, S.Hopkins (+13), A.Davies; 20 J.Wingham (+1); 18 C.Tarbuck (+1), R.Milner, A.Gillooly, D.Bailey (+9); 17 P.Bale; 16 A.Gallagher (+5); 15 J.Withers (+11); 14 D.Rees, M.Jasnikowski (+3); 13 D.Evans (+9); 10 P.Thompson (+1); 8 B.Pain (+4), Matt.Davies (+6); 7 S.Evans (+3); 6 B.Harrison (+3), T.Harrison, R.Burdett; 5 N.Underhill (+4), D.Bishop (+1); 4 R.Harding (+3), F.Gladstone (+2); 3 C.Morley (+1), J.Czerpak (+3); 2 D.Docherty (+1); 1 R.Robinson (+1), G.Blaize, M.Bedden (+1).

WAKEFIELD

Formation of club: 1901
Ground: College Grove, Eastmoor Road, Wakefield WF1 3RR
Capacity: 2,450 (Seated 450)
Colours: Black and gold
Honours: Division Three Champions – 1987-88
Best League finish: 2nd in Division Two 1994-95
Best Cup run: SF 1975-76
Last season: Premiership Two – 12th. Tetley's Bitter Cup – 3rd round (lost 8-16 to Kendal)
Owners: Members
Director of rugby: Steve Townend.
Coach: Roger Burman, Clive Harris, Max Greenwood, David Heroy
Player-coach: Matt Greenwood
Captain: Neil Summers

BIRKBY, Alex Mark (Scrum-half)
Born Sheffield, 21.07.77. 5′9″, 12st 5lb. **ADPR:** Wakefield (1995-99, 22, 3t-15pts).

BREHENY, Ian John (Full-back)
Born Harold Wood, 02.01.78. 5′10″, 13st 10lb. **ADPR:** Wakefield (1997-99, 25, 10t-50pts). Exciting talent at full-back who was the club's leading try-scorer with 10 last season.

BROOKING, Keith Simon (Hooker/prop)
Born Torquay, 07.05.73. 6′, 16st. **ADPR:** Exeter (1994-97, 36, 1t-5pts), Wakefield (1997-99, 34). West Country man who was one of the mainstays of Wakefield's pack. Formerly with Newton Abbot and Bath before beginning his senior career with Exeter. South West Divisional representative. Has also represented the Welsh Exiles.

DIXON, Stuart John (Centre)
Born Bradford, 21.02.77. **ADPR:** Wakefield (1998-99, 20, 3t, 6c, 13pg-66pts). Formerly with Bradford & Bingley.

EDWARDS, Owen David (Fly-half)
Born Hatfield, 14.12.78. 6′, 13st 7lb. **ADPR:** Wakefield (1998-99, 11, 3t, 1c, 1pg-20pts).

ELISARA, Faimafili **Caine** (No 8)
Born Auckland, New Zealand, 30.11.75. **Rep hons:** Netherlands. **ADPR:** Wakefield (1997-99, 26, 6t-30pts). Learned his rugby in New Zealand but his Dutch parentage saw him line up for the Netherlands in their World Cup qualifiers against England and Italy at Huddersfield last November. Also captained the Netherlands in their repechage games against South Korea in April 1999.

FLINT, Jonathan David (Centre)
Born Harrogate, 06.06.71. 6′2″, 13st 8lb. **ADPR:** Nottingham (1990-91, 1), Otley (1993-96, 36, 6t, 1dg-33pts), Wakefield (1997-99, 32, 7t-35pts).

GREENWOOD, Matthew James (Lock/flanker)
Born Leeds, 25.09.64. 6′5″, 17st. **Rep hons:** England A (13, Sp92, 1t-5pts), Barbarians (93-94). **ADPR:** Nottingham (1988-92, 27, 1t-4pts), Wasps (1992-97, 78, 5t-25pts), Wakefield (1997-99, 46, 1t-5pts). Vastly experienced former England A cap who won championship honours with Wasps before returning from London. Started his career with Roundhay and toured New Zealand with England B in 1992 before joining Wasps. Continues to defy a serious knee injury to remain the most consistent of forwards.

GUILFORD, Bryan Raymond (Prop)
Born Timaru, New Zealand, 19.06.69. **ADPR:** Wakefield (1998-99, 9). Formerly with Cleckheaton.

HARDCASTLE, Dean (Prop)
Born Doncaster, 26.01.76. 5′10″, 16st 7lb. **ADPR:** Wakefield (1996-99, 29). Former England U21 cap.

HUGHES, Richard Alexander (Flanker)
Born Dewsbury, 12.06.76. **ADPR:** Wakefield (1997-99, 12).

HURDLEY, Andrew James (Flanker)
Born Wollongong, Australia, 14.02.72. **ADPR:** Wakefield (1998-99, 18). Formerly with Terrigal in Australia.

LATHAM, Rhodri (Prop)
Born Ghana, 01.08.69. 6′1″, 18st 4lb. **ADPR:** Wakefield (1987-99, 126). Ever-present last season and one of the great servants of Wakefield rugby. Developed his game as a youngster in Ghana where his father worked as a mining engineer. Played for Selby before joining Wakefield. A builder by trade and a keen fisherman, he claims to have landed a 32lb pike. Still hoping to score his first League try.

LLOYD, Nicholas James (Prop)
Born London, 12.10.76. **ADPR:** Wakefield (1998-99, 16, 1t-5pts). Formerly with Old Alleynians.

McKENZIE, Leroy (Wing)
Born Birmingham, 02.09.69. **ADPR:** Coventry (1988-93, 43, 6t-24pts), Moseley (1993-94, 10), Wakefield (1998-99, 12, 5t-25pts). Blockbusting wing who returned to rugby union last season after a spell with Hull Sharks RL.

MAYNARD, Philip Michael (Centre)
Born Wakefield, 08.01.70. 5′11″, 14st 7lb. **ADPR:** Wakefield (1989-99, 95, 13t-62pts). Former England Schools and Colts cap.

MILLS, Matthew Peter (Lock)
Born Leeds, 29.12.73. 6′4″, 16st. **ADPR:** Rotherham (1994-98, 30, 1t-5pts), Wakefield (1998-99, 11). Formerly with Selby.

MORGAN, Matthew (Prop)
Born Sydney, Australia, 11.11.73. **ADPR:** Wakefield (1998-99, 7). Tough Australian who has played for Randwick, Sunnybank and Brothers back home.

PLEVEY, Scott Gary (Hooker)
Born Doncaster, 28.09.76. 5′10″, 13st 7lb. **ADPR:** Wakefield (1996-99, 16, 1t-5pts). Former Yorkshire U21 hooker.

RHODES, Thomas Edward (Fly-half/centre)
Born Bradford, 29.11.78. 6′2″, 14st. **ADPR:** Leeds (1998-99, 16, 1t, 1c-7pts). Has also played for Bradford Bulls RL.

SHINE, Benjamin John (Wing)
Born Sydney, Australia, 19.12.77. **ADPR:** Wakefield (1998-99, 10, 3t-15pts). Has played representative rugby for ACT.

SIMPSON-DANIEL, Christopher Paul (Scrum-half)
Born York, 15.07.78. 5′9″, 13st 7lb. **ADPR:** Newcastle (1997-98, 1), Wakefield (1998-99, 13, 4t-20pts).

SKURR, Jon Anthony (Flanker)
Born Basildon, 08.07.79. **ADPR:** Wakefield (1997-99, 8, 1t-5pts), Morley (1998-99, 2t-10pts).

SOWERBY, Mark (No 8)
Born 05.09.69. 6′4″, 16st 5lb. **ADPR:** Wakefield (1989-99, 93, 1t-5pts). Former England Students cap who is getting back into the swing after putting his rugby career on hold for two years while working in Turkey as a site manager for a chemical company.

SUMMERS, Neil Gary (Fly-half/full-back)
Born Leeds, 10.10.68. **ADPR:** Headingley (1987-90, 31, 8t-32pts), Wakefield (1997-99, 39, 8t-40pts). Hard-working captain who returned to rugby union in 1997 after seven years playing with Featherstone Rovers and Bradford RL.

URE, Philip Michael (Fly-half)
Born Malden, Surrey, 05.04.77. **ADPR:** London Irish (1996-97, 2, 2c, 1pg-7pts), Wakefield (1998-99, 13, 14c, 16pg-76pts). Leading points-scorer last season. Narrowly missed out on a Blue while at Oxford. Formerly with Richmond.

WHITE, Paul Joseph (Utility back)
Born 15.12.64. 5′10″, 12st 7lb. **ADPR:** Morley (1987-93, 37, 6t, 2dg-30pts), Wakefield (1993-99, 74, 11t-55pts).

WILSON, Glen Richard (Flanker)
Born Wakefield, 31.07.76. 6′1″, 15st 2lb. **ADPR:** Morley (1990-91, 2t-8pts), Wakefield (1996-99, 54, 5t-25pts). Former North U21 and England Students flanker who was ever-present last season.

YATES, Kern Clinton (Flanker)
Born Wegberg, Germany, 12.02.74. **ADPR:** Wakefield (1994-96, 13, 1t-5pts), Leeds (1995-97, 16, 5t-25pts), Wakefield (1997-99, 29, 2t-10pts). Dynamic openside flanker enjoying a second spell at the club. Former captain of England 16 Group.

REVIEW

Wakefield, for so long the standard-bearers of Yorkshire rugby and now ranked only third behind Rotherham and Leeds, did well to avoid relegation after another disappointing campaign. Just six games were won all season, the pick probably being a 25-13 home triumph over Orrell. Phil Ure was the leading points-scorer with just 76 while Ian Breheny crossed for 10 tries. In the pack, player-coach Matt Greenwood grafted hard all season as did Caine Elisara who achieved fame, of sorts, by playing for the Netherlands in their World Cup games against England and Italy at Huddersfield.

WAKEFIELD in Premiership Two 1998-99

Sep	5	A	Moseley	Won	33	32	A.Birkby (2T) C.Elisara (T) P.Ure (3C, 4P)
	12	H	Worcester	Lost	22	48	R.Hitchmough (T) P.Maynard (T) C.Simpson-Daniel (T) P.Ure (2C, P)
	19	A	Waterloo Drummers	Lost	25	36	J.Flint (T) L.McKenzie (T) C.Elisara (T) P.Ure (2C, 2P)
	26	H	Exeter	Lost	19	27	C.Simpson-Daniel (T) R.Hitchmough (T) P.Ure (3P)
Oct	3	A	Fylde	Lost	18	20	J.Flint (T) L.McKenzie (T) P.Ure (C, 2P)
	10	H	Rugby Lions	Lost	22	26	A.Birkby (T) G.Wilson (T) L.McKenzie (T) P.Ure (2C, P)

17	A	London Welsh	Lost	21	45	C.Elisara (T) L.McKenzie (T) J.Flint (T) P.Ure (3C)
24	H	Blackheath	Won	19	9	L.McKenzie (T) S.Dixon (T) P.Ure (3P)
31	A	Orrell	Lost	5	24	S.Plevey (T)
Nov 7	H	Bristol	Lost	15	46	N.Summers (T) C.Simpson-Daniel (T) J.Flint (T)
21	A	Rotherham	Lost	7	34	J.Flint (T) P.Ure (C)
Dec 12	H	Coventry	Lost	10	18	G.Wilson (T) O.Edwards (C, P)
20	A	Leeds Tykes	Lost	0	38	
Jan 2	H	Rotherham	Lost	13	40	P.White (T) S.Dixon (C, 2P)
16	A	Bristol	Lost	19	35	I.Breheny (T) S.Dixon (C, 4P)
23	H	Orrell	Won	25	13	B.Shine (2T) N.Lloyd (T) J.Flint (T) S.Dixon (C, P)
Feb 6	A	Blackheath	Lost	20	28	I.Breheny (T) C.Simpson-Daniel (T) S.Dixon (2C, 2P)
13	H	London Welsh	Lost	16	30	N.Summers (T) C.Elisara (T) S.Dixon (2P)
27	A	Rugby Lions	Won	23	17	K.Yates (T) N.Summers (T) I.Breheny (T) R.Ashforth (C, 2P)
Mar 13	H	Fylde	Won	27	11	O.Edwards (2T) J.Flint (T) R.Ashforth (4P)
27	A	Exeter	Lost	13	37	N.Summers (T) R.Ashforth (C, P) S.Dixon (P)
Apr 3	H	Waterloo Drummers	Lost	14	20	I.Breheny (T) R.Ashforth (3P)
17	A	Worcester	Lost	19	67	B.Shine (T) N.Summers (T) S.Dixon (T) R.Ashforth (2C)
24	H	Moseley	Won	38	20	I.Breheny (4T) R.Ashforth (T, 2P) S.Dixon (T, C)
May 2	H	Leeds Tykes	Lost	13	51	J.Skurr (T) I.Breheny (T) R.Ashforth (P)
8	A	Coventry	Lost	13	40	I.Breheny (T) O.Edwards (T) S.Dixon (P)

Summary of Premiership scorers:

76 P.Ure (14C, 16P); 66 S.Dixon (3T, 6C, 13P); 52 R.Ashforth (T, 4C, 13P); 50 I.Breheny (10T); 35 J.Flint (7T); 25 N.Summers (5T), L.McKenzie (5T); 20 C.Simpson-Daniel (4T), C.Elisara (4T), O.Edwards (3T, C, P); 15 B.Shine (3T), A.Birkby (3T); 10 G.Wilson (2T), R.Hitchmough (2T); 5 K.Yates (T), P.White (T), J.Skurr (T), S.Plevey (T), P.Maynard (T), N.Lloyd (T).

Summary of Premiership appearances:

26 G.Wilson, R.Latham (+1); 24 N.Summers, M.Sowerby (+8), M.Greenwood; 22 J.Flint, K.Brooking (+3); 20 S.Dixon (+2); 19 I.Breheny (+1); 18 A.Hurdley (+2); 17 K.Yates (+5), D.Hardcastle (+10), C.Elisara; 16 N.Lloyd (+7); 13 P.Ure

(+3), C.Simpson-Daniel (+3), S.Plevey (+6), R.Hitchmough; 12 P.White, L.McKenzie (+1), R.Hughes (+7), A.Birkby (+2); 11 M.Mills (+7), O.Edwards (+1), M.Burrow (+1); 10 B.Shine (+1); 9 B.Guilford (+2); 8 R.Ashforth; 7 M.Morgan (+3); 6 R.Thompson (+4); 5 J.Skurr (+3), P.Maynard (+2); 2 R.Wilson (+2), N.Dykes (+2); 1 E.Smithies (+1), A.Platt (+1).

WATERLOO DRUMMERS

Formation of club: 1882
Ground: The Pavilion, St Anthony's Road, Blundellsands, Liverpool L23 8TW
Capacity: 8,900 (Seated 900)
Colours: Myrtle, scarlet and white
Best League finish: 10th in Division One 1987-88
Best Cup run: Losing finalist 1975-76
Last season: Premiership Two – 9th. Tetley's Bitter Cup – 5th round (lost 10-27 to Wasps)
Owners: Members
Chairman: Raymond Wilson
Director of rugby/Coach: Tony Russ
Captain: David Blyth

BECKETT, Mark Douglas (Prop)
Born Hartlepool, 16.10.65. 6′2″, 19st 7lb. **ADPR:** Waterloo (1991-99, 120, 8t-39pts). Reliable front row man who started out as a No 8 before moving to Blundellsands. Played for Waterloo in their famous Pilkington Cup win over Bath. Graduate of Sheffield University and works as a financial advisor.

BLYTH, David John (Backrow)
Born Liverpool, 14.03.71. 6′3″, 17st. **ADPR:** Newcastle (1991-92, 1), Waterloo (1991-92, 6), West Hartlepool (1992-93, 9), Waterloo (1993-99, 91, 12t-60pts).

BRITTIN, Jason Mark (Prop/hooker)
Born Hastings, New Zealand, 24.10.73. 5′11″, 14st 2lb. **ADPR:** Waterloo (1996-99, 18). Arrived at Waterloo from Hawkes Bay. Keen cricketer.

CHARLES, Andrew John (Prop)
Born Rome, 04.07.73. 6′, 15st. **ADPR:** Waterloo (1998-99, 25). Previously with Bayonne in France and Powerhouse in Australia. Made an immediate impact after joining the club last summer.

DAVIES, Gareth Martin (Centre)
Born Widnes, 07.08.73. **ADPR:** Waterloo (1998-99, 19, 1t-5pts). Formerly with Warrington RL.

EDWARDS, James William (Fly-half)
Born Liverpool, 28.11.79. **ADPR:** Waterloo (1998-99, 4).

EVANS, Gerallt Lloyd (Prop)
Born St Asaph, 30.12.75. **ADPR:** Waterloo (1998-99, 12). Formerly with Bangor in North Wales and Fraser Tech in New Zealand.

GRAHAM, Philip John (Wing)
Born Carlisle, 02.12.76. 5′10″, 13st. **ADPR:** Liverpool St Helens (1995-97, 30, 8t-40pts), Waterloo (1997-99, 47, 8t-40pts). Formerly with Wigton.

GRIFFITHS, Lyndon Alun (Fly-half)
Born Bridgend, 17.02.74. **ADPR:** Waterloo (1996-99, 58, 4t, 71c, 132pg-558pts). Prolific points-scorer who has garnered 558 in just two seasons at Blundellsands since moving from Wales where he had first-class experience with Swansea and Bridgend.

HACKNEY, Stephen Thomas (Wing)
Born Stockton-on-Tees, 13.06.68. 5′11″, 13st 10lb. **Rep hons:** England A (13, Aus88, 13t-61pts), Barbarians (87-88). **ADPR:** Nottingham (1988-91, 25, 2t-8pts), Leicester (1991-97, 77, 25t-121pts), Moseley (1997-98, 5, 1t-5pts), Waterloo (1997-99, 23, 6t-30pts). A proven try-scorer with every club he has played for, Steve scored 13 tries in 13 England A appearances and can consider himself unlucky to miss out on England honours.

HANDLEY, Anthony Francis (Utility back)
Born Salford, 12.11.73. 5′11″, 13st 5lb. **ADPR:** Waterloo (1992-99, 107, 3t, 10c, 15pg, 4dg-92pts). Former England Colt and U21 cap who has played regularly for Lancashire. Educated at De la Salle College, Salford and St Ambrose Barlow HS. Played soccer for Salford Boys and the North.

HILL, Nigel David (Centre)
Born Amersham, 04.12.67. 6′, 14st 7lb. **ADPR:** Waterloo (1989-94, 43, 1t-5pts), Moseley (1994-95, 5), Waterloo (1995-99, 52, 1t-5pts). Has played cricket for British Polytechnics and Oxfordshire. Joined Waterloo after attending a sports science course at Liverpool Polytechnic. Educated at King Alfred's, Wantage. Teaches at Meole Brace School, Shrewsbury. Has also played for Oxford RFC.

HOLT, Matthew Robert (Hooker)
Born Ipswich, Australia, 30.10.71. **ADPR:** Waterloo (1996-99, 55, 8t-40pts).

JOHNSON, Steven John (Lock/flanker)
Born Swansea, 10.10.73. 6′6″, 15st 7lb. **ADPR:** Blackheath (1996-98, 5), Waterloo (1998-99, 2).

LARUE, Stephane Daniel Dominique (Flanker)
Born Bezons, France, 08.09.72. 6′5″, 15st 10lb. **ADPR:** Waterloo (1998-99, 15, 3t-15pts). Formerly with Grenoble and Rumilly in France.

McGOWAN, Louis Joseph (Lock)
Born Liverpool, 17.10.77. 6′5″, 16st 4lb. **ADPR:** Waterloo (1997-99, 9). Educated at Nugent HS and formerly with Sefton RFC.

MORRIS, Stewart **Wayne** (Scrum-half)
Born Swansea, 06.12.72. **ADPR:** Waterloo (1996-99, 40, 13t-65pts). Former Welsh Schools cap who enjoyed spells at Bridgend, Pontypool and Aberavon before moving to Lancashire.

O'KEEFE, Martin David (Prop)
Born Birkenhead, 28.04.78. 6′2″, 17st. **ADPR:** Waterloo (1997-99, 11). Formerly with Winnington Park. Educated at St Anselm's College and Manchester Metropolitan University. Has represented Merseyside at badminton.

O'KEEFE, Stephen James (Prop)
Born Birkenhead, 30.10.71. 6′, 17st. **ADPR:** Waterloo (1997-99, 6). Martin's older brother. Educated at Nottingham University, works as quality control engineer. Formerly with Liverpool St Helen's.

O'REILLY, John Paul (Scrum-half)
Born Belebi Pikwe, Botswana, 07.01.76. 5′10″, 13st 8lb. **ADPR:** Sale (1996-97, 7), Waterloo (1997-99, 28, 3t-15pts). Former England U21 cap.

STEWART, Lee (Flanker)
Born Johannesburg, South Africa, 26.03.71. 6′3″, 15st 6lb. **ADPR:** Waterloo (1998-99, 23, 2t-10pts). Typically aggressive South African loose forward who played for Transvaal and Treviso in Italy.

SWETMAN, Michael Andrew (Wing)
Born Rinteln, Germany, 26.11.80. **ADPR:** Waterloo (1998-99, 8, 2t, 1pg-13pts).

TEMMEN, Karl (Lock)
Born Salisbury, 23.09.74. 6′9″, 18st 10lb. **ADPR:** Waterloo (1996-99, 52, 1t-5pts). Missed just one League game last season and continues to be a major force in the Waterloo pack. Educated at Wellfield HS, Leyland. Works as a mechanical engineer.

WANDS, Stephen (Flanker)
Born Edinburgh, 07.12.75. **ADPR:** Waterloo (1998-99, 20, 1t-5pts). Formerly with Boroughmuir.

WHITE, Paul Andrew (Lock)
Born Brighton, 08.05.70. 6′4″, 17st 7lb. **ADPR:** Waterloo (1990-99, 87, 7t-35pts).

WOLFENDEN, Christopher Thomas (Flanker)
Born Waterloo, 05.02.69. 6′2″, 15st 11lb. **ADPR:** Waterloo (1993-99, 43, 6t-30pts).

WOOF, Shaun Anthony (Centre)
Born Liverpool, 06.03.77. 6′2″, 14st 7lb. **ADPR:** Waterloo (1996-99, 53, 15t-75pts). England U21 cap who was ever-present last season and joint leading try-scorer with five. Formerly with Caldy and educated at Caldy GS.

REVIEW

After starting the season with a sensational 22-7 win over Rotherham, Waterloo's season declined markedly and they had to be content with 9th place, which in no way reflects their ability and potential. Waterloo were nothing if not unpredictable. This was a side that could defeat Worcester (31-26) and Leeds (13-12) in consecutive games and then capitulate 41-14 to Exeter next time out. The consistent Lyndon Griffiths was again their top scorer, this time with 198, while Shaun Woof and Wayne Morris were joint top try-scorers on five apiece.

WATERLOO DRUMMERS in Premiership Two 1998-99

Sep	5	H	Rotherham	Won	22	7	G.Davies (T) L.Griffiths (C, 5P)
	12	A	Coventry	Lost	15	21	S.Larue (T) J.O'Reilly (T) L.Griffiths (C, P)
	19	H	Wakefield	Won	36	25	J.O'Reilly (T) M.Mullins (T) S.Woof (T) S.Larue (T) L.Griffiths (2C, 4P)
	26	A	Moseley	Won	15	13	M.Mullins (T) M.Beckett (T) L.Griffiths (C, P)
Oct	3	H	Worcester	Won	31	26	L.Stewart (T) P.White (T) S.Woof (T) L.Griffiths (2C, 4P)
	10	H	Leeds Tykes	Won	13	12	S.Woof (T) L.Griffiths (C, 2P)
	17	A	Exeter	Lost	14	41	M.Mullins (T) N.Hill (T) L.Griffiths (2C)
	24	H	Fylde	Won	27	6	S.Larue (T) L.Griffiths (T, C, 5P)
	31	A	Rugby Lions	Lost	9	20	L.Griffiths (3P)

Nov 7	H	London Welsh	Won	12	10	L.Griffiths (4P)
21	A	Blackheath	Won	24	18	S.Hackney (2T) P.Graham (T) L.Griffiths (3C, P)
Dec 12	H	Orrell	Lost	10	17	P.White (T) L.Griffiths (C, P)
19	A	Bristol	Lost	8	36	L.Griffiths (T, P)
Jan 2	H	Blackheath	Won	31	25	S.Woof (T) M.Holt (T) S.Wands (T) L.Griffiths (2C, 3P) T.Handley (D)
16	A	London Welsh	Lost	17	49	P.Graham (T) M.Holt (T) J.O'Reilly (T) T.Handley (C)
23	H	Rugby Lions	Won	11	3	S.Hackney (T) L.Griffiths (2P)
Feb 6	A	Fylde	Lost	5	24	M.Beckett (T)
13	H	Exeter	Lost	11	13	P.Graham (T) L.Griffiths (2P)
28	A	Leeds Tykes	Won	10	9	W.Morris (T) L.Griffiths (C) T.Handley (D)
Mar 13	A	Worcester	Lost	15	41	P.Graham (T) M.Swetman (T) L.Griffiths(C, P)
27	H	Moseley	Lost	8	32	M.Swetman (T) L.Griffiths (P)
Apr 3	A	Wakefield	Won	20	14	M.Holt (T) L.Stewart (T) L.Griffiths (2C, 2P)
17	H	Coventry	Lost	24	25	W.Morris (2T) M.Holt (T) L.Griffiths (3C, P)
24	A	Rotherham	Lost	3	44	L.Griffiths (P)
May 1	H	Bristol	Lost	13	44	C.Wolfenden (T) S.Woof (T) M.Swetman (P)
8	A	Orrell	Lost	15	59	W.Morris (2T) L.Griffiths (C, P)

Summary of Premiership scorers:

198 L.Griffiths (2T, 25C, 46P); 25 S.Woof (5T), W.Morris (5T); 20 M.Holt (4T), P.Graham (4T); 15 J.O'Reilly (3T), M.Mullins (3T), S.Larue (3T), S.Hackney (3T); 13 M.Swetman (2T, P); 10 P.White (2T), L.Stewart (2T), M.Beckett (2T); 8 T.Handley (C, 2D); 5 C.Wolfenden (T), S.Wands (T), N.Hill (T), G.Davies (T).

Summary of Premiership appearances:

26 S.Woof (+3), M.Holt (+7), P.Graham, L.Griffiths (+1); 25 A.Charles (+1), M.Beckett (+1); 24 K.Temmen (+4); 23 L.Stewart (+7), B.Kay, T.Handley (+4); 20 S.Wands (+4), J.O'Reilly (+6), N.Hill (+9), D.Blyth (+3); 19 C.Wolfenden (+10), G.Davies (+1); 18 W.Morris (+6), S.Hackney (+2); 16 P.White (+1); 15 S.Larue (+2); 12 G.Evans (+8), J.Brittin (+5); 11 M.Mullins; 8 M.Swetman (+4), L.McGowan (+7); 4 M.O'Keefe (+4), J.Edwards (+2); 3 S.O'Keefe (+3); 2 S.Johnson (+2); 1 D.Tully (+1), A.Towner (+1), B.Thomson (+1), L.Smith, R.Saverimutto (+1), I.Orford (+1), C.Inkson (+1).

WEST HARTLEPOOL

Formation of club: 1881
Ground: Victoria Park, Clarence Road, Hartlepool TS24 8BZ
Capacity: 7,500 (Seated 4,000)
Colours: Blue, red and white
Honours: Division Three Champions – 1990-91
Best League finish: 9th in Division One 1994-95
Best Cup run: QF 1982-83, 1992-93, 1995-96, 1997-98
Last season: Premiership One – 14th (relegated). Tetley's Bitter Cup – 5th round (lost 21-32 to Newcastle)
Owner: Members
Chief executive: Paul Mackings
Director of rugby: TBC
Captain: TBC

BEAL, Paul Andrew (Prop)
Born Malton, 10.02.68. 6′, 18st. **ADPR:** West Hartlepool (1994-99, 51). Formerly with Redcar.

BENTLEY, Mark James (Flanker)
Born Rinteln, Germany, 09.03.78. **ADPR:** West Hartlepool (1998-99, 3).

CASSIDY, Shaun (Flanker)
Born Middlesbrough, 13.10.69. 6′, 14st 10lb. **ADPR:** Wasps (1988-90, 2), West Hartlepool (1990-92, 7), Newcastle (1993-96, 31, 1t-5pts), Bedford (1996-97, 2), West Hartlepool (1997-99, 33, 1t-5pts). Former England Students representative who has travelled the world playing rugby, enjoying stays with Durban HSOB and the Olympic Club in the USA.

CULLINANE, Brett John (Hooker/prop)
Born Otahuhu, New Zealand, 14.05.73. 6′2″, 17st 4lb. **ADPR:** West Hartlepool (1997-99, 18). Reliable back-up hooker who hails from the Pukekohe club in New Zealand.

FARNER, Philippe Albert (Lock)
Born Dar-es-Salaam, Tanzania, 09.01.70. 6′7″, 17st 4lb. **Rep hons:** USA (4, Ton99), France A (1, En96). **ADPR:** West Hartlepool (1997-99, 40, 3t-15pts). Powerful former France A who now plays his international rugby for USA, qualifying through his American mother. Previously played for the famous Racing Club in France and for Invercargill.

FARRELL, Emmet Anthony (Fly-half/full-back)
Born Dublin, 06.03.77. 5′9″, 14st. **ADPR:** West Hartlepool (1997-99, 48, 15t, 2dg-81pts). Exceptionally talented young Irishman who was ever-present for West Hartlepool during their Premiership campaign last season. Has played Gaelic Football for Dublin and had soccer trials with Leeds United. A member of the Irish Schools squad who were unbeaten in Australia in 1996. Former Ireland U21 cap who has also played for Blackrock and University College Dublin.

GIACHERI, Mark Renato Giulio (Second row)
Born Sydney, Australia, 01.02.69. 6′8″, 17st 11lb. **Rep hons:** Italy (29, Rom92), Barbarians (95-96). **ADPR:** West Hartlepool (1997-99, 19, 2t-10pts). Australian-reared Italian who has been struggling with injuries but still hopes to play in the 1999 World Cup for Italy. Has played for the Randwick club in Sydney, the ACT Brumbies and Treviso.

GILBERT, Mark (Lock)
Born Wolverhampton, 24.09.75. **ADPR:** Walsall (1997-98, 19), Worcester (1998-99, 2), West Hartlepool (1998-99, 1).

HYDE, Daniel Wade (Flanker)
Born Holmfirth, 06.01.76. 6′3″, 15st 3lb. **ADPR:** West Hartlepool (1997-99, 16, 3t-15pts). Formerly with Huddersfield.

JOHN, Stephen (Wing/centre)
Born Cardiff, 11.10.73. 5′10″, 13st. **ADPR:** West Hartlepool (1996-99, 67, 25t, 1pg-128pts). Former Welsh Schools and U21 cap who was the club's top try-scorer in the League with six. Formerly with Cardiff, he was also a PE student at Loughborough University.

McDONALD, Shane Richard (Hooker)
Born Stratford, New Zealand, 21.06.71. 5′11″, 17st 2lb. **Rep hons:** Ireland A (1, It99, 1t-5pts). **ADPR:** West Hartlepool (1998-99, 15, 2t-10pts). New Zealand-reared hooker from Taranaki whose ability has already been spotted by the Ireland selectors.

MACLURE, Gareth Roderick (Centre)
Born Bury, 01.03.80. **ADPR:** West Hartlepool (1998-99, 9, 2t-10pts).

MONKLEY, Duane Innes (Flanker)
Born Morrinsville, New Zealand, 31.10.66. 6′1″, 15st 2lb. **ADPR:** Plymouth Albion (1990-91, 4, 1t-4pts), West Hartlepool (1998-99, 14, 1t-5pts). Superb hard-grafting flanker in the best New Zealand traditions who made an immediate impact when he became available. Also plays for Waikato.

NU'UALI'ITIA, Toetu (Scrum-half)
Born Auckland, New Zealand, 22.06.66. 5′8″, 14st 2lb. **Rep hons:** Manu Samoa. **ADPR:** West Hartlepool (1997-99, 43, 8t-40pts). Tough New Zealand-reared Western Samoan who played in the 1995 World Cup. His provinces in New Zealand include Counties, North Harbour and Auckland.

PEACOCK, Andrew (Hooker)
Born Newport, 03.12.68. 5′11″, 15st 7lb. **ADPR:** West Hartlepool (1996-99, 46, 1t-5pts). Former Wales Schools and U21 prop who experienced Welsh League rugby with Pontypool and Newport.

SALTER, Matthew (Flanker)
Born Greenwich, 02.12.76. **ADPR:** Blackheath (1995-96, 2), West Hartlepool (1998-99, 7). Formerly with London Broncos RL.

SCHRADER, Russell John (Lock)
Born Featherston, New Zealand, 02.05.74. 6′7″, 16st 7lb. **ADPR:** West Hartlepool (1997-99, 15). New Zealand lock who learned his trade with the Petone club.

SEYMOUR, Patrick John (Prop)
Born Northallerton, 18.07.78. 6′, 17st 7lb. **ADPR:** West Hartlepool (1997-99, 10). Formerly with Harrogate and Middlesbrough.

STONE, Richard John (Scrum-half)
Born Lincoln, 04.11.72. 5′10″, 13st 12lb. **ADPR:** Bedford (1995-98, 26, 8t-40pts), West Hartlepool (1998-99, 13). A graduate of Loughborough University who has also enjoyed a spell at Welford Road with Leicester.

TANGINOA, Peter Lawrence (Centre)
Born Vava'u, Tonga, 09.12.73. 6′, 15st. **Rep hons:** Tonga. **ADPR:** West Hartlepool (1998-99, 15, 2t-10pts). Tongan international who is returning to full fitness after a serious spinal injury incurred when playing for Tonga in the first leg of their World Cup repechage game against South Korea. Formerly with Northland in New Zealand and the Brisbane Broncos RL.

VAN DER ESCH, John Julian (Prop)
Born Lower Hutt, New Zealand, 07.06.69. 6′3″, 17st 7lb. **Rep hons:** Netherlands. **ADPR:** West Hartlepool (1998-99, 11). Formerly with Dundee HSFP, Edinburgh, and Petone (New Zealand).

WEBB, Christopher Andrew Cunningham (Lock)
Born Nottingham, 08.02.75. 6′5″, 17st 4lb. **ADPR:** West Hartlepool (1997-99, 4). Formerly with UWIC.

WHITEHEAD, Stuart David (Hooker)
Born Edinburgh, 21.01.70. 5′8″. **ADPR:** West Hartlepool (1996-99, 23).

REVIEW

A bitterly disappointing season for West Hartlepool who again found themselves unable to cement a place in the top flight having won promotion the previous season. Financially unable to sign the big-name players who can ensure survival, West's move to Victoria Park also backfired with much smaller than anticipated gates. Under coach Mike Brewer, West remained competitive at home, especially after the arrival of Waikato flanker Duane Monkley. Australian Stephen Vile was another marvellously consistent performer and will be missed after his move to Bristol.

WEST HARTLEPOOL in Premiership One 1998-99

Sep	13	H	London Irish	Lost	20	44	S.John (2T) S.Vile (2P) P.Belgian (2C)
	20	A	Gloucester	Lost	3	36	P.Belgian (P)
	27	A	Wasps	Lost	14	71	Penalty (T) S.Vile (T, 2C)
Oct	4	H	Newcastle Falcons	Lost	19	24	E.Farrell (T) J.Benson (T) S.Vile (3P)
	10	A	Richmond	Lost	23	41	J.Benson (T) S.John (T) S.Vile (2C, 3P)
	17	H	Bath	Lost	20	50	Penalty (T) E.Farrell (T) S.Vile (2C, 2P)
	20	H	Saracens	Lost	3	52	S.Vile (P)
	24	A	Harlequins	Lost	10	25	J.Connolly (T) S.Vile (C, P)
Nov	1	H	Leicester Tigers	Lost	15	45	Penalty (T) T.Nu'uali'itia (T) J.Benson (C, P)
	13	A	Manchester Sale	Lost	26	42	Penalty (T) S.John (T) S.Vile (C, 3P) J.Benson (C, P)
	22	H	London Scottish	Lost	7	37	T.Louth (T) S.Vile (C)
Dec	12	A	Bedford	Won	23	10	E.Farrell (T) M.Brewer (T) S.Vile (2C, 3P)
	20	H	Northampton Saints	Lost	9	33	S.Vile (3P)
	27	A	Newcastle Falcons	Lost	13	29	S.John (T) S.McDonald (T) S.Vile (P)
Jan	3	H	Wasps	Won	21	17	J.Ponton (T) T.Handley (T) S.Vile (C, 2P) E.Farrell (D)
	16	A	London Irish	Lost	21	43	T.Nu'uali'itia (2T) S.McDonald (T) S.Vile (3C)
	23	A	Northampton Saints	Lost	14	19	P.Tanginoa (T) S.Vile (T, 2C)
Feb	14	A	Saracens	Lost	27	48	S.John (T) P.Tanginoa (T) S.Vile (C, 5P)

Mar 14	H	Gloucester	Won	33	32	S.Vile (T, C, 6P D) D.Monkley (T)
28	H	Manchester Sale	Drew	33	33	J.Ponton (T) S.Vile (T, 2C, 3P) P.Farner (T) M.Mullins (T)
Apr 18	H	Richmond	Lost	35	36	M.Mullins (T) S.Vile (T, 2C, 7P)
21	H	Harlequins	Lost	37	47	K.Fourie (2T) J.Benson (T) D.Hyde (T) S.Vile (4C, 3P)
24	A	Bath	Lost	24	56	P.Greaves (T) E.Farrell (T) S.Vile (C, 4P)
May 2	H	Bedford	Lost	0	39	
8	A	London Scottish	Lost	14	26	D.Hyde (T) P.Greaves (T) J.Benson (2C)
16	A	Leicester Tigers	Lost	37	72	G.Maclure (2T) M.Brewer (T) P.Beal (T) E.Farrell (T) J.Benson (3C, 2P)

Summary of Premiership scorers:

240 S.Vile (5T, 28C, 52P, D); 41 J.Benson (3T, 7C, 4P); 30 S.John (6T); 28 E.Farrell (5T, D); 20 Penalty (4T); 15 T.Nu'uali'itia (3T); 10 P.Tanginoa (2T), J.Ponton (2T), M.Mullins (2T), S.McDonald (2T), G.Maclure (2T), D.Hyde (2T), P.Greaves (2T), K.Fourie (2T), M.Brewer (2T); 7 P.Belgian (2C, P); 5 D.Monkley (T), T.Louth (T), T.Handley (T), P.Farner (T), J.Connolly (T), P.Beal (T).

Summary of Premiership appearances:

26 E.Farrell (+1); 25 S.Sparks (+4), J.Ponton (+1), S.John; 23 M.Brewer (+1); 22 S.Vile, T.Nu'uali'itia, P.Beal (+4); 21 P.Farner; 20 J.Benson (+5); 17 J.Connolly (+1); 15 P.Tanginoa (+2), S.McDonald; 14 D.Monkley, T.Handley (+9), S.Cassidy (+4); 13 R.Stone (+9), P.Greaves (+3); 11 J.J.Van Der Esch (+6), M.Mullins, D.Hyde (+4); 10 A.Peacock (+6), B.Fuller (+2); 9 S.Whitehead (+9), G.Maclure (+5), M.Giacheri (+1), K.Fourie (+2), B.Cullinane (+4); 7 P.Seymour (+6), M.Salter (+2); 6 T.Louth; 4 H.Bishop (+1); 3 C.Webb (+2), R.Schrader, T.Herbert (+1), T.Collier, M.Bentley; 2 P.Belgian (+1); 1 M.Gilbert.

WORCESTER

Formation of club: 1871
Ground: Sixways, Pershore Lane, Hindlip, Worcester WR3 8SU
Capacity: 7,000
Colours: Navy blue and gold
Honours: Champions North Midlands One – 1989-90, Midlands One – 1994-95, Division Four North – 1996-97, Jewson One – 1997-98
Best League finish: 3rd in Division Two 1998-99
Best Cup run: Last 16 1997-98
Last season: Premiership Two – 3rd. Tetley's Bitter Cup – 4th round (lost 17-31 to Gloucester)
Owner & chief executive: Cecil Duckworth
Director of rugby: Les Cusworth.
Coach: TBC
Captain: Bruce Fenley

BALL, Dean John (Hooker)
Born Bromsgrove, 24.07.71. 5'7", 15st 4lb. **ADPR:** Moseley (1991-97, 62, 2t-10pts), Worcester (1997-99, 46, 3t-15pts). Formerly with Bromsgrove.

BAXTER, Nicholas Anthony (Wing)
Born Birmingham, 13.04.73. 6', 15st 8lb. **ADPR:** Worcester (1995-99, 66, 63t-315pts). Prodigious try-scorer who joined Worcester from King's Norton. Represented England at the 1998 Commonwealth Games Sevens tournament in Kuala Lumpur.

BEDDOW, Timothy Arthur Ronald (Hooker)
Born Dudley, 20.12.69. 6', 15st 11lb. **ADPR:** Moseley (1990-91, 3), Bath (1991-95, 3), Northampton (1995-98, 13, 1t-5pts), Worcester (1998-99, 1). Member of the England Students side at the 1992 World Students Cup. Educated at High Arcal, Dudley, and St Paul's College, Cheltenham.

CARTER, Nathan Edwin (Flanker)
Born Gloucester, 22.06.72. 6', 15st 10lb. **ADPR:** Gloucester (1996-99, 63, 5t-25pts). Arrives at Worcester from Premiership One Gloucester where he has been a first-team regular for the last three years. Formerly with Gordon League.

CLARK, Gary John (Flanker)
Born Coventry, 03.05.65. 6'3", 17st 7lb. **ADPR:** Saracens (1996-97, 9, 2t-10pts), Worcester (1997-99, 39, 4t-20pts). Former Saracens Second XV captain who has blossomed since arriving at Sixways.

COCKLE, James Christian (Flanker)
Born Clifton, 29.10.76. 6'3", 16st 6lb. **ADPR:** Moseley (1996-98, 28, 2t-10pts), Bedford (1998-99, 24, 1t-5pts). **Other clubs:** Bath, Keynsham. A feisty, talented flanker who made his presence felt in a fine backrow unit. Has already represented English Schools and England Under 21. Member of England's Commonwealth Games squad.

CONNOLLY, James Francis (Centre)
Born Wellington, New Zealand, 06.02.73. 6', 14st 4lb. **ADPR:** West Hartlepool (1996-99, 56, 7t-35pts). Consistent young New Zealand centre who was educated at St Bede's College and Lincoln University in New Zealand. Has represented Canterbury.

DENHARDT, Richard David Ian (Lock)
Born Birmingham, 13.09.67. 6'4", 18st 8lb. **ADPR:** Moseley (1987-98, 59, 3t-15pts), Worcester (1998-99, 21, 3t-15pts). Rugged lock and former Moseley captain who previously played for Wellington in New Zealand.

DEVEREUX, Simon (No 8/lock)
Born Gloucester, 20.10.68. 6'3", 17st. **ADPR:** Gloucester (1992-99, 66, 2t-10pts). **Other clubs:** Spartans. Former Spartans backrow forward, rarely far away from the fiercest action. Hit the headlines in 1995 after receiving a nine-month prison sentence, having been found guilty of assault in a second-team match against Rosslyn Park, when he broke an opponent's jaw with a punch.

FENLEY, Bruce (Scrum-half)
Born Cheltenham, 07.09.68. 5'8", 13st. **ADPR:** Moseley (1987-93, 38, 3t-14pts), Gloucester (1993-96, 41, 4t-20pts), Worcester (1996-99, 76, 25t-125pts). Terrific grafter for Worcester since arriving from Gloucester. Inspiring club captain. Former Midlands representative player.

HARVEY, Ben (Scrum-half)
Born Redruth, 26.06.74. 5'9", 13st. **ADPR:** Bristol (1995-96, 4), Richmond (1996-98, 7, 1t-5pts), Worcester (1998-99, 10, 1t-5pts). Opportunities restricted by the presence of Fenley at scrum-half. Member of England's sevens squad at the Commonwealth Games. Nephew of actress Jan Harvey.

HILTON-JONES, Richard (No 8)
Born New Zealand, 10.10.69. 6'4", 17st. **ADPR:** Worcester (1997-99, 31, 5t-25pts). Formerly played for Northland in New Zealand.

HOLFORD, Paul Curtis (Wing)
Born Gloucester, 02.12.69. 5'11", 13st 6lb. **Rep hons:** England A (2, Vic95, 1t-5pts). **ADPR:** Gloucester (1992-97, 56, 17t-85pts), Worcester (1997-99, 37, 18t-90pts). Gloucester's loss was Worcester's gain when Holford moved to Sixways. South West Divisional player.

HOUSTON, Gordon Patrick (Hooker)
Born Bangor, Northern Ireland, 22.03.67. 6'1", 15st 7lb. **ADPR:** Worcester (1996-99, 40, 4t-20pts). Formerly with Selly Oak, Instonians and Edinburgh.

HUGHES, Duncan Andrew (Centre)
Born Derby, 14.07.72. 5'11", 14st 6lb. **ADPR:** Worcester (1991-99, 82, 21t, 11c, 7pg-148pts). Class performer who numbers Newport and Llanelli among his former clubs.

JENNER, James William Clutton (No 8)
Born Reading, 27.11.71. 6'4", 17st 5lb. **ADPR:** Worcester (1997-99, 38, 20t-100pts). Athletic backrow man and another from Worcester to play for England in the 1998 Commonwealth Games. Formerly with Bristol and Exeter.

LILEY, John Garin (Full-back)
Born Wakefield, 21.08.67. 6', 13st 10lb. **Rep hons:** England A (4, Nam90, 6c, 7pg-33pts). **ADPR:** Wakefield (1987-88, 5, 2t, 4c, 2pg-22pts), Leicester (1988-97, 102, 25t, 129c, 232pg, 1dg-1070pts), Moseley (1997-98, 10, 2t, 8c, 7pg-47pts), Worcester (1997-99, 22, 2t, 11c, 36pg-140pts). Second most prolific points-scorer, behind Rob Andrew, in the history of English League rugby. Toured Argentina with England in 1990. Played his early rugby with Sandal.

LINNETT, Mark Stuart (Prop)
Born Rugby, 17.02.63. 5'11", 17st. **Rep hons:** England (1, Fiji89, 1t-4pts), A (4, It88, 2t-8pts), Barbarians (89-90). **ADPR:** Moseley (1987-95, 86, 11t-52pts), Worcester (1995-99, 86, 14t-70pts). At the very heart of Worcester's revival since joining from Moseley four years ago. Educated at Dunsmore CS in Rugby.

LLOYD, Stephen John (Lock)
Born Montevideo, Uruguay, 11.07.68. 6'6", 19st. **ADPR:** Moseley (1988-95, 63, 1t-5pts), Harlequins (1995-96, 2),Worcester (1996-99, 57, 5t-25pts). Former Wales squad member and Midlands representative.

LOFTHOUSE, James Christopher Michael (Fly-half)
Born Sunderland, 01.10.78. 5'11", 13st 4lb. **ADPR:** Worcester (1998-99, 8, 9c, 5pg-33pts). Former Sedbergh Schoolboy and England Schools captain, led England 18 Group on their successful tour of Australia in 1997. Has also enjoyed spells with Sale and Bath.

LYMAN, Neil Michael (Prop)
Born Bedford, 06.05.70. 6'1", 19st 7lb. **ADPR:** Moseley (1990-93, 13), Worcester (1994-99, 59, 7t-35pts). Former England U21 cap who has also played for Kidderminster.

McLAUGHLIN, Alastair James David (Centre)
Born Darlington, 31.05.76. 5'10", 15st. **ADPR:** Worcester (1994-99, 32, 8t-40pts). Has also played for Waterloo and Birkenhead Park.

MITCHELL, Peter John (Prop)
Born Cheltenham, 31.01.67. 6', 17st 7lb. **ADPR:** Moseley (1989-93, 11), Waterloo (1993-94, 2), Orrell (1995-96, 14), Worcester (1996-99, 51, 3t-15pts).

MORRIS, Simon Paul (Centre/wing)
Born Gloucester, 03.05.69. 6′, 13st 7lb. **ADPR:** Lydney (1989-90, 1t-4pts), Gloucester (1990-95, 48, 12t-55pts), Worcester (1997-99, 24, 6t-30pts).

MYLER, Robert (Centre/wing)
Born Widnes, 04.03.70. 6′, 15st. **ADPR:** Worcester (1997-99, 21, 11t-55pts). Formerly with Warrington RL and Oldham Bears RL.

ORGEE, Edward Rodney (Flanker)
Born 29.02.76. 6′4″, 17st 4lb. **ADPR:** Worcester (1996-99, 23, 2t-10pts).

RAYMOND, Christopher John (Lock)
Born Cheltenham, 01.03.68. 6′5″, 18st 4lb. **ADPR:** Moseley (1988-94, 45, 1t-5pts), Gloucester (1994-96, 21, 5t, 20c, 25pg, 4dg-152pts), Worcester (1996-99, 68, 6t-30pts).

RICHARDS, James Mervyn (Hooker)
Born Pembrokeshire, 11.09.75. 5′9″, 15st 3lb. **ADPR:** Bedford (1997-99, 35, 1t-5pts). Made the No 2 shirt his own and enjoyed a successful season in a formidable front row.

RICHARDSON, Nigel David (Flanker)
Born Worcester, 01.02.71. 6′3″, 15st 4lb. **ADPR:** Leicester (1992-94, 6, 3t-15pts), London Irish (1996-97, 5, 1t-5pts), Worcester (1997-99, 33, 1t-5pts). Educated at King's, Worcester, Loughborough University and St Edmund's House, Cambridge, winning Blues in 1993 and 1994.

ROBINSON, Tom William James (Hooker)
Born Birmingham, 08.01.77. 5′11″, 15st. **ADPR:** Worcester (1998-99, 3). Formerly with Gloucester, Bristol and Villagers in South Africa.

SCOTT, Christopher Clarke (Flanker)
Born Cheltenham, 14.02.64. 5′11″, 14st 7lb. **ADPR:** Worcester (1997-99, 15, 7t-35pts). Vastly experienced flanker who played for Newport and Neath in the Premiership.

SIMS, David (Lock)
Born Gloucester, 22.11.69. 6′7″, 17st 12lb. **Rep hons:** England (3, NZ98), A (23, Sp92, 1t-5pts), Barbarians (95-96). **ADPR:** Gloucester (1990-99, 138, 9t-43pts). Former Gloucester captain who moved from Kingsholm in the summer having turned down a chance to join Leicester. Educated at Churchdown CS.

SMITH, Timothy John (Full-back)
Born Gloucester, 10.05.62. 5′11″, 13st 10lb. **ADPR:** Gloucester (1987-96, 94, 11t, 58c, 141pg, 2dg-596pts), Worcester (1996-99, 54, 13t, 72c, 48pg-353pts).

TOMLINSON, Richard George (Centre)
Born Worcester, 25.11.71. 5′10″, 14st. **ADPR:** Worcester (1990-91, 1), Rugby Lions (1992-94, 16, 1pg-3pts), Nottingham (1994-97, 16, 3t, 2c, 3pg-28pts), Worcester (1996-99, 50, 12t, 11c, 10pg-112pts).

WALKER, Matthew (Wing)
Born Sheffield, 01.09.78. **ADPR:** Rotherham (1998-99, 21, 8t-40pts). Summer signing from Rotherham. Rapidly developing wing who made his England U21 debut last season.

WINDO, Anthony John (Prop)
Born Gloucester, 30.04.69. 6′, 17st 4lb. **ADPR:** Gloucester (1989-99, 89, 9t-45pts). Another to move from Gloucester in the summer. Formerly with Longlevens.

YAPP, Anthony (Fly-half)
Born Ludlow, 26.07.77. 5′10″, 12st 6lb. **ADPR:** Worcester (1996-97, 2, 1dg-3pts), Bedford (1997-99, 39, 5t, 18c, 23pg, 7dg-151pts). Took on the responsibility of

kicking with aplomb. Finished up top scorer with 138 points including three tries and six drop goals. Educated at Ludlow School, Tony learned much of his rugby at Worcester and also spent a season in Australia before joining Bedford where he worked closely with Paul Turner. Sister Jo has emerged as a star scrum-half for the England Women's side.

REVIEW

Ambitious Worcester lost five of their last six games and trailed in a distant third behind Bristol and Rotherham as their dream of Premiership One rugby came undone. During the season multi-millionaire owner Cecil Duckworth even tried to take over Sale in an attempt to secure Premiership One rugby, a bid which at the time of publication was being considered by the RFU. During the season kicking duties were shared by Rob Le Bas, who scored 162 points, and John Liley who amassed 140. Nick Baxter scored 13 tries to make it 64 in four seasons of League rugby.

WORCESTER in Premiership Two 1998-99

Sep	5	H	Coventry	Won	22	7	N.Baxter (T) R.Tomlinson (T) R.Denhardt (T) B.Fenley (T) R.Le Bas (C)
	12	A	Wakefield	Won	48	22	R.Myler (3T) D.Hughes (2T) T.Smith (T) M.Linnett (T) R.Le Bas (5C, P)
	19	H	Moseley	Won	23	8	R.Denhardt (2T) Penalty (T) R.Le Bas (C, 2P)
	27	H	Leeds Tykes	Won	24	19	D.Hughes (T) N.Baxter (T) R.Le Bas (C, 4P)
Oct	3	A	Waterloo Drummers	Lost	26	31	M.Linnett (T) J.Jenner (T) R.Le Bas (2C, 4P)
	10	H	Exeter	Won	40	15	R.Le Bas (T, 4C, 4P) D.Hughes (T) R.Hilton-Jones (T) N.Baxter (T)
	17	A	Fylde	Won	17	8	B.Fenley (T) R.Le Bas (T, P) J.Liley (2C)
	24	H	Rugby Lions	Won	29	6	P.Holford (T) D.Hughes (T) J.Liley (2C, 5P)
	31	A	London Welsh	Won	22	14	R.Myler (2T) J.Liley (4P)
Nov	7	H	Blackheath	Won	21	9	N.Baxter (T) P.Holford (T) J.Liley (C, 3P)
	21	A	Orrell	Won	13	9	Penalty (T) J.Liley (C, 2P)
Dec	13	H	Bristol	Won	20	9	J.Jenner (T) J.Liley (5P)
	19	A	Rotherham	Lost	19	29	A.McLaughlin (T) J.Liley (C, 4P)
Jan	2	H	Orrell	Won	17	0	A.McLaughlin (T) J.Liley (4P)
	16	A	Blackheath	Won	51	3	J.Devereux (2T) S.Morris (T) J.Jenner (T) J.Liley (T, 2C, P) B.Fenley (T) N.Malone (T, 2C) R.Myler (T)
	23	H	London Welsh	Won	14	12	R.Myler (T) J.Liley (3P)

Feb	6	A	Rugby Lions	Won	36	23	J.Jenner (T) R.Hilton-Jones (T) R.Myler (T) N.Lyman (T) R.Le Bas (2C, 4P)
	13	H	Fylde	Won	56	0	S.Morris (2T) Penalty (T) R.Le Bas (T, 4C, 2P) J.Jenner (T) S.Powell (T) P.Holford (T) A.McLaughlin (T) N.Malone (C)
	27	A	Exeter	Lost	23	27	R.Le Bas (T, 2C, 3P) Penalty (T)
Mar	13	H	Waterloo Drummers	Won	41	15	N.Baxter (2T) P.Holford (T) M.Linnett (T) S.Morris (T) B.Fenley (T) R.Le Bas (C, P) J.Lofthouse (3C)
	28	A	Leeds Tykes	Lost	16	24	S.Turner (T) J.Lofthouse (P) J.Liley (C, 2P)
Apr	3	A	Moseley	Lost	16	18	J.Goodwin (T) J.Liley (C, 3P)
	17	H	Wakefield	Won	67	19	N.Baxter (3T) A.McLaughlin (2T) B.Harvey (T) J.Goodwin (T) M.Crisp (T) S.Turner (T) S.Lloyd (T) J.Liley (T) J.Lofthouse (6C)
	24	A	Coventry	Lost	17	26	N.Baxter (T) J.Lofthouse (4P)
May	1	H	Rotherham	Lost	27	35	N.Baxter (2T) R.Hilton-Jones (T) R.Le Bas (3C, 2P)
	9	A	Bristol	Lost	11	21	N.Baxter (T) R.Le Bas (2P)

Summary of Premiership scorers:

162 R.Le Bas (4T, 26C, 30P); 140 J.Liley (2T, 11C, 36P); 65 N.Baxter (13T); 40 R.Myler (8T); 33 J.Lofthouse (9C, 5P); 25 A.McLaughlin (5T), J.Jenner (5T), D.Hughes (5T); 20 Penalty (4T), S.Morris (4T), P.Holford (4T), B.Fenley (4T); 15 M.Linnett (3T), R.Hilton-Jones (3T), R.Denhardt (3T); 11 N.Malone (T, 3C); 10 S.Turner (2T), J.Goodwin (2T), J.Devereux (2T); 5 R.Tomlinson (T), T.Smith (T), S.Powell (T), N.Lyman (T), S.Lloyd (T), B.Harvey (T), M.Crisp (T).

Summary of Premiership appearances:

26 C.Raymond (+2), D.Hughes; 25 M.Linnett (+6), B.Fenley (+3); 24 J.Jenner (+7), D.Ball (+3); 23 R.Le Bas (+1); 21 J.Liley (+9), R.Hilton-Jones (+2), R.Denhardt (+7); 18 N.Richardson (+3), P.Mitchell (+5), S.Lloyd (+4); 17 N.Lyman (+2); 16 N.Baxter (+1); 15 R.Myler (+4), S.Morris (+2), P.Holford (+1); 14 G.Clark (+2); 13 E.Orgee (+5); 12 G.Houston (+7); 11 A.McLaughlin (+1); 10 B.Harvey (+6); 9 S.Turner (+4), N.Malone (+3); 8 R.Tomlinson, J.Lofthouse (+2); 7 T.Smith (+2), J.Devereux (+2); 4 P.Manley (+2); 3 C.Scott, T.Robinson (+3); 2 A.Martin (+2), S.Hobson, J.Goodwin (+1), M.Gilbert (+2); 1 S.Powell (+1), L.Hinton (+1), P.Hassan (+1), L.Feurer, M.Crisp, J.Broady (+1), T.Beddow (+1).

Rugby in England 1998-99

Allied Dunbar Premiership

A season of high drama, tension and crisis off the pitch – London Scottish and Richmond were eventually merged with London Irish in mid-June – finished with Leicester deservedly being crowned Premiership champions. Leicester led almost throughout; Bath had their moments at the top of the table around October, but it was a brief flirtation with the leadership and Leicester had wrested it back from them by November. Thereafter the most serious challenge came from an unexpected quarter. While not left for dead, the nouveaux riches such as Newcastle and their ilk, who had dominated the previous season, did not add much life to the championship challenge. It was left to Northampton, guided by the guru of gurus Ian McGeechan, to provide Leicester with their only worry. But Saints blew it at home when they lost to Saracens in early February, that defeat providing the initial stuffing for a cushion of points on which Leicester sat until it was Tigers' turn to visit Saints. Leicester eased through in front of 10,000 fanatics at Franklin's Gardens and that was that, an achievement all the more praiseworthy since they were crippled by injuries throughout. Centre Will Greenwood was the most serious casualty, a groin injury ending his season back in November. But they also had to do without Joel Stransky for a sizeable chunk of the campaign and of course they lost the services of Austin Healey after he was cited for stamping on London Irish's Kevin Putt and banned for eight weeks. Captain Martin Johnson was not without his problems, but did appear to be unfortunate in the number of white and yellow cards that he picked up. His utter professionalism and dedication to the cause saw him through and he finished the season on a personal high, lifting nearly every individual award going. His leadership qualities were honed throughout a difficult programme and under him Leicester proved uncatchable. Among those who tried were London Irish who, under the canny coaching of Dick Best and Andy Keast, prospered in the most unlikely of situations. They were one of only four teams to beat Leicester, a Conor O'Shea drop goal in injury time at Sunbury doing the trick and seeing the Exiles home by a solitary point.

The incentive of European Cup rugby for the top six finishers concentrated minds and tension right to the end. After Northampton and Leicester had secured the top two places there was a regular scrap for the remaining four. At one point it looked as if London Irish would take one of them, but they were falsely placed having played more games than their rivals and in the end they just lost on points difference to Bath. The West Country side, aggrieved at having missed out on a chance to defend their European title this season because of the English clubs' boycott, had appeared to be out of it themselves until their final match, against London Scottish at the Recreation Ground. Bath ran in a dozen tries, a result which meant that Newcastle had to beat Saracens by a clear 30 points in their final Premiership match of the season. The game was to be played four days after Newcastle's Cup final defeat and understandably they lost. So Saracens, Harlequins, Wasps and Bath join the Saints and the Tigers in Europe.

There was only one runner in it at the other end of the table. West Hartlepool just could not compete. They did pull off a shocking victory over Wasps in the New Year and there were further triumphs over Bedford and Gloucester, as well as a high-scoring draw at home to Sale – indeed they went close to victory in a couple of other matches – but overall they were outclassed. Bedford survived but only after undergoing the prolonged torture of the play-offs against Rotherham. The first leg went Rotherham's way up at Clifton Lane, but Bedford won the second leg at Goldington Road and Alistair Murdoch's solo try early in the second half clinched Premiership One rugby for them, because having finished level on aggregate play-off points (38 each) Bedford slipped through on try count. There was a distinctly soccer-like feel to the game for much of the season as clubs began to turf out players and coaches. Richard Hill parted company with Gloucester, John Mitchell left Sale, Rob Smith was shunted aside at Wasps (who then signed up Mitchell) and Saracens dispensed with Paul Turner's help on the coaching front.

Premiership Two was crammed with intrigue and excitement. Essentially there were only ever three teams in it: Bristol, Worcester and Rotherham. True, Coventry, London Welsh and Leeds did rattle their sabres from time to time, but they were never serious contenders. In November Worcester suffered a setback which could have had a bearing on the outcome, although thankfully it did not. They were deducted two points for fielding an ineligible player, hooker Tom Robinson signed from Bath, and although they protested that administrative errors had been made by the Rugby Football Union, the points were not restored. Leeds also suffered. Their insistence on playing Rugby League star Wendell Sailor when confusion reigned over his eligibility cost them four points in the end – still not enough, as it turned out, to take them into the play-offs. Bristol, after long months when their own destiny looked in doubt, got everything in place to buy their way into the top flight. Struggling London Scottish were to have been the vehicle, but thankfully it was unnecessary, Bristol returning to Premiership One on their own recognisance, or to be more accurate, on points difference from Rotherham – a far more satisfactory route to the top. It was the second season on the trot that the Yorkshire club had reached the play-offs. They were nearer this time than last and it is surely only a matter of time before they join the elite.

Down in the relegation zone Blackheath and Fylde fought a desperate battle to avoid the drop and ultimately failed, while in Jewson National League One Henley Hawks and Manchester were in a different class to their rivals and were duly promoted.

Premiership One

	P	*W*	*D*	*L*	*F*	*A*	*Pts*
Leicester	26	22	0	4	771	423	44
Northampton	26	19	0	7	754	556	38
Saracens	26	16	1	9	748	583	33
NEC Harlequins	26	16	1	9	690	653	33
Wasps	26	15	1	10	717	506	31
Bath	26	15	0	11	698	574	30
London Irish	26	15	0	11	703	607	30
Newcastle Falcons	26	14	0	12	719	639	28
Richmond	26	11	2	13	720	715	22*
Gloucester	26	9	1	16	554	643	19
Manchester Sale	26	9	1	16	604	731	19
London Scottish	26	8	0	18	491	734	16
Bedford	26	6	0	20	552	859	12
West Hartlepool	26	3	1	22	501	1007	7

* 2 points deducted for not fulfilling fixtures on specified dates.

Play-offs (two legs): Rotherham 19 Bedford 11; Bedford 27 Rotherham 19. Bedford win by scoring more tries. Bedford and Rotherham stay in their respective divisions.

Premiership Two

	P	*W*	*D*	*L*	*F*	*A*	*Pts*
Bristol	26	22	0	4	848	418	44
Rotherham	26	22	0	4	775	347	44
Worcester	26	18	0	8	716	409	34*
London Welsh	26	17	0	9	662	552	34
Exeter	26	14	1	11	591	598	29
Leeds Tykes	26	16	0	10	713	367	28†
Coventry	26	14	0	12	652	560	28
Orrell	26	12	0	14	566	483	24
Waterloo	26	12	0	14	419	634	24
Moseley	26	10	0	16	498	633	20
Rugby Lions	26	9	0	17	425	660	18
Wakefield	26	6	0	20	469	812	12
Blackheath	26	5	0	21	419	842	10
Fylde	26	4	1	21	375	805	9

* 2 points deducted for fielding ineligible player.
† 4 points deducted for fielding ineligible player.

Top Premiership points-scorers: 331 J.Schuster (Harlequins); 318 G.Johnson (Saracens); 306 J.Wilkinson (Newcastle); 305 S.Gough (Coventry); 294 M.Catt (Bath); 263 K.Logan (Wasps); 250 S.Tuipulotu (Leeds); 242 S.Howarth (Manchester Sale); 241 B.Easson (Exeter); 240 S.Vile (West Hartlepool); 224 S.Verbickas (Orrell); 215 N.Woods (London Irish); 203 E.Va'a (Richmond); 202 J.Stransky (Leicester).

Top Premiership try-scorers (excluding play-offs): 18 D.Lax (Rotherham); 16 N.Back (Leicester), B.Wade (Rotherham); 15 A.Currier (London Welsh), A.Smallwood (Coventry); 14 P.Lam (Northampton), J.Guscott (Bath), L.Woodard (London Welsh); 13 I.Balshaw (Bath), L.Nabaro (Bristol), N.Baxter (Worcester), S.Verbickas (Orrell), A.Larkin (Bristol).

Note: D.Lax also scored a try in a play-off game against Bedford.

1000 points in the English National Leagues 1987-99:

1,318 Rob Andrew (Wasps/Newcastle) 39, 103, 90, 126, –, 29, 159, 135, 93, 292, 226, 26
1,279 John Liley (Wakefield/Leicester/Moseley/Worcester) 22, 9, 126, 110, 125, 106, 28, 99, 272, 195, 47, 140
1,160 Paul Grayson (Waterloo/Northampton) –, –, –, –, –, 126, 132, 189, 218, 129, 210, 156
1,090 Andy Green (Exeter) 42, 6, 97, 92, 77, 122, 130, 32, 192, 300, –, –
1,053 Mark Mapletoft (Rugby/Gloucester) –, –, 4, –, 60, 26, 115, 85, 21, 269, 275, 198
1,048 Steve Gough (Fylde/Coventry) 20, 4, –, 7, 6, 13, 17, 36, 138, 404, 98, 305
1,042 Jon Callard (Bath) –, –, 27, –, –, 29, 178, 150, 236, 224, 183, 15

Leading try-scorers in the English National Leagues 1987-99:

77 Eddie Saunders (Rugby) 7, 9, 7, 7, 2, 3, 2, 7, 9, 8, 12, 4
71 Mark Sephton (Liverpool St Helens) –, –, 6, 3, 3, 8, 9, 7, 7, 11, 8, 9
67 Jeremy Guscott (Bath) 1, 10, 4, 5, 1, 3, 2, 1, 9, 12, 5, 14
65 Nick Baxter (Worcester) –, –, –, –, –, –, –, –, 5, 18, 29, 13
62 Rory Underwood (Leicester/Bedford) 1, 1, 4, 8, 9, 2, –, 3, 8, 7, 7, 12
61 Daren O'Leary (Saracens/Harlequins) –, –, –, –, –, 3, 11, 1, 14, 15, 9, 8
57 Dave Scully (Wakefield/Rotherham) 6, 8, 4, 4, 3, –, 3, 2, 7, 9, 5, 6

Jewson One

	P	W	D	L	F	A	Pts
Henley Hawks	26	22	1	3	644	299	45
Manchester	26	20	1	5	758	372	41
Rosslyn Park	26	17	1	8	588	371	35
Nottingham	26	16	0	10	590	469	32
Otley	26	15	1	10	508	416	31
Newbury	26	14	1	11	552	476	29
Wharfedale	26	13	1	12	477	421	27
Lydney	26	11	2	13	438	482	24
Camberley	26	10	1	15	529	661	21
Reading	26	10	0	16	468	635	20
Birmingham & Solihull	26	9	0	17	422	523	18
Harrogate	26	8	2	16	311	461	18
Morley	26	7	1	18	468	643	15
Liverpool St Helens	26	4	0	22	335	859	8

Jewson Two (North)

	P	W	D	L	F	A	Pts
Preston Grasshoppers	26	23	0	3	822	341	46
Stourbridge	26	22	0	4	895	413	44
New Brighton	26	20	0	6	703	329	40
Kendal	26	18	0	8	635	347	36
Nuneaton	26	14	2	10	597	533	30
Sheffield	26	15	0	11	497	455	30
Sandal	26	13	0	13	697	611	26
Sedgley Park	26	12	1	13	710	554	25
Walsall	26	10	1	15	515	720	21
Aspatria	26	10	0	16	578	675	20
Whitchurch	26	9	1	16	450	599	19
Hinckley	26	7	1	18	445	733	15
Lichfield	26	3	0	23	371	950	6
Winnington Park	26	3	0	23	310	965	6

Jewson Two (South)

	P	W	D	L	F	A	Pts
Bracknell	26	23	1	2	631	317	47
Esher	26	23	0	3	864	308	46
North Walsham	26	22	0	4	627	306	44
Barking	26	19	1	6	644	327	39
Metropolitan Police	26	14	1	11	470	545	29
Norwich	26	11	0	15	383	427	22
Clifton	26	10	1	15	415	483	21
Tabard	26	9	1	16	461	501	19
Weston-super-Mare	26	9	1	16	417	588	19
Bridgwater	26	8	2	16	462	624	18
Redruth	26	8	1	17	503	654	17
Plymouth Albion	26	7	1	18	455	666	15
Cheltenham	26	7	0	19	335	608	14
Havant	26	7	0	19	361	674	14

Other Champions 1998-99

NORTH

North One: Doncaster. North Two: Bradford & Bingley. North West One: Aldwinians. North West Two: Stockport. North West Three: Wigan. North East One: Darlington Mowden Park. North East Two: Darlington. North East Three: Selby. North Lancs/Cumbria: Blackpool. North Lancs One: De La Salle. North Lancs Two: Burnage. Cumbria: Millom. South Lancs/Cheshire One: St Edward Old Boys. South Lancs/Cheshire Two: Dukinfield. South Lancs/Cheshire Three: Moore. South Lancs/Cheshire Four: Halton. Durham/Northumberland One: Medicals. Durham/Northumberland Two: Houghton. Durham/Northumberland Three: Wallsend. Durham/Northumberland Four: Jarrovians. Yorkshire One: Huddersfield YMCA. Yorkshire Two: Scarborough. Yorkshire Three: York R.I. Yorkshire Four: Old Rishworthians. Yorkshire Five: Rotherham Clifton.

MIDLANDS

Midlands One: Bedford Athletic. Midlands Two: Longton. Midlands West One: Malvern. Midlands West Two: Newcastle-under-Lyme. Midlands East One: Wellingborough. Midlands East Two: Luton. Staffordshire/Warwickshire: Silhillians. Staffordshire: Uttoxeter. Warwickshire: Atherstone. North Midlands One: Bridgnorth. North Midlands Two: Veseyans. Notts, Lincs & Derbyshire One: Ashfield. Notts, Lincs & Derbyshire Two: Barton & District. Notts, Lincs & Derbyshire Three: Bolsover. East Midlands/Leicestershire One: Market Bosworth. East Midlands/Leicestershire Two: Wellingborough OG. East Midlands/Leicestershire Three: Corby.

SOUTH WEST

South West One: Penzance & Newlyn. South West Two West: Cinderford. South West Two East: Dorchester. Western Counties West: Truro. Western Counties North: Hornets. Southern Counties North: Olney. Southern Counties South: Chippenham. Cornwall/Devon: Newton Abbot. Gloucestershire/Somerset: Barton Hill OB. Bucks/Oxfordshire One: Witney. Bucks/Oxfordshire Two: Wheatley. Berks, Dorset & Wilts One: Ivel Barbarians. Berks, Dorset & Wilts Two: Minety. Berks, Dorset & Wilts Three: Bradford on Avon. Devon One: Wessex. Devon Two: Totnes. Devon Three: Plymouth YMCA. Cornwall One: St Just. Cornwall Two: St Agnes. Gloucestershire One: Chipping Sodbury. Gloucestershire Two: Westbury-on-Severn. Gloucestershire Three: Gloucester CS Tigers. Somerset One: Avon. Somerset Two: Broad Plain. Somerset Three: Castle Cary.

LONDON & SOUTH EAST

London One: Westcombe Park. London Two North: Cambridge. London Two South: Winchester. London Three North East: Chelmsford. London Three North West: London Nigerian. London Three South East: Maidstone. London South West: Effingham & Leatherhead. Herts/Middlesex One: Imperial Medicals. Herts/Middlesex Two: Bank of England. Herts/Middlesex Three: Northolt. Herts/Middlesex Four North: Chess Valley. Herts/Middlesex Four South: London Tribes. Eastern Counties One: Thetford. Eastern Counties Two: Billericay. Eastern Counties Three North: Wisbech. Eastern Counties Three South: East London. Eastern Counties Four North: Brightlingsea. Eastern Counties Four South: Millwall Albion. Kent One: Dartfordians. Kent Two: New Ash Green. Kent Three: Greenwich. Sussex One: Hove. Sussex Two: Pulborough. Sussex Three: Plumpton. Hampshire One: Tottonians. Hampshire Two: Romsey. Hampshire Three: AC Delco. Surrey One: Cobham. Surrey Two: Old Tiffinians. Surrey Three: Haslemere. Surrey Four: Old Bevonians.

TETLEY'S BITTER CUP 1998-99

Final

Newcastle 19 Wasps 29 (Twickenham, 15 May 1999)

This was the day Wasps finally came in from the cold. Having frozen on four previous Twickenham appearances including a humiliating defeat last year, Wasps at last got their name on the Tetley's Bitter Cup. It was also something of a personal victory for Wasps fly-half Alex King and successfully ended an unhappy year of injury and poor form for him. King set Wasps on the way with a superbly taken try in the 27th minute; breaking through the midfield shackles with the Newcastle defence bemused by Mark Denney's decoy run at a scrum, he kicked ahead and beat Gary Armstrong in the dive for the ball as it came to rest under the Newcastle posts. His compelling and influential performance left Jonny Wilkinson, one of his rivals for the England shirt, in the shade. Wilkinson, England's boy wonder, was at stand-off in the absence of the injured Rob Andrew, whose tactical alertness and experience was sorely missed. In contrast, Wasps had in Gareth Rees one of the most experienced players on the pitch, Rees having been an 18-year-old schoolboy when he appeared for Wasps in the first of their five final appearances.

Newcastle had their moments, but no luck. The forwards put in some massive drives, one taking them up the Wasps line, but when the defence was penalised for infringing, referee Steve Lander awarded a kick not a penalty try. Vai'aiga Tuigamala also got close after an interception, but he was brilliantly and bravely tackled by Josh Lewsey a stride away from the line and bundled out of play into the corner. As if that was not enough, later in the game Lewsey himself intercepted a Tuigamala pass meant for Stuart Legg and raced away to score Wasps' second try. The conversion by Rees took the Canadian's personal tally to a Cup final record of 16 points. At least there was some consolation for Tuigamala when he managed in his turn to intercept a Lewsey pass in the final minute and score the Falcons' only try.

For Lewsey, after the nightmare of England's antipodean tour last summer, the game marked his final rehabilitation. Although he had a decent tour on a personal level, he was still scarred by the battering England received and has not been included in any international get-together since. 'It has been disappointing,' admitted Lewsey, who filled the No 10 shirt on the tour. 'No one has spoken to me about it, where I should play or what I need to do.' Lewsey saw the queue for the stand-off berth at Twickenham and after turning out at full-back for Wasps this season, will no doubt be glad he had such a good game on the wing, coming in as he did for the injured Kenny Logan.

There was a string of fine performances by Wasps, in particular openside flanker Joe Worsley, the former England schools international. His performance underlined why he had earned a place on England's summer tour of Australia. 'You have to stick with these youngsters,' said Wasps' director of rugby Nigel Melville afterwards. 'They can be frustrating sometimes, but they can be brilliant too. Players like Joe are the future of English rugby. I'd have him on the Test bench now because he is outstanding in the impact role.'

Newcastle: S.Legg; J. Naylor, M.Shaw, T.May, V.Tuigamala; J.Wilkinson, G.Armstrong (capt); G.Graham, R.Nesdale, M.Hurter, G.Archer, D.Weir, P.Walton, R.Arnold, R.Beattie.

Replacements: T.Underwood for Naylor (40), I.Peel for Hurter (69), J. Cartmell for Walton (40).

Scorers: T: Tuigamala. C: Wilkinson. P: Wilkinson (4).

Wasps: G.Rees; J.Lewsey, F.Waters, M.Denney, P.Sampson; A.King, A.Gomarsall; D. Molloy, T.Leota, W.Green, M.Weedon, S.Shaw, L.Dallaglio (capt), J.Worsley, P.Scrivener.

Replacements: R.Henderson for Denney (6), K.Logan for Sampson (46), M.Friday for Gomarsall (48), D.Alexopoulos for Leota (32-40), P.Volley for Scrivener (59-62).

Scorers: T: King, Lewsey. C: Rees (2). P: Rees (4). DG: King.

Referee: S.Lander (Liverpool).

Attendance: 48,000.

Earlier Rounds

There was an FA Cup look to the competition this year with the introduction of a preliminary round and a veritable shoal of minnows. Sadly glory eluded the amateur ranks, although there were one or two notable performances such as those of Launceston, Macclesfield and Tynedale, who all reached the second round from the preliminary before falling foul of superior opposition. Henley pulled off two of the shocks of the competition when they beat Rosslyn Park at Roehampton and then Premiership side Bedford at Goldington Road. They also claimed the distinction of being the only team to rack up a century, against Havant. Exeter, Leeds, Henley, Lydney and Waterloo all perished in the fifth round, which was a stage further than Bath managed. But while their exit up at Newcastle in the fourth round was not exactly a bolt from the blue, Leicester's defeat at unfancied Richmond in the quarter-finals was certainly contrary to all expectations. Richmond had never gone so far in the Cup, although the achievement was lost on their fans, only 7,000 or so of whom turned up at the Madejski Stadium to see them tame the Tigers. Their first semi-final appearance at home to Newcastle drew some 3,000 more, but there was a sense of anti-climax to the end of their historic Cup run, made against a background of financial problems and a clouded future. In the other semi-final Wasps found Gloucester no problem; the West Country side brought an army of support with them but there were still fewer than 10,000 in Loftus Road to witness Wasps' triumph.

Tetley's Bitter Cup Results 1998-99

Preliminary round:
North: Aspull 46 W Hartlepool TDSOB 13; Darlington Mowden Park 8 Tynedale 12; Egremont 17 Bridlington 16; Hull Ionians 26 Broughton Park 3; Morpeth 34 Wigton 16; Stockport 3 Doncaster 44; Warrington 18 Macclesfield 26. Midlands: Barkers Butts 35 Belgrave 26; Bromsgrove 20 Longton 19; Malvern 23 Westleigh 3; Mansfield 13 Bedford Athletic 25; Nottingham Moderns 0 Scunthorpe 34; Stafford 13 Kenilworth 41; Wellingborough 20 Broadstreet 26; Woodrush 8 Banbury 53. South East: Charlton Park 16 Wimbledon 18; Finchley 10 Cheshunt 29; Guildford & Godalming 54 Old Emanuel 17; Harlow 6 Cambridge 14; Ipswich 26 Old Albanians 3; Lewes 11 Ruislip 33; Old Colfeians 13 Haywards Heath 10; Westcombe Park 40 Staines 20; Winchester 32 Jersey 8. South West: Abbey 35 Chinnor 9; Keynsham 15 Launceston 21; Marlow 10 Penzance & Newlyn 44; Matson 19 Torquay Athletic 27; Slough 0 Maidenhead 25; Spartans 13 Salisbury 9; Swanage & Wareham 14 Stroud 13; Tiverton 29 Clevedon 34.

Round 1:
North: Aspatria 17 Bedford Athletic 32; Banbury 15 Scunthorpe 17; Barkers Butts 17 Macclesfield 27; Bromsgrove 10 Sedgley Park 34; Cheshunt 33 Morpeth 26; Clevedon 7 Barking 32; Clifton 3 Esher 60; Doncaster 20 Walsall 19; Hinckley 20 Nuneaton 24; Hull Ionians 59 Egremont 0; Kendal 13 Broadstreet 12; Malvern 14 Sandal 52; New Brighton 38 Lichfield 8; Preston Grasshoppers 43 Kenilworth 6; Stourbridge 32 Sheffield 6; Tynedale 47 Winnington Park 10; Whitchurch 32 Aspull 10. South: Guildford & Godalming 18 Bridgwater & Albion 28; Launceston 32 North Walsham 18; Metropolitan Police 34 Cheltenham 8; Norwich 15 Winchester 23; Penzance & Newlyn 32 Cambridge 13; Plymouth Albion 32 Redruth 18; Ruislip 9 Old Colfeians 43; Spartans 10 Havant 24; Swanage & Wareham 44 Abbey 7;

Tabard 26 Wimbledon 23; Torquay Athletic 15 Maidenhead 29; Westcombe Park 14 Bracknell 21; Weston-super-Mare 26 Ipswich 24.

Round 2:
Bridgwater & Albion 15 Rosslyn Park 49; Esher 41 Tabard 3; Henley 100 Havant 19; Hull Ionians 13 Macclesfield 3; Kendal 20 Liverpool St Helens 7; Lydney 44 Camberley 34; Maidenhead 22 Launceston 21; Metropolitan Police 25 Winchester 14; New Brighton 25 Nuneaton 10; Newbury 37 Cheshunt 13; Nottingham 50 Preston Grasshoppers 3; Old Colfeians 23 Swanage & Wareham 32; Otley 18 Morley 20; Plymouth Albion 13 Barking 18; Reading 21 Penzance & Newlyn 5; Sandal 6 Doncaster 3; Scunthorpe 0 Harrogate 29; Sedgley Park 20 Manchester 17; Tynedale 22 Stourbridge 30; Weston-super-Mare 15 Bracknell 43; Wharfedale 27 Birmingham-Solihull 5; Whitchurch 23 Bedford Athletic 15.

Round 3:
Blackheath 21 Sedgley Park 22; Bracknell 13 Metropolitan Police 6; Coventry 26 Worcester 36; Esher 42 Harrogate 17; Exeter 81 Whitchurch 11; Hull Ionians 7 Newbury 31; Lydney 44 Stourbridge 5; Morley 39 Maidenhead 25; Nottingham 27 Wharfedale 17; Reading 12 Orrell 23; Rosslyn Park 12 Henley 16; Rotherham 8 London Welsh 6; Swanage & Wareham 6 Barking 36; Wakefield 8 Kendal 16; Waterloo 34 New Brighton 23; Bristol 55 Sandal 0; Moseley 22 Fylde 15; Rugby 7 Leeds 68.

Round 4:
Bedford 22 Henley 29; Bristol 19 London Irish 43; Gloucester 31 Worcester 17; Harlequins 46 Esher 10; Kendal 20 London Scottish 25; Leicester 65 Barking 6; Morley 8 Saracens 26; Moseley 24 Lydney 25; Newcastle 25 Bath 22; Nottingham 8 Exeter 24; Rotherham 24 Leeds 27; Richmond 46 Newbury 12; Sale 31 Northampton 47; Sedgley Park 3 Wasps 53; Waterloo 18 Orrell 11; West Hartlepool 34 Bracknell 14.

Round 5:
Gloucester 31 Henley 9; Leicester 49 Leeds 0; London Scottish 33 Harlequins 37; Lydney 0 Saracens 40; Northampton 6 London Irish 21; Richmond 37 Exeter 10; Wasps 27 Waterloo 10; West Hartlepool 21 Newcastle 32.

Quarter-finals:
Gloucester 15 Harlequins 13; Newcastle 15 Saracens 0; Richmond 15 Leicester 13; Wasps 19 London Irish 3.

Semi-finals:
Richmond 3 Newcastle 20; Wasps 35 Gloucester 21.

Rugby in Wales 1998-99

While the fortunes of the national side took an encouraging upturn under Graham Henry, domestic club rugby in Wales was severely disrupted by the split with rebel clubs Cardiff and Swansea, who chose to drop out of the Premiership and play friendlies against English Premiership opposition. Harsh words were exchanged on a regular basis throughout a long winter although, happily, peace broke out in June when the two clubs signed eight-year loyalty agreements with the WRU. The Welsh Premier Division should prove a much stronger testing ground this season as a result. Cardiff and Swansea have both been granted places in the European Cup, provoking much anger at Ebbw Vale who had finished fourth in the Premiership and were expecting a European berth themselves. In the final analysis it seems incredible that such a dispute was allowed to persist and tarnish an absolutely vital season leading into the 1999 World Cup, hosted by the WRU. Perhaps the only positive outcome of the dispute was that, relieved of the burden of facing Swansea and Cardiff on a regular basis, Llanelli were able to stabilise, on and off the field, after a disastrous 1997-98 season and began to play and look like the great club of yesteryear. Welsh rugby is always the stronger for a strong Llanelli. The Scarlets, who happily welcomed back Scott Quinnell from Richmond, were clearly the class act in a truncated Premiership – any side which can defeat Pontypridd on four occasions deserve to be champions – and they also defeated the same opponents to take the WRU Challenge Trophy. They were, however, very much second best when they tackled Swansea in the SWALEC Cup final. Swansea's power-packed performance at Ninian Park underlined exactly what the Welsh public had been missing and it is probably no coincidence that peace talks were rapidly concluded thereafter.

In Division One, Dunvant, coached by Mark Perdue and well captained by Mark Harris, emerged from a long season of 30 games to take the title comfortably from Bonymaen. Dunvant clocked up 1,046 points and scored 150 tries, 21 coming from experienced Fijian centre Tevita Manaseitava, who also scored three for Pyle earlier in the season. Winger Mark Jones enlivened Llandovery's season with 23 tries and Jonathan Mason again performed well for Rumney. In Division Two Abercynon's pack, which included former Wales lock Mark Rowley, proved too powerful for most teams, as illustrated by the fact that captain Neil Edwards scored 28 tries from No 8 and the side were also awarded 13 penalty tries. Glamorgan Wanderers, captained by Garan Treharne who scored 21 tries, won their last three home games to take the title in Division Three East while the experienced Huw Woodland skippered Tonyrefail to success in Division Four East. Croesyceiliog looked like going unbeaten en route to the Division Five East championship but lost their final game to Newport HSOB, Caldicot emerged from the pack in Division Six East and fly-half Phil Lewis steered Abercwmboi to victory in Division Seven East. Elsewhere veteran fly-half Mike Lewis came out of retirement to inspire his Cwmllynfell side in Division Four West, while in Division Six West Penclawdd ran up a record 35 bonus points, their top score being a 112-5 canter against Milford Haven.

Premier Division

Pool A

	P	*W*	*D*	*L*	*F*	*A*	*Pts*
Llanelli	20	15	1	4	768	341	64
Pontypridd	20	12	0	8	646	468	46
Neath	20	12	0	8	568	491	44
Ebbw Vale	20	12	1	7	541	468	44

Pool B

	P	W	D	L	F	A	Pts
Caerphilly	20	10	2	8	550	562	37
Bridgend	20	9	2	9	522	597	34
Newport	20	5	0	15	499	629	23
Aberavon	20	2	0	18	391	929	10

Leading points-scorers: 257 B.Davey (Caerphilly); 196 B.Hayward (Llanelli); 179 G.Cull (Bridgend); 178 J.Strange (Ebbw Vale); 175 C.Rees (Aberavon) 163 N.Jenkins (Pontypridd); 153 S.Jones (Llanelli); 140 M.Pearce (Neath).

Division One

	P	W	D	L	F	A	Pts
Dunvant	30	24	1	5	1046	503	97
Bonymaen	30	22	2	6	827	392	91
Pontypool	30	23	0	7	766	494	80
Treorchy	30	16	2	12	808	567	64
Cross Keys	30	18	1	11	725	603	62
Merthyr	30	16	2	12	643	624	59
Llandovery	30	15	2	13	771	688	56
Tredegar	30	16	1	13	676	620	55
Rumney	30	12	1	17	626	753	51
Newbridge	30	14	0	16	628	611	48
Abertillery	30	12	2	16	565	615	48
UWIC	30	12	1	17	585	719	42
Blackwood	30	10	1	19	570	707	40
Tondu	30	10	1	19	502	673	38
South Wales Police	30	9	1	20	503	864	29
Maesteg	30	2	0	28	363	1171	8

Other champions:

Division Two: Abercynon
Division Three East: Glamorgan Wanderers
Division Three West: Carmarthen Quins
Division Four East: Tonyrefail
Division Four West: Cwmllynfell
Division Five East: Croesyceiliog
Division Five West: Mumbles
Division Five Central: Ystalyfera
Division Six East: Caldicot
Division Six West: Penclawdd
Division Six Central: Cwmavon
Division Seven East: Abercwmboi
Division Seven West: Loughor

Leading aggregate points in Welsh League rugby (1990-99)

1,896 Neil Jenkins (Pontypridd) 127, 173, 203, 285, 249, 285, 254, 157, 163
1,349 Aled Williams (Llandovery) 120, 132, 195, 176, 198, 198, 77, 160, 93
1,326 Byron Hayward (Ebbw Vale) 28, 121, 82, 236, 65, 205, 239, 154, 196
1,242 Jason Williams (Newbridge) –, 67, 119, 51, 121, 220, 132, 228, 304
1,228 Jonathan Mason (Rumney) 46, 16, 221, 101, 138, 187, 180, 249, 90

1,109 Ioan Bebb (Cross Keys) –, 29, 91, 75, 5, 152, 218, 280, 259
1,082 Justin Price (Tenby) –, 63, 56, 156, 139, 141, 212, 121, 194
852 Adrian Davies (Cardiff) 6, –, 264, 209, 207, 166, –, –, –
847 Paul Parry (Builth Wells) –, –, 222, 199, 149, 144, 105, 28, –
771 Jimmy Morris (Llanelli) 189, 161, 204, 97, 109, 11, –, –, –

SWALEC Cup 1998-99

Final

Swansea 37 Llanelli 10 (Ninian Park, Cardiff, 15 May 1999)

Swansea, condemned by their own political stance to play friendlies against English opposition throughout the season, looked on with quiet amusement as the Welsh media proclaimed their old rivals Llanelli as the top team in the land. After winning the WRU Premiership and Challenge Cup the Scarlets were indeed chasing the treble when they lined up against Swansea at Ninian Park, but they faced determined opposition with a point to prove. After a fiery but scrappy opening from both sides Swansea moved through the gears in a blistering second quarter to score three tries and establish a stranglehold on the game they were never to relinquish. Their 27-point winning margin was comfortably the biggest ever seen in a SWALEC final. Colin Charvis – playing after a midweek team announcement suggested otherwise – was in no way inconvenienced by a recently healed fractured cheekbone and muscled his way over for two tries to cap a commanding performance. But the dynamic flanker was just pipped for the man of the match award by fly-half Arwel Thomas, who combined his trademark flashes of genius with a mature kicking game. Wales coach Graham Henry can rest assured that quality cover for Neil Jenkins does exist. Wayne Proctor sneaked a Llanelli try but South African lock Tyronne Maulin crashed over for a third Swansea score before the interval, courtesy of a slashing Thomas break. After half-time Thomas kicked a drop goal to add to his first-half effort and a short-range penalty before replacement flanker Dean Thomas sealed victory with a fourth try. The match, and the argument, were Swansea's and captain Scott Gibbs, who broke a bone in his hand during the fray, remained unrepentant: 'We might have been playing against Second XVs towards the end but 70 per cent of our games against English sides this season have been more useful than anything I have seen in the Welsh Premiership. From what I've seen of Llanelli's opposition they've been playing against boys until they met us.'

Swansea: D.Weatherley; R.Rees, M.Taylor, S.Gibbs (capt), M.Robinson; A.Thomas, R.Jones; D.Morris, G.Jenkins, B.Evans, T.Maulin, A.Moore, P.Moriarty, C.Charvis, L.Jones.

Replacements: D.Thomas for Moriarty (68), C.Anthony for Evans (71), C.Van Rensburg for Gibbs (79), C.Wells for Jenkins (79), J.Griffiths for A Moore (79), L.Davies for Thomas (79).

Scorers: T: Charvis (2), Maulin, D.Thomas. C: A.Thomas (3), Davies. P: A.Thomas. DG: A.Thomas (2).

Llanelli: B.Hayward; W.Proctor, S.Finau, N.Davies, G.Evans; S.Jones, R.Moon; M.Madden, R.McBryde (capt), J.Davies, C.Wyatt, M.Voyle, H.Jenkins, I.Boobyer, S.Quinnell.

Replacements: V.Cooper for Voyle (71), A.Copsey for Jenkins (71), C.Warlow for N.Davies (78), A.Thomas for Moon (78), I.Jones for Boobyer (78).

Scorers: T: Proctor. C: Hayward. P: Hayward.

Referee: R.Davies (Dunvant).

Round 1:
Abercrave 14 Neath Athletic 17; Aberdare 25 Blaenau Gwent 14; Aberystwyth 92 Pontarddulais 0; Alltwen 43 Denbigh 5; Ammanford 31 Mold 7; Amman United bt Llanidloes (w/o); Bangor Normal College 0 Caldicot 82; Bargoed 10 Taibach 22; Bethesda 10 Pill Harriers 24; Blaenavon 29 Trinant 17; Blaengarw 44 Ystalafera 5; BP Llandarcy 12 St Albans 5; Bridgend Athletic 20 Neyland 10; Bridgend Sports 12 Betws 15; Bryncoch 22 Dinas Powys 32; BSC Port Talbot 33 Porthcawl 3; Burry Port 7 Croesyceiliog 43; Bynea 27 Gwernyfed 7; Caernarfon 10 Newport Saracens 29; Canton 17 Pontardawe 6; Cardiff HSOB Quins 5 Pontyclun 11; Cardiff Medicals 0 Rhiwbina 60; Cardiff University 0 Newcastle Emlyn 36; Cefneithin 12 Pembroke Dock Quins 15; Chepstow 22 Machen 0; Colwyn Bay 5 Rhydyfelin 46; Cwmbran 12 Llanishen 10; Cwmgwrach 16 Hendy 13; Cwmllynfell 42 Swansea University 8; Dolgellau 11 Ynysybwl 30; Fairwater 28 Senghennydd 18; Fishguard and Goodwick 3 Skewen 27; Fleur de Lys 23 Aberaeron 13; Gorseinon 30 Maesteg Quins 15; Haverfordwest 12 Tonyrefail 15; Laugharne 22 Aberystwyth University 0; Llandaff North 19 Tonna 14; Llandybie 5 Beddau 31; Llangadog 10 Ogmore Vale 26; Llangwm 0 Bangor 49; Llanhilieth 39 Ruthin 7; Llantwit Fardre 29 Nantyglo 10; Loughor 26 Pentyrch 14; Monmouth 29 Pontllanffraith 0; Morriston bt Carmarthen College (w/o); Nantymoel 17 Birchgrove 13; Newtown 8 Cilfynnydd 16; Old Illtydians 30 Barry 6; Penygroes 5 Welshpool 10; Pontyates 10 Mumbles 31; Pontyberem 13 Penclawdd 14; Pontypool United 25 Crumlin 18; Pwllheli 30 Baglan 13; Rhigos 15 Tylorstown 7; Rhyl 12 Cefn Cribwr 21; RTB Ebbw Vale 13 Abercarn 8; St Clears 16 Pembroke 14; St Davids 0 Cwmtwrch 46; St Josephs 24 Banwen 0; Taffs Well 16 Maesteg Celtic 12; Tredegar Ironsides 13 Brynamman 25; Trimsaran 51 Crymych 7; Univ Wales Inst Newport 27 Cowbridge 8; Waunarlwydd 29 Llandudno 15; Ynysddu 12 New Dock Stars 5.

Round 2:
Aberavon Green Stars 5 Cefn Coed 52; Abergavenny 70 Cwmtwrch 5; Amman United 7 Swansea 100; Bedwas 22 Nantyfyllon 5; Betws (Ammanford) 32 Usk 23; Blaengarw 27 Brynmawr 0; BP Llandarcy 42 Cwmgors 5; Bridgend Athletic 44 Bynea 18; Brynamman 9 Llantwit Fardre 13; Caldicot 7 Llangennech 25; Canton 17 Chepstow 16; Cardigan 89 St Clears 3; Carmarthen Quins 15 Tonmawr 12; Cefn Cribwr 12 Fairwater 15; Cilfynydd 0 Cardiff 93; Crynant 38 Betws (Newport) 5; Cwmavon 19 New Tredegar 10; Cwmbran 5 Carmarthen Athletic 36; Cwmgwrach 9 Croesyceiliog 5; Cwmllynfell bt Bangor University (w/o); Fleur de Lys 10 Seven Sisters 41; Furnace United 29 Llandaff North 11; Garndiffaith 46 Llandeilo 5; Glamorgan Wanderers 61 Felinfoel 8; Glyncoch 21 Llanelli Wanderers 3; Gorseinon 31 Bedlinog 0; Gowerton 6 Brynithel 3; Heol-y-Cyw 31 Aberystwyth 16; Kidwelly 29 Newcastle Emlyn 20; Lampeter 5 Taffs Well 14; Laugharne 9 Ynysybwl 34; Llandaff 15 Talywain 23; Llangefni 8 Cowbridge 11; Llanhilieth 32 Brecon 7; Llanybydder 7 Pontyclun 49; Milford Haven 10 Morriston 59; Mumbles 8 Blaina 11; Nantymoel 39 Blaenavon 3; Neath Athletic 8 Penclawdd 21; Nelson 14 Treherbert 18; Newport HSOB 15 Glynneath 30; Ogmore Vale 44 Loughor 7; Old Illtydians 5 Builth Wells 15; Old Penarthians 0 Hirwaun 11; Pembroke Dock Quins 8 St Josephs 5; Penarth 15 Gilfach Goch 51; Pencoed 10 Llantwit Major 3; Penygraig 29 Ammanford 10; Pill Harriers 32 RTB Ebbw Vale 5; Pontycymmer 11 Rhigos 23; Pontypool United 31 Alltwen 11; Rhiwbina 10 Dinas Powys 20; Skewen 9 Newport Saracens 5; Swansea Uplands 0 Trimsaran 43; Tonyrefail 26 Rhydyfelin 5; Tumble 41 Glais 14; Tygroes 13 BSC Port Talbot 10; Waunarlwydd 10 Monmouth 15; Welshpool 0 Beddau 17; Vardre 44 Briton Ferry 10; Ystrad Rhondda 21 Bangor 5.

Round 3:
Abercwmboi 21 Pill Harriers 7; Betws 21 Llangennech 20; Blaengarw 20 Penclawdd 19; Blaina 14 Rhymney 18; Bridgend Athletic 6 Ynysybwl 14; Carmarthen Quins 50 BP Llandarcy 3; Cefn Coed 0 Bedwas 60; Cardiff 84 Seven Sisters 10; Cowbridge 5 Whitland 22; Crynant 0 Swansea 48; Cwmavon 16 Tumble 13; Cwmllynfell 13 Carmarthen Athletic 0; Dinas Powys 86 Furnace United 0; Gilfach Goch 12 Builth

Wells 34; Glyncoch 3 Nantymoel 24; Glynneath 14 Fairwater 12; Gorseinon 12 Aberavon Quins 28; Heol-y-Cyw 47 Pembroke Dock Quins 10; Hirwaun 31 Skewen 6; Llanharan 90 Gowerton 0; Llanhilieth 27 Cardigan 20; Monmouth 29 Tygroes 14; Morriston 11 Ystradgynlais 18; Narberth 52 Ogmore Vale 17; Oakdale 27 Canton 11; Pencoed 34 Abercynon 21; Penygraig 21 Tenby United 8; Pontyclun 22 Cwmgwrach 13; Risca 23 Resolven 21; St Peter's 18 Pontypool United 19; Taffs Well 24 Garndiffaith 21; Talywain 35 Pyle 3; Tonyrefail 15 Kidwelly 18; Treherbert 23 Abergavenny 7; Trimsaran 16 Llantrisant 10; Vardre 37 Llantwit Fardre 15; Wrexham 31 Glamorgan Wanderers 22; Ystrad Rhondda 32 Kenfig Hill 13.

Round 4:
Group A: Ebbw Vale 73 Treherbert 15; Dinas Powys 5 Pontypool United 16. Group B: Glynneath 10 Trimsaran 25; Cross Keys 25 Dunvant 14. Group C: Bridgend 29 Treorchy 24; Talywain 9 Nantymoel 14. Group D: Pontypool 64 Rhigos 6; Beddau 0 Whitland 35. Group E: Wrexham 15 Neath 46; Penygraig 10 Rhymney 8. Group F: Ystradgynlais 32 Vardre 20; Monmouth 11 Llanhilieth 20. Group G: Llanharan 19 Newport 25; Risca 8 Swansea 57. Group H: Hirwaun 19 Kidwelly 9; Heol-y-Cyw 10 Tondu 27. Group I: Narberth 19 Caerphilly 29; Cwmavon 17 Bedwas 21. Group J: Abercwmboi 5 Maesteg 29; Betws (Ammanford) 3 Blackwood 17. Group K: Pontyclun 0 Llanelli 80; Blaengarw 10 Ynysybwl 10 (away team through). Group L: Pencoed 11 Abertillery 25; Cardiff 40 Llandovery 22 (at Llandovery). Group M: Pontypridd 71 Aberavon Quins 15; Cwmllynfell 13 Taffs Well 7. Group N: Tredegar 20 Merthyr 16; Builth Wells 5 Rumney 26. Group O: Aberavon 49 Carmarthen Quins 22; Ystrad Rhondda 19 South Wales Police 13. Group P: Bonymaen 51 Newbridge 12; Oakdale 7 UWIC 12.

Round 5:
Bonymaen 82 UWIC 19; Caerphilly 53 Bedwas 10; Cardiff 33 Abertillery 3; Cross Keys 38 Trimsaran 7; Cwmllynfell 0 Pontypridd 41; Hirwaun 13 Tondu 36; Llanelli 100 Ynysybwl 0; Llanhilieth 26 Ystradgynlais 19; Maesteg 8 Blackwood 31; Nantymoel 0 Bridgend 29; Penygraig 3 Neath 47; Pontypool United 3 Ebbw Vale 61; Swansea 60 Newport 38; Tredegar 35 Rumney 14; Whitland 13 Pontypool 15; Ystrad Rhondda 7 Aberavon 37.

Round 6:
Aberavon 12 Cardiff 20; Blackwood 9 Tredegar 12 (aet); Bridgend 16 Swansea 43; Caerphilly 15 Ebbw Vale 20; Cross Keys 39 Tondu 11; Llanelli 91 Llanhilieth 0; Pontypool 15 Neath 14; Pontypridd 47 Bonymaen 12.

Quarter-finals:
Pontypool 26 Cardiff 52; Pontypridd 17 Llanelli 22; Swansea 42 Ebbw Vale 14; Tredegar 12 Cross Keys 17.

Semi-finals:
Cross Keys 3 Swansea 60 (at Pontypridd); Llanelli 39 Cardiff 10 (at Bridgend).

Past Finals

	Winners		*Runners-up*		*Lloyd Lewis MOM Award*	
1972	Neath	15	Llanelli	9		
1973	Llanelli	30	Cardiff	7		
1974	Llanelli	12	Aberavon	10		
1975	Llanelli	15	Aberavon	6	Phil Bennett	(Llanelli)
1976	Llanelli	16	Swansea	4	Phil Bennett	(Llanelli)
1977	Newport	16	Cardiff	15	Ian Barnard	(Newport)
1978	Swansea	13	Newport	9	David Richards	(Swansea)
1979	Bridgend	18	Pontypridd	12	Steve Fenwick	(Bridgend)
1980	Bridgend	15	Swansea	9	Gareth Williams	(Bridgend)
1981	Cardiff	14	Bridgend	6	Rob Lakin	(Cardiff)
1982	Cardiff	12	Bridgend	12	Mark Titley	(Bridgend)
	(Cardiff win by scoring try)					

1983	Pontypool	16	Swansea	6	David Bishop	(Pontypool)
1984	Cardiff	24	Neath	19	Gareth Jones	(Neath)
1985	Llanelli	15	Cardiff	14	Gary Pearce	(Llanelli)
1986	Cardiff	28	Newport	21	Adrian Hadley	(Cardiff)
1987	Cardiff	16	Swansea	15	Anthony Clement	(Swansea)
1988	Llanelli	28	Neath	13	Jonathan Davies	(Llanelli)
1989	Neath	14	Llanelli	13	Chris Bridges	(Neath)
1990	Neath	16	Bridgend	10	Kevin Ellis	(Bridgend)
1991	Llanelli	24	Pontypool	9	Rupert Moon	(Llanelli)
1992	Llanelli	10	Swansea	7	Rupert Moon	(Llanelli)
1993	Llanelli	21	Neath	18	Gareth Llewellyn	(Neath)
1994	Cardiff	15	Llanelli	8	Andy Moore	(Cardiff)
1995	Swansea	17	Pontypridd	12	Paul Arnold	(Swansea)
1996	Pontypridd	29	Neath	22	Paul John	(Pontypridd)
1997	Cardiff	33	Swansea	26	Leigh Davies	(Cardiff)
1998	Llanelli	19	Ebbw Vale	12	Siua Taumalolo	(Ebbw Vale)
1999	Swansea	37	Llanelli	10	Arwel Thomas	(Swansea)

WRU Challenge Trophy 1999

Pool A:

Caerphilly 11 Canada 7; Aberavon 42 Georgia 0; Neath 18 Natal Wildebeests 36; Aberavon 0 Canada 10; Pontypridd 32 Natal Wildebeests 14; Neath 59 Georgia 14; Aberavon 20 Natal Wildebeests 14; Caerphilly 36 Georgia 17; Neath 16 Edinburgh Reivers 18; Pontypridd 52 Canada 10; Caerphilly 32 Natal Wildebeests 37; Aberavon 14 Edinburgh Reivers 39; Neath 11 Canada 14; Caerphilly 0 Edinburgh Reivers 64; Pontypridd 69 Georgia 7. *Winners*: Pontypridd. *Runners-up*: Edinburgh Reivers.

Pool B:

Bridgend 44 Romania 10; Llanelli 23 Northern Bulls 10; Ebbw Vale 22 Glasgow Caledonians 22; Newport 21 Gauteng Falcons 19; Newport 46 Romania 20; Ebbw Vale 20 Northern Bulls 13; Llanelli 36 Gauteng Falcons 15; Bridgend 17 Gauteng Falcons 15; Newport 24 Northern Bulls 39; Llanelli 21 Glasgow Caledonians 19; Ebbw Vale 28 Romania 0; Bridgend 28 Northern Bulls 5; Newport 7 Glasgow Caledonians 18; Ebbw Vale 25 Gauteng Falcons 19; Llanelli 57 Romania 12; Bridgend 10 Glasgow Caledonians 8. *Winners*: Llanelli. *Runners-up*: Bridgend.

Final:

Llanelli 41 Pontypridd 18.

Play-off:

Bridgend 25 Edinburgh Reivers 23.

Welsh Schools' Cup

Final

Neath College 30 Cross Keys College 24.

Past Finals

1990: Neath College 42 Nantyglo CS 21
1991: Neath College 24 Ysgol Glantaf 9
1992: Neath College 38 Stradey 0
1993: Cross Keys College 27 Maesteg CS 15
1994: Neath College 34 Cross Keys College 6
1995: St David's College 22 Neath College 15
1996: Ysgol Glantaf 20 Gowerton 8
1997: Cowbridge CS 8 Brynteg 6
1998: Neath College 39 Brynteg 0
1999: Neath College 30 Cross Keys College 24

Rugby in Ireland 1998-99

AIB League

Cork Constitution, winners of the inaugural competition back in 1991, emerged from a compelling dogfight with Munster rivals Garryowen to win the All-Ireland final in a game deserving a bigger crowd than the 10,000 that travelled up country to Lansdowne Road. Cork eventually triumphed courtesy of a Ronan O'Gara penalty just before the break in extra time. Stout defence led by dynamic hooker Frankie Sheehan, who was voted man of the match, saw them hang on for the remainder of the game. Had Garryowen replied in kind and the scores still been level at the end of extra time the Limerick side would have prevailed by virtue of finishing top of the table in the regular season. That would have been tough on Cork Constitution who finished their campaign with nine successive wins, including a 32-20 semi-final win over Buccaneers and a 26-19 victory over Shannon in the last regular game. By the middle of May they were clearly the class team in the land and deserving of honours.

Cork began the showpiece final in style. The hard-working John Fogarty set up quick ruck ball after a line-out; from Brian O'Meara's typically crisp service, O'Gara floated a clever flat pass for Kelly to break Keane's tackle and offload for Conor Mahony, who put Anthony Horgan over in the corner. O'Gara and Killian Keane swapped two penalties apiece before Garryowen forced extra time in the 79th minute with a well-crafted try for Jack Clarke. Garryowen, it has to be said, were distracted by an injury to young fly-half Jeremy Staunton who pulled a thigh muscle during training the previous day. Staunton could only kick with his left foot and his running game was also hindered, so captain Keane frequently stepped in to take on kicking duties though he endured a poor afternoon with his place-kicking, landing only two out of six attempts. Ironically Keane himself was suffering from a knee injury which ultimately required another operation – his sixth on the offending joint.

In the semi-final play-offs Garryowen had trailed St Mary's 17-0 just before half-time and there seemed little chance of them making the final. The Dublin side had started in great form with tries from John McWeeney and Peter McKenna and a conversion and penalty from Fergal Campion. Their place in the final looked even more certain when Garryowen prop Kieran Ronan was sent off for stamping but from this low point – 17 points down and 14 men against 15 – Garryowen began to prosper. Keane was the inspiration, landing four penalties and converting a penalty try. One of the great comebacks was complete and it was achieved in such a manner as to suggest that perhaps this year their name was on the trophy, which would have been particularly sweet after watching great rivals Shannon take the title for four consecutive years. Away in the West hopes were high that the Buccaneers – an amalgam of Athlone and Ballinasloe – could complete their fairytale rise to prominence. The atmosphere was certainly conducive, the home fans striking up with their signature tune 'Fields of Athenry', and after John O'Driscoll had scored an early try for Cork Constitution, Buccaneers came storming back with two penalties from Simon Allnutt and a try for busy flanker Eoin Brennan. But although the Buccaneers forwards – including powerful men like Martin Cahill, Jimmy Screene and the Rigney brothers – fought a brave fight they were gradually subdued by the Cork Constitution pack, backed up by half-backs O'Meara and O'Gara who enjoyed another fine game in tandem. Cork's John Kelly and David O'Brien scored early second-half tries and O'Gara kicked 17 points, the Buccs gaining a late consolation try through Michael Devine.

Final

Cork Constitution 14 Garryowen 11 (aet) (Lansdowne Road, 15 May 1999)

Cork Constitution: B.Walsh; A.Horgan, J.Kelly, C.Mahony, D.O'Brien; R.O'Gara, B.O'Meara; I.Murray, F.Sheehan, J.O'Driscoll, K.Murphy, D.Sheehan, D.Corkery (capt), J.Murray, J.Fogarty.

Replacements: D.O'Callaghan for Murphy (69), P.Soden for O'Driscoll (72), C.Kehelly for Fogarty (85), A.Byrne for D.Sheehan (99).

Scorers: T: Horgan. P: O'Gara (3).

Garryowen: D.Crotty; J.Clarke, K.Hartigan, K.Keane (capt), K.O'Riordan; J.Staunton, T.Tierney; N.Hartigan, P.Cunningham, R.Laffan, S.Leahy, D.Peters, P.Hogan, B.Cronin, D.Wallace.

Replacements: P.Humphreys for Cunningham (56), R.Leahy for Peters (85), C.Varley for Hogan (90).

Scorers: T: Clarke. P: Keane (2).

Referee: D.McHugh (Munster).

Division One

	P	*W*	*D*	*L*	*F*	*A*	*Pts*
Garryowen	11	8	0	3	237	140	16
Cork Constitution	11	8	0	3	265	170	16
Buccaneers	11	8	0	3	196	202	16
St Mary's College	11	7	0	4	215	177	14
Lansdowne	11	7	0	4	189	184	14
Shannon	11	6	0	5	224	164	12
Young Munster	11	4	1	6	134	135	9
Terenure College	11	4	1	6	175	182	9
Ballymena	11	4	0	7	190	224	8
Clontarf	11	4	0	7	198	246	8
Blackrock College	11	4	0	7	180	232	8
Galwegians	11	1	0	10	117	264	2

Championship Play-offs:

Semi-finals: Garryowen 19 St Mary's College 17; Cork Constitution 32 Buccaneers 20.

Final: Cork Constitution 14 Garryowen 11 (aet).

Leading try-scorers: 5 E.Elwood (Galwegians), M.Horan (Shannon), K.O'Riordan (Garryowen), A.Guinan (Blackrock). 4 B.Rigney (Buccaneers), D.O'Brien (Cork Constitution), B.Walsh (Cork Constitution), J.Lacey (Shannon), V.Costello (St Mary's), G.Dempsey (Terenure), D.O'Dowd (Young Munster). 3 O.Winchester (Clontarf), J.Kelly (Cork Constitution), C.Mahony (Cork Constitution), R.O'Gara (Cork Constitution), M.McNamara (Garryowen), G.D'Arcy (Lansdowne), M.Dillon (Lansdowne), R.Kearns (Lansdowne), J.Hayes (Shannon), P.McKenna (St Mary's), J.McWeeney (St Mary's), M.Smyth (Terenure). 2 M.Blair, R.Irwin, S.Stewart (all Ballymena), B.Carey, P.Jordan, M.Roche, R Wheeler (all Blackrock), R.Lee, M.Steffert (both Buccaneers), D.Moore, P.Noble, R.Vorster (all Clontarf), D.Corkery, J.Kiernan, B.O'Meara (all Cork Constitution), P.Duigan (Galwegians), D.Crotty, K.Keane, K.Ronan, J.Staunton, D.Wallace (all Garryowen), C.McEntee,

S.McEntee (both Lansdowne), A.Foley, M.Galwey, C.McMahon, P.McMahon (all Shannon), M.Cuddihy, C.McGuinness, R.McIlreavy (all St Mary's), B.Treacy (Terenure), P.Clohessy, G.Earls, D.Tobin (all Young Munster).

Leading goal-kickers: 112 R.O'Gara (Cork Constitution); 110 S.Mason (Ballymena); 106 S.Allnutt (Buccaneers); 98 R.Murphy (Clontarf), 90 R.Kearns (Lansdowne); 80 K.Keane (Garryowen), A.Thompson (Shannon); 65 F.Campion (St Mary's); 57 E.Elwood (Galwegians); 39 A.McGowan (Blackrock).

In Division Two there was no stopping big-spending Dungannon, captained by Charlie Simpson and coached by Willie Anderson. They had recruited heavily during the summer, attracting David Humphreys back from London Irish and Jonathan Bell from Northampton. Ulster's magnificent effort in the European Cup took its toll on their squad a little and they did lose two games they might otherwise expected to have won, but their promotion into Division One was never in doubt. In Division Three University College Dublin reaped the benefit of being coached by the IRB's New Zealand development officer Lee Smith, who is based in Dublin, and strode to the title in style. Most impressive in the centre was the strapping Brian O'Driscoll who deservedly won a place on tour to Australia where he played in both Tests. The Division Four title went to Cork club Midleton, captained by Niall Murphy and coached by scrum-half Damon Ulrich and Tom Mulcahy. After qualifying from the Munster Junior League the previous season Midleton maintained their momentum and clinched promotion on the final day with a win over CIYMS. In the Junior League play-offs Dublin club Barnhall came through powerfully with wins over Dromore, Connemara and Thomond, who also won promotion by defeating Collegians in a play-off.

Division Two

	P	*W*	*D*	*L*	*F*	*A*	*Pts*
Dungannon	15	13	0	2	479	259	26
DLS Palmerston	15	10	2	3	284	211	22
Wanderers	15	10	0	5	342	293	20
Old Belvedere	15	9	1	5	276	212	19
Malone	15	9	1	5	233	206	19
Bective Rangers	15	8	2	5	240	269	18
Portadown	15	8	1	6	250	268	17
Greystones	15	8	0	7	334	313	16
Old Crescent	15	7	1	7	305	236	15
Sunday's Well	15	7	0	8	270	246	14
City of Derry	15	7	0	8	284	293	14
UC Cork	15	5	4	6	248	303	14
Dolphin	15	5	1	9	218	256	11
Skerries	15	3	1	11	199	262	7
Old Wesley	15	2	2	11	181	315	6
Ballynahinch	15	1	0	14	171	372	2

Leading try-scorers: 11 S.Bell (Dungannon); 6 I.Orr (City of Derry), M.Cunningham (DLSP), S.Stephens (DLSP), Alan Clarke (Dungannon), M.Logue (Greystones), W.Robertson (Greystones), D.Finnegan (Wanderers). 5 S.Smyth (Derry), Alistair Clarke (Dungannon), S.Carroll (Malone), B.Doharty (Old Wesley), J.Park (Portadown), P.Barry (UC Cork), A.McSweeney (UC Cork).

Leading goal-kickers: 160 E.Olazabel (Wanderers); 143 R.McIlmoyle (Portadown); 141 B.Begley (Old Crescent); 139 E.Costigan (Greystones); 129 D.Martin (Old

Belvedere); 124 J.O'Mahony (Dolphin); 117 W.Johnston (Bective); 115 R.Daly (Sunday's Well); 113 I.McGregor (City of Derry).

Division Three

	P	*W*	*D*	*L*	*F*	*A*	*Pts*
University College Dublin	13	10	0	3	362	176	20
NIFC	13	9	0	4	246	186	18
Monkstown	13	8	0	5	209	238	16
Instonians	13	7	1	5	277	178	15
Bohemians	13	6	0	7	179	225	12
Richmond	13	7	0	6	156	208	14
Carlow	13	6	0	7	212	209	12
Galway Corinthians	13	5	1	7	257	223	11
Dublin University	13	4	0	9	193	255	8
Highfield	13	2	0	11	130	325	4

Leading try-scorers: 10 B.O'Driscoll (UCD). 6 I.Dwyer (Carlow), B.Glynn (Galway Corinthians), C.Bleakley (NIFC), C.Scally (UCD). 5 D.Watts (Monkstown), G. O'Loan (NIFC). 4 J.Waddock (Carlow), N.Tuwhanguai (Galway Corinthians), M.McHugh (Dublin University), G.McCullough (Instonians). 3 T.Allnutt (Galway Corinthians), G.Hayes (Dublin University), S.McLoughlin (Dublin University), K.Hilman (Instonians), I.McMullen (Instonians), P.Shields (Instonians), C.Lupton (Monkstown), G.Harron (NIFC), S.Iafeta (NIFC), J.Park (NIFC), S.Dogget (UCD), J.Shine (UCD), J.Smith (UCD). 2 D.Murphy (Bohemians), J.Fahy, P.Guckian, I.Place, A.White (all Galway Corinthians), W. Martel (Dublin University), W.Allen, M.Hayden (both Highfield), A.Campbell, K.McKee (both Instonians), D.Dent, J.Gibson, J.Kennedy, R.McInerney, S.Newton (all Monkstown), C.Weiniger (NIFC), E.Buckley (Richmond), P.Bredin, G.Cantwell, M.Cooling, C.Kearne, H.McMahon, M.Moynagh (all UCD).

Leading goal-kickers: 125 G.McCullough (Instonians); 106 G.Harron (NIFC); 103 M.McHugh (Dublin University); 102 K.Kanohi (Bohemians); 84 B.O'Driscoll (UCD); 78 T.James (Carlow); 60 G.Wright (Galway Corinthians); 57 E.Buckley (Richmond); 49 G.McWilliams (Monkstown); 41 M.Hayden (Highfield).

Division Four

	P	*W*	*D*	*L*	*F*	*A*	*Pts*
Midleton	10	7	1	2	194	83	15
Ballina	10	7	1	2	167	96	15
Banbridge	10	7	0	3	161	129	14
Waterpark	10	5	0	5	155	121	10
Omagh	10	5	0	5	142	123	10
Suttonians	10	5	0	5	161	146	10
Queen's University	10	5	0	5	152	226	10
Bangor	10	4	1	5	113	153	9
Ards	10	4	0	6	134	153	8
Collegians	10	3	1	6	150	159	7
CIYMS	10	1	0	9	55	195	2

Barnhall and Thomond promoted from provincial League play-offs.

Leading try-scorers: 7 S.McKearney (Omagh), N.O'Reilly (Suttonians). 6 T.Sneddon (Banbridge). 5 M.Humphreys (Collegians). 4 J.Mescal (Ballina), G.Lynch

(Midleton). 3 G.Brady (Ballina), G.Peterson (Ballina), B.Fisher (Collegians), J.Holland (Midleton), D.Flack (Omagh), P.Archibold (Queen's Univ), N.Beggs (Queen's Univ), M.Fitzsimmons (Suttonians), J.Fahy (Waterpark). 2 B.Gadsen, R.Gardiner, C.Stocker (all Ards), B.Kelly, D.Murphy (both Bangor), S.Aldred, S.Armstrong, P.McAteer (all Collegians), M.Chambers (CIYMS), I.Dunne, N.Murphy, M.O'Mahoney (all Midleton), A.Anderson, A.Hamilton (both Omagh), J.Goodrich, A.Kirkpatrick, T.Trainor (all Queen's Univ), B.Davis, C.O'Mahony, J.Walsh (all Suttonians), G.Jones, T.Keogh, G.Muir, J.Walsh (all Waterpark).

Leading goal-kickers: 76 J.Carey (Ballina); 69 B.Boss (Ards); 58 S.Aldred (Collegians); 54 J.Walsh (Suttonians); 45 J.Holland (Midleton); 41 S.Naden (Waterpark); 29 D.Soper (Banbridge); 26 R.Chambers (Banbridge), C.Magenis (Bangor).

Guinness Inter-Provincial Championship 1998-99

	P	*W*	*D*	*L*	*F*	*A*	*Bonus pts*	*Pts*
Munster	6	4	0	2	125	92	2	18
Ulster	6	3	0	3	137	119	3	15
Leinster	6	3	0	3	135	136	2	14
Connacht	2	2	0	4	95	145	3	11

Results: Leinster 14 Ulster 34; Connacht 13 Munster 18; Munster 18 Leinster 24; Connacht 21 Ulster 18; Leinster 29 Connacht 24; Ulster 29 Munster 12; Ulster 11 Leinster 35; Munster 21 Connacht 7; Connacht 24 Leinster 23; Munster 31 Ulster 9; Leinster 10 Munster 25; Ulster 36 Connacht 6.

Past Inter-Provincial Champions

1946 Ulster
1947 Munster
1948 Leinster
1949 Leinster
1950 Ulster
1951 Ulster
1952 Munster
1953 Ulster
1954 Leinster-Munster
1955 Ulster-Connacht
1956 Leinster-Ulster-Connacht
1957 Munster
1958 Leinster
1959 Munster
1960 Leinster
1961 Leinster
1962 Munster
1963 Leinster
1964 Leinster
1965 Munster
1966 Ulster-Munster
1967 Ulster
1968 Munster
1969 Ulster
1970 Ulster
1971 Leinster
1972 Leinster-Munster-Ulster
1973 Munster
1974 Ulster
1975 Leinster-Ulster-Munster
1976 Ulster
1977 Leinster-Munster-Ulster
1978 Munster
1979 Leinster
1980 Leinster
1981 Leinster
1982 Leinster-Ulster-Munster
1983 Leinster-Ulster-Munster
1984 Ulster
1985 Ulster
1986 Ulster
1987 Ulster
1988 Ulster
1989 Ulster
1990 Ulster
1991 Ulster

1992 Ulster
1993 Ulster
1994 Ulster
1995 Munster
1996 Leinster
1997 Munster
1998 Leinster
1999 Munster

Branch Competitions 1998-99

LEINSTER

Heineken Senior Cup: Clontarf
Kitty O'Shea Senior League: Terenure College
Heineken Metropolitan Cup: Clontarf
Smithwicks Provincial Towns Cup: Navan
Heineken Junior League Division One: Terenure College
ACC Qualifying League: Barnhall
Under 20 League: Lansdowne
McCorry U20 Cup: Old Belvedere
Coca-Cola Senior Schools Cup: Blackrock College
Coca-Cola Junior Schools Cup: Belvedere College

ULSTER

First Trust Bank Senior Cup: Instonians
Senior League: Ballymena
Junior Cup: Dungannon II
Smithwicks Provincial Towns Cup: Dungannon
Junior League Division One: Coleraine II
AIB Qualifying League: Dromore
Renault Senior Schools Cup: Campbell College
Schools Second XV Cup: Royal Belfast Academical Institute

MUNSTER

Heineken Senior Cup: Garryowen
Heineken Senior League: Old Crescent or Sunday's Well
Heineken Provincial Towns Cup: Bruff
Heineken Junior League Division One: Thomond
Heineken Senior Seconds League: Garryowen.
Heineken Junior Cup: Young Munster or Kilfeacle
Coca Cola Senior Schools Cup: Christian Brothers Cork
Coca Cola Junior Schools Cup: Christian Brothers Cork

CONNACHT

Heineken Senior Cup: Buccaneers
Heineken Senior League: Buccaneers
Heineken Junior League Division One: Connemara
AIB Qualifying League: Connemara
Heineken Junior Cup: Sligo
Statoil Senior Schools Cup: Sligo Grammar
Statoil Junior Schools Cup: Garbally College

Rugby in Scotland 1998-99

Whatever conclusions Lord Mackay of Clashfern and his panel arrive at in their review of the game in Scotland and the running of the Scottish Rugby Union, there is no doubt what the people in the stands thought of things. The creation of the two Super Districts – ostensibly done in the pursuit of rugby excellence, but now under a cloud of suspicion that halving the number of districts did the same to the expense of running them – was not a howling success. Big matches involving touring sides and European Cup opponents did not attract the sort of crowds that sponsors and administrators had hoped for. The decision to stage matches at football grounds, Hibernian's Easter Road Stadium and Partick Thistle's Firhill, proved to be a poor one. And neither Edinburgh Reivers nor Glasgow Caledonians succeeded in uniting the two bands of supporters which comprised their following under the new banners; for example, when Reivers played in the Borders the Edinburgh element did not follow them down, and when matches were staged in the capital, the Borders fans stayed at home.

On the field it was little better. The Tri-series between the two sides – all that was left to them after the European Cup and before the Five Nations Championship – was won by Edinburgh, although Glasgow were victorious in the opening fixture. But the trophy at which they had originally been aimed, the European Cup, eluded both teams. This was even worse when considered in the light of Caledonians' claim before the tournament had got under way that they would win it. Confidence is all very admirable in sport, but it is not everything; ability, teamwork and luck also have their part to play in success. Still, they tried. And even if Lord Mackay's review concludes that the *status quo ante* should prevail and that four districts are better than two, it is unlikely that the cream will return to club rugby – in fact as far as they are concerned the Super Districts have been a success. The professional players have made it clear that they want to train and play together all the time. If they can't then they may well leave Scotland. A sort of Rugby Clearance.

Even without them, though, club rugby is not doing too badly. A youthful Heriot's FP skipped to the Tennents Premiership Division One title in style. They were an invigorating team, their emphasis on fast, open rugby. And with the veteran prop Jocky Bryce at the helm they had someone with a lot of nous who knew when to apply the brakes. They were always looking to be expansive; they did get caught out once or twice, notably against Melrose, but not enough to lose out in the title race. Melrose were worthy runners-up, a win fewer, a defeat extra being enough to leave them a place adrift. Glasgow Hawks pushed them hard throughout and eventually took third place. Currie's fourth place was a disappointment, since they had promised so much at the beginning of the season. It was even gloomier in Stirling, where County were relegated for the first time in their history in the top flight. Boroughmuir had never been out of the first division since leagues were introduced in 1973, but they too were relegated, on points difference (nine in total) from West of Scotland. Gala waltzed off with the Second Division title and the first leg of their deserved double. They and Kelso turned it into a two-horse race. At the other end of the Division Kilmarnock Falcons were brought to earth; they finished ahead of bottom club Edinburgh Academicals – relegated for the second season in succession – but not enough to save them from the drop. Peebles, the champions, and East Kilbride from Division Three, will take their places.

Tennents Velvet Premiership

Division One

	P	*W*	*D*	*L*	*F*	*A*	*PD*	*Bonus pts*	*Pts*
Heriot's FP	18	14	0	4	620	322	298	13	69
Melrose	18	13	0	5	491	300	191	11	63
Glasgow Hawks	18	13	1	4	437	273	164	7	61
Currie	18	12	0	6	434	343	91	8	56
Hawick	18	9	0	9	344	455	–111	5	41
Watsonians	18	7	2	9	391	428	–37	6	38
Jed-Forest	18	7	2	9	356	449	–93	3	35
West of Scotland	18	6	0	12	355	418	–63	10	34
Boroughmuir	18	6	0	12	382	454	–72	10	34
Stirling County	18	0	1	17	300	668	–368	6	8

Leading points-scorers: 268 Ross (Heriot's FP); 195 Curtis (West of Scotland); 147 Donaldson (Currie); 143 Richards (Jed-Forest); 122 Murdio (Hawick); 113 Martin (Glasgow Hawks).

Leading try-scorers: 16 Walker (Heriot's FP); 9 Di Rollo (Watsonians), Taylor (Heriot's FP); 8 Cook (Hawick), Kiddie (Boroughmuir), Nichol (Melrose).

Division Two

	P	*W*	*D*	*L*	*F*	*A*	*PD*	*Bonus pts*	*Pts*
Gala	18	14	0	4	524	242	282	14	70
Kelso	18	14	1	3	436	235	201	8	66
Kirkcaldy	18	11	0	7	372	298	74	12	56
Dundee HSFP	18	8	1	9	446	431	15	8	38*
Biggar	18	8	1	9	249	341	–92	4	38
Aberdeen GSFP	18	6	2	10	299	341	–42	8	36
Selkirk	18	8	1	9	279	341	–62	6	36*
Musselburgh	18	7	0	11	379	475	–96	6	34
Kilmarnock Falcons	18	6	0	12	329	475	–146	7	31
Edinburgh Academicals	18	5	0	13	281	415	–134	8	28

* Deducted four championship points.

Leading points-scorers: 221 Aitchison (Kelso); 191 Newton (Dundee); 148 Livingstone (Musselburgh); 147 Parker (Gala); 124 Blair (Selkirk); 106 Oddie (Aberdeen).

Leading try-scorers: 9 Amos (Gala); 8 Walker (Biggar); 7 Aitchison (Kelso), Parker (Gala), Utterson (Kelso); 6 Dickson (Selkirk).

Division Three

	P	*W*	*D*	*L*	*F*	*A*	*PD*	*Bonus pts*	*Pts*
Peebles	18	14	0	4	398	294	104	6	62
East Kilbride	18	12	1	5	364	260	104	7	57
Preston Lodge FP	18	12	0	6	378	243	135	8	56
Berwick	18	11	0	7	360	271	89	6	50
Gordonians	18	9	2	7	445	267	178	8	48
Grangemouth	18	10	1	7	310	269	41	5	47
Ayr	18	8	1	9	291	277	14	8	42
Stewart's Melville FP	18	4	1	13	358	470	–112	9	27
Glenrothes	18	4	0	14	217	491	–274	4	20
Glasgow Southern	18	3	0	15	210	499	–289	2	14

Other honours:

Tennents National League – Division One: Hutchesons' Aloysians. Division Two: Ross High. Division Three: Perthshire. Division Four: Aberdeenshire. Division Five: Helensburgh. Division Six: Cumnock. Division Seven: Strathendrick.

SRU TENNENTS VELVET CUP 1998-99

Final

Gala 8 Kelso 3 (Murrayfield, 24 April 1999)

For the second season running the final was an all-Second Division shooting match. This time, though, there was nothing freakish about it. While last year Glasgow Hawks were wolves in Division Two clothing, this year's was the real thing, with properly registered Second Division members and not a Super District player in sight. Both finalists had sorted out some big boys on their way through – Kelso had accounted for Boroughmuir and Gala for Melrose, each of the lesser lights beating their betters in the semi-finals. Victory in the last final to be sponsored by Tennents, who opted to quit with two years to run on their present contract, had a sharp little twist for Gary Parker, Gala's player-coach. Parker had left Melrose a couple of seasons earlier when they achieved a League, Cup and Melrose Sevens treble. He shared in the first leg of that treble, but his contract as kicker with the Scottish Claymores American Football side prevented him from taking part in either the Cup final or the sevens tournament. This year, having coached Gala to a semi-final victory over the First Division outfit, then having masterminded their lifting of the Cup, he also presided over their Melrose Sevens title. A week after the Cup win Melrose announced they had re-signed Parker as their player-coach.

The final itself was not exactly bristling with great plays. Kelso had begun the game by taking a gamble with Kosie Alberts. Their South African full-back appeared at the start with a heavily bandaged knee and lasted just 11 minutes; thereafter Kelso decided to channel everything through their more powerful forwards. Flanker Stewart Bennet, who had an outstanding match, went within an ant's waistline of touching down to add to Graeme Aitchison's second-minute penalty, while prop Darren Howlett also crossed the line only for the touchdown to be disallowed. So it was that in the 76th minute Chris Paterson, the Gala stand-off half, looped around his centres and scored the only try. He then made absolutely certain with a drop goal a minute from full time.

Gala: M.Dods; G.Parker, C.Townsend, D.Gray, K.Amos; C.Paterson, D.Boland; A.Johnston, S.Scott, E.Johnston, R.Gray (capt), N.Hines, G.Brown, T.Weir, J.Amos.

Replacements: G.Robson for Boland (55), G.Easson for Johnston (62), P.Harrison for Brown (68).

Scorers: T: Paterson. DG: Paterson.

Kelso: K.Alberts; S.Ross, G.Laing, K.Utterson, D.Baird; G.Aitchison, G.Cowe (capt); B.Hogarth, K.Thompson, D.Howlett, S.Rowley, C.Rutherford, S.Bennet, S.Forsyth, D.Rankin.

Replacements: J.Fleming for Alberts (11), S.Laing for Rutherford (24).

Scorer: P: Aitchison.

Referee: R.Dickson (Madras FP).

Round 3:
Alloa 17 Strathmore 7; Ayr 109 Carrick 5; Biggar 46 Annan 16; Boroughmuir 117 Howe of Fife 8; Cumnock 20 Stewart's Melville FP 14; Dalziel 12 Kirkcaldy 46; Dunfermline 9 Langholm 17; East Kilbride 28 Selkirk 18; Gala 76 Gordonians 19; Glasgow Southern 17 Glasgow Hawks 71; Greenock Wanderers 10 Melrose 99; Haddington 19 Ross High 17; Hawick 40 Berwick 18; Hawick Linden 7 Edinburgh Academicals 17; Heriots FP 73 Glenrothes 11; Hillhead-Jordanhill 13 St Boswells 6; Hutchesons' Aloysians 72 Allan Glen's 0; Irvine 8 Stewartry 21; Jed-Forest 25 Preston Lodge 27; Kelso 73 Lenzie 5; Kilmarnock 109 Hyndland FP 0; Linlithgow 15 Stirling County 8; Morgan Academy FP 20 Ellon 8; Musselburgh 24 Grangemouth 9; Peebles 50 Livingston 5; Perthshire 47 Royal 'Dick' Vet College 3; Portobello FP 0 Currie 64; Strathaven 12 Dundee HSFP 60; Waysiders-Drumpeille 6 Aberdeen GSFP 31; West of Scotland 53 Cambuslang 10.

Round 4:
Alloa 3 Stewartry 13; Biggar 7 Kelso 23; Edinburgh Academicals 6 Boroughmuir 44; Gala 32 Ayr 7; Glasgow Hawks 49 Dundee HSFP 12; Hawick 19 Currie 13; Kilmarnock 18 East Kilbride 12; Kirkcaldy 13 Aberdeen GSFP 10; Langholm 20 Linlithgow 15; Melrose 45 Hillhead-Jordanhill 7; Morgan Academy FP 0 Heriot's FP 70; Musselburgh 23 West of Scotland 17; Peebles 16 Haddington 9; Perthshire 17 Murrayfield 7; Preston Lodge 44 Cumnock 6; Watsonians 44 Hutchesons' Aloysians 9.

Round 5:
Glasgow Hawks 10 Kelso 13; Hawick 8 Boroughmuir 16; Heriot's FP 45 Perthshire 10; Kilmarnock 12 Musselburgh 10; Langholm 16 Gala 39; Preston Lodge 33 Peebles 23; Stewartry 25 Kirkcaldy 22; Watsonians 0 Melrose 33.

Quarter-finals:
Boroughmuir 16 Heriot's FP 15; Kelso 38 Preston Lodge 10; Melrose 42 Kilmarnock 13; Stewartry 19 Gala 35.

Semi-finals:
Boroughmuir 15 Kelso 40; Gala 28 Melrose 22.

Tennents Velvet Shield: *Final*: Garnock 23 Jed-Forest 35.

Tennents Velvet Bowl: *Final*: Duns 34 Gordonians 17.

Lloyds TSB Five Nations Championship 1999

The Five Nations bowed out in truly spectacular fashion with a classic tournament, decided in the third minute of injury time in the last game when Scott Gibbs' last-gasp try at Wembley secured a shock Wales win – and ensured that Scotland took possession of a title they richly deserved. Over 700,000 paying spectators watched this year's event – figures which few, if any, annual sporting events in the world can match – and the inclusion of Italy in the 2000 tournament should further widen its appeal. The 1999 competition included three games that will live in the memory forever, namely Scotland's win in Paris and Wales' incredible back-to-back victories over France and England, while in any other season Scotland's pulsating triumph over Ireland would have been considered a classic.

Above all, Scotland's Five Nations Championship was just and fitting reward for their coach Jim Telfer, one of the great men of rugby. His last ever Five Nations side is arguably a better team than the 1990 and 1984 Grand Slam sides, who were magnificent, feisty battlers but lacked the adventure and ambition of their modern-day successors. They are also younger and have the potential to improve significantly. Their success has been achieved despite the psychological scars of the 1997-98 season and serious injuries to influential players such as Bryan Redpath, Duncan Hodge, Eric Peters, Doddie Weir and Tom Smith. New stars have stepped into the breach. Locks Scott Murray and Stuart Grimes displayed the ball-handling skills and appetite for work of backrow stalwarts; the Leslie brothers galvanised key areas in attack and defence and senior internationals such as Gary Armstrong, Alan Tait and Paul Burnell were rejuvenated figures. Fly-half Gregor Townsend, meanwhile, climbed on to a new plateau of consistency and excellence. To score tries in all four Championship matches, and in the friendly against Italy for good measure, is a remarkable achievement but no more than his general play merited.

England can reflect on a season of steady improvement – the emergence of Jonny Wilkinson, Dan Luger and Steve Hanley was a massive bonus – but in the cool light of day must realise they had only themselves to blame for defeat against Wales. When you are on top in Test rugby you fail to put your chances away at your peril. Graham Henry's Wales fulfilled his wish 'to be bold' and were rewarded in consequence. Their greatest achievement was victory in Paris – they travelled as complete no-hopers after defeats against Scotland and Ireland but shook France rigid with their adventurous play. Ireland, yet again, disappointed desperately after promising so much – what a difference an early win over France would have made.

And what of the French? After two consecutive Grand Slams they started the season aiming for a unique third consecutive clean sweep – instead they were left with the wooden spoon. Yes, they suffered from injuries but they were also arrogant, dismissive and lacked focus. Given the talent at their disposal their performances bordered on the disgraceful and possibly the biggest surprise of the season was that Jean-Claude Skrela and Pierre Villepreux hung on to their jobs.

FINAL TABLE

	P	*W*	*D*	*L*	*F*	*A*	*Pts*
Scotland	4	3	0	1	120	79	6
England	4	3	0	1	103	78	6
Wales	4	2	0	2	109	126	4
Ireland	4	1	0	3	66	90	2
France	4	1	0	3	75	100	2

Top Points-scorers

	T	C	P	DG	Pts
Neil Jenkins (Wales)		8	16		64
Jonny Wilkinson (England)		6	16		60
David Humphreys (Ireland)		3	13	2	51
Kenny Logan (Scotland)		11	5		37
Thomas Castaignede (France)	1	4	5		28
Alan Tait (Scotland)	5				25
Emile Ntamack (France)	4				20
Gregor Townsend (Scotland)	4				20
Scott Gibbs (Wales)	2				10
Shane Howarth (Wales)	2				10
Dafydd James (Wales)	2				10
Martin Leslie (Scotland)	2				10
Dan Luger (England)	2				10
Cameron Murray (Scotland)	2				10
Craig Quinnell (Wales)	2				10
Tim Rodber (England)	2				10
Nick Beal (England)	1				5
Colin Charvis (Wales)	1				5
Franck Comba (France)	1				5
Christophe Dominici (France)	1				5
Richard Dourthe (France)	1				5
Stuart Grimes (Scotland)	1				5
Steve Hanley (England)	1				5
Richard Hill (England)	1				5
Christophe Juillet (France)	1				5
John Leslie (Scotland)	1				5
Kevin Maggs (Ireland)	1				5
Scott Murray (Scotland)	1				5
Matt Perry (England)	1				5
Keith Wood (Ireland)	1				5
Penalty try	1				5

IRELAND 9 FRANCE 10 (Lansdowne Road, 6 February 1999)

The most exciting of Five Nations campaigns made a comparatively low-key start in the rain and gloom of Dublin, where genuine Irish expectations of victory were cruelly denied in a flurry of late activity – Thomas Castaignede landing a penalty to put France in front, David Humphreys missing a similar-range effort by the narrowest of margins at the death. In retrospect this game demonstrated that Irish hopes had been lifted unrealistically by the euphoria of Ulster's success in the European Cup and that France, double Grand Slam winners in the previous two seasons, were creaking badly. Ireland began in predictable fashion. Keith Wood led the forward charges and Humphreys and McGuinness hoisted a succession of garryowens. The French, on the other hand, looked hesitant and disjointed. Within five minutes referee Peter Marshall caught France offside and Humphreys kicked the penalty. Though Ireland lost centre Jonathan Bell after just 15 minutes, his replacement Rob Henderson made an immediate impact as a short pass from Humphreys put the stocky Wasps centre clean through. The French cover got across but from the ensuing scrum their front row was penalised and Humphreys kicked Ireland to a six-point lead. The game turned when impressive No 8 Victor Costello left the field after only 10 minutes of the second half with damaged ribs, to be replaced by the less effective Trevor Brennan. Despite a third penalty from Humphreys extending Ireland's lead to nine points, Ireland lost their forward initiative and the French sensed their chance.

Inspired by captain Raphael Ibanez and lock Fabien Pelous, the French pack began to force Ireland into their own half and from a line-out, centre Richard Dourthe was driven over by his forwards. Castaignede converted and as the weather worsened France retained their control, going ahead for the first time in the game with a minute left when Castaignede found the target. Ireland refused to give up, launching themselves into the French from the restart and winning possession. France were penalised and in a gut-wrenching moment of irony, the man who had led Ulster to glory in the same ground just a week before had the chance to kick the international side to an even more dramatic victory. Alas not.

Ireland: C.O'Shea (London Irish); G.Dempsey (Terenure), K.Maggs (Bath), J.Bell (Dungannon), J.Bishop (London Irish); D.Humphreys (Dungannon), C.McGuinness (St Mary's); P.Clohessy (Young Munster), K.Wood (Harlequins), P.Wallace (Saracens), J.Davidson (Castres), P.Johns (Saracens, capt), D.O'Cuinneagain (Sale), E.Miller (Terenure), V.Costello (St Mary's).

Replacements: R.Henderson (Wasps) for Bell (15), T.Brennan (St Mary's) for Costello (50), J.Fitzpatrick (Dungannon) for Clohessy (63).

Scorers: P: Humphreys (3).

France: E.Ntamack (Toulouse); T.Lombard (Stade Francais), F.Comba (Stade Francais), R.Dourthe (Stade Francais), P.Bernat-Salles (Biarritz); T.Castaignede (Castres), P.Carbonneau (Brive); C.Califano (Toulouse), R.Ibanez (Perpignan, capt), F.Tournaire (Toulouse), O.Brouzet (Begles-Bordeaux), F.Pelous (Toulouse), P.Benetton (Agen), O.Magne (Brive), T.Lievremont (Perpignan).

Replacements: S.Marconnet (Stade Francais) for Califano (40), T.Cleda (Pau) for Pelous (69), A.Gomes (Stade Francais) for Lombard (80).

Scorers: T: Dourthe. C: Castaignede. P: Castaignede.

Referee: P.Marshall (Australia).

SCOTLAND 33 WALES 20 (Murrayfield, 6 February 1999)

Scotland's most important victory in years. After a disastrous 1998 season, and with a growing discontent over the running of their domestic game, this adventurous and ultimately successful performance from the national side finally got the Scottish public back on side. They liked what they saw and thereafter offered the kind of unconditional support that has always inspired Scottish sides. The game started in dramatic fashion, Duncan Hodge surprising the Welsh with a switch kick, and just 10 seconds were on the clock when centre John Leslie, making his Five Nations debut, touched down. Murrayfield was as stunned as Wales. Wales replied with a Neil Jenkins penalty and the Welsh forwards, led by Colin Charvis, began to make an impact. The pressure resulted in a penalty and captain Robert Howley took a quick tap-penalty and chip kick to open up the Scottish midfield. He gathered his own kick and sidestepped Glenn Metcalfe before unloading to Dafydd James, who cantered in untouched beneath the posts to score. A Hodge penalty meant Wales led 10-8 at half-time. After the break Jenkins re-established Wales' five-point cushion with a penalty but almost immediately the game swung back to the home side. Howley took another quick penalty and moved the ball to Jenkins, but as the Pontypridd fly-half attempted to offload the ball to Scott Quinnell it fell to Townsend, who galloped 60 yards for the score. Kenny Logan converted before the best try of the game, superb running and handling creating a score for Scott Gibbs. Jenkins converted for a 20-15 lead. Alan Tait then scored for Scotland, and though Logan missed the conversion to leave the game tied at 20-20, the Scots were beginning to fire in every department. Townsend visibly grew in confidence and within three minutes Scotland had killed the game. Logan made no mistake with a penalty and from the restart the Scots won back possession and started to pound the Welsh line. From a five-metre scrum Scott Murray completed an outstanding performance – the first of many in the tournament – by driving over for a try which was converted by Logan to give the Scots a 30-20 lead. An injury-time penalty completed the win.

Scotland: G.Metcalfe (Glasgow Caledonians); C.Murray (Edinburgh Reivers), G.Townsend (Brive), J.Leslie (Sanix, Japan), K.Logan (Wasps); D.Hodge (Edinburgh Reivers), G.Armstrong (Newcastle, capt); T.Smith (Glasgow Caledonians), G.Bulloch (Glasgow Caledonians), P.Burnell (London Scottish), S.Murray (Bedford), D.Weir (Newcastle), P.Walton (Newcastle), M.Leslie (Edinburgh Reivers), E.Peters (Bath).

Replacements: S.Grimes (Glasgow Caledonians) for Weir (40), A.Tait (Newcastle) for Hodge (46), B.Pountney (Northampton) for M. Leslie (21-27), Walton (69), D.Hilton (Bath) for Burnell (72).

Scorers: T: J Leslie, Townsend, Tait, S.Murray. C: Logan (2). P: Hodge, Logan (2).

Wales: S.Howarth (Sale); D.James (Pontypridd), A.Bateman (Richmond), S.Gibbs (Swansea), M.Robinson (Swansea); N.Jenkins (Pontypridd), R.Howley (Cardiff, capt); D.Morris (Swansea), J.Humphreys (Cardiff), C.Anthony (Llanelli), I.Gough (Llanelli), C.Wyatt (Llanelli), C.Charvis (Swansea), M.Williams (Pontypridd), S.Quinnell (Llanelli).

Replacements: B.Williams (Richmond) for Humphreys (56), M.Voyle (Llanelli) for Gough (66).

Scorers: T: James, Gibbs. C: Jenkins (2). P: Jenkins (2).

Referee: E.Morrison (England).

WALES 23 IRELAND 29 (Wembley Stadium, 20 February 1999)

Ireland, and in particular David Humphreys who contributed 19 points, bounced back from the disappointment of defeat against France with this spirited win over Wales, who were strangely ill-disciplined up front and lacked cohesion for much of the game. From the kick-off both sides were fired up. Within two minutes the fists were flying and Wales were soon to pay the price. Ireland were penalised just inside the Welsh half but some unnecessary aggression from Craig Quinnell after the whistle saw Australian referee Scott Young reverse the decision, David Humphreys making no mistake with the kick. On 23 minutes Wales pushed forward but as Neil Jenkins attempted to hoist a high ball, Humphreys blocked his effort and Ireland poured through for Kevin Maggs to score. Suddenly Ireland had their tails up. Another penalty a minute later extended their lead as the Welsh forwards continued to struggle to secure possession. Neil Jenkins managed to kick his second penalty before the break but not before Humphreys had punished Wales for being offside. If Welsh supporters thought half-time might bring a turnaround they were soon disappointed. A Welsh handling error soon after the break let in Ireland and winger Niall Woods surged into the Welsh 22. Quick second-phase ball followed and Keith Wood sidestepped his way over from 12 yards. Humphreys made no mistake with the conversion and soon added a drop goal. Ireland had raced to a 20-point lead. Wales, however, refused to crumble. A perfect line-out 10 yards from the Irish line gave Craig Quinnell a chance to drive and he ploughed over for the score. An easy conversion from Jenkins and Wales were back in the game. A sweeping move and a deft one-handed pass from Chris Wyatt on 65 minutes put Shane Howarth over in the corner. Again Jenkins made no mistake, slotting home the kick, and Wales were now just three points adrift. Ireland had to steady the ship before they were washed away and Humphreys stepped forward to do exactly that; under pressure from two red shirts, Humphreys coolly sent over his second drop goal of the game on 75 minutes. Ireland were not to be denied this time around.

Wales: S.Howarth (Sale); M.Robinson (Swansea), M.Taylor (Swansea), S.Gibbs (Swansea), D.James (Pontypridd); N.Jenkins (Pontypridd), R.Howley (Cardiff, capt); D.Morris (Swansea), B.Williams (Richmond), D.Young (Cardiff), C.Quinnell (Richmond), C.Wyatt (Llanelli), C.Charvis (Swansea), M.Williams (Pontypridd), S.Quinnell (Llanelli).

Replacements: M.Voyle (Llanelli) for M.Williams (27-33), G.Jenkins (Swansea) for B.Williams (52), C.Anthony (Swansea) for Young (66).

Scorers: T: C.Quinnell, Howarth. C: Jenkins (2). P: Jenkins (3).

Ireland: C.O'Shea (London Irish); N.Woods (London Irish), K.Maggs (Bath), R.Henderson (Wasps), J.Bishop (London Irish); D.Humphreys (Dungannon), C.McGuinness (St Mary's); P.Clohessy (Young Munster), K.Wood (Harlequins), P.Wallace (Saracens), J.Davidson (Castres), P.Johns (Saracens, capt), D.O'Cuinneagain (Sale), A.Ward (Ballynahinch), E.Miller (Terenure).

Replacements: J.Fitzpatrick (Dungannon) for Clohessy (66), V.Costello (St Mary's) for Miller (66), M.Galwey (Shannon) for Johns (80).

Scorers: T: Maggs, Wood. C: Humphreys (2). P: Humphreys (3). DG: Humphreys (2).

Referee: S.Young (Australia).

ENGLAND 24 SCOTLAND 21 (Twickenham, 20 February 1999)

When tries by Dan Luger and Tim Rodber saw England cruise into a 14-0 lead in the first 20 minutes of this match, most of the Twickenham crowd, English and Scottish, expected a 40-point demolition. England were so dominant at forward that they were opening huge gaps in the Scottish defence every time they ran with the ball. But in an astonishing turnaround, the following 60 minutes saw England lose direction, while Scotland grew in stature and confidence by the minute. By the end England, who stirred themselves to score a second-half try through Nick Beal, were simply hanging on. The Scotland pack, with lock Scott Murray once again to the fore, gave their side a route back into the game by gradually achieving parity with their counterparts. Their line-out work was very efficient while England's started to fall apart, and their frontrow began to counter the English dominance in the scrum. This total shift in initiative allowed the ever-dangerous Scotland midfield to capitalise. Alan Tait scored a wonderful brace of tries either side of half-time – the third successive Twickenham Five Nations game in which an opponent has scored two tries and still been on the losing side (Alan Bateman for Wales and Ireland's Denis Hickie were the others). Gregor Townsend also repeated his try from a fortnight before by pouncing on a mix-up in the England midfield to race 60 yards under the posts. But for Kenny Logan enduring a poor day with his kicking Scotland would have emerged as victors. In contrast the 19-year-old Jonny Wilkinson had a superb kicking day, converting all three tries and the one penalty opportunity he was offered. Indeed he was the pick of the England backs in all areas. The two massive tackles he made deep in the second half when England were desperately holding on to a three-point lead probably saved them the match. In the end Clive Woodward's side hung on but there was little glory in victory. Scotland will be bitterly disappointed. Only three times in the last 60 years have they won at Twickenham and their forwards' huge physical contribution so nearly allowed this year to be Scotland's.

England: N.Beal (Northampton); D.Luger (Harlequins), J.Guscott (Bath), J.Wilkinson (Newcastle), D.Rees (Sale); M.Catt (Bath), M.Dawson (Northampton);

J.Leonard (Harlequins), R.Cockerill (Leicester), D.Garforth (Leicester), M.Johnson (Leicester), T.Rodber (Northampton), L.Dallaglio (Wasps, capt), N.Back (Leicester), R.Hill (Saracens).

Replacements: D.Grewcock (Saracens) for Johnson (60), K.Bracken (Saracens) for Dawson (70).

Scorers: T: Rodber, Luger, Beal. C: Wilkinson (3). P: Wilkinson.

Scotland: G.Metcalfe (Glasgow Caledonians); C.Murray (Edinburgh Reivers), A.Tait (Edinburgh Reivers), J.Leslie (Sanix, Japan), K.Logan (Wasps); G.Townsend (Brive), G.Armstrong (Newcastle, capt); T.Smith (Glasgow Caledonians), G.Bulloch (Glasgow Caledonians), P.Burnell (London Scottish), S.Murray (Bedford), S.Grimes (Glasgow Caledonians), P.Walton (Newcastle), M.Leslie (Edinburgh Reivers), E.Peters (Bath).

Replacements: B.Pountney (Northampton) for Walton (60), D.Hilton (Bath) for Burnell (65).

Scorers: T: Tait (2), Townsend. C: Logan (3).

Referee: D.McHugh (Ireland).

FRANCE 33 WALES 34 (Stade de France, 6 March 1999)

One of the great Five Nations matches in history – in fact for drama and excitement it's impossible to recall anything better. Coach Graham Henry told his men to be bold – his favourite word – as well as disciplined, and every Welshman obeyed his instructions to the letter. Gone was the senseless fighting and intimidation that marred their performance against Ireland. Instead one could only admire a team determined to stand or fall by their pure rugby ability. France may have outscored them 4 to 3 in tries but Wales created at least another three cast-iron opportunities and at one point you had to rub your eyes in disbelief as Neil Jenkins missed four consecutive penalty attempts. In truth a 20-point winning margin would not have flattered them. From the moment Jenkins scythed through the French defence in the second minute with a slashing break from his own 22, France were on the back foot. Jenkins continued to catch France by surprise for the next 80 minutes, breaking superbly throughout and finally nailing the lie that he is not a good distributor. After kicking an early penalty he converted Charvis' foraging try before Castaignede belatedly ignited France with an astonishing break, also from his own 22. Soon afterwards Emile Ntamack claimed the first of his three tries by successfully chasing down Franck Comba's clever chip ahead. Back came Jenkins with a brace of penalties before Ntamack scored an exact replica of his first try, and France finally took the lead on 30 minutes with another Castaignede penalty. The French have weathered the storm, we sagely nodded. Not a bit of it. Jenkins stroked home his third penalty before Wales struck with two cracking tries in quick succession, first through Dafydd James and then Craig Quinnell. Was a 10-point buffer at half-time enough? France steadied their nerves and drew level, Ntamack completing a sensational hat-trick and Castaignede kicking his goals. Jenkins was struggling with his goal-kicking but he recovered and landed a beauty. France pressed as the final whistle approached and a glorious darting Castaignede try saw them regain the lead. Then Jenkins struck again and finally Castaignede blew hard, offered a little prayer and attempted to deliver the spoils, just as he did against Ireland. It was sport at its agonising, intoxicating best.

France: E.Ntamack (Toulouse); P.Bernat-Salles (Biarritz), R.Dourthe (Stade Francais), F.Comba (Stade Francais), T.Lombard (Stade Francais); T.Castaignede (Castres), P.Carbonneau (Brive); C.Califano (Toulouse), R.Ibanez (Perpignan, capt), F.Tournaire (Toulouse), O.Brouzet (Begles-Bordeaux), F.Pelous (Toulouse), P.Benetton (Agen), M.Raynaud (Narbonne), T.Lievremont (Perpignan).

Replacements: D.Aucagne (Pau) for Dourthe (5), X.Garbajosa (Toulouse) for Bernat-Salles (40), S.Marconnet (Stade Francais) for Tournaire (40), R.Castel (Beziers) for Benetton (64).

Scorers: T: Ntamack (3), Castaignede. C: Castaignede (2). P: Castaignede (3).

Wales: S.Howarth (Sale); M.Robinson (Swansea), M.Taylor (Swansea), S.Gibbs (Swansea), D.James (Pontypridd); N.Jenkins (Pontypridd), R.Howley (Cardiff, capt); P.Rogers (London Irish), G.Jenkins (Swansea), B.Evans (Swansea), C.Quinnell (Richmond), C.Wyatt (Llanelli), C.Charvis (Swansea), B.Sinkinson (Neath), S.Quinnell (Llanelli).

Replacements: G.Thomas (Cardiff) for Robinson (52), D.Llewellyn (Ebbw Vale) for Howley (66), for Rogers (66) A.Lewis (Cardiff).

Scorers: T: Charvis, James, C.Quinnell. C: Jenkins (2). P: Jenkins (5).

Referee: J.Fleming (Scotland).

IRELAND 15 ENGLAND 27 (Lansdowne Road, 6 March 1999)

The excitement was intense before this game but after the crowd and players, warming up on the pitch, had watched the remarkable events from Paris on the big screen a sense of anti-climax almost inevitably descended on Lansdowne Road. In addition England, though rarely engaging top gear, were at their ruthless, pragmatic best and rarely looked like giving way to the Irish. Much had been made of the mighty Irish pack before this showdown but England's forwards, inspired by Martin Johnson and Lawrence Dallaglio, were in mean and dominant form. It was probably apt that England's killer punch in the dying minutes of this contest was delivered by Johnson and Tim Rodber, who both swatted the defence aside for the latter to crash over for a try that silenced the home crowd. England had seized the initiative in the first half with a well-worked try by Matt Perry but the accurate goal-kicking of David Humphreys sustained Ireland and they actually began to threaten in the final quarter when, with time running out, they threw caution to the wind and discovered some fluency in attack. As was the case against Scotland, young Jonny Wilkinson was the key figure defensively, putting in a number of huge tackles that belied his size. At one point the inspirational Keith Wood fielded a long kick in his own 22 and set off at pace towards the English midfield. Who was there to stop him but Wilkinson, who stood firm and stopped the rampant hooker in his tracks. This was enough to crush the spirits of the Irish team, who only kept in touch through the boot of David Humphreys and occasional mistakes by the English forwards. Wilkinson also seized the opportunity to counter-attack whenever possible, being dragged down a yard short on one occasion. His goal-kicking, of course, was close to immaculate, with four penalties and a conversion. Elsewhere Kyran Bracken may have been slightly fortunate in coming in ahead of Matt Dawson but the Saracens man was at his busy best, adding pace and incisiveness to England's play around the fringes. Perry did little wrong after being preferred to Nick Beal at full-back and Dan Luger again hinted at his potential on the wing. Not a vintage performance but impressive nonetheless.

Ireland: C.O'Shea (London Irish); G.Dempsey (Terenure), K.Maggs (Bath), R.Henderson (Wasps), J.Bishop (London Irish); D.Humphreys (Dungannon), C.McGuinness (St Mary's); P.Clohessy (Young Munster), K.Wood (Harlequins), P.Wallace (Saracens), P.Johns (Saracens, capt), J.Davidson (Castres), D.O'Cuinneagain (Sale), A.Ward (Ballynahinch), V.Costello (St Mary's).

Replacements: E.Miller (Terenure) for Costello (64), J.Fitzpatrick (Dungannon) for Clohessy (66).

Scorers: P: Humphreys (5).

England: M.Perry (Bath); D.Luger (Harlequins), J.Guscott (Bath), J.Wilkinson (Newcastle), D.Rees (Sale); P.Grayson (Northampton), K.Bracken (Saracens); J.Leonard (Harlequins), R.Cockerill (Leicester), D.Garforth (Leicester), M.Johnson (Leicester), T.Rodber (Northampton), L.Dallaglio (Wasps, capt), N.Back (Leicester), R.Hill (Saracens).

Replacement: N.McCarthy (Gloucester) for Cockerill (66-68).

Scorers: T: Perry, Rodber. C: Wilkinson. P: Wilkinson (4). DG: Grayson.

Referee: P.O'Brien (New Zealand).

SCOTLAND 30 IRELAND 13 (Murrayfield, 20 March 1999)

A typically frenetic Celtic encounter played at breakneck speed that in any other season might have rated as the game of the tournament. Above all it confirmed the quality of Jim Telfer's class of '99, some of their attacking play taking the breath away. Scotland played with invigorating wit, pace and vision to dispatch the Irish and on this form it was no surprise that they subsequently went on to win in Paris and claim the title. Four tries to one Scotland outscored Ireland – Cameron Murray bagging two and Gregor Townsend and Stuart Grimes claiming one apiece – as they recorded a third consecutive win at Murrayfield in a major international for the first time since the 1991 World Cup. The only downbeat note for Scotland, apart from too many missed tackles for Telfer's liking, was a depressing broken leg for Tom Smith, who has suffered so cruelly with injuries since returning from the 1997 British Lions tour. Smith missed all of the 1998 season with a complicated groin strain but remains a key player in their future plans. The cupboard was not entirely bare for Ireland who, in short bursts, played some of their best rugby of the tournament. Former South Africa Sevens captain Dion O'Cuinneagain enjoyed a stunning game in the loose and David Humphreys, who scored their early try, matched Townsend break for break, but elsewhere there was a woeful inability to make the final telling pass and their habit of coughing up the ball in contact proved costly – Scotland scoring their two second-half tries after counter-attacking, albeit brilliantly, from turnovers. Not for the first time, Keith Wood overplayed his hand charging around the fringes of ruck and maul. Scotland knew what was coming, clinically lined him up and then sent him flying back yards at a time. Ireland have to learn to use the Harlequins hooker as a decoy as well as a front-line runner, for his safety and their general good. They also strangely ignored Rob Henderson in their original selection – once again the Wasps centre was their most penetrative back when he came on as replacement. On the evidence of another disappointing campaign, coach Warren Gatland faced a tough summer as Ireland work towards the World Cup.

Scotland: G.Metcalfe (Glasgow Caledonians); C.Murray (Edinburgh Reivers), A.Tait (Edinburgh Reivers), J.Leslie (Sanix, Japan), K.Logan (Wasps); G.Townsend (Brive), G.Armstrong (Newcastle, capt); T.Smith (Glasgow Caledonians), G.Bulloch (Glasgow Caledonians), P.Burnell (London Scottish), S.Murray (Bedford), S.Grimes (Glasgow Caledonians), P.Walton (Newcastle), M.Leslie (Edinburgh Reivers), E.Peters (Bath).

Replacements: D.Hilton (Bath) for Smith (39), B.Pountney (Northampton) for Walton (67), S.Longstaff (Glasgow Caledonians) for C.Murray (76), S.Brotherstone (Edinburgh Reivers) for Bulloch (77), I.Fairley (Edinburgh Reivers) for Armstrong (80).

Scorers: T: Murray (2), Grimes, Townsend. C: Logan (2). P: Logan (2).

Ireland: C.O'Shea (London Irish); J.Bishop (London Irish), K.Maggs (Bath), J.Bell (Dungannon), G.Dempsey (Terenure); D.Humphreys (Dungannon), C.McGuinness (St Mary's); P.Clohessy (Young Munster), K.Wood (Harlequins), P.Wallace (Saracens), P.Johns (Saracens, capt), J.Davidson (Castres), D.O'Cuinneagain (Sale), A.Ward (Ballynahinch), E.Miller (Terenure).

Replacements: V.Costello (St Mary's) for Miller (16), T.Brennan (St Mary's) for Ward (64), R.Henderson (Wasps) for Bell (64), C.Scally (UCD) for McGuinness (76).

Scorers: T: Pen try (Humphreys). C: Humphreys. P: Humphreys (2).

Referee: D.Bevan (Wales).

ENGLAND 21 FRANCE 10 (Twickenham, 20 March 1999)

A disappointing, almost routine game in front of a strangely muted Twickenham crowd saw England record their first win over France for four years, courtesy of the remarkable Jonny Wilkinson who landed seven penalties in seven attempts. Generally speaking, defences held sway, although France's impressive centre Franck Comba did escape to score the game's only try in the dying seconds. England did have a number of scoring opportunities but fate and lack of real finishing class ensured that Wilkinson's kicks were their only reward for long periods of dominance. France had come to Twickenham with history in their favour and a fifth consecutive victory over 'Les Rosbifs' in their sights, but it was not to be. England's forwards were too strong and the defence too well organised. Three early penalties for Wilkinson put England in charge before they took the opportunity to spread the ball wide, both Perry and Guscott being thwarted just yards from the French try-line. Matt Dawson replaced the injured Kyran Bracken just before the break and referee Colin Hawke was also forced to retire on the stroke of half-time, Scot Jim Fleming replacing the New Zealander with minimum disruption. A charge-down on Emile Ntamack's kick nearly led to an England try but again France conceded the penalty just inches from their try-line. In the last quarter, England strung a series of attacks together until they were awarded yet another penalty near the French line. They inevitably opted for a line-out and drive, but it was no mere formality and the ball was spread wide with Rees nearly breaking free on the right. The French were adjudged offside and Wilkinson kicked an easy penalty from in front of the posts to make it 15-3. The stifled attack was a costly one for England with David Rees breaking his ankle and being replaced by Northampton's Nick Beal. France attempted to inject more urgency into proceedings, bringing on fresh legs in the form of Marc Reynaud and David Auradou, but after another period of English dominance, Wilkinson kicked a further two penalties to make it 21-3 going into the last ten minutes before Comba's late try.

England: M.Perry (Bath); D.Luger (Harlequins), J.Guscott (Bath), J.Wilkinson (Newcastle), D.Rees (Sale); M.Catt (Bath), K.Bracken (Saracens); J.Leonard (Harlequins), R.Cockerill (Leicester), D.Garforth (Leicester), M.Johnson (Leicester), T.Rodber (Northampton), L.Dallaglio (Wasps, capt), N.Back (Leicester), R.Hill (Saracens).

Replacements: N.Beal (Northampton) for Rees (33), M.Dawson (Northampton) for Bracken (35), M.Corry for Hill (50), V.Ubogu (Bath) for Garforth (78).

Scorers: P: Wilkinson (7).

France: E.Ntamack (Toulouse); X.Garbajosa (Toulouse), P.Giodarni (Dax), F.Comba (Stade Francais), C.Dominici (Stade Francais); T.Castaignede (Castres), P.Carbonneau (Brive); S.Marconnet (Stade Francais), R.Ibanez (Perpignan, capt), F.Tournaire (Toulouse), O.Brouzet (Begles-Bordeaux), F.Pelous (Toulouse), R.Castel (Beiers), T.Lievremont (Perpignan), C.Juillet (Toulouse).

Replacements: C.Califano (Toulouse) for Marconnet (47), M.Raynaud (Narbonne) for Lievremont (65), D.Auradou (Stade Francais) for Pelous (65).

Scorers: T: Comba. C: Castaignede. P: Castaignede.

Referee: C.Hawke (New Zealand), replaced by J.Fleming (40).

FRANCE 22 SCOTLAND 36 (Stade de France, 10 April 1999)

Has Paris ever seen anything like it? In an astonishing performance that ultimately earned Gary Armstrong and his team the Championship, Scotland destroyed France with a remarkable five-try burst midway through the first half that took the breath away. With their forwards providing a constant stream of quality possession, Scotland's backs, as they had done all season, ran and handled with the courage of their convictions. The result was a victory to cherish, and before those who weren't there start carping about powder-puff tackling, let it be stated that exactly the same French back division denied England a single try at Twickenham three weeks earlier. Curiously Scotland made a hesitant start, fumbling the ball twice and then conceding an early try to Ntamack after an electric break by Thomas Castaignede who, unfortunately, badly twisted a knee when he was ankle-tapped en route to the line. Thereafter it was all Scotland. Alan Tait scored twice to hoist his Five Nations total to five for the season, muscular flanker Martin Leslie, enjoying his best game in a Scotland shirt, also scored a brace and the irrepressible Gregor Townsend added another to complete a proud record of scoring a try in every game in the 1999 Championship. France hit back momentarily with tries from Christophe Dominici and Christophe Juillet before half-time but after the break there was just one further score, a penalty by Kenny Logan. An extraordinary game, and what a way for Scotland's coach Jim Telfer to bow out of the Five Nations fray. 'That performance was Jim's legacy,' enthused assistant coach John Rutherford afterwards. 'The first half was all about attack and accepting opportunities, the second half obstinate defence.' France's assistant coach Pierre Villepreux spoke afterwards, in his normal philosophical fashion, about how the French team must cut the 1999 Five Nations from their memories: 'It did not happen.' Villepreux, on this occasion, got it badly wrong. Rather than forget, the French must remember every last agonising detail of a miserable campaign. They departed Paris needing to work as never before, firstly to regain their self-respect and then the respect of others. After this defeat a massive dose of honesty and realism was required, not self-deceiving delusion.

France: E.Ntamack (Toulouse); X.Garbajosa (Toulouse), P.Giordani (Dax), F.Comba (Stade Francais), C.Dominici (Stade Francais); T.Castaignede (Castres), P.Carbonneau (Brive); F.Tournaire (Toulouse), R.Ibanez (Perpignan, capt), C.Califano (Toulouse), T.Cleda (Pau), O.Brouzet (Begles-Bordeaux), R.Castel (Beziers), C.Labit (Toulouse), C.Juillet (Toulouse).

Replacements: D.Aucagne (Pau) for Castaignede (4), C.Laussucq (Stade Francais) for Carbonneau (38), S.Marconnet (Stade Francais) for Califano (55), D.Auradou (Stade Francais) for Cleda (55), P.Benetton (Agen) for Castel (55), T.Lombard (Stade Francais) for Giordani (62).

Scorers: T: Ntamack, Dominici, Juillet. C: Aucagne (2). P: Aucagne.

Scotland: G.Metcalfe (Glasgow Caledonians); C.Murray (Edinburgh Reivers), A.Tait (Edinburgh Reivers), J.Leslie (Sanix, Japan), K.Logan (Wasps); G.Townsend (Brive); G.Armstrong (Newcastle, capt); D.Hilton (Bath), G.Bulloch (Glasgow Caledonians), P.Burnell (London Scottish), S.Murray (Bedford), S.Grimes (Glasgow Caledonians), B.Pountney (Northampton), M.Leslie (Edinburgh Reivers), S.Reid (Leeds).

Replacements: G.Graham (Newcastle) for Hilton (66), P.Walton (Newcastle) for Pountney (73), A.Reed (Wasps) for Murray (80).

Scorers: T: Tait (2), M.Leslie (2), Townsend. C: Logan (4). P: Logan.

Referee: C.Thomas (Wales).

WALES 32 ENGLAND 31 (Wembley Stadium, 11 April 1999)

The Five Nations signed off in sensational style, Wales gaining the sweetest and most unlikely of victories in the third minute of injury time when Scott Gibbs powered his way past four defenders to score under the posts. Neil Jenkins administered the coup de grace with a nerveless conversion and there was just time for Mike Catt to bungle a drop-goal attempt before South African referee Andre Watson brought proceedings to a halt. England's Grand Slam hopes were left in tatters but Wales, after back-to-back victories over France and England, could start dreaming of a bright future. Despite a warm-up routine featuring Max Boyce and Tom Jones – congratulations to the WRU for showing real imagination in staging their games – it was England who initially seemed inspired by the occasion. Playing their best rugby of the tournament, they crossed for three tries through Dan Luger, Steve Hanley and Richard Hill. Strangely, however, they showed an untypical lack of discipline and a series of unnecessary penalties, some for backchat and failing to retreat 10 metres, saw the immaculate Jenkins land six penalties. For all their domination England only led 25-18 at half-time and already the alarm bells were beginning to ring among experienced observers. Moments after the restart England's cause was further undermined when Neil Back made an unforced error attempting to retrieve a loose kick deep in his 22. From the ensuing scrum the impressive Shane Howarth waltzed over to level the scores and from then on an upset was always possible. Two well-struck penalties from Jonny Wilkinson eased England's fears a little, but Barrie-Jon Mather and Matt Perry managed to squander an overlap situation and as the game went into injury time Wales were still scrapping. At that point they a received a huge boost from a controversial decision when Tim Rodber was penalised by Watson for a huge tackle on Colin Charvis, considered by many to be the 'hit' of the tournament. Initially Watson saw nothing wrong with the challenge but he reversed his decision after the intervention of his Irish touchjudge Allan Lewis. Jenkins pushed Wales downfield with a 45-yard touchfinder and from the resulting line-out Gibbs worked his magic, a try applauded in Scotland as much as Wales!

Wales: S.Howarth (Sale); G.Thomas (Cardiff), M.Taylor (Swansea), S.Gibbs (Swansea), D.James (Pontypridd); N.Jenkins (Pontypridd), R.Howley (Cardiff, capt); P.Rogers (London Irish), G.Jenkins (Swansea), B.Evans (Swansea), C.Quinnell (Richmond), C.Wyatt (Llanelli), C.Charvis (Swansea), B.Sinkinson (Neath), S.Quinnell (Llanelli).

Replacements: N.Walne (Richmond) for Thomas (64), A.Lewis (Cardiff) for Rogers (69), D.Young (Cardiff) for Evans (69).

Scorers: T: Howarth, Gibbs. C: Jenkins (2). P: Jenkins (6).

England: M.Perry (Bath); D.Luger (Harlequins), B-J.Mather (Sale), J.Wilkinson (Newcastle), S.Hanley (Sale); M.Catt (Bath), M.Dawson (Northampton); J.Leonard (Harlequins), R.Cockerill (Leicester), D.Garforth (Leicester), M.Johnson (Leicester), T.Rodber (Northampton), L.Dallaglio (Wasps, capt), N.Back (Leicester), R.Hill (Saracens).

Replacement: V.Ubogu (Bath) for Garforth (69).

Scorers: T: Luger, Hanley, Hill. C: Wilkinson (2). P: Wilkinson (4).

Referee: A.Watson (South Africa).

Five Nations Championship

Winners, Triple Crowns and Grand Slams

CHAMPIONS		WHITEWASH
1883	England†	Ireland
1884	England†	Ireland
1885	Not completed	
1886	England and Scotland	
1887	Scotland	
1888	Ireland, Scotland, Wales	
1889	Scotland	
1890	England and Scotland	
1891	Scotland†	Ireland
1892	England†	
1893	Wales†	
1894	Ireland†	
1895	Scotland†	Ireland
1896	Ireland	
1897	Not completed	
1898	Not completed	
1899	Ireland†	England
1900	Wales†	
1901	Scotland†	England
1902	Wales†	Scotland
1903	Scotland†	England
1904	Scotland	
1905	Wales†	England
1906	Ireland and Wales	
1907	Scotland†	
1908	Wales*	
1909	Wales*	
1910	England	France
1911	Wales*	Scotland
1912	England and Ireland	France
1913	England*	France
1914	England*	France, Scotland
1915-19	World War 1	
1920	England, Scotland, Wales	Ireland
1921	England*	
1922	Wales	

CHAMPIONS		WHITEWASH
1923	England*	
1924	England*	France
1925	Scotland*	France
1926	Ireland and Scotland	France
1927	Ireland and Scotland	
1928	England*	
1929	Scotland	France
1930	England	
1931	Wales	
1932	England, Ireland, Wales	
1933	Scotland†	
1934	England†	
1935	Ireland	
1936	Wales	
1937	England†	
1938	Scotland†	
1939	England, Ireland, Wales	
1940-46	World War 2	
1947	England and Wales	Scotland
1948	Ireland*	
1949	Ireland†	
1950	Wales*	
1951	Ireland	
1952	Wales*	Scotland
1953	England	Scotland
1954	England†, Wales, France	Scotland
1955	France, Wales	
1956	Wales	
1957	England*	France
1958	England	
1959	France	
1960	England†, France	Ireland
1961	France	
1962	France	
1963	England	
1964	Scotland, Wales	
1965	Wales†	
1966	Wales	
1967	France	
1968	France*	Scotland
1969	Wales†	

CHAMPIONS		WHITEWASH
1970	France, Wales	
1971	Wales*	
1972	Not completed	England
1973	Five-way tie	
1974	Ireland	
1975	Wales	
1976	Wales*	England
1977	France*	Ireland
1978	Wales*	Scotland
1979	Wales†	
1980	England†	
1981	France*	Ireland
1982	Ireland†	
1983	France, Ireland	
1984	Scotland*	Ireland
1985	Ireland†	Scotland
1986	France, Scotland	Ireland
1987	France*	
1988	France, Wales	
1989	France	
1990	Scotland*	Wales
1991	England*	
1992	England*	Ireland
1993	France	
1994	Wales	
1995	England*	Wales
1996	England†	
1997	France*	
1998	France*	Ireland
1999	Scotland	

*Denotes Grand Slam
†Denotes Triple Crown

Notes: Whitewash is losing all Championship games in a season. The tournament became Five Nations contest when France joined in 1910. Reverted to Four Nations from 1932-39 when France were banned because players were paid at club level. England did not compete in 1888 and 1889, declining membership of the new International Rugby Board. Disputes marred uncompleted Championships in 1885, 1897 and 1898. In 1972 Scotland and Wales refused to play in Dublin because of violence in Ulster. The trophy was first awarded in 1993. Wales won the 1994 title on tie-break. Until 1993 teams level on points shared title.

Italy Enter the Six Nations

Timing is everything in sport and unfortunately Italy's has been badly awry as they prepare for their historic entry into the Lloyds TSB Six Nations tournament, their first match being against Scotland in Rome on 5 February. Just when they need to be at their very best, it has all gone horribly wrong. A long, tough season of friendlies against Six Nations opposition ended without a victory but with their pride intact. However an end-of-season visit to South Africa with a tired and under-strength squad proved disastrous, resulting in calamitous 101-0 and 74-3 defeats. A few weeks later coach Georges Coste resigned, to be replaced by former national captain Massimo Mascioletti.

Before their visit to South Africa Italy's results ranged from an unlucky, but encouraging, 23-15 defeat against England in a World Cup qualifier at Huddersfield – a scoreline that would have looked even better had Alessandro Troncon not had a perfectly legitimate try disallowed – to more painful reverses against France (49-24), Scotland (30-12) and Wales (60-21). And then came South Africa! There is a tangible sense that having toiled so long to achieve admittance into an enlarged Five Nations they have relaxed a little – and suffered the consequences. The tragic death of the much loved and admired Ivan Francescato, a richly talented utility back, plunged the squad into depression and a long injury list has scarcely helped their cause. The latter, however, is something that the Italians will have to get used to as they prepare for the Six Nations fray.

Despite their depressing setbacks few would deny that Italy have earned the right to join the northern hemisphere's premier competition. In the last four years they have defeated Ireland on no less than three occasions, recorded a first-ever win over France, defeated Scotland 25-21 in Treviso and triumphed 23-19 against Argentina in Piacenza.

Rugby was introduced into Italy in 1910 by Piero Mariana, a student returning from Paris where he learned the game. Gradually a small nucleus of 16 clubs was established, the national federation was formed in 1929 and the following year Italy competed in their first international – losing 9-0 to Spain in Barcelona. In 1934 Italy became members of FIRA and competed with mixed fortunes until the Second World War. Benito Mussolini was reportedly keen on the game and certainly Italy staged a number of wartime internationals, including a surprise 22-3 win over Romania. After the war Italian rugby visibly grew in strength, the national side losing just two FIRA games between 1950 and 1966 and regularly performing well against powerful French A XVs. Onwards into the 70s and 80s the Italians continued the learning process by seeking out tougher opposition. Always enthusiastic travellers around Europe, they spread their wings, visiting South Africa, Australia, Argentina and New Zealand. In 1978 they surprised the Pumas with a 19-6 win and in 1980 demonstrated a hitherto unsuspected steel while going down 18-12 to the Junior All Blacks. Flying out of Auckland that night they stopped off in the Cook Islands, the other side of the international dateline, and played the Pacific islanders in a hastily arranged international – thus becoming on 5 July 1980 the only side in history to play two internationals on the same day.

In recent years the French influence has been huge with Pierre Villepreux serving as technical director for a number of years and Bertrand Foucarde taking over for the 1991 World Cup. Prior to the 1995 World Cup he was succeeded by Georges Coste, a fiery disciplinarian who contributed hugely to the Italian ascendancy, bringing organisation and consistency to the national side. On the field, aided by Italy's laissez-faire approach to player payments before the days of full professionalism, a myriad of stars have come and made their distinctive contribution to the Italian game – Mark Ella, Andy Haden, Roger Gould, David Campese, Frano Botica, John Kirwan, Zinzan Brooke, Rob Louw, Michael Lynagh and many others. The sceptics argued that their presence did little to strengthen the domestic game but perhaps they underestimated the increased profile and respectability such world stars gave to Italian rugby. Gradually the general standard has risen to a position where they can at least live with the best.

They acquitted themselves well in the 1995 World Cup against England and Argentina though they slumped to a disappointing 42-18 defeat in their final pool game against Western Samoa. Four years earlier they were memorably defiant against the All Blacks at Welford Road, scoring two tries before going down 31-21, and in 1987 they recovered from a heavy 70-6 defeat against New Zealand in their opening game to lose unluckily 25-16 to Argentina and then defeat Fiji 18-15.

Italy's solid record of achievement in recent years has been based on an exceptional generation of players – individuals such as wing Marcello Cuttitta, twin brother and prop Massimo, wing Paulo Vaccari who has missed all this season with a complicated hand injury, fly-half Diego Dominguez, flanker Massimo Giovanelli, scrum-half Alessandro Troncon, No 8 Carlo Checcinato and the late Ivan Francescato. Now they are backed up by a new breed such as powerful centres Manuel Dallan and Christian Stoica and livewire openside flanker Mauro Bergamasco, who was outstanding against England.

Nobody expects them to flourish immediately in the Six Nations tournament next year but if they can learn from recent mistakes they will surely provide tricky opposition, especially in front of their own volatile crowds. Italians always get behind their national sporting sides when something is at stake – the concept of a friendly in the sense of a non-competitive game is alien to their nature – and if their rugby players can pull off an early Six Nations victory thousands of new supporters will come flocking to the Italian game.

Italian roll of honour

Most-capped players: 66 Massimo Cuttitta; 60 Serafino Ghizzoni; 55 Stefano Bettarello; 55 Marcello Cuttitta; 54 Massimo Giovanelli; 54 Massimo Mascioletti; 53 Giancarlo Pivetta; 50 Ambrogio Bona, Diego Dominguez, Paulo Vaccari.

Leading points-scorers: 687 Diego Dominguez; 483 Stefano Bettarello; 294 Luigi Troiani; 133 Enrico Ponzi; 115 Marcello Cuttitta; 97 Paulo Vaccari; 93 Massimo Bonomi; 84 Manrico Marchetto; 77 Ivan Francescato, Serafino Ghizzoni.

Leading try-scorers: 26 Marcello Cuttitta; 21 Manrico Marchetto; 20 Paulo Vaccari; 17 Serafino Ghizzoni, Massimo Mascioletti; 16 Ivan Francescato; 11 Carlo Checchinato, Edgardo Venturi; 10 Vittorio Ambron; 9 Gianni Zano.

Recent results against Six Nations opposition

10/04/99 v Ireland lost 39-30 (Lansdowne Road)
20/03/99 v Wales lost 21-60 (Treviso)
06/03/99 v Scotland lost 30-12 (Murrayfield)
30/01/99 v France lost 49-24 (Genoa)
22/11/98 v England lost 23-15 (Huddersfield)
07/02/98 v Wales lost 20-23 (Llanelli)
24/01/98 v Scotland won 25-21 (Treviso)
20/12/97 v Ireland won 37-22 (Bologna)
18/10/97 v France lost 30-19 (Auch)
22/03/97 v France won 40-32 (Grenoble)
04/01/97 v Ireland won 37-29 (Lansdowne Road)
14/12/96 v Scotland lost 29-22 (Murrayfield)
23/11/96 v England lost 54-21 (Twickenham)
05/10/96 v Wales lost 31-22 (Rome)
16/01/96 v Wales lost 31-26 (Cardiff)
14/10/95 v France lost 34-22 (Buenos Aires)
31/05/95 v England lost 27-20 (Durban)
06/05/95 v Ireland won 22-12 (Treviso)
07/01/95 v Scotland lost 18-16 (Perth)
04/12/94 v France lost 14-9 (Dijon)
12/10/94 v Wales lost 29-19 (Cardiff)

European Cup 1998-99

A record crowd for the tournament of 49,000 filled Lansdowne Road with a sonic boom as Ulster lifted the European Cup, uniting all of Ireland under their red and white colours at a historic moment. Ulster's achievement on becoming the first Irish side to win the Cup is worthy of praise. If their coach Harry Williams was angry he had every right to be. Ulster won the Cup not because the English clubs had boycotted it but because they played well and hard and because Williams had succeeded in moulding a team from a number of different places – England and Scotland as well as Ulster – and getting them to play for each other and to a game plan. And this was no rollover of a tournament without the English. The French were widely expected to do well, so the fact that Ulster saw off three French sides on the way to this glorious triumph is further testament to their quality. Throughout the campaign they defended superbly and showed nous and a streetwise approach to games. And however poor Colomiers were on the day, no one could accuse Toulouse or Stade Francais of that on the run-in. They, indeed, had been much fancied for the title themselves.

The final itself was not a pretty sight and no Ulsterman would claim that. They took ruthless advantage of the fact that Jean-Luc Sadourny had only been back in action for a month since rupturing knee ligaments the previous May. He may well need treatment for shell-shock after being bombarded throughout the match by David Humphreys and company. And the kicking did not stop there. Ulster's automaton of a bootboy, the full-back Simon Mason, took his points tally for the competition to a distinguished 144 with the six out of six penalties he landed, punishing every French transgression, his first four establishing a half-time lead which ensured that Ulster could restart with confidence. That self-belief was further enhanced with the sight of the departing Laurent Labit in the 53rd minute. The Colomiers fly-half and goal-kicker had taken a heavy knock in the first half and never recovered. When Humphreys dropped his fourth goal of the tournament there was no catching the Ulstermen. Two more Mason penalties left the destination of the trophy in no doubt.

Final

Ulster 21 Colomiers 6 (Lansdowne Road, 30 January 1999)

Ulster: S.Mason; S.Coulter, J.Cunningham, J.Bell, A.Park; D.Humphreys (capt), A.Matchett; J.Fitzpatrick, A.Clarke, R.Irwin, M.Blair, G.Longwell, S.McKinty, A.Ward, T.McWhirter.

Replacements: S.McDowell for Cunningham (40), G.Leslie for Irwin (72), D.Topping for McWhirter (75).

Scorers: P: Mason (6). DG: Humphreys.

Colomiers: J-L.Sadourny (capt); M.Biboulet, S.Roque, J.Sieurac, B.Lhande; L.Labit, F.Galthie; S.Delpuech, M.Dal Maso, S.Graou, J-M.Lorenzi, G.Moro, B.de Giusti, P.Tabacco, S.Peysson.

Replacements: D.Skrela for Lhande (19), M.Carre for Labit (53), P.Pueyo for Peysson (67).

Scorers: P: Labit, Carre.

Referee: C.Thomas (Wales).

Semi-finals

A staggering result. Yet again Ulster's chances had been written off and yet again they proved the detractors and doubters wrong. This was not simply a beating for the French, it was a warning to everyone that Ulster were a serious side. They were given plenty of help; 20,000 screaming, yelling, hysterical supporters urged them to greater heights, simultaneously condemning a more than useful Stade Francais to the depths of despair. Stade Francais, the glamour club with a host of glittering stars from the rugby firmament, were the ones expected to set Belfast alight with their exciting approach to the game. Remarkably, though, it was the Irish who turned on the style and, in perfect rugby conditions, outplayed the French in a thrilling spectacle which kept the crowd on the edge of their seats until the last. Simon Mason was his usual unflappable self, landing five penalties, and he and Humphreys slotted a drop goal apiece as well. Humphreys also scored a try for good measure.

The other semi-final had its moments, most of them late in the tie. Perpignan were threatening to ease through until David Skrela, the powerful Colomiers threequarter and son of France coach Jean-Claude, came on and saved the day. Skrela, still only 19, replaced Michel Carre in the centre at half-time and he it was who settled matters when he flung his 6ft 3in, 15 stone frame over the line for a late try, which he also converted. It was a welcome score. Until then Colomiers had trailed to two Benoit Bellot penalties and had lost regular kicker Laurent Labit after an hour had elapsed. At that point all Colomiers had to show was a solitary Labit penalty. But Skrela junior, who normally plays at full-back or on the wing, stepped into the breach to underline his pedigree and ensure a place in the final.

Colomiers 10 Perpignan 6 (Stade Selery, 9 January 1999)

Colomiers: J-L.Sadourny (capt); M.Biboulet, M.Carre, J.Sieurac, B.Lhande; L.Labit, F.Galthie; S.Delpuech, M.Dal Maso, S.Graou, J-P.Revallier, G.Moro, B.de Giusti, P.Tabacco, S.Peysson.

Replacements: D.Skrela for Carre (40), S.Milhas for Galthie (41), P.Pueyo for de Giusti (58), R.Bastide for Labit (63), R.Nones for Delpuech (63).

Scorers: T: Skrela. C: Skrela. P: Labit.

Perpignan: G.Arandiga; A.Joubert, D.Plana, N.Martin, H.Laporte; B.Bellot, M.Barrau; S.de Besombes, M.Koniekiewicz, R.Peillard, O.Olibeau, P.Furet, S.Deroeux, B.Goutta, T.Lievremont (capt).

Replacements: E.Champagnac for Goutta (68), D.Camberabero for Bellot (70).

Scorers: P: Bellot (2).

Referee: J.Dume (France).

Ulster 33 Stade Francais 27 (Ravenhill, 9 January 1999)

Ulster: S.Mason; S.Coulter, J.Cunningham, J.Bell, A.Park; D.Humphreys (capt), A.Matchett; J.Fitzpatrick, A.Clarke, R.Irwin, M.Blair, G.Longwell, S.McKinty, A.Ward, T.McWhirter.

Replacements: D.Topping for McWhirter (33), G.Leslie for Irwin (54).

Scorers: T: McKinty, Humphreys. C: Mason. P: Mason (5). DG: Mason, Humphreys.

Stade Francais: S.Viars; A.Gomes, R.Dourthe, C.Mytton, T.Lombard; D.Dominguez (capt), C.Laussucq; S.Marconnet, L.Pedrosa, P.de Villiers, H.Chaffardon, D.George, C.Moni, R.Pool-Jones, C.Juillet.

Replacements: M.Lievremont for Pool-Jones (50), V.Moscato for Pedrosa (50), S.Simon for Marconnet (50).

Scorers: T: Juillet (2), Lievremont. C: Dominguez (3). P: Dominguez (2).

Referee: J.Fleming (Scotland).

Quarter-finals

A round of ugliness, upset and humiliation and one which saw the big Welsh hopes Llanelli and Pontypridd, as well as French side Toulouse, crashing out of the competition. The saddest sight, though, was not the bowed heads of the aforementioned teams. Rather it was that of Welsh referee Nigel Whitehouse being escorted off the field by security staff after a punchy second half in which yellow cards were shown to Stephane Delpuech, Frederic Pedoussant and Des Clohessy. The points all came in the first half, when Munster did not have the firepower to overcome their opponents. For Pontypridd, the drubbing they received at the hands of a rampant Stade Francais side was their heaviest defeat in the European Cup. They conceded an incredible 10 tries and the French club's outside half Diego Dominguez, the Italy international, scored a massive 31 points, comprising nine conversions, two tries and a penalty. Pontypridd kept up with their opponents only for the first 30 minutes; thereafter it was all one-way traffic. Second-half replacement Benoit Bellot did for Llanelli, who got themselves to within a point at half-time. Bellot punished them for falling foul of the laws with three penalties after the interval and then capped a fine performance with his side's final try. Toulouse were left shattered by Ulster who completely outplayed and out-thought their opponents. David Humphreys masterminded operations in superlative fashion and landed two drop goals to go with Simon Mason's three penalties. Toulouse had the consolation of scoring the game's only try, but they never came to terms with Ulster's tactics of launching mortar bombs of kicks high over enemy territory and were left pinned for long periods deep in their own half.

Ulster 15 Toulouse 13 (Ravenhill, 11 December 1998)

Ulster: S.Mason; S.Coulter, S.McDowell, J.Bell, J.Cunningham; D.Humphreys (capt), A.Matchett; J.Fitzpatrick, A.Clarke, R.Irwin, M.Blair, G.Longwell, S.McKinty, A.Ward, T.McWhirter.

Replacements: A.Park for McDowell (10), D.Topping for McKinty (42-44) and for Ward (49), G.Leslie for Irwin (56), R.Weir for Clarke (65), B.Cunningham for Humphreys (83).

Scorers: P: Mason (3). DG: Humphreys (2).

Toulouse: S.Ougier; X.Garbajosa, R.Paillet, L.Stensness, M.Marfaing; Y.Delaigue, J.Cazalbou (capt); C.Califano, Y.Bru, J-L.Jordana, F.Pelous, F.Belot, S.Dispagne, C.Labit, D.Lacroix.

Replacements: H.Miorin for Lacroix (53), M.Lievremont for Dispagne (69).

Scorers: T: Pelous. C: Ougier. P: Delaigue (2).

Referee: B.Campsall (England).

Perpignan 34 Llanelli 17 (Stade Aime-Giral, 12 December 1998)

Perpignan: G.Arandiga; A.Joubert, D.Plana, N.Martin, H.Laporte; D.Camberabero, M.Barrau; R.Peillard (capt), R.Ibanez, S.de Besombes, O.Olibeau, P.Furet, S.Deroeux, B.Goutta, T.Lievremont.

Replacements: B.Bellot for Camberabero (38), G.Majoral for Goutta (72).

Scorers: T: Laporte, Joubert, Bellot. C: Camberabero, Arandiga. P: Bellot (3), Camberabero (2).

Llanelli: D.Williams; W.Proctor, N.Davies, R.Boobyer, G.Evans; S.Jones, R.Moon; P.Booth, R.McBryde (capt), M.Madden, V.Cooper, M.Voyle, D.Hodges, I.Boobyer, C.Wyatt.

Replacement: S.Gale for Booth (55).

Scorers: T: Williams. P: Jones (4).

Referee: A.Lewis (Ireland).

Stade Francais 71 Pontypridd 14 (Stade Jean Bouin, 12 December 1998)

Stade Francais: S.Viars; A.Gomes, R.Dourthe, C.Mytton, T.Lombard; D.Dominguez (capt), C.Laussucq; S.Marconnet, L.Pedrosa, P.de Villiers, H.Chaffardon, D.George, C.Moni, R.Pool-Jones, C.Juillet.

Replacements: D.Auradou for George (56), V.Moscato for Pedrosa (56), L.Loustau for Laussucq (66), S.Keith for Moni (75), T.Malet for de Villiers (75).

Scorers: T: Dominguez (2), Laussucq, Mytton, Pool-Jones, George, Gomes, de Villiers, Loustau, Moscato. C: Dominguez (9). P: Dominguez.

Pontypridd: K.Morgan; G.Wyatt, J.Lewis, D.James, G.O.Lewis; N.Jenkins (capt), P.John; A.Griffiths, A.Lamerton, N.Tau, G.Prosser, I.Gough, G.P.Lewis, M.Williams, D.McIntosh.

Replacements: S.Enoch for Jenkins (40), S.Lewis for J.Lewis (44), A.Freeman for Prosser (57), N.Eynon for Tau (75), M.Griffiths for A.Griffiths (75), M.Lloyd for McIntosh (75), M.Taylor for John (70).

Scorers: T: Wyatt, G.P.Lewis. C: Jenkins, Wyatt.

Referee: C.Muir (Scotland).

Colomiers 23 Munster 9 (Stade Selery, 13 December 1998)

Colomiers: D.Skrela; B.Lhande, M.Carre, S.Roque, M.Biboulet; L.Labit, S.Milhas; S.Delpuech, M.Dal Maso (capt), S.Graou, G.Moro, J-M.Lorenzi, B.de Giusti, P.Tabacco, S.Peysson.

Replacements: R.Tremoulet for Dal Maso (61), R.Rysman for Moro (68), F.Pedoussaut for Milhas (69).

Scorers: T: Peysson, de Giusti. C: Labit (2). P: Labit (3).

Munster: B.Roche; J.O'Neill, K.Keane, R.Ellison, M.Lynch; B.Everitt, P.Stringer; P.Clohessy, M.McDermott, J.Hayes, M.Galwey (capt), M.O'Driscoll, D.Corkery, E.Halvey, A.Foley.

Replacements: D.Clohessy for Hayes (41), T.Tierney for Stringer (57), D.Wallace for Corkery (65), S.Leahy for O'Driscoll (74).

Scorer: P: Keane (3).

Referee: N.Whitehouse (Wales).

Pool stages

With the exception of Pool A where Stade Francais were runaway winners, finishing four points clear of their nearest rivals Llanelli, it was relatively close in the four groups. Toulouse and Stade Francais both hit three figures in their points differentials, but that was no indicator of one-sidedness. Toulouse finished in second place behind Ulster in Pool C and considering they had begun their campaign with a 38-38 draw at home to Edinburgh Reivers, the Irishmen did particularly well to top their group. The critical victory was the 29-24 victory over Toulouse after the French side had won the opening leg. At least the French side had the satisfaction of recording the biggest win of the tournament when they hammered Ebbw Vale 108-16. Llanelli and Pontypridd were Wales' only successes, both finishing in runners-up spot in their respective groups. Llanelli, though, had a negative points differential, and a substantial one at that of minus 67, but that was better than either Neath or Ebbw Vale managed, the pair of them finishing bottom but one and bottom of Pool B and C respectively. No one remained unbeaten in the round-robin stage of the tournament. Perpignan's 238 was the best points aggregate of the 16 teams and they didn't concede the fewest – that honour went to Toulouse with 103 – but even so they only leaked 108 along with Munster, who were runners-up to the French side. Understandably Ebbw Vale let in most points, 307, and unsurprisingly next worst was Neath with 194.

Pool A

	P	*W*	*D*	*L*	*F*	*A*	*Pts*	*Diff*
Stade Francais	6	5	0	1	219	117	10	+102
Llanelli	6	3	0	3	113	180	6	–67
Begles-Bordeaux	6	2	0	4	141	124	4	+17
Leinster	6	2	0	4	127	179	4	–52

Results: Llanelli 27 Leinster 33; Begles-Bordeaux 28 Stade Francais 39; Llanelli 22 Begles-Bordeaux 10; Leinster 17 Stade Francais 28; Leinster 9 Begles-Bordeaux 3; Stade Francais 49 Llanelli 3; Stade Francais 56 Leinster 31; Begles-Bordeaux 48 Llanelli 10; Begles-Bordeaux 31 Leinster 10; Llanelli 17 Stade Francais 13; Leinster 27 Llanelli 34; Stade Francais 34 Begles-Bordeaux 21.

Pool B

	P	*W*	*D*	*L*	*F*	*A*	*Pts*	*Diff*
Perpignan	6	5	0	1	238	108	10	+130
Munster	6	4	1	1	144	108	9	+36
Neath	6	1	1	4	118	194	3	–76
Padova	6	1	0	5	79	169	2	–90

Results: Munster 20 Padova 13; Neath 33 Perpignan 51; Munster 34 Neath 10; Perpignan 67 Padova 8; Padova 28 Neath 17; Perpignan 41 Munster 24; Padova 6 Perpignan 14; Neath 18 Munster 18; Neath 16 Padova 3; Munster 13 Perpignan 5; Perpignan 60 Neath 24; Padova 21 Munster 35.

Pool C

	P	*W*	*D*	*L*	*F*	*A*	*Pts*	*Diff*
Ulster	6	4	1	1	197	168	9	+29
Toulouse	6	4	0	2	234	103	8	+131
Edinburgh Reivers	6	2	1	3	179	146	5	+33
Ebbw Vale	6	1	0	5	114	307	2	–193

Results: Ulster 38 Edinburgh Reivers 38; Toulouse 108 Ebbw Vale 16; Toulouse 39 Ulster 3; Edinburgh Reivers 41 Ebbw Vale 17; Ebbw Vale 28 Ulster 61; Edinburgh Reivers 25 Toulouse 29; Ebbw Vale 16 Edinburgh Reivers 43; Ulster 29 Toulouse 24; Ulster 43 Ebbw Vale 18; Toulouse 23 Edinburgh Reivers 11; Ebbw Vale 19 Toulouse 11; Edinburgh Reivers 21 Ulster 23.

Pool D

	P	*W*	*D*	*L*	*F*	*A*	*Pts*	*Diff*
Colomiers	6	4	0	2	176	121	8	+55
Pontypridd	6	3	0	3	160	141	6	+19
Benetton Treviso	6	3	0	3	142	150	6	–8
Glasgow Caledonians	6	2	0	4	121	187	4	–66

Results: Benetton Treviso 19 Colomiers 22; Glasgow Caledonians 21 Pontypridd 43; Pontypridd 32 Colomiers 27; Benetton Treviso 34 Glasgow Caledonians 15; Pontypridd 13 Benetton Treviso 22; Colomiers 34 Glasgow Caledonians 16; Colomiers 35 Pontypridd 21; Glasgow Caledonians 40 Benetton Treviso 27; Colomiers 41 Benetton Treviso 7; Glasgow Caledonians 26 Colomiers 17; Benetton Treviso 33 Pontypridd 19; Pontypridd 32 Glasgow Caledonians 3.

Leading Scorers 1998-99

Leading points-scorers: 144 S.Mason (Ulster); 100 D.Dominguez (Stade Francais); 97 N.Jenkins (Pontypridd); 68 A.McGowan (Leinster); 66 L.Labit (Colomiers); 54 K.Rolleston (Padova), C.Chalmers (Edinburgh Reivers), K.Keane (Munster).

Leading try-scorers: 7 M.Marfaing (Toulouse), E.Ntamack (Toulouse), T.Lombard (Stade Francais); 4 S.Peysson (Colomiers), M.Barrau (Perpignan), M.Galwey (Munster), J.Mayer (Edinburgh Reivers), D.James (Pontypridd), G.Tutard (Perpignan), D.Plana (Perpignan), P.Bondouy (Toulouse), S.McKinty (Ulster), D.Skrela (Colomiers), P.Lapoutge (Toulouse).

Suspensions

Jean-Philippe Revallier (Colomiers) 7 days from 19/9/98.
Marco Baroni (Padova) 21 days from 10/10/98.
Cyril Vancheri (Toulouse) 28 days from 7/11/98.

EUROPEAN SHIELD

Final

Bourgoin 16 Montferrand 35 (Stade Gerland, Lyon, 28 February 1999)

The weather finally relented and, a month later than scheduled, Montferrand duly dispatched Bourgoin to earn themselves a place in next season's European Cup competition. Bourgoin were the inaugural winners of this tournament two years ago when it was known as the European Conference. The pulling power of the competition should never be underestimated, these two clubs drawing 31,986 people into Lyon's Stade Gerland. Montferrand fly-half Gerald Merceron kicked 20 of their points, converting a penalty try and knocking over six penalty goals for good measure. The cheering thing, though, was the fact that Montferrand outscored Bourgoin by three tries to one. The first came when Bourgoin full-back Nigel Geany held back Jimmy Marlu and referee Joel Dume awarded the penalty try. Bourgoin stayed in touch thanks to three penalties by Benjamin Boyet but after the break Montferrand really opened up. Three more penalties followed from Merceron and then wing Marlu scored a superb try, set up by man of the match Stephane Castaignede when he made a sniping break from a scrum near the halfway line. Marlu's power and pace did the rest as he covered the last 30 metres, leaving two defenders for dead. Bourgoin did hit back with a stunning try of their own through McLaren when there was still more than a quarter of an hour and a lot of hope left, but Merceron's final penalty kept them in control and the game was wrapped up by replacement scrum-half Christophe Larrue's touchline run and try.

Bourgoin: N.Geany; L.Saunier, J.McLaren, E.Tuni, L.Giolitti; B.Boyet, E.Galon; O.Milloud, J-F.Martin-Cullet, P.Peyron, M.Cecillon, J.Daude, L.Nallet, J-F.Tordo, P.Raschi (capt).

Replacements: A.Peclier for Tuni (43), R.Magellan for Peyron (50), A.Studer for Daude (66).

Scorers: T: McLaren. C: Boyet. P: Boyet (3).

Montferrand: N.Nadau; J.Marlu, F.Ribeyrolles (capt), F.Azema, D.Bory; G.Merceron, S.Castaignede; E.Menieu, O.Azam, F.Heyer, D.Barrier, C.Sarraute, A.Costes, J-M.Lhermet, E.Lecomte.

Replacements: J.Morante for Ribeyrolles (26-29 and 33-37), C.Larrue for Castaignede (72), G.Allison for Lhermet (79), L.Gunter for Sarraute (79).

Scorers: T: Marlu, Larrue, pen try. C: Merceron. P: Merceron (6).

Referee: J.Dume (France).

Leading Scorers 1998-99

Leading points-scorers: 94 C.Lamaison (Brive); 90 B.Davey (Caerphilly); 85 G.Merceron (Montferrand); 84 D.Aucagne (Pau); 76 S.Prosper (Agen); 63 N.Dubosc (Castres); 58 G.Cull (Bridgend); 57 G.Peens (Roma).

Leading try-scorers: 7 E.Tuni (Bourgoin); 6 O.Slusariuc (Dinamo Bucharest), G.Fabre (Agen); 5 P.Labeyrie (Dax), J.Bonvoisin (Montferrand), P.Bomati (Brive), F.Benaech (Narbonne), V.Tufa (Dinamo Bucharest).

Suspensions

Nathan Jones (Caerphilly) 21 days from 19/9/98.
Lancelot Eymard (Perigueux) 21 days from 19/9/98.
Andrea Lo Cicero (Rovigo) 14 days from 19/9/98.
Willie Begarie (Agen) 21 days from 19/9/98 reduced on appeal to 12 days.
Serge Betsen (Biarritz) 21 days from 19/9/98 reduced on appeal to 12 days.
Philippe Carbonneau (Brive) 28 days from 19/9/98 reduced on appeal to 12 days.
Mario Vella (Rovigo) 14 days from 27/9/98.
Sean Marshall (Caerphilly) 14 days from 27/9/98.
Fabrice Landrau (Racing CF) 30 days from 18/10/98.

Other Test Matches

(From 11 July 1998 to 30 June 1999)

Tri-Nations

Australia 24 New Zealand 16 (Melbourne, 11 July 1998)

Australia: M.Burke (NSW); B.N.Tune (Queensland), D.J.Herbert (Queensland), T.J.Horan (Queensland), J.W.C.Roff (ACT); S.J.Larkham (ACT), G.M.Gregan (ACT); R.L.L.Harry (NSW), P.N.Kearns (NSW), A.T.Blades (NSW), T.M.Bowman (NSW), J.A.Eales (Queensland, capt), M.J.Cockbain (Queensland), R.S.T.Kefu (Queensland), D.J.Wilson (Queensland).

Replacements: D.J.Crowley (Queensland) for Harry (16), V.Ofahengaue (NSW) for Kefu (46), J.A.Paul (ACT) for Kearns (46-59), O.Finegan (ACT) for Ofahengaue (76).

Scorers: T: Burke (2). C: Burke. P: Burke (4).

New Zealand: C.M.Cullen (Wellington); J.W.Wilson (Otago), S.J.McLeod (Waikato), W.K.Little (North Harbour), J.Vidiri (Counties); A.P.Mehrtens (Canterbury), J.W.Marshall (Canterbury); C.W.Dowd (Auckland), A.D.Oliver (Otago), O.M.Brown (Auckland), I.D.Jones (North Harbour), R.M.Brooke (Auckland), M.N.Jones (Auckland), T.C.Randell (Otago, capt), J.A.Kronfeld (Otago).

Replacements: C.J.Spencer (Auckland) for Mehrtens (46-73) and for McLeod (73), I.Maka (Otago) for M.Jones (61), J.T.Lomu (Counties) for Vidiri (61).

Scorers: T: I.Jones, Kronfeld. P: Mehrtens, Spencer.

Referee: C.Thomas (Wales)

Australia 13 South Africa 14 (Perth, 18 July 1998)

Australia: M.Burke (NSW); B.N.Tune (Queensland), D.J.Herbert (Queensland), T.J.Horan (Queensland), J.W.C.Roff (ACT); S.J.Larkham (ACT), G.M.Gregan (ACT); D.J.Crowley (Queensland), P.N.Kearns (NSW), A.T.Blades (NSW), T.M.Bowman (NSW), J.A.Eales (Queensland, capt), M.J.Cockbain (Queensland), R.S.T.Kefu (Queensland), D.J.Wilson (Queensland).

Replacements: J.A.Paul (ACT) for Kearns (20-46), V.Ofahengaue (NSW) for Kefu (45), D.P.P.Smith (Queensland) for Tune (49), O.Finegan (ACT) for Cockbain (50-70).

Scorers: T: Tune, Gregan. P: Burke.

South Africa: P.C.Montgomery (W Province); C.S.Terblanche (Boland), A.H.Snyman (Blue Bulls), P.G.Muller (Natal), P.W.G.Rossouw (W Province); H.W.Honiball (Natal), J.H.Van Der Westhuizen (Blue Bulls); R.B.Kempson (Natal), J.Dalton (Gauteng), A.C.Garvey (Natal), K.Otto (Blue Bulls), M.G.Andrews (Natal), J.Erasmus (Free State), G.H.Teichmann (Natal, capt), A.G.Venter (Free State).

Replacements: C.M.Williams (W Province) for Montgomery (10-22), A-H.Le Roux (Free State) for Kempson (59).

Scorers: T: Van Der Westhuizen. P: Montgomery (3).

Referee: C.J.Hawke (New Zealand)

New Zealand 3 South Africa 13 (Wellington, 25 July 1998)

New Zealand: C.M.Cullen (Wellington); J.W.Wilson (Otago), M.A.Mayerhofler (Canterbury), W.K.Little (North Harbour), J.T.Lomu (Counties); C.J.Spencer (Auckland), J.W.Marshall (Canterbury); C.W.Dowd (Auckland), A.D.Oliver (Otago), O.M.Brown (Auckland), I.D.Jones (North Harbour), R.M.Brooke (Auckland), M.N.Jones (Auckland), T.C.Randell (Otago, capt), J.A.Kronfeld (Otago).

Replacements: O.F.J.Tonu'u (Auckland) for Marshall (28), A.P.Mehrtens (Canterbury) for Spencer (48), I.Maka (Otago) for M.Jones (59), S.J.McLeod (Waikato) for Mayerhofler (66).

Scorer: P: Mehrtens.

South Africa: P.C.Montgomery (W Province); C.S.Terblanche (Boland), A.H.Snyman (Blue Bulls), P.G.Muller (Natal), P.W.G.Rossouw (W Province); H.W.Honiball (Natal), J.H.Van Der Westhuizen (Blue Bulls); R.B.Kempson (Natal), J.Dalton (Gauteng), A.C.Garvey (Natal), K.Otto (Blue Bulls), M.G.Andrews (Natal), A.D.Aitken (W Province), G.H.Teichmann (Natal, capt), A.G.Venter (Free State).

Replacements: C.M.Williams (W Province) for Rossouw (14-20), P.F.Smith (Gauteng) for Snyman (40), R.B.Skinstad (W Province) for Andrews (52), A-H.Le Roux (Free State) for Kempson (52).

Scorers: T: Rossouw. C: Montgomery. P: Montgomery (2).

Referee: E.F.Morrison (England)

New Zealand 23 Australia 27 (Christchurch, 1 August 1998)

New Zealand: C.M.Cullen (Wellington); J.W.Wilson (Otago), M.A.Mayerhofler (Canterbury), W.K.Little (North Harbour), J.T.Lomu (Counties); A.P.Mehrtens (Canterbury), J.W.Marshall (Canterbury); C.W.Dowd (Auckland), A.D.Oliver (Otago), O.M.Brown (Auckland), I.D.Jones (North Harbour), R.M.Brooke (Auckland), M.N.Jones (Auckland), T.C.Randell (Otago, capt), M.P.Carter (Auckland).

Replacements: C.H.Hoeft (Otago) for Dowd (40), S.M.Robertson (Canterbury) for Carter (63).

Scorers: T: Cullen, Lomu. C: Mehrtens (2). P: Mehrtens (3).

Australia: M.Burke (NSW); J.S.Little (Queensland), D.J.Herbert (Queensland), T.J.Horan (Queensland), J.W.C.Roff (ACT); S.J.Larkham (ACT), G.M.Gregan (ACT); D.J.Crowley (Queensland), P.N.Kearns (NSW), A.T.Blades (NSW), T.M.Bowman (NSW), J.A.Eales (Queensland, capt), M.J.Cockbain (Queensland), R.S.T.Kefu (Queensland), D.J.Wilson (Queensland).

Replacements: V.Ofahengaue (NSW) for Kefu (67).

Scorers: T: Burke, Little, Larkham, Bowman. C: Eales (2). P: Burke.

Referee: W.D.Bevan (Wales)

South Africa 24 New Zealand 23 (Durban, 15 August 1998)

South Africa: P.C.Montgomery (W Province); C.S.Terblanche (Boland), A.H.Snyman (Blue Bulls), P.G.Muller (Natal), P.W.G.Rossouw (W Province); H.W.Honiball (Natal), J.H.Van Der Westhuizen (Blue Bulls); R.B.Kempson (Natal), J.Dalton (Gauteng), A.C.Garvey (Natal), K.Otto (Blue Bulls), M.G.Andrews (Natal), J.Erasmus (Free State), G.H.Teichmann (Natal, capt), A.G.Venter (Free State).

Replacements: R.B.Skinstad (W Province) for Otto (40-70), A-H.Le Roux (Free State) for Garvey (52), P.F.Smith (Gauteng) for Snyman (65), A.D.Aitken (W Province) for Erasmus (65).

Scorers: T: Terblanche, Van Der Westhuizen, Dalton, Skinstad. C: Montgomery (2).

New Zealand: C.M.Cullen (Wellington); J.W.Wilson (Otago), E.Clarke (Auckland), M.A.Mayerhofler (Canterbury), J.T.Lomu (Counties); A.P.Mehrtens (Canterbury), J.W.Marshall (Canterbury); C.H.Hoeft (Otago), A.D.Oliver (Otago), O.M.Brown (Auckland), R.K.Willis (Waikato), R.M.Brooke (Auckland), T.C.Randell (Otago, capt), I.Maka (Otago), J.A.Kronfeld (Otago).

Replacements: S.M.Robertson (Canterbury) for Maka (50), N.R.Berryman (Northland) for Clarke (62).

Scorers: T: Marshall, Randell. C: Mehrtens (2). P: Mehrtens (3).

Referee: P.L.Marshall (Australia)

South Africa 29 Australia 15 (Johannesburg, 22 August 1998)

South Africa: P.C.Montgomery (W Province); C.S.Terblanche (Boland), A.H.Snyman (Blue Bulls), P.G.Muller (Natal), P.W.G.Rossouw (W Province); H.W.Honiball (Natal), J.H.Van Der Westhuizen (Blue Bulls); R.B.Kempson (Natal), J.Dalton (Gauteng), A.C.Garvey (Natal), K.Otto (Blue Bulls), M.G.Andrews (Natal), J.Erasmus (Free State), G.H.Teichmann (Natal, capt), A.G.Venter (Free State).

Replacements: A-H.Le Roux (Free State) for Kempson (51), R.B.Skinstad (W Province) for Andrews (57), A.D.Aitken (W Province) for Erasmus (77), P.F.Smith (Gauteng) for Snyman (88).

Scorers: T: Garvey, Skinstad. C: Montgomery (2). P: Montgomery (5).

Australia: M.Burke (NSW); B.N.Tune (Queensland), D.J.Herbert (Queensland), T.J.Horan (Queensland), J.W.C.Roff (ACT); S.J.Larkham (ACT), G.M.Gregan (ACT); D.J.Crowley (Queensland), P.N.Kearns (NSW), A.T.Blades (NSW), T.M.Bowman (NSW), J.A.Eales (Queensland, capt), M.J.Cockbain (Queensland), R.S.T.Kefu (Queensland), D.J.Wilson (Queensland).

Replacements: J.S.Little (Queensland) for Herbert (8), V.Ofahengaue (NSW) for Kefu (53), O.Finegan (ACT) for Cockbain (58), G.M.Panoho (Queensland) for Blades (73), N.P.Grey (NSW) for Tune (85), C.Whitaker (NSW) for Larkham (88).

Scorer: P: Burke (5).

Referee: J.M.Fleming (Scotland)

Australia 19 New Zealand 14 (Sydney, 29 August 1998)

Australia: M.Burke (NSW); B.N.Tune (Queensland), J.S.Little (Queensland), T.J.Horan (Queensland), J.W.C.Roff (ACT); S.J.Larkham (ACT), G.M.Gregan (ACT); D.J.Crowley (Queensland), P.N.Kearns (NSW), A.T.Blades (NSW),

T.M.Bowman (NSW), J.A.Eales (Queensland, capt), M.J.Cockbain (Queensland), R.S.T.Kefu (Queensland), D.J.Wilson (Queensland).

Replacements: V.Ofahengaue (NSW) for Kefu (52), G.M.Panoho (Queensland) for Blades (60), O.Finegan (ACT) for Cockbain (77), D.P.P.Smith (Queensland) for Burke (80).

Scorers: T: Burke. C: Eales. P: Eales (4).

New Zealand: C.M.Cullen (Wellington); J.W.Wilson (Otago), E.Clarke (Auckland), M.A.Mayerhofler (Canterbury), J.T.Lomu (Counties); A.P.Mehrtens (Canterbury), J.W.Marshall (Canterbury); C.H.Hoeft (Otago), A.D.Oliver (Otago), K.J.Meeuws (Otago), R.K.Willis (Waikato), R.M.Brooke (Auckland), T.C.Randell (Otago, capt), X.J.Rush (Auckland), J.A.Kronfeld (Otago).

Replacements: I.D.Jones (North Harbour) for Brooke (51), S.M.Robertson (Canterbury) for Kronfeld (62), C.J.Spencer (Auckland) for Mehrtens (72), C.W.Dowd (Auckland) for Hoeft (75).

Scorers: T: Cullen. P: Mehrtens (2). DG: Mehrtens.

Referee: D.T.M.McHugh (Ireland)

Other Tests

Italy 23 Argentina 19 (Piacenza, 7 November 1998)

Italy: P.Vaccari (Calvisano); F.Roselli (Rugby Roma), A.Stoica (Narbonne), F.Mazzariol (Treviso), Marcello Cuttitta (Amatori Calvisano); D.Dominguez (Stade Francais), A.Troncon (Treviso); G.P.De Carli (Rugby Roma), A.Moscardi (Rovigo), F.Properzi-Curti (Amatori Calvisano), C.Checchinato (Treviso), W.Cristofoletto (Treviso), M.Giovanelli (Narbonne, capt), C.Caione (L'Aquila), O.Arancio (Amatori Calvisano).

Replacements: M.Dallan (Treviso) for Cuttitta (14), Massimo Cuttitta (Amatori Calvisano) for De Carli (70).

Scorers: T: Moscardi, Checchinato. C: Dominguez (2). P: Dominguez (3).

Argentina: M.Contepomi (Newman); D.L.Albanese (San Isidro), E.Simone (Liceo Naval), L.Arbizu (Brive), F.Soler (Tala); G.Quesada (Hindu), A.Pichot (Richmond); R.D.Grau (Saracens), F.E.Mendez (Northampton), M.Reggiardo (Castres), P.L.Sporleder (Curupayti, capt), A.Allub (Jockey Club), S.Phelan (CASI), C.I.Fernandez Lobbe (Liceo Naval), R.A.Martin (San Isidro).

Replacements: O.J.Hasan Jalil (ACT) for Reggiardo (18), M.Durand (Chambery) for Phelan (46), M.A.Ruiz (Teque) for Martin (48), E.Jurado (Jockey Club) for Soler (51), J.C.Fernandez Miranda (Hindu) for Quesada (60), N.Fernandez Miranda (Hindu) for Pichot (60).

Scorers: T: Pen try. C: J.C.Fernandez Miranda. P: Quesada (3), J.C.Fernandez Miranda.

Referee: C.White (England)

France 34 Argentina 14 (Nantes, 14 November 1998)

France: A.Gomes (Stade Francais); E.Ntamack (Toulouse), F.Comba (Stade Francais), S.Glas (Bourgoin-Jallieu), T.Lombard (Stade Francais); D.Aucagne (Pau), P.Carbonneau (Brive); S.Marconnet (Stade Francais), R.Ibanez (Perpignan, capt), F.Tournaire (Toulouse), F.Pelous (Toulouse), O.Brouzet (Begles-Bordeaux), M.Lievremont (Stade Francais), T.Lievremont (Perpignan), O.Magne (Brive).

Replacements: P.Bernat-Salles (Biarritz) for Ntamack (41), C.Lamaison (Brive) for Lombard (80), R.Castel (Beziers) for M.Lievremont (80), T.Cleda (Pau) for Pelous (80).

Scorers: T: Comba, Glas (2), Carbonneau, Bernat-Salles. C: Aucagne (3). P: Aucagne.

Argentina: M.Contepomi (Newman); D.L.Albanese (San Isidro), E.Simone (Liceo Naval), J.Orengo (Rosario), I.Corleto (CUBA); L.Arbizu (Brive), A.Pichot (Richmond); R.D.Grau (Saracens), F.E.Mendez (Northampton), O.J.Hasan Jalil (ACT), P.L.Sporleder (Curupayti, capt), A.Allub (Jockey Club), M.Durand (Chambery), P.J.Camerlinckx (Regatas de Bella Vista), M.A.Ruiz (Teque).

Replacements: M.Scelzo (Banco Hipotecario) for Hasan Jalil (45), M.Ledesma Arocena (Curupayti) for Grau (55), F.Contepomi (Newman) for Simone (73), R.A.Martin (San Isidro) for Ruiz (80).

Scorers: T: Camerlinckx. P: Arbizu (3).

Referee: A.Cole (Australia)

Wales 20 South Africa 28 (Wembley, 14 November 1998)

Wales: S.P.Howarth (Sale); G.Thomas (Cardiff), M.Taylor (Swansea), I.S.Gibbs (Swansea), D.R.James (Pontypridd); N.R.Jenkins (Pontypridd), R.Howley (Cardiff, capt); A.L.P.Lewis (Cardiff), J.M.Humphreys (Cardiff), C.T.Anthony (Swansea), J.C.Quinnell (Richmond), C.P.Wyatt (Llanelli), C.L.Charvis (Swansea), L.S.Quinnell (Llanelli), M.E.Williams (Pontypridd).

Replacements: D.R.Morris (Swansea) for Lewis (48), B.R.Evans (Swansea) for Anthony (67).

Scorers: T: Thomas. P: Jenkins (5).

South Africa: P.C.Montgomery (W Province); C.S.Terblanche (Boland), A.H.Snyman (Blue Bulls), P.F.Smith (Gauteng), P.W.G.Rossouw (W Province); H.W.Honiball (Natal), J.H.Van Der Westhuizen (Blue Bulls); R.B.Kempson (Natal), J.Dalton (Gauteng), A.C.Garvey (Natal), K.Otto (Blue Bulls), M.G.Andrews (Natal), J.Erasmus (Free State), G.H.Teichmann (Natal, capt), A.G.Venter (Free State).

Replacements: A-H.Le Roux (Natal) for Garvey (46), R.B.Skinstad (W Province) for Andrews (46).

Scorers: T: Van Der Westhuizen, Venter, pen try. C: Smith (2). P: Smith (3).

Referee: S.Dickinson (Australia)

France 21 Australia 32 (Paris, 21 November 1998)

France: A.Gomes (Stade Francais); P.Bernat-Salles (Biarritz), C.Lamaison (Brive), S.Glas (Bourgoin-Jallieu), T.Lombard (Stade Francais); D.Aucagne (Pau), P.Carbonneau (Brive); S.Marconnet (Stade Francais), R.Ibanez (Perpignan, capt), F.Tournaire (Toulouse), O.Brouzet (Begles-Bordeaux), F.Pelous (Toulouse), M.Lievremont (Stade Francais), T.Lievremont (Perpignan), O.Magne (Brive).

Replacements: R.Castel (Beziers) for M.Lievremont (68).

Scorers: T: Lombard, Carbonneau. C: Lamaison. P: Lamaison (3).

Australia: C.E.Latham (Queensland); J.S.Little (Queensland), D.J.Herbert (Queensland), N.P.Grey (NSW), J.W.C.Roff (ACT); S.J.Larkham (ACT), G.M.Gregan (ACT); E.P.Noriega (ACT), P.N.Kearns (Queensland), A.T.Blades (NSW), T.M.Bowman (NSW), J.A.Eales (Queensland, capt), M.J.Cockbain (Queensland), R.S.T.Kefu (Queensland), D.J.Wilson (Queensland).

Replacements: O.Finegan (ACT) for Cockbain (56), V.Ofahengaue (NSW) for Kefu (58), M.A.Foley (Queensland) for Kearns (58).

Scorers: T: Bowman, Kefu, Wilson. C: Eales. P: Eales (5).

Referee: A.Watson (South Africa)

Scotland 10 South Africa 35 (Murrayfield, 21 November 1998)

Scotland: D.J.Lee (London Scottish); A.V.Tait (Edinburgh Reivers), M.J.MacM.Mayer (Edinburgh Reivers), J.A.Leslie (Glasgow Caledonians), C.A.Murray (Edinburgh Reivers); D.W.Hodge (Edinburgh Reivers), B.W.Redpath (Edinburgh Reivers, capt); T.J.Smith (Glasgow Caledonians), G.C.Bulloch (Glasgow Caledonians), A.P.Burnell (London Scottish), S.Murray (Bedford), G.W.Weir (Newcastle), P.Walton (Newcastle), E.W.Peters (Bath), A.C.Pountney (Northampton).

Replacements: G.P.J.Townsend (Brive) for Lee (15), M.D.Leslie (Edinburgh Reivers) for Walton (53), D.I.W.Hilton (Bath) for Burnell (56), K.McK.Logan (Wasps) for Tait (71), G.Armstrong (Newcastle) for Redpath (77).

Scorers: T: Hodge. C: Hodge. P: Hodge.

South Africa: P.C.Montgomery (W Province); C.S.Terblanche (Boland), A.H.Snyman (Blue Bulls), J.C.Stewart (W Province), P.W.G.Rossouw (W Province); H.W.Honiball (Natal), J.H.Van Der Westhuizen (Blue Bulls); R.B.Kempson (Natal), J.Dalton (Gauteng), A.C.Garvey (Natal), K.Otto (Blue Bulls), M.G.Andrews (Natal), J.Erasmus (Free State), G.H.Teichmann (Natal, capt), R.B.Skinstad (W Province).

Replacements: A-H.Le Roux (Natal) for Garvey (53), A.G.Venter (Free State) for Otto (56).

Scorers: T: Terblanche, Snyman, Rossouw, Van Der Westhuizen, Skinstad. C: Montgomery (2). P: Montgomery (2).

Referee: C.White (England)

Wales 43 Argentina 30 (Llanelli, 21 November 1998)

Wales: S.P.Howarth (Sale); G.Thomas (Cardiff), M.Taylor (Swansea), I.S.Gibbs (Swansea), D.R.James (Pontypridd); N.R.Jenkins (Pontypridd), R.Howley (Cardiff, capt); A.L.P.Lewis (Cardiff), J.M.Humphreys (Cardiff), C.T.Anthony (Swansea), J.C.Quinnell (Richmond), C.P.Wyatt (Llanelli), C.L.Charvis (Swansea), L.S.Quinnell (Llanelli), M.E.Williams (Pontypridd).

Replacements: M.J.Voyle (Llanelli) for S.Quinnell (42), B.H.Williams (Richmond) for Humphreys (70).

Scorers: T: Taylor, James, Charvis (2). C: Jenkins (4). P: Jenkins (5).

Argentina: M.Contepomi (Newman); I.Corleto (CUBA), J.Orengo (Rosario), L.Arbizu (Brive), F.Soler (Tala); F.Contepomi (Newman), A.Pichot (Richmond); M.Reggiardo (Castres), F.E.Mendez (Northampton), O.J.Hasan Jalil (ACT), A.Allub (Jockey Club), P.L.Sporleder (Curupayti, capt), M.Durand (Chambery), P.J.Camerlinckx (Regatas de Bella Vista), M.A.Ruiz (Teque).

Replacements: R.A.Martin (San Isidro) for Durand (57), E.Simone (Liceo Naval) for Orengo (65), M.Ledesma Arocena (Curupayti) for Reggiardo (70), D.L.Albanese (San Isidro) for Soler (71).

Scorers: T: F.Contepomi, Pichot, Sporleder, pen try. C: F.Contepomi (2). P: F.Contepomi (2).

Referee: A.Lewis (Ireland)

England 11 Australia 12 (Twickenham, 28 November 1998)

England: M.B.Perry (Bath); T.Underwood (Newcastle), P.R.De Glanville (Bath), J.C.Guscott (Bath), A.S.Healey (Leicester); P.J.Grayson (Northampton), M.J.S.Dawson (Northampton); J.Leonard (Harlequins), R.Cockerill (Leicester), D.J.Garforth (Leicester), M.O.Johnson (Leicester), T.A.K.Rodber (Northampton), L.B.N.Dallaglio (Wasps, capt), R.A.Hill (Saracens), N.A.Back (Leicester).

Replacement: M.J.Catt (Bath) for Grayson (32).

Scorers: T: Guscott. P: Catt (2).

Australia: C.E.Latham (Queensland); J.S.Little (Queensland), D.J.Herbert (Queensland), N.P.Grey (NSW), J.W.C.Roff (ACT); S.J.Larkham (ACT), G.M.Gregan (ACT); E.P.Noriega (ACT), P.N.Kearns (Queensland), A.T.Blades (NSW), T.M.Bowman (NSW), J.A.Eales (Queensland, capt), M.J.Cockbain (Queensland), R.S.T.Kefu (Queensland), D.J.Wilson (Queensland).

Replacements: M.A.Foley (Queensland) for Kearns (46), O.Finegan (ACT) for Cockbain (49).

Scorer: P: Eales (4).

Referee: P.Honiss (New Zealand)

Ireland 13 South Africa 27 (Dublin, 28 November 1998)

Ireland: C.M.P.O'Shea (London Irish); J.P.Bishop (London Irish), J.C.Bell (Dungannon), K.M.Maggs (Bath), G.Dempsey (Terenure College); E.P.Elwood (Galway), C.D.McGuinness (St Mary's College); J.M.Fitzpatrick (Dungannon), K.G.M.Wood (Harlequins), P.M.N.Clohessy (Young Munster), P.S.Johns (Saracens, capt), M.E.O'Kelly (London Irish), D.O'Cuinneagain (Sale), V.C.P.Costello (St Mary's College), A.J.Ward (Ballynahinch).

Replacements: J.W.Davidson (Castres) for O'Kelly (54), R.Corrigan (Greystones) for Fitzpatrick (54), R.P.Nesdale (Newcastle) for Wood (82).

Scorers: T: Wood. C: Elwood. P: Elwood (2).

South Africa: P.C.Montgomery (W Province); C.S.Terblanche (Boland), A.H.Snyman (Blue Bulls), J.C.Stewart (W Province), P.W.G.Rossouw (W Province); H.W.Honiball (Natal), J.H.Van Der Westhuizen (Blue Bulls); R.B.Kempson (Natal), J.Dalton (Gauteng), A.C.Garvey (Natal), K.Otto (Blue Bulls), M.G.Andrews (Natal), J.Erasmus (Free State), G.H.Teichmann (Natal, capt), R.B.Skinstad (W Province).

Replacements: A.E.Drotske (Free State) for Dalton (11), A.G.Venter (Free State) for Andrews (51), A-H.Le Roux (Natal) for Kempson (51).

Scorers: T: Van Der Westhuizen, Erasmus, Skinstad. C: Montgomery (3). P: Montgomery (2).

Referee: C.Thomas (Wales)

England 13 South Africa 7 (Twickenham, 5 December 1998)

England: N.D.Beal (Northampton); T.Underwood (Newcastle), P.R.De Glanville (Bath), J.C.Guscott (Bath), D.D.Luger (Harlequins); M.J.Catt (Bath), M.J.S.Dawson (Northampton); J.Leonard (Harlequins), R.Cockerill (Leicester), D.J.Garforth (Leicester), M.O.Johnson (Leicester), T.A.K.Rodber (Northampton), L.B.N.Dallaglio (Wasps, capt), R.A.Hill (Saracens), N.A.Back (Leicester).

Replacements: D.L.Rees (Sale) for Underwood (9), A.D.King (Wasps) for De Glanville (59), A.S.Healey (Leicester) for Rees (22), M.E.Corry (Leicester) for Catt (60-62), D.J.Grewcock (Saracens) for Rodber (67).

Scorers: T: Guscott. C: Dawson. P: Dawson (2).

South Africa: P.C.Montgomery (W Province); C.S.Terblanche (Boland), A.H.Snyman (Blue Bulls), J.C.Stewart (W Province), P.W.G.Rossouw (W Province); H.W.Honiball (Natal), J.H.Van Der Westhuizen (Blue Bulls); R.B.Kempson (Natal), J.Dalton (Gauteng), A.C.Garvey (Natal), K.Otto (Blue Bulls), M.G.Andrews (Natal), J.Erasmus (Free State), G.H.Teichmann (Natal, capt), R.B.Skinstad (W Province).

Replacements: A-H.Le Roux (Natal) for Kempson (27-40) and for Garvey (59), A.G.Venter (Free State) for Andrews (49), W.Swanepoel (Free State) for Van Der Westhuizen (60).

Scorers: T: Rossouw. C: Montgomery.

Referee: P.D.O'Brien (New Zealand)

Argentina 26 Wales 36 (Buenos Aires, 1st Test, 5 June 1999)

Argentina: D.L.Albanese (San Isidro); O.Bartolucci (Atletico del Rosario), E.Simone (Liceo Naval), L.Arbizu (Brive), E.Jurado (Jockey Club); G.Quesada (Hindu), A.Pichot (Richmond); R.D.Grau (Saracens), F.E.Mendez (Northampton), M.Reggiardo (Castres), P.L.Sporleder (Curupayti, capt), A.Allub (Jockey Club), R.A.Martin (San Isidro Club), P.J.Camerlinckx (Regatas Bella Vista), C.I.Fernandez Lobbe (Liceo Naval).

Replacements: O.J.Hasan Jalil (Auch) for Grau (40), L.Ostiglia (Hindu) for Allub (56), G.Longo (San Isidro Club) for Camerlinckx (76).

Scorers: T: Bartolucci, Quesada. C: Quesada (2). P: Quesada (4).

Wales: S.P.Howarth (Sale); M.F.D.Robinson (Swansea), M.Taylor (Swansea), A.G.Bateman (Northampton), D.R.James (Pontypridd); N.R.Jenkins (Pontypridd), R.Howley (Cardiff, capt); J.P.D.Rogers (Newport), G.R.Jenkins (Swansea), B.R.Evans (Swansea), J.C.Quinnell (Cardiff), C.P.Wyatt (Llanelli), C.L.Charvis (Swansea), L.S.Quinnell (Llanelli), B.D.Sinkinson (Neath).

Replacements: D.Young (Cardiff) for Rogers (75), A.L.P.Lewis (Cardiff) for Evans (75).

Scorers: T: James, Wyatt, Sinkinson. C: N.Jenkins (3). P: N.Jenkins (4). DG: Howarth.

Referee: B.Campsall (England)

Argentina 16 Wales 23 (Buenos Aires, 2nd Test, 12 June 1999)

Argentina: D.L.Albanese (San Isidro); O.Bartolucci (Atletico del Rosario), J.Orengo (Rosario), L.Arbizu (Brive), G.F.Camardon (Asociation Alumni); F.Contepomi (Newman), A.Pichot (Richmond); R.D.Grau (Saracens), F.E.Mendez

(Northampton), M.Reggiardo (Castres), P.L.Sporleder (Curupayti, capt), C.I.Fernandez Lobbe (Liceo Naval), R.A.Martin (San Isidro), G.Longo (San Isidro), M.A.Ruiz (Teque).

Replacements: J.L.Cilley (San Isidro) for Contepomi (55), A.Allub (Jockey Club) for Fernandez-Lobbe (61), M.Ledesma Arocena (Curupayti) for Mendez (66), L.Ostiglia (Hindu) for Martin (73), O.J.Hasan Jalil (Auch) for Reggiardo (78).

Scorers: T: Orengo. C: Cilley. P: Contepomi (3).

Wales: S.P.Howarth (Sale); G.Thomas (Cardiff), M.Taylor (Swansea), A.G.Bateman (Northampton), D.R.James (Pontypridd); N.R.Jenkins (Pontypridd), R.Howley (Cardiff, capt); J.P.D.Rogers (Newport), G.R.Jenkins (Swansea), B.R.Evans (Swansea), J.C.Quinnell (Cardiff), C.P.Wyatt (Llanelli), G.P.Lewis (Pontypridd), L.S.Quinnell (Llanelli), B.D.Sinkinson (Neath).

Replacements: D.Young (Cardiff) for Evans (60), J.M.Humphreys (Cardiff) for G.Jenkins (73), A.L.P.Lewis (Cardiff) for Rogers (77).

Scorers: T: G.Jenkins. P: N.Jenkins (5). DG: N.Jenkins.

Referee: C.White (England)

Australia 46 Ireland 10 (Brisbane, 1st Test, 12 June 1999)

Australia: C.E.Latham (Queensland); B.N.Tune (Queensland), D.J.Herbert (Queensland), T.J.Horan (Queensland), J.W.C.Roff (ACT); N.Spooner (Queensland), G.M.Gregan (ACT); D.J.Crowley (Queensland), J.A.Paul (ACT), E.P.Noriega (ACT), T.M.Bowman (NSW), D.Giffin (ACT), M.J.Cockbain (Queensland), R.S.T.Kefu (Queensland), D.J.Wilson (Queensland, capt).

Replacements: C.P.Strauss (NSW) for Kefu (46), J.Williams (ACT) for Giffin (47-56) and for Cockbain (71), J.S.Little (Queensland) for Tune (48), A.T.Blades (NSW) for Crowley (49).

Scorers: T: Tune, Herbert, Wilson, Strauss (3). C: Spooner (5). P: Spooner (2).

Ireland: C.M.P.O'Shea (London Irish); J.P.Bishop (London Irish), B.O'Driscoll (UC Dublin), K.M.Maggs (Bath), M.Mostyn (Begles-Bordeaux); D.G.Humphreys (Dungannon), T.Tierney (Garryowen); P.M.N.Clohessy (Young Munster), K.G.M.Wood (Harlequins), P.S.Wallace (Saracens), P.S.Johns (Saracens), J.W.Davidson (Castres), D.O'Cuinneagain (Sale, capt), V.C.P.Costello (St Mary's College), A.J.Ward (Ballynahinch).

Replacements: M.E.O'Kelly (London Irish) for Johns (53), R.Corrigan (Lansdowne) for Clohessy (53), S.D.Corkery (Cork Constitution) for Costello (61).

Scorers: T: Maggs. C: Humphreys. P: Humphreys.

Referee: A.Watson (South Africa)

Australia 32 Ireland 26 (Perth, 2nd Test, 19 June 1999)

Australia: C.E.Latham (Queensland); J.S.Little (Queensland), D.J.Herbert (Queensland), T.J.Horan (Queensland), J.W.C.Roff (ACT); N.Spooner (Queensland), G.M.Gregan (ACT); G.M.Panoho (Queensland), J.A.Paul (ACT), E.P.Noriega (ACT), T.M.Bowman (NSW), D.Giffin (ACT), M.J.Cockbain (Queensland), R.S.T.Kefu (Queensland), D.J.Wilson (Queensland, capt).

Replacements: J.Williams (ACT) for Cockbain (21-28 and 74), D.J.Crowley (Queensland) for Panoho (28), C.P.Strauss (NSW) for Kefu (46), N.P.Grey (NSW) for Spooner (58), M.Burke (NSW) for Latham (76), P.N.Kearns (Queensland) for Paul (80).

Scorers: T: Latham, Horan. C: Roff (2). P: Roff (3), Spooner (3).

Ireland: G.Dempsey (Terenure College); J.P.Bishop (London Irish), B.O'Driscoll (UC Dublin), K.M.Maggs (Bath), J.C.Bell (Dungannon); D.G.Humphreys (Dungannon), T.Tierney (Garryowen); P.M.N.Clohessy (Young Munster), K.G.M.Wood (Harlequins), P.S.Wallace (Saracens), P.S.Johns (Saracens), M.E.O'Kelly (London Irish), T.Brennan (St Mary's College), D.O'Cuinneagain (Sale, capt), A.J.Ward (Ballynahinch).

Replacements: R.P.Nesdale (Newcastle) for Wood (55), J.W.Davidson (Castres) for Johns (66), R.Corrigan (Lansdowne) for Clohessy (70), S.D.Corkery (Cork Constitution) for Brennan (75).

Scorers: T: Bishop, Maggs, Clohessy. C: Humphreys. P: Humphreys (3).

Referee: A.Watson (South Africa)

Australia 22 England 15 (Sydney 26 June 1999)

Australia: C.E.Latham (Queensland); B.N.Tune (Queensland), D.J.Herbert (Queensland), N.P.Grey (NSW), J.W.C.Roff (ACT); T.J.Horan (Queensland), G.M.Gregan (ACT); D.J.Crowley (Queensland), J.A.Paul (ACT), E.P.Noriega (ACT), J.P.Welborn (NSW), D.Giffin (ACT), M.J.Cockbain (Queensland), R.S.T.Kefu (Queensland), D.J.Wilson (Queensland, capt).

Replacements: G.M.Panoho (Queensland) for Crowley (20-30), C.P.Strauss (NSW) for Kefu (46), J.Williams (ACT) for Cockbain (80), M.Burke (NSW) for Tune (81).

Scorers: T: Tune (2), Roff, Wilson. C: Roff.

England: M.B.Perry (Bath); D.L.Rees (Sale), M.J.Catt (Bath), J.C.Guscott (Bath), D.D.Luger (Saracens); J.P.Wilkinson (Newcastle), K.P.P.Bracken (Saracens); J.Leonard (Harlequins), R.Cockerill (Leicester), D.J.Garforth (Leicester), M.O.Johnson (Leicester, capt), T.A.K.Rodber (Northampton), R.A.Hill (Saracens), M.E.Corry (Leicester), N.A.Back (Leicester).

Replacements: M.J.S.Dawson (Northampton) for Bracken (51), P.B.T.Greening (Sale) for Cockerill (53), N.D.Beal (Northampton) for Perry (54-61), D.J.Grewcock (Saracens) for Rodber (64), B.B.Clarke (Richmond) for Corry (73), V.E.Ubogu (Bath) for Garforth (73), P.R.De Glanville (Bath) for Catt (79).

Scorers: T: Perry (2). C: Wilkinson. P: Wilkinson.

Referee: C.J.Hawke (New Zealand)

New Zealand 54 France 7 (Wellington, 26 June 1999)

New Zealand: J.W.Wilson (Otago); C.M.Cullen (Wellington), A.I.Ieremia (Wellington), D.P.E.Gibson (Canterbury), T.J.F.Umaga (Wellington); A.P.Mehrtens (Canterbury), J.W.Marshall (Canterbury); C.H.Hoeft (Otago), A.D.Oliver (Otago), K.J.Meeuws (Otago), N.M.Maxwell (Canterbury), R.M.Brooke (Auckland), D.G.Mika (Auckland), T.C.Randell (Otago, capt), J.A.Kronfeld (Otago).

Replacements: A.F.Blowers (Auckland) for Mika (57), P.F.Alatini (Otago) for Ieremia (61), T.E.Brown (Otago) for Mehrtens (68), I.D.Jones (North Harbour) for Maxwell (70), M.G.Hammett (Canterbury) for Kronfeld (78).

Scorers: T: Cullen (2), Umaga (3), Marshall (2). C: Mehrtens (5). P: Mehrtens (3).

France: X.Garbajosa (Toulouse); O.Sarramea (Castres), T.Castaignede (Castres), E.Ntamack (Toulouse), C.Dominici (Stade Francais); U.Mola (Dax), P.Mignoni (Beziers); C.Califano (Toulouse), R.Ibanez (Perpignan, capt), F.Tournaire (Toulouse), F.Pelous (Toulouse), D.Auradou (Stade Francais), A.Costes (Montferrand), C.Juillet (Stade Francais), O.Magne (Brive).

Replacements: J-L.Sadourny (Colomiers) for Dominici (40), C.Lamaison (Brive) for Castaignede (52), F.Galthie (Colomiers) for Mignoni (55), J-L.Aqua (Toulon) for Juillet (69), M.Dal Maso (Colomiers) for Ibanez (69), J-J.Crenca (Agen) for Califano (69).

Scorers: T: Mola. C: Castaignede.

Referee: S.Dickinson (Australia)

Wales 29 South Africa 19 (Cardiff, 26 June 1999)

Wales: S.P.Howarth (Sale); G.Thomas (Cardiff), M.Taylor (Swansea), A.G.Bateman (Northampton), D.R.James (Pontypridd); N.R.Jenkins (Pontypridd), R.Howley (Cardiff, capt); J.P.D.Rogers (Newport), G.R.Jenkins (Swansea), D.Young (Cardiff), J.C.Quinnell (Cardiff), C.P.Wyatt (Llanelli), C.L.Charvis (Swansea), L.S.Quinnell (Llanelli), B.D.Sinkinson (Neath).

Replacements: M.J.Voyle (Llanelli) for C.Quinnell (18), A.L.P.Lewis (Cardiff) for Rogers (81), J.M.Humphreys (Cardiff) for G.Jenkins (83).

Scorers: T: Thomas, Taylor. C: N.Jenkins (2). P: N.Jenkins (5).

South Africa: P.C.Montgomery (W Province); C.S.Terblanche (Boland), P.G.Muller (Natal), J.C.Mulder (Gauteng), P.W.G.Rossouw (W Province); A.J.J.Van Straaten (Gauteng Falcons), W.Swanepoel (Free State); R.B.Kempson (Natal), A.E.Drotske (Free State), I.J.Visagie (W Province), C.S.Boome (W Province), K.Otto (Blue Bulls), C.J.P.Krige (W Province), G.H.Teichmann (Natal, capt), J.Erasmus (Free State).

Replacements: A-H.Le Roux (Natal) for Kempson (49), A.G.Venter (Free State) for Boome (49), D.J.B.Von Hoesslin (Griqualand West) for Swanepoel (58), G.S.Du Toit (Griqualand West) for Van Straaten (58).

Scorers: T: Montgomery, Swanepoel. P: Van Straaten (2), Du Toit.

Referee: E.F.Morrison (England)

A Internationals – Results

16/11/98 France A 9 Australia 24 (Lille)
18/11/98 Wales A 19 Argentina 28 (Pontypridd)
01/12/98 Ireland A 19 South Africa 50 (Belfast)
05/02/99 Ireland A 26 France A 25 (Donnybrook)
05/02/99 Wales A 20 Scotland A 8 (Myreside)
19/02/99 Ireland A 29 Wales A 40 (Ebbw Vale)
19/02/99 England A 27 Scotland A 16 (Headingley)
05/03/99 Scotland A 61 Italy A 6 (Galashiels)
05/03/99 Ireland A 21 England A 28 (Donnybrook)
05/03/99 France A 17 Wales A 20 (Perigeaux)
19/03/99 Scotland A 31 Ireland A 21 (Myreside)
19/03/99 England A 24 France A 21 (Redruth)
09/04/99 Ireland A 73 Italy A 17 (Donnybrook)
09/04/99 Wales A 32 England A 25 (Wrexham)
09/04/99 France A 23 Scotland A 16 (Bourges)

Commonwealth Games

Rugby made a striking debut at the Commonwealth Games with excellent crowds and great excitement at the Petaling Jaya Stadium in Kuala Lumpur. New Zealand, who always raise their game when gold medals or world championships are at stake, beat old rivals Fiji in a marvellous final which provided one of the enduring memories of the Games. It seems certain that rugby will again be one of the focal points of the Manchester Games in 2002. Happily one of the stars of the tournament was Jonah Lomu who first came to prominence as a schoolboy star of the 1994 and 1995 Hong Kong Sevens. He loves the abbreviated form of the game, in which he uses his skill as well as extraordinary strength and pace, and he is never happier than when playing sevens for New Zealand. Lomu may have failed to get on the scoresheet in New Zealand's 21-12 win over Fiji but he blasted enormous holes in the Pacific islanders' defence, while one chase-back and tackle against Senirusi Rauqe was the *mano a mano* confrontation of the tournament. New Zealand were also indebted to Christian Cullen, entitled more than most to a rest after a murderous season, but determined to win gold. 'Sevens improves my game every time I play,' insists one of rugby's most extraordinary talents. A lesson perhaps for those big names in Britain who shy away from the unforgiving arena of sevens rugby?

The All Blacks' victory – courtesy of tries by the unsung Dallas Seymour, Christian Cullen and replacement Caleb Ralph – sealed a splendid final day of action. By nightfall a capacity 15,000 crowd were packed into the Petaling Jaya Stadium. While there were some mismatches, inevitable in the early stages of an 18-team field, there were as many contests of the highest quality at all levels of the 52-match, three-day event. Given the sporting tendencies of the Commonwealth countries this was virtually a rerun of the 1997 World Championships – more's the pity that Scotland, supposedly the home of sevens, felt unable to send a squad and England felt that their league programme must take precedence, though they did at least turn up and proceeded to the quarter-finals before they were outclassed by Australia.

New Zealand and Australia had started an epic final day as the top two seeds, based on their results the previous day, Sunday, but a David Campese-led Australia, 28-14 semi-final losers to Fiji after their convincing 49-14 win over England, had to be satisfied with a third-place finish by virtue of a 33-12 play-off victory over Samoa. The Samoans in turn had nailed their colours to the mast with an impressive 26-5 defeat of South Africa before losing 19-14 to New Zealand, a courageous effort with so many of their best players in Australia preparing for the Pacific RWC qualifying tournament. Youthful Canada also made the very most of their opportunities to impress on the world stage, taking Fiji to the limit before going out 26-19. With less than three minutes left, Canada were 19-14 ahead but then lost a five-metre attacking scrum on the Fijian line and saw their opponents break out for the first of two scores.

In between, Canada had one last chance, taking the ball to halfway from their own line only to run out of support as the incomparable Fijian captain Waisale Serevi regained possession to dart away virtually unopposed. If any team, other than Malaysia of course, endeared itself to the steadily growing crowd it was Canada, for this was a most spirited effort against all the odds.

Quarter-finals: Australia 49 England 14; Fiji 26 Canada 19; New Zealand 38 Wales 14; Samoa 26 South Africa 5. *Semi-finals*: Fiji 28 Australia 14; New Zealand 19 Samoa 14. *Bronze medal*: Australia 33 Samoa 12. *Gold/silver medal final*: New Zealand 21 Fiji 12.

Plate: *Quarter-finals*: Cook Islands 45 Trinidad and Tobago 12; Malaysia 26 Swaziland 7; Papua New Guinea 40 Sri Lanka 17; Tonga 35 Kenya 19. *Semi-finals*: Cook Islands 22 Tonga 21; Papua New Guinea 35 Malaysia 5. *Final*: Cook Islands 31 Papua New Guinea 12.

Bowl: *Final*: Bahamas 48 Cayman Islands 17.

IRB/FIRA World Junior Cup

Final

Wales 0 New Zealand 25 (Stradey Park, Llanelli, 4 April 1999)

A marvellous competition, jointly sponsored by the IRB and FIRA, reached a predictable climax when the impressive young New Zealand side, coached by former All Black flanker Mark 'Cowboy' Shaw, proved comfortable winners over a plucky Welsh team. Although Wales, coached by John Bevan, the former Wales and British Lions wing, had excelled in reaching the final for the first time since 1996, when they were beaten by Argentina, they were always second best against a complete New Zealand outfit. The Welsh were unable to reproduce the form which had accounted for England, Argentina and South Africa on the way to the final – the latter decided by virtue of Wales' penalty to South Africa's drop goal after the score finished level at 10-10. The Welsh tried to play with the same kind of expansive style that had brought them so much reward but a deluge of rain before the kick-off hindered rather than helped their cause. They knocked on with disconcerting regularity, having achieved parity in the set-piece, and they gifted New Zealand a 10-0 interval advantage. Gerrard Fasaualu, who scored two tries in the semi-final defeat of Ireland, claimed the first here after 10 minutes and then made Wales pay for losing possession in midfield four minutes later. Wales continued to compete but nine minutes into the second half a searching kick from Riki Flutey gave Junior Muliaina the chance to pick up and slide over the line for the conclusive try. The All Blacks clinched victory when Richard McGaw, the outstanding openside flanker, drove over for their fourth try. The junior All Blacks, participating in this event for the first time, were clinical in their execution and cruised through the half without ever really stretching themselves. In the 3rd/4th place play-off Ireland, champions in 1998 and brave semi-final losers to New Zealand this time around, again performed well before losing 27-20 to South Africa.

Wales: R.Williams; K.James, J.Robinson, M.Price, R.Johnston; C.Sweeney, R.Powell; D.Pattison, C.Thomas, G.Wood, D.Adams, A.Jones (capt), J.Bater, T.Morris, M.Owen.

Replacements: D.Peel for Williams (45), C.Bowen for Adams (45), M.Griffiths for Owen (56), A.Chiffi for Bater (60), R.Mills for Wood (67).

New Zealand: S.Paku; J.Muliaina, A.Mauger, G.Fasaualu, J.Stewart; R.Flutey, D.Gibson; C.Dermody, J.Ward (capt), C.Johnson, B.Mika, D.Quate, S.Bates, R.McGaw, J.Collins.

Replacements: R.Wallace for Collins (43), J.Shoemark for Mauger (68), T.Woodcock for Dermody (68), L.Mahoney for Flutey (68).

Scorers: T: Fasaualu (2), Muliaina, McGaw. C: Flutey. P: Flutey.

Referee: S.Lander (England).

Rankings:

Division One:
1 New Zealand; 2 Wales; 3 South Africa; 4 Ireland; 5 France; 6 Canada; 7 Argentina; 8 Italy; 9 Scotland;10 Chile; 11 England; 12 Romania; 13 Japan; 14 Uruguay; 15 Poland; 16 Georgia.

Division Two:
1 Spain; 2 Russia; 3 Portugal; 4 Czech Republic; 5 Ukraine; 6 Paraguay; 7 Germany; 8 Belgium.

Division Three:
1 Morocco; 2 Cote D'Ivoire; 3 Chinese Taipei; 4 Netherlands; 5 Brazil; 6 Croatia; 7 Andorra; 8 Luxembourg.

Principal Fixtures 1999-2000

Saturday 28 August

INTERNATIONALS
Australia v New Zealand (Sydney)
England v Canada (Twickenham)
Ireland v Argentina (Lansdowne Rd)
Italy v Fiji (L'Aquila)
Scotland v Romania (Murrayfield)
Spain v Uruguay (L'Aquila)
Wales v France (Cardiff)

TETLEY'S BITTER CUP
Preliminary Round

JEWSON ONE
Birmingham/Solihull v Harrogate
Bracknell v Otley
Fylde v Rosslyn Park
Newbury v Preston Grasshoppers
Reading v Camberley
Wharfedale v Nottingham

Sunday 29 August

JEWSON ONE
Lydney v Blackheath

Saturday 4 September

JEWSON ONE
Birmingham/Solihull v Newbury
Camberley v Preston Grasshoppers
Harrogate v Wharfedale
Lydney v Bracknell
Nottingham v Blackheath
Otley v Fylde
Rosslyn Park v Reading

WRU LEAGUE
Premier Division
Bridgend v Swansea
Caerphilly v Edinburgh Reivers
Dunvant v Neath
Glasgow Caledonians v Pontypridd
Llanelli v Ebbw Vale
Newport v Cardiff
Division One
Aberavon v Bonymaen
Abercynon v Treorchy Rhondda
Blackwood v Merthyr
Llandovery v UWIC
Pontypool v Llanharan
Rumney v Newbridge
Tredegar v Abertillery
Cross Keys v Tondu

SRU TENNENTS LEAGUE
Premiership One
Hawick v Watsonians
Heriot's FP v Currie
Jed-Forest v Glasgow Hawks
Melrose v Gala
West of Scotland v Kelso
Premiership Two
Boroughmuir v Aberdeen GSFP
Kirkcaldy v Stirling County
Musselburgh v Dundee HSFP
Peebles v East Kilbride
Selkirk v Biggar

Tuesday 7 September

WORLD CUP WARM-UP MATCH
England XV v ERP All Stars (Anfield)

ALLIED DUNBAR TWO
Exeter Chiefs v Waterloo Drummers
Henley Hawks v London Welsh
Manchester v Worcester
Moseley v West Hartlepool
Orrell v Leeds Tykes
Rugby Lions v Coventry
Wakefield v Rotherham

Saturday 11 September

ALLIED DUNBAR ONE
Bristol v Bedford
Gloucester v Newcastle Falcons
Harlequins v Bath
Manchester Sale v London Wasps
Northampton Saints v Leicester Tigers
Saracens v London Irish

ALLIED DUNBAR TWO
Coventry v Henley Hawks
Leeds Tykes v Exeter Chiefs (2: 30)
London Welsh v Rotherham
Orrell v Wakefield
Waterloo Drummers v Moseley
West Hartlepool v Manchester
Worcester v Rugby Lions

JEWSON ONE
Blackheath v Harrogate
Bracknell v Nottingham
Fylde v Lydney
Newbury v Camberley
Preston Grasshoppers v Rosslyn Park
Reading v Otley
Wharfedale v Birmingham/Solihull

WRU LEAGUE
Premier Division
Bridgend v Cardiff
Ebbw Vale v Caerphilly
Edinburgh Reivers v Glasgow Caledonians
Neath v Newport
Pontypridd v Dunvant
Swansea v Llanelli
Division One
Llanharan v Cross Keys
Merthyr v Abercynon
Newbridge v Abertillery
Pontypool v Aberavon
Tondu v Llandovery
Tredegar v Blackwood
Treorchy Rhondda v Bonymaen
UWIC v Rumney

SRU TENNENTS LEAGUE
Premiership One
Currie v Melrose
Gala v Hawick
Glasgow Hawks v Heriot's FP
Kelso v Jed-Forest
Watsonians v West of Scotland
Premiership Two
Aberdeen GSFP v Kirkcaldy
Biggar v Musselburgh
Dundee HSFP v Boroughmuir
East Kilbride v Selkirk
Stirling County v Peebles

SRU TENNENTS CUP
1st Round

Wednesday 15 September

WRU LEAGUE
Division One
Aberavon v Treorchy Rhondda
Abertillery v UWIC
Abercynon v Tredegar
Blackwood v Newbridge
Bonymaen v Merthyr
Llandovery v Llanharan
Rumney v Tondu
Cross Keys v Pontypool

Saturday 18 September

WORLD CUP WARM-UP MATCH
England XV v ERP All Stars (Twickenham)

ALLIED DUNBAR TWO
Exeter Chiefs v Orrell
Henley Hawks v Worcester
Rotherham v Coventry
Manchester v Waterloo Drummers
Moseley v Leeds Tykes
Rugby Lions v West Hartlepool
Wakefield v London Welsh

TETLEY'S BITTER CUP
1st Round

JEWSON ONE
Birmingham/Solihull v Blackheath
Harrogate v Bracknell
Lydney v Reading
Nottingham v Fylde
Otley v Preston Grasshoppers
Rosslyn Park v Camberley
Wharfedale v Newbury

WRU LEAGUE
Premier Division
Caerphilly v Swansea
Dunvant v Edinburgh Reivers
Glasgow Caledonians v Ebbw Vale
Llanelli v Bridgend
Neath v Cardiff
Newport v Pontypridd
Division One
Llanharan v Rumney
Merthyr v Treorchy Rhondda
Newbridge v Abercynon
Pontypool v Llandovery
Tondu v Abertillery
Tredegar v Bonymaen
UWIC v Blackwood
Cross Keys v Aberavon

SRU TENNENTS LEAGUE
Premiership One
Hawick v Currie
Jed-Forest v Heriot's FP
Kelso v Watsonians
Melrose v Glasgow Hawks

West of Scotland v Gala
Premiership Two
Boroughmuir v Biggar
East Kilbride v Stirling County
Kirkcaldy v Dundee HSFP
Peebles v Aberdeen GSFP
Selkirk v Musselburgh

Saturday 25 September

ALLIED DUNBAR ONE
Bath v Northampton Saints
Bedford v London Irish
Harlequins v Saracens
Leicester Tigers v Manchester Sale
London Wasps v Gloucester
Newcastle Falcons v Bristol

ALLIED DUNBAR TWO
Coventry v London Welsh
Exeter Chiefs v Wakefield
Orrell v Moseley
Waterloo Drummers v Rugby Lions
West Hartlepool v Henley Hawks
Worcester v Rotherham

JEWSON ONE
Blackheath v Wharfedale
Bracknell v Birmingham/Solihull
Camberley v Otley
Fylde v Harrogate
Newbury v Rosslyn Park
Preston Grasshoppers v Lydney
Reading v Nottingham

WRU CHALLENGE CUP
1st Round

WRU LEAGUE
Premier Division
Bridgend v Caerphilly
Ebbw Vale v Dunvant
Edinburgh Reivers v Newport
Llanelli v Cardiff
Pontypridd v Neath
Swansea v Glasgow Caledonians
Division One
Aberavon v Merthyr
Abertillery v Llanharan
Abercynon v UWIC
Blackwood v Tondu
Bonymaen v Newbridge
Llandovery v Cross Keys
Rumney v Pontypool
Treorchy Rhondda v Tredegar

Saturday 25 September

SRU TENNENTS LEAGUE
Premiership One
Currie v West of Scotland
Gala v Kelso
Glasgow Hawks v Hawick
Heriot's FP v Melrose
Watsonians v Jed-Forest
Premiership Two
Aberdeen GSFP v East Kilbride
Biggar v Kirkcaldy
Dundee HSFP v Peebles
Musselburgh v Boroughmuir
Stirling County v Selkirk

Monday 27 September

ALLIED DUNBAR TWO
Leeds Tykes v Manchester (8: 00)

Wednesday 29 September

WRU LEAGUE
Division One
Llandovery v Aberavon
Llanharan v Blackwood
Newbridge v Treorchy Rhondda
Pontypool v Abertillery
Tondu v Abercynon
Tredegar v Merthyr
UWIC v Bonymaen
Cross Keys v Rumney

Friday 1 October

RUGBY WORLD CUP
Wales v Argentina (Cardiff)
Fiji v Namibia (Beziers)

SRU TENNENTS LEAGUE
Premiership One
Hawick v Heriot's FP
Jed-Forest v Melrose
Kelso v Currie
Watsonians v Gala
Premiership Two
Peebles v Biggar
Selkirk v Boroughmuir

Saturday 2 October

RUGBY WORLD CUP
England v Italy (Twickenham)
France v Canada (Beziers)
Ireland v United States (Lansdowne Rd)
Spain v Uruguay (Galashiels)

ALLIED DUNBAR ONE
Bristol v London Wasps
Gloucester v Leicester Tigers
London Irish v Newcastle Falcons
Manchester Sale v Bath
Northampton Saints v Harlequins
Saracens v Bedford

ALLIED DUNBAR TWO
Henley Hawks v Waterloo Drummers (2: 30)
London Welsh v Worcester
Manchester v Orrell
Moseley v Exeter Chiefs
Rotherham v West Hartlepool
Rugby Lions v Leeds Tykes
Wakefield v Coventry

JEWSON ONE
Birmingham/Solihull v Fylde
Blackheath v Newbury
Harrogate v Reading
Lydney v Camberley
Nottingham v Preston Grasshoppers
Otley v Rosslyn Park
Wharfedale v Bracknell

WRU LEAGUE
Premier Division
Caerphilly v Llanelli
Cardiff v Pontypridd
Dunvant v Swansea
Glasgow Caledonians v Bridgend
Neath v Edinburgh Reivers
Newport v Ebbw Vale
Division One
Aberavon v Tredegar
Abertillery v Cross Keys
Abercynon v Llanharan
Blackwood v Pontypool
Bonymaen v Tondu
Merthyr v Newbridge
Rumney v Llandovery
Treorchy Rhondda v UWIC

SRU TENNENTS LEAGUE
Premiership One
West of Scotland v Glasgow Hawks
Premiership Two
East Kilbride v Dundee HSFP
Kirkcaldy v Musselburgh
Stirling County v Aberdeen GSFP

Sunday 3 October

RUGBY WORLD CUP
Australia v Romania (Belfast)
New Zealand v Tonga (Bristol)
Scotland v South Africa (Murrayfield)
Western Samoa v Japan (Wrexham)

Friday 8 October

RUGBY WORLD CUP
France v Namibia (Bordeaux)
Scotland v Uruguay (Murrayfield)

Saturday 9 October

RUGBY WORLD CUP
England v New Zealand (Twickenham)
Fiji v Canada (Bordeaux)
United States v Romania (Lansdowne Rd)
Wales v Japan (Cardiff)

ALLIED DUNBAR ONE
Bath v Gloucester
Harlequins v Manchester Sale
London Wasps v London Irish
Newcastle Falcons v Bedford
Northampton Saints v Saracens

ALLIED DUNBAR TWO
Exeter Chiefs v Manchester (2: 30)
Leeds Tykes v Henley Hawks
Moseley v Wakefield
Orrell v Rugby Lions
Waterloo Drummers v Rotherham
West Hartlepool v London Welsh
Worcester v Coventry

JEWSON ONE
Bracknell v Blackheath
Camberley v Nottingham
Fylde v Wharfedale
Newbury v Otley
Preston Grasshoppers v Harrogate
Reading v Birmingham/Solihull

Rosslyn Park v Lydney

WRU LEAGUE
Premier Division
Bridgend v Dunvant
Caerphilly v Cardiff
Ebbw Vale v Neath
Glasgow Caledonians v Llanelli
Pontypridd v Edinburgh Reivers
Swansea v Newport
Division One
Aberavon v Rumney
Llandovery v Abertillery
Llanharan v Bonymaen
Newbridge v Tredegar
Pontypool v Abercynon
Tondu v Treorchy Rhondda
UWIC v Merthyr
Cross Keys v Blackwood

SRU TENNENTS LEAGUE
Premiership One
Currie v Watsonians
Gala v Jed-Forest
Glasgow Hawks v Kelso
Heriot's FP v West of Scotland
Melrose v Hawick
Premiership Two
Aberdeen GSFP v Selkirk
Biggar v East Kilbride
Boroughmuir v Kirkcaldy
Dundee HSFP v Stirling County
Musselburgh v Peebles

Sunday 10 October

RUGBY WORLD CUP
Argentina v Western Samoa (Llanelli)
Ireland v Australia (Lansdowne Road)
Italy v Tonga (Leicester)
South Africa v Spain (Murrayfield)

Thursday 14 October

RUGBY WORLD CUP
Australia v United States (Limerick)
Canada v Namibia (Toulouse)
New Zealand v Italy (Huddersfield)
Wales v Western Samoa (Cardiff)

Friday 15 October

RUGBY WORLD CUP
England v Tonga (Twickenham)
Ireland v Romania (Lansdowne Road)
South Africa v Uruguay (Glasgow)

Saturday 16 October

RUGBY WORLD CUP
Argentina v Japan (Cardiff)
France v Fiji (Toulouse)
Scotland v Spain (Murrayfield)

ALLIED DUNBAR ONE
Bedford v London Wasps
Bristol v Bath
Gloucester v Harlequins
London Irish v Leicester Tigers
Manchester Sale v Northampton Saints
Saracens v Newcastle Falcons

ALLIED DUNBAR TWO
Coventry v West Hartlepool
Henley Hawks v Orrell
London Welsh v Waterloo Drummers (2: 30)
Manchester v Moseley (2: 15)
Rotherham v Leeds Tykes
Rugby Lions v Exeter Chiefs
Wakefield v Worcester

TETLEY'S BITTER CUP
2nd Round

WRU LEAGUE
Premier Division
Cardiff v Edinburgh Reivers
Dunvant v Llanelli
Glasgow Caledonians v Caerphilly
Neath v Swansea
Newport v Bridgend
Pontypridd v Ebbw Vale
Division One
Abertillery v Rumney
Abercynon v Cross Keys
Blackwood v Llandovery
Bonymaen v Pontypool
Merthyr v Tondu
Newbridge v Aberavon
Tredegar v UWIC
Treorchy Rhondda v Llanharan

Sunday 17 October

SRU TENNENTS LEAGUE
Premiership One
Gala v Currie
Jed-Forest v Hawick
Kelso v Heriot's FP
Watsonians v Glasgow Hawks
West of Scotland v Melrose
Premiership Two
Aberdeen GSFP v Dundee HSFP
East Kilbride v Musselburgh
Peebles v Boroughmuir
Selkirk v Kirkcaldy
Stirling County v Biggar

SRU TENNENTS CUP
2nd Round

Wednesday 20 October

RUGBY WORLD CUP
Quarter-final play-offs at Lens, Murrayfield and Twickenham

Saturday 23 October

RUGBY WORLD CUP
Quarter-final at Cardiff

ALLIED DUNBAR ONE
Leicester Tigers v Bristol (1: 00)

ALLIED DUNBAR TWO
Exeter Chiefs v Henley Hawks
Leeds Tykes v London Welsh
Manchester v Wakefield (2: 15)
Moseley v Rugby Lions
Orrell v Rotherham
Waterloo Drummers v Coventry
West Hartlepool v Worcester

JEWSON ONE
Birmingham/Solihull v Preston Grasshoppers
Blackheath v Fylde
Bracknell v Newbury
Harrogate v Camberley
Lydney v Otley
Nottingham v Rosslyn Park
Wharfedale v Reading

WRU CHALLENGE CUP
2nd Round

WRU LEAGUE
Premier Division
Bridgend v Neath
Caerphilly v Dunvant
Ebbw Vale v Edinburgh Reivers
Glasgow Caledonians v Cardiff
Llanelli v Newport
Swansea v Pontypridd
Division One
Aberavon v Abertillery
Llandovery v Abercynon
Llanharan v Merthyr
Pontypool v Treorchy Rhondda
Rumney v Blackwood
Tondu v Tredegar
UWIC v Newbridge
Cross Keys v Bonymaen

SRU TENNENTS LEAGUE
Premiership One
Glasgow Hawks v Gala
Hawick v West of Scotland
Heriot's FP v Watsonians
Jed-Forest v Currie
Melrose v Kelso
Premiership Two
Biggar v Aberdeen GSFP
Boroughmuir v East Kilbride
Kirkcaldy v Peebles
Musselburgh v Stirling County
Selkirk v Dundee HSFP

Sunday 24 October

RUGBY WORLD CUP
Quarter-finals at Lansdowne Road, Murrayfield and Stade de France

Saturday 30 October

RUGBY WORLD CUP
Semi-final at Twickenham

ALLIED DUNBAR ONE
Bath v London Irish
Harlequins v Bristol
Leicester Tigers v Bedford (1: 00)
London Wasps v Newcastle Falcons
Manchester Sale v Saracens
Northampton Saints v Gloucester

JEWSON ONE
Camberley v Birmingham/Solihull
Fylde v Bracknell
Newbury v Lydney
Otley v Nottingham
Preston Grasshoppers v Wharfedale
Reading v Blackheath
Rosslyn Park v Harrogate

WRU LEAGUE
Premier Division
Dunvant v Glasgow Caledonians
Ebbw Vale v Cardiff
Edinburgh Reivers v Swansea
Neath v Llanelli
Newport v Caerphilly
Pontypridd v Bridgend
Division One
Abercynon v Rumney
Blackwood v Abertillery
Bonymaen v Llandovery
Merthyr v Pontypool
Newbridge v Tondu
Tredegar v Llanharan
Treorchy Rhondda v Cross Keys
UWIC v Aberavon

Sunday 31 October

RUGBY WORLD CUP
Semi-final at Twickenham

Tuesday 2 November

WRU LEAGUE
Division One
Abertillery v Abercynon
Blackwood v Aberavon
Llandovery v Treorchy Rhondda
Llanharan v Newbridge
Pontypool v Tredegar
Rumney v Bonymaen
Tondu v UWIC
Cross Keys v Merthyr

Wednesday 3 November

WRU LEAGUE
Premier Division
Bridgend v Edinburgh Reivers
Caerphilly v Neath
Cardiff v Dunvant
Glasgow Caledonians v Newport
Llanelli v Pontypridd
Swansea v Ebbw Vale

Thursday 4 November

RUGBY WORLD CUP
3rd place play-off at Cardiff

Saturday 6 November

RUGBY WORLD CUP
Final at Cardiff

ALLIED DUNBAR ONE
Bedford v Bath
Bristol v Northampton Saints
Gloucester v Manchester Sale
London Irish v Harlequins
Newcastle Falcons v Leicester Tigers
Saracens v London Wasps

JEWSON ONE
Birmingham/Solihull v Rosslyn Park
Blackheath v Preston Grasshoppers
Fylde v Newbury
Harrogate v Otley
Nottingham v Lydney
Wharfedale v Camberley

Sunday 7 November

JEWSON ONE
Bracknell v Reading

WRU CHALLENGE CUP
3rd Round

Saturday 13 November

ALLIED DUNBAR ONE
Bath v Newcastle Falcons
Gloucester v Saracens
Harlequins v Bedford
Leicester Tigers v London Wasps
Manchester Sale v Bristol
Northampton Saints v London Irish

TETLEY'S BITTER CUP
3rd Round

WRU LEAGUE
Premier Division
Dunvant v Newport
Ebbw Vale v Bridgend
Glasgow Caledonians v Neath
Llanelli v Edinburgh Reivers

Pontypridd v Caerphilly
Swansea v Cardiff
Division One
Aberavon v Tondu
Blackwood v Abercynon
Bonymaen v Abertillery
Llandovery v Merthyr
Pontypool v Newbridge
Treorchy Rhondda v Rumney
UWIC v Llanharan
Cross Keys v Tredegar

SRU TENNENTS CUP
3rd Round

Saturday 20 November

EUROPEAN CUP
Pool A: Stade Francais/CASG v Glasgow Caledonians
Pool A: Leinster v Leicester
Pool B: Bath v Toulouse
Pool B: Swansea v Padova
Pool C: Bourgoin v Ulster
Pool C: Wasps v Llanelli
Pool D: Colomiers v Saracens
Pool D: Munster v Pontypridd
Pool E: Cardiff v Harlequins
Pool E: Treviso v Montferrand
Pool F: Northampton v Neath
Pool F: Edinburgh Reivers v Grenoble

EUROPEAN SHIELD
Pool A: Dax v Bristol
Pool A: Amatori Calvisano v Begles-Bordeaux
Pool B: Bedford v Newport
Pool B: Castres v Italy 3
Pool C: Manchester Sale v Perpignan
Pool C: Caerphilly v Pau
Pool D: Ebbw Vale v Connacht
Pool D: Romania v Toulon
Pool E: Bridgend v Spain
Pool E: Gloucester v Biarritz
Pool F: Portugal v Dunvant
Pool F: Narbonne v Newcastle
Pool G: Rugby Roma v Agen
Pool G: London Irish v Brive

ALLIED DUNBAR TWO
Coventry v Leeds Tykes
Henley Hawks v Moseley
London Welsh v Orrell
Rotherham v Exeter Chiefs
Rugby Lions v Manchester
Wakefield v West Hartlepool
Worcester v Waterloo Drummers

JEWSON ONE
Camberley v Blackheath
Lydney v Harrogate
Newbury v Nottingham
Otley v Birmingham/Solihull
Preston Grasshoppers v Bracknell
Reading v Fylde
Rosslyn Park v Wharfedale

WRU CHALLENGE CUP
4th Round

WRU LEAGUE
Division One
Abercynon v Aberavon
Bonymaen v Blackwood
Merthyr v Rumney
Newbridge v Cross Keys
Tondu v Llanharan
Tredegar v Llandovery
Treorchy Rhondda v Abertillery
UWIC v Pontypool

SRU TENNENTS LEAGUE
Premiership One
Currie v Glasgow Hawks
Gala v Heriot's FP
Kelso v Hawick
Watsonians v Melrose
West of Scotland v Jed-Forest
Premiership Two
Aberdeen GSFP v Musselburgh
Dundee HSFP v Biggar
East Kilbride v Kirkcaldy
Peebles v Selkirk
Stirling County v Boroughmuir

Saturday 27 November

EUROPEAN CUP
Pool A: Leicester v Stade Francais/CASG
Pool A: Glasgow Caledonians v Leinster
Pool B: Toulouse v Swansea
Pool B: Padova v Bath
Pool C: Llanelli v Bourgoin
Pool C: Ulster v Wasps
Pool D: Pontypridd v Colomiers
Pool D: Saracens v Munster
Pool E: Montferrand v Cardiff

Pool E: Harlequins v Treviso
Pool F: Grenoble v Northampton
Pool F: Neath v Edinburgh Reivers

EUROPEAN SHIELD
Pool A: Begles-Bordeaux v Dax
Pool A: Bristol v Amatori Calvisano
Pool B: Italy 3 v Bedford
Pool B: Newport v Castres
Pool C: Pau v Manchester Sale
Pool C: Perpignan v Caerphilly
Pool D: Toulon v Ebbw Vale
Pool D: Connacht v Romania
Pool E: Biarritz v Bridgend
Pool E: Spain v Gloucester
Pool F: Newcastle v Portugal
Pool F: Dunvant v Narbonne
Pool G: Brive v Rugby Roma
Pool G: Agen v London Irish

ALLIED DUNBAR TWO
Exeter Chiefs v London Welsh
Leeds Tykes v Worcester
Manchester v Henley Hawks
Moseley v Rotherham
Orrell v Coventry
Rugby Lions v Wakefield
Waterloo Drummers v West Hartlepool

JEWSON ONE
Birmingham/Solihull v Lydney
Blackheath v Rosslyn Park
Bracknell v Camberley
Fylde v Preston Grasshoppers
Harrogate v Nottingham
Otley v Wharfedale
Reading v Newbury

IRU – AIB LEAGUE
Division Two
Belfast Harlequins v Sunday's Well
Dolphin v Bective Rangers
Greystones v City of Derry
Malone v Galwegians
Old Belvedere v Blackrock College
Old Crescent v Portadown
Wanderers v UC Dublin

WRU LEAGUE
Division One
Aberavon v Llanharan
Abertillery v Merthyr
Abercynon v Bonymaen
Blackwood v Treorchy Rhondda
Llandovery v Newbridge
Pontypool v Tondu
Rumney v Tredegar
Cross Keys v UWIC

SRU TENNENTS LEAGUE
Premiership One
Currie v Heriot's FP
Gala v Melrose
Glasgow Hawks v Jed-Forest
Kelso v West of Scotland
Watsonians v Hawick
Premiership Two
Aberdeen GSFP v Boroughmuir
Biggar v Selkirk
Dundee HSFP v Musselburgh
East Kilbride v Peebles
Stirling County v Kirkcaldy

Saturday 4 December

ALLIED DUNBAR ONE
Bedford v Northampton Saints
Bristol v Gloucester
London Irish v Manchester Sale
London Wasps v Bath
Newcastle Falcons v Harlequins
Saracens v Leicester Tigers

ALLIED DUNBAR TWO
Coventry v Exeter Chiefs
Henley Hawks v Rugby Lions
London Welsh v Moseley
Rotherham v Manchester
Wakefield v Waterloo Drummers
West Hartlepool v Leeds Tykes
Worcester v Orrell

JEWSON ONE
Camberley v Fylde
Lydney v Wharfedale
Newbury v Harrogate
Nottingham v Birmingham/Solihull
Otley v Blackheath
Preston Grasshoppers v Reading
Rosslyn Park v Bracknell

IRU – AIB LEAGUE
Division One
Ballymena v DLS Palmerston
Buccaneers v Cork Constitution
Dungannon v St Mary's College
Garryowen v Terenure College
Lansdowne v Shannon
Young Munster v Clontarf

Division Two
Bective Rangers v Greystones
Belfast Harlequins v UC Cork
Blackrock College v Dolphin
City of Derry v Portadown
Old Crescent v Wanderers
Sunday's Well v Malone
UC Dublin v Old Belvedere

WRU LEAGUE
Premier Division
Cardiff v Newport
Ebbw Vale v Llanelli
Edinburgh Reivers v Caerphilly
Neath v Dunvant
Pontypridd v Glasgow
Swansea v Bridgend
Division One
Abertillery v Tredegar
Bonymaen v Aberavon
Llanharan v Pontypool
Merthyr v Blackwood
Newbridge v Rumney
Tondu v Cross Keys
Treorchy Rhondda v Abercynon
UWIC v Llandovery

SRU TENNENTS LEAGUE
Premiership One
Hawick v Gala
Heriot's FP v Glasgow Hawks
Jed-Forest v Kelso
Melrose v Currie
West of Scotland v Watsonians
Premiership Two
Boroughmuir v Dundee HSFP
Kirkcaldy v Aberdeen GSFP
Musselburgh v Biggar
Peebles v Stirling County
Selkirk v East Kilbride

Saturday 11 December

EUROPEAN CUP
Pool A: Glasgow Caledonians v Leicester
Pool A: Stade Francais/CASG v Leinster
Pool B: Padova v Toulouse
Pool B: Swansea v Bath
Pool C: Ulster v Llanelli
Pool C: Bourgoin v Wasps
Pool D: Saracens v Pontypridd
Pool D: Colomiers v Munster
Pool E: Harlequins v Montferrand
Pool E: Cardiff v Treviso
Pool F: Neath v Grenoble
Pool F: Northampton v Edinburgh Reivers

EUROPEAN SHIELD
Pool A: Bristol v Begles-Bordeaux
Pool A: Dax v Amatori Calvisano
Pool B: Newport v Italy 3
Pool B: Bedford v Castres
Pool C: Perpignan v Pau
Pool C: Manchester Sale v Caerphilly
Pool D: Connacht v Toulon
Pool D: Ebbw Vale v Romania
Pool E: Spain v Biarritz
Pool E: Bridgend v Gloucester
Pool F: Dunvant v Newcastle
Pool F: Portugal v Narbonne
Pool G: Agen v Brive
Pool G: Rugby Roma v London Irish

ALLIED DUNBAR TWO
Exeter Chiefs v Worcester
Henley Hawks v Wakefield
Leeds Tykes v Waterloo Drummers
Manchester v London Welsh
Moseley v Coventry
Orrell v West Hartlepool
Rugby Lions v Rotherham

JEWSON ONE
Birmingham/Solihull v Otley
Blackheath v Camberley
Bracknell v Preston Grasshoppers
Fylde v Reading
Harrogate v Lydney
Nottingham v Newbury
Wharfedale v Rosslyn Park

IRU – AIB LEAGUE
Division Two
Bective Rangers v Blackrock College
Dolphin v City of Derry
Galwegians v Sunday's Well
Greystones v Old Crescent
Portadown v Wanderers
UC Cork v Old Belvedere

WRU LEAGUE
Division One
Aberavon v Pontypool
Abertillery v Newbridge
Abercynon v Merthyr
Blackwood v Tredegar

Bonymaen v Treorchy Rhondda
Llandovery v Tondu
Rumney v UWIC
Cross Keys v Llanharan

SRU TENNENTS LEAGUE
Premiership One
Currie v Hawick
Gala v West of Scotland
Glasgow Hawks v Melrose
Heriot's FP v Jed-Forest
Watsonians v Kelso
Premiership Two
Aberdeen GSFP v Peebles
Biggar v Boroughmuir
Dundee HSFP v Kirkcaldy
Musselburgh v Selkirk
Stirling County v East Kilbride

Saturday 18 December

EUROPEAN CUP
Pool A: Leicester v Glasgow Caledonians
Pool A: Leinster v Stade Francais/CASG
Pool B: Toulouse v Padova
Pool B: Bath v Swansea
Pool C: Llanelli v Ulster
Pool C: Wasps v Bourgoin
Pool D: Pontypridd v Saracens
Pool D: Munster v Colomiers
Pool E: Montferrand v Harlequins
Pool E: Treviso v Cardiff
Pool F: Grenoble v Neath
Pool F: Edinburgh Reivers v Northampton

EUROPEAN SHIELD
Pool A: Begles-Bordeaux v Bristol
Pool A: Amatori Calvisano v Dax
Pool B: Italy 3 v Newport
Pool B: Castres v Bedford
Pool C: Pau v Perpignan
Pool C: Caerphilly v Manchester Sale
Pool D: Toulon v Connacht
Pool D: Romania v Ebbw Vale
Pool E: Biarritz v Spain
Pool E: Gloucester v Bridgend
Pool F: Newcastle v Dunvant
Pool F: Narbonne v Portugal
Pool G: Brive v Agen
Pool G: London Irish v Rugby Roma

ALLIED DUNBAR TWO
Coventry v Manchester
London Welsh v Rugby Lions
Rotherham v Henley Hawks
Wakefield v Leeds Tykes
Waterloo Drummers v Orrell
West Hartlepool v Exeter Chiefs
Worcester v Moseley

JEWSON ONE
Camberley v Wharfedale
Lydney v Nottingham
Newbury v Fylde
Otley v Harrogate
Preston Grasshoppers v Blackheath
Reading v Bracknell
Rosslyn Park v Birmingham/Solihull

IRU – AIB LEAGUE
Division Two
City of Derry v Bective Rangers
Malone v Dolphin
Old Belvedere v Portadown
Old Crescent v Galwegians
Sunday's Well v Greystones
UC Dublin v UC Cork
Wanderers v Belfast Harlequins

WRU CHALLENGE CUP
5th Round

SRU TENNENTS CUP
4th Round

Sunday 26 December

ALLIED DUNBAR ONE
Bath v Leicester Tigers
Bristol v Saracens
Gloucester v London Irish
Harlequins v London Wasps
Manchester Sale v Bedford
Northampton Saints v Newcastle Falcons

Monday 27 December

JEWSON ONE
Wharfedale v Otley

WRU LEAGUE
Premier Division
Caerphilly v Ebbw Vale
Cardiff v Bridgend
Dunvant v Pontypridd

Glasgow Caledonians v Edinburgh Reivers
Llanelli v Swansea
Newport v Neath
Division One
Llanharan v Llandovery
Merthyr v Bonymaen
Newbridge v Blackwood
Pontypool v Cross Keys
Tondu v Rumney
Tredegar v Abercynon
Treorchy Rhondda v Aberavon
UWIC v Abertillery

Tuesday 28 December

IRU – AIB LEAGUE
Division One
Clontarf v Dungannon
Cork Constitution v Garryowen
DLS Palmerston v Lansdowne
Shannon v Young Munster
St Mary's College v Buccaneers
Terenure College v Ballymena
Division Two
Malone v Blackrock College

Wednesday 29 December

ALLIED DUNBAR ONE
Bedford v Gloucester
Leicester Tigers v Harlequins
London Irish v Bristol
London Wasps v Northampton Saints
Newcastle Falcons v Manchester Sale
Saracens v Bath

Sunday 2 January

TETLEY'S BITTER CUP
4th Round

Monday 3 January

WRU LEAGUE
Premier Division
Bridgend v Llanelli
Cardiff v Neath
Ebbw Vale v Glasgow Caledonians
Edinburgh Reivers v Dunvant
Pontypridd v Newport
Swansea v Caerphilly
Division One
Aberavon v Cross Keys
Abertillery v Tondu
Abercynon v Newbridge
Blackwood v UWIC
Bonymaen v Tredegar
Llandovery v Pontypool
Rumney v Llanharan
Treorchy Rhondda v Merthyr

Saturday 8 January

EUROPEAN CUP
Pool A: Stade Francais/CASG v Leicester
Pool A: Leinster v Glasgow Caledonians
Pool B: Swansea v Toulouse
Pool B: Bath v Padova
Pool C: Bourgoin v Llanelli
Pool C: Wasps v Ulster
Pool D: Colomiers v Pontypridd
Pool D: Munster v Saracens
Pool E: Cardiff v Montferrand
Pool E: Treviso v Harlequins
Pool F: Northampton v Grenoble
Pool F: Edinburgh Reivers v Neath

EUROPEAN SHIELD
Pool A: Dax v Begles-Bordeaux
Pool A: Amatori Calvisano v Bristol
Pool B: Bedford v Italy 3
Pool B: Castres v Newport
Pool C: Manchester Sale v Pau
Pool C: Caerphilly v Perpignan
Pool D: Ebbw Vale v Toulon
Pool D: Romania v Connacht
Pool E: Bridgend v Biarritz
Pool E: Gloucester v Spain
Pool F: Portugal v Newcastle
Pool F: Narbonne v Dunvant
Pool G: Rugby Roma v Brive
Pool G: London Irish v Agen

ALLIED DUNBAR TWO
Coventry v Orrell
Henley Hawks v Manchester
London Welsh v Exeter Chiefs
Rotherham v Moseley
Wakefield v Rugby Lions
West Hartlepool v Waterloo Drummers
Worcester v Leeds Tykes

JEWSON ONE
Birmingham/Solihull v Camberley
Blackheath v Reading
Bracknell v Fylde
Harrogate v Rosslyn Park
Lydney v Newbury
Nottingham v Otley
Wharfedale v Preston Grasshoppers

IRU – AIB LEAGUE
Division Two
Belfast Harlequins v Old Belvedere
City of Derry v Old Crescent
Dolphin v UC Dublin
Galwegians v Wanderers
Greystones v Blackrock College
Malone v UC Cork
Portadown v Bective Rangers

Saturday 8 January

WRU LEAGUE
Division One
Llanharan v Abertillery
Merthyr v Aberavon
Newbridge v Bonymaen
Pontypool v Rumney
Tondu v Blackwood
Tredegar v Treorchy Rhondda
UWIC v Abercynon
Cross Keys v Llandovery

SRU TENNENTS CUP
5th Round

Saturday 15 January

EUROPEAN CUP
Pool A: Glasgow Caledonians v Stade Francais/CASG
Pool A: Leicester v Leinster
Pool B: Padova v Swansea
Pool B: Toulouse v Bath
Pool C: Ulster v Bourgoin
Pool C: Llanelli v Wasps
Pool D: Saracens v Colomiers
Pool D: Pontypridd v Munster
Pool E: Harlequins v Cardiff
Pool E: Montferrand v Treviso
Pool F: Neath v Northampton
Pool F: Grenoble v Edinburgh Reivers

EUROPEAN SHIELD
Pool A: Bristol v Dax
Pool A: Begles-Bordeaux v Amatori Calvisano
Pool B: Newport v Bedford
Pool B: Italy 3 v Castres
Pool C: Perpignan v Manchester Sale
Pool C: Pau v Caerphilly
Pool D: Connacht v Ebbw Vale
Pool D: Toulon v Romania
Pool E: Spain v Bridgend
Pool E: Biarritz v Gloucester
Pool F: Dunvant v Portugal
Pool F: Newcastle v Narbonne
Pool G: Agen v Rugby Roma
Pool G: Brive v London Irish

ALLIED DUNBAR TWO
Exeter Chiefs v Coventry
Leeds Tykes v West Hartlepool
Manchester v Rotherham
Moseley v London Welsh
Orrell v Worcester
Rugby Lions v Henley Hawks
Waterloo Drummers v Wakefield

JEWSON ONE
Camberley v Harrogate
Fylde v Blackheath
Newbury v Bracknell
Otley v Lydney
Preston Grasshoppers v Birmingham/Solihull
Reading v Wharfedale
Rosslyn Park v Nottingham

IRU – AIB LEAGUE
Division Two
Bective Rangers v Galwegians
Old Belvedere v Greystones
Old Crescent v Dolphin
Sunday's Well v City of Derry
UC Cork v Portadown
UC Dublin v Belfast Harlequins
Wanderers v Malone

Saturday 15 January

WRU LEAGUE
Division One
Aberavon v Llandovery
Abertillery v Pontypool
Abercynon v Tondu
Blackwood v Llanharan

Bonymaen v UWIC
Merthyr v Tredegar
Rumney v Cross Keys
Treorchy Rhondda v Newbridge

SRU TENNENTS LEAGUE
Premiership One
Hawick v Glasgow Hawks
Jed-Forest v Watsonians
Kelso v Gala
Melrose v Heriot's FP
West of Scotland v Currie
Premiership Two
Boroughmuir v Musselburgh
East Kilbride v Aberdeen GSFP
Kirkcaldy v Biggar
Peebles v Dundee HSFP
Selkirk v Stirling County

Saturday 22 January

ALLIED DUNBAR ONE
Bath v London Wasps
Gloucester v Bristol
Harlequins v Newcastle Falcons
Leicester Tigers v Saracens
Manchester Sale v London Irish
Northampton Saints v Bedford

ALLIED DUNBAR TWO
Exeter Chiefs v Rotherham
Leeds Tykes v Coventry
Manchester v Rugby Lions
Moseley v Henley Hawks
Orrell v London Welsh
Waterloo Drummers v Worcester
West Hartlepool v Wakefield

JEWSON ONE
Birmingham/Solihull v Reading
Blackheath v Bracknell
Harrogate v Preston Grasshoppers
Lydney v Rosslyn Park
Nottingham v Camberley
Otley v Newbury
Wharfedale v Fylde

IRU – AIB LEAGUE
Division One
Ballymena v Clontarf
Buccaneers v Shannon
Dungannon v Cork Constitution
Garryowen v St Mary's College
Lansdowne v Terenure College
Young Munster v DLS Palmerston
Division Two
Bective Rangers v Malone
Blackrock College v Belfast Harlequins
City of Derry v Galwegians
Dolphin v Old Belvedere
Portadown v Sunday's Well
UC Cork v Greystones
UC Dublin v Old Crescent

WRU CHALLENGE CUP
6th Round

SRU TENNENTS LEAGUE
Premiership One
Currie v Kelso
Gala v Watsonians
Glasgow Hawks v West of Scotland
Heriot's FP v Hawick
Melrose v Jed-Forest
Premiership Two
Aberdeen GSFP v Stirling County
Biggar v Peebles
Boroughmuir v Selkirk
Dundee HSFP v East Kilbride
Musselburgh v Kirkcaldy

Tuesday 25 January

ALLIED DUNBAR ONE
Bedford v Harlequins
Bristol v Manchester Sale
London Irish v Northampton Saints
London Wasps v Bristol
Newcastle Falcons v Bath
Saracens v Gloucester

Saturday 29 January

TETLEY'S BITTER CUP
5th Round

IRU – AIB LEAGUE
Division One
Clontarf v Lansdowne
Cork Constitution v Young Munster
DLS Palmerston v Garryowen
Shannon v Dungannon
St Mary's College v Ballymena
Division Two
Belfast Harlequins v Dolphin
Galwegians v UC Cork
Greystones v UC Dublin
Malone v Old Belvedere
Old Crescent v Sunday's Well

Portadown v Blackrock College
Wanderers v Bective Rangers

WRU LEAGUE
Premier Division
Caerphilly v Bridgend
Cardiff v Llanelli
Dunvant v Ebbw Vale
Glasgow Caledonians v Swansea
Neath v Pontypridd
Newport v Edinburgh Reivers
Division One
Llandovery v Rumney
Llanharan v Abercynon
Newbridge v Merthyr
Pontypool v Blackwood
Tondu v Bonymaen
Tredegar v Aberavon
UWIC v Treorchy Rhondda
Cross Keys v Abertillery

SRU TENNENTS LEAGUE
Premiership One
Hawick v Melrose
Jed-Forest v Gala
Kelso v Glasgow Hawks
Watsonians v Currie
West of Scotland v Heriot's FP
Premiership Two
East Kilbride v Biggar
Kirkcaldy v Boroughmuir
Peebles v Musselburgh
Selkirk v Aberdeen GSFP
Stirling County v Dundee HSFP

Sunday 30 January

IRU – AIB LEAGUE
Division One
Terenure College v Buccaneers

Saturday 5 February

SIX NATIONS CHAMPIONSHIP
England v Ireland (Twickenham)
Italy v Scotland (Rome)
Wales v France (Cardiff)

Wednesday 9 February

IRU – AIB LEAGUE
Division One
Lansdowne v St Mary's College

Saturday 12 February

ALLIED DUNBAR ONE
Bath v Bedford
Harlequins v London Irish
Leicester Tigers v Newcastle Falcons
London Wasps v Saracens
Manchester Sale v Gloucester
Northampton Saints v Bristol

ALLIED DUNBAR TWO
Coventry v Waterloo Drummers
Henley Hawks v Exeter Chiefs
London Welsh v Leeds Tykes
Rotherham v Orrell
Rugby Lions v Moseley
Wakefield v Manchester
Worcester v West Hartlepool

JEWSON ONE
Bracknell v Wharfedale
Camberley v Lydney
Fylde v Birmingham/Solihull
Newbury v Blackheath
Preston Grasshoppers v Nottingham
Reading v Harrogate
Rosslyn Park v Otley

IRU – AIB LEAGUE
Division One
Ballymena v Cork Constitution
Buccaneers v Clontarf
Dungannon v DLS Palmerston
Young Munster v Terenure College
Division Two
Bective Rangers v Belfast Harlequins
Blackrock College v UC Dublin
Galwegians v Portadown
Malone v City of Derry
Old Belvedere v Old Crescent
Sunday's Well v Wanderers

WRU LEAGUE
Premier Division
Bridgend v Glasgow Caledonians
Ebbw Vale v Newport
Edinburgh Reivers v Neath
Llanelli v Caerphilly
Pontypridd v Cardiff
Swansea v Dunvant
Division One
Abertillery v Llandovery
Abercynon v Pontypool
Blackwood v Cross Keys
Bonymaen v Llanharan

Merthyr v UWIC
Rumney v Aberavon
Tredegar v Newbridge
Treorchy Rhondda v Tondu

SRU TENNENTS CUP
Quarter-finals

Sunday 13 February

IRU – AIB LEAGUE
Division One
Garryowen v Shannon
Division Two
Dolphin v UC Cork

Saturday 19 February

SIX NATIONS CHAMPIONSHIP
France v England (Stade de France)
Ireland v Scotland (Lansdowne Road)
Wales v Italy (Cardiff)

Saturday 26 February

TETLEY'S BITTER CUP
Quarter-finals

ALLIED DUNBAR TWO
Exeter Chiefs v Rugby Lions
Leeds Tykes v Rotherham
Moseley v Manchester
Orrell v Henley Hawks
Waterloo Drummers v London Welsh
West Hartlepool v Coventry
Worcester v Wakefield

JEWSON ONE
Birmingham/Solihull v Bracknell
Harrogate v Fylde
Lydney v Preston Grasshoppers
Nottingham v Reading
Otley v Camberley
Rosslyn Park v Newbury
Wharfedale v Blackheath

IRU – AIB LEAGUE
Division One
Clontarf v Garryowen
Cork Constitution v Lansdowne
DLS Palmerston v Buccaneers
Shannon v Ballymena
St Mary's College v Young Munster
Terenure College v Dungannon
Division Two
Belfast Harlequins v Malone
Blackrock College v Sunday's Well
Dolphin v Portadown
Greystones v Wanderers
Old Belvedere v City of Derry
UC Cork v Bective Rangers
UC Dublin v Galwegians

WRU CHALLENGE CUP
7th Round

SRU TENNENTS LEAGUE
Premiership One
Currie v Gala
Glasgow Hawks v Watsonians
Hawick v Jed-Forest
Heriot's FP v Kelso
Melrose v West of Scotland
Premiership Two
Biggar v Stirling County
Boroughmuir v Peebles
Dundee HSFP v Aberdeen GSFP
Kirkcaldy v Selkirk
Musselburgh v East Kilbride

Saturday 4 March

SIX NATIONS CHAMPIONSHIP
England v Wales (Twickenham)
Ireland v Italy (Lansdowne Road)
Scotland v France (Murrayfield)

Saturday 11 March

ALLIED DUNBAR ONE
Bedford v Leicester Tigers
Bristol v Harlequins
Gloucester v Northampton Saints
London Irish v Bath
Newcastle Falcons v London Wasps
Saracens v Manchester Sale

ALLIED DUNBAR TWO
Coventry v Worcester
Henley Hawks v Leeds Tykes
London Welsh v West Hartlepool
Manchester v Exeter Chiefs
Rotherham v Waterloo Drummers
Rugby Lions v Orrell
Wakefield v Moseley

JEWSON ONE
Blackheath v Birmingham/Solihull
Bracknell v Harrogate
Camberley v Rosslyn Park
Fylde v Nottingham
Newbury v Wharfedale
Preston Grasshoppers v Otley
Reading v Lydney

IRU – AIB LEAGUE
Division One
Ballymena v Young Munster
DLS Palmerston v Cork Constitution
Dungannon v Lansdowne
Garryowen v Buccaneers
Terenure College v Shannon
Division Two
City of Derry v Blackrock College
Galwegians v Old Belvedere
Greystones v Belfast Harlequins
Old Crescent v Bective Rangers
Portadown v UC Dublin
Sunday's Well v UC Cork
Wanderers v Dolphin

WRU LEAGUE
Premier Division
Cardiff v Caerphilly
Dunvant v Bridgend
Edinburgh Reivers v Pontypridd
Llanelli v Glasgow Caledonians
Neath v Ebbw Vale
Newport v Swansea
Division One
Aberavon v Newbridge
Llandovery v Blackwood
Llanharan v Treorchy Rhondda
Pontypool v Bonymaen
Rumney v Abertillery
Tondu v Merthyr
UWIC v Tredegar
Cross Keys v Abercynon

SRU TENNENTS CUP
Semi-final

SRU TENNENTS LEAGUE
Premiership One
Currie v Jed-Forest
Gala v Glasgow Hawks
Kelso v Melrose
Watsonians v Heriot's FP
West of Scotland v Hawick
Premiership Two
Aberdeen GSFP v Biggar
Dundee HSFP v Selkirk
East Kilbride v Boroughmuir
Peebles v Kirkcaldy
Stirling County v Musselburgh

Sunday 12 March

IRU – AIB LEAGUE
Division One
St Mary's College v Clontarf

SRU TENNENTS CUP
Semi-final

Saturday 18 March

SIX NATIONS CHAMPIONSHIP
Italy v England (Rome)
Wales v Scotland (Cardiff)

JEWSON ONE
Birmingham/Solihull v Wharfedale
Camberley v Newbury
Harrogate v Blackheath
Lydney v Fylde
Nottingham v Bracknell
Otley v Reading
Rosslyn Park v Preston Grasshoppers

Sunday 19 March

SIX NATIONS CHAMPIONSHIP
France v Ireland (Stade de France)

Saturday 25 March

ALLIED DUNBAR ONE
Bath v Bristol
Harlequins v Gloucester
Leicester Tigers v London Irish
London Wasps v Bedford
Newcastle Falcons v Saracens
Northampton Saints v Manchester Sale

ALLIED DUNBAR TWO
Coventry v Wakefield
Exeter Chiefs v Moseley
Leeds Tykes v Rugby Lions
Orrell v Manchester
Waterloo Drummers v Henley Hawks
West Hartlepool v Rotherham

Worcester v London Welsh

JEWSON ONE
Blackheath v Nottingham
Bracknell v Lydney
Fylde v Otley
Newbury v Birmingham/Solihull
Preston Grasshoppers v Camberley
Reading v Rosslyn Park
Wharfedale v Harrogate

IRU – AIB LEAGUE
Division One
Buccaneers v Ballymena
Clontarf v DLS Palmerston
Cork Constitution v Terenure College
Shannon v St Mary's College
Young Munster v Dungannon
Division Two
Bective Rangers v Sunday's Well
Belfast Harlequins v Old Crescent
Blackrock College v Galwegians
Dolphin v Greystones
Old Belvedere v Wanderers
UC Cork v City of Derry
UC Dublin v Malone

WRU CHALLENGE CUP
Quarter-finals

WRU LEAGUE
Division One
Abertillery v Aberavon
Abercynon v Llandovery
Blackwood v Rumney
Bonymaen v Cross Keys
Merthyr v Llanharan
Newbridge v UWIC
Tredegar v Tondu
Treorchy Rhondda v Pontypool

SRU TENNENTS LEAGUE
Premiership One
Glasgow Hawks v Currie
Hawick v Kelso
Heriot's FP v Gala
Jed-Forest v West of Scotland
Melrose v Watsonians
Premiership Two
Biggar v Dundee HSFP
Boroughmuir v Stirling County
Kirkcaldy v East Kilbride
Musselburgh v Aberdeen GSFP
Selkirk v Peebles

Saturday 1 April

SIX NATIONS CHAMPIONSHIP
France v Italy (Stade de France)
Ireland v Wales (Lansdowne Road)

Sunday 2 April

SIX NATIONS CHAMPIONSHIP
Scotland v England (Murrayfield)

Wednesday 5 April

IRU – AIB LEAGUE
Division Two
Wanderers v Blackrock College

Saturday 8 April

TETLEY'S BITTER CUP
Semi-finals

ALLIED DUNBAR ONE
Bedford v Newcastle Falcons
Bristol v Leicester Tigers
Gloucester v Bath
London Irish v London Wasps
Manchester Sale v Harlequins
Saracens v Northampton Saints

ALLIED DUNBAR TWO
Henley Hawks v West Hartlepool
London Welsh v Coventry
Manchester v Leeds Tykes
Moseley v Orrell
Rotherham v Worcester
Rugby Lions v Waterloo Drummers
Wakefield v Exeter Chiefs

JEWSON ONE
Blackheath v Lydney
Camberley v Reading
Harrogate v Birmingham/Solihull
Nottingham v Wharfedale
Otley v Bracknell
Preston Grasshoppers v Newbury
Rosslyn Park v Fylde

IRU – AIB LEAGUE
Division One
Ballymena v Dungannon
Clontarf v Terenure College
Lansdowne v Buccaneers
Shannon v Cork Constitution
St Mary's College v DLS Palmerston

Division Two
City of Derry v UC Dublin
Galwegians v Dolphin
Malone v Greystones
Portadown v Belfast Harlequins
Sunday's Well v Old Belvedere
UC Cork v Old Crescent

WRU LEAGUE
Premier Division
Bridgend v Newport
Caerphilly v Glasgow
Ebbw Vale v Pontypridd
Edinburgh Reivers v Cardiff
Llanelli v Dunvant
Swansea v Neath
Division One
Aberavon v UWIC
Abertillery v Blackwood
Llandovery v Bonymaen
Llanharan v Tredegar
Pontypool v Merthyr
Rumney v Abercynon
Tondu v Newbridge
Cross Keys v Treorchy Rhondda

Sunday 9 April

IRU – AIB LEAGUE
Division One
Garryowen v Young Munster

Saturday 15 April

EUROPEAN CUP
Quarter-finals

EUROPEAN SHIELD
Quarter-finals

ALLIED DUNBAR TWO
Coventry v Rotherham
Leeds Tykes v Moseley
London Welsh v Wakefield
Orrell v Exeter Chiefs
Waterloo Drummers v Manchester
West Hartlepool v Rugby Lions
Worcester v Henley Hawks

JEWSON ONE
Birmingham/Solihull v Nottingham
Blackheath v Otley
Bracknell v Rosslyn Park
Fylde v Camberley
Harrogate v Newbury
Reading v Preston Grasshoppers
Wharfedale v Lydney

IRU – AIB LEAGUE
Division One
Lansdowne v Garryowen

WRU LEAGUE
Division One
Aberavon v Blackwood
Abercynon v Abertillery
Bonymaen v Rumney
Merthyr v Cross Keys
Newbridge v Llanharan
Tredegar v Pontypool
Treorchy Rhondda v Llandovery
UWIC v Tondu

Tuesday 18 April

ALLIED DUNBAR ONE
Bath v Manchester Sale
Bedford v Saracens
Harlequins v Northampton Saints
Leicester Tigers v Gloucester
London Wasps v Bristol
Newcastle Falcons v London Irish

Saturday 22 April

ALLIED DUNBAR ONE
Bristol v Newcastle Falcons
Gloucester v London Wasps
London Irish v Bedford
Manchester Sale v Leicester Tigers
Northampton Saints v Bath
Saracens v Harlequins

ALLIED DUNBAR TWO
Exeter Chiefs v Leeds Tykes
Henley Hawks v Coventry
Manchester v West Hartlepool
Moseley v Waterloo Drummers
Rotherham v London Welsh
Rugby Lions v Worcester
Wakefield v Orrell

JEWSON ONE
Camberley v Bracknell
Lydney v Birmingham/Solihull
Newbury v Reading
Nottingham v Harrogate
Preston Grasshoppers v Fylde
Rosslyn Park v Blackheath

IRU – AIB LEAGUE
Division One
Ballymena v Lansdowne
Cork Constitution v Clontarf
DLS Palmerston v Shannon
Dungannon v Garryowen
Terenure College v St Mary's College
Young Munster v Buccaneers
Division Two
Belfast Harlequins v Galwegians
Blackrock College v UC Cork
Greystones v Portadown
Old Belvedere v Bective Rangers
Old Crescent v Malone
UC Dublin v Sunday's Well
Wanderers v City of Derry

WRU CHALLENGE CUP
Semi-finals

WRU LEAGUE
Division One
Abertillery v Bonymaen
Abercynon v Blackwood
Llanharan v UWIC
Merthyr v Llandovery
Newbridge v Pontypool
Rumney v Treorchy Rhondda
Tondu v Aberavon
Tredegar v Cross Keys

SRU TENNENTS CUP
Final

Tuesday 25 April

WRU LEAGUE
Premier Division
Cardiff v Glasgow Caledonians
Dunvant v Caerphilly
Edinburgh Reivers v Ebbw Vale
Neath v Bridgend
Newport v Llanelli
Pontypridd v Swansea

Saturday 29 April

ALLIED DUNBAR ONE
Bath v Harlequins
Bedford v Bristol
Leicester Tigers v Northampton Saints
London Irish v Saracens
London Wasps v Manchester Sale
Newcastle Falcons v Gloucester

ALLIED DUNBAR TWO
Coventry v Rugby Lions
Leeds Tykes v Orrell
London Welsh v Henley Hawks
Rotherham v Wakefield
Waterloo Drummers v Exeter Chiefs
West Hartlepool v Moseley
Worcester v Manchester

IRU – AIB LEAGUE
Division One
Buccaneers v Dungannon
DLS Palmerston v Terenure College
Garryowen v Ballymena
Lansdowne v Young Munster
Shannon v Clontarf
St Mary's College v Cork Constitution
Division Two
Bective Rangers v UC Dublin
Blackrock College v Old Crescent
City of Derry v Belfast Harlequins
Galwegians v Greystones
Portadown v Malone
Sunday's Well v Dolphin
UC Cork v Wanderers

WRU LEAGUE
Premier Division
Bridgend v Pontypridd
Caerphilly v Newport
Cardiff v Ebbw Vale
Glasgow Caledonians v Dunvant
Llanelli v Neath
Swansea v Edinburgh Reivers
Division One
Aberavon v Abercynon
Abertillery v Treorchy Rhondda
Blackwood v Bonymaen
Llandovery v Tredegar
Llanharan v Tondu
Pontypool v UWIC
Rumney v Merthyr
Cross Keys v Newbridge

Saturday 6 May

EUROPEAN CUP
Semi-finals

EUROPEAN SHIELD
Semi-finals

ALLIED DUNBAR ONE
Bath v Saracens
Bristol v London Irish
Gloucester v Bedford

Harlequins v Leicester Tigers
Manchester Sale v Newcastle Falcons
Northampton Saints v London Wasps

ALLIED DUNBAR TWO
Exeter Chiefs v West Hartlepool
Henley Hawks v Rotherham
Leeds Tykes v Wakefield
Manchester v Coventry
Moseley v Worcester
Orrell v Waterloo Drummers
Rugby Lions v London Welsh

Saturday 6 May

IRU – AIB LEAGUE
Semi-finals

WRU LEAGUE
Premier Division
Dunvant v Cardiff
Ebbw Vale v Swansea
Edinburgh Reivers v Bridgend
Neath v Caerphilly
Newport v Glasgow Caledonians
Pontypridd v Llanelli
Division One
Bonymaen v Abercynon
Llanharan v Aberavon
Merthyr v Abertillery
Newbridge v Llandovery
Tondu v Pontypool
Tredegar v Rumney
Treorchy Rhondda v Blackwood
UWIC v Cross Keys

Saturday 13 May

TETLEY'S BITTER CUP
Final

ALLIED DUNBAR TWO
Coventry v Moseley
London Welsh v Manchester
Rotherham v Rugby Lions
Wakefield v Henley Hawks
Waterloo Drummers v Leeds Tykes
West Hartlepool v Orrell
Worcester v Exeter Chiefs

IRU – AIB LEAGUE
Final

WRU LEAGUE
Premier Division
Bridgend v Ebbw Vale
Caerphilly v Pontypridd
Cardiff v Swansea
Edinburgh Reivers v Llanelli
Neath v Glasgow Caledonians
Newport v Dunvant

Saturday 20 May

ALLIED DUNBAR ONE
Bedford v Manchester Sale
Leicester Tigers v Bath
London Irish v Gloucester
London Wasps v Harlequins
Newcastle Falcons v Northampton Saints
Saracens v Bristol

WRU CHALLENGE CUP
Final

Saturday 27 May

EUROPEAN CUP
Final

EUROPEAN SHIELD
Final